FAMILY LAW

FAMILY LAW

An account of the Law of Domestic Relations in England
and Wales in the last quarter of the twentieth century,
with some comparisons

Olive M. Stone

*LL.B., B.Sc.(Econ.) Ph.D., of Gray's Inn, Barrister
Reader in Law to the University of London at the
London School of Economics and Political Science*

First published 1977 by
THE MACMILLAN PRESS LTD
London and Basingstoke
Associated companies in New York Dublin
Melbourne Johannesburg and Madras

ISBN 0 333 19629 5 (hard cover)
0 333 19630 9 (paper cover)

Photoset, printed and bound in Great Britain by
R. J. ACFORD LIMITED
Industrial Estate, Chichester, Sussex

Contents

Preface

This book is based on the lectures on the Law of Domestic Relations for students for the Bachelor of Laws degree that I have delivered for some years at the London School of Economics and Political Science. Much of it was written during special leave in the law libraries of Monash University, Australia and the University of Singapore, and my thanks are due to the staff of these and other law libraries for their ever-ready help and co-operation. I thank also those, especially Mss Jacquie Fleming and Mary Choo, who produced a fair typescript. In the later stages my colleague Mr David Bradley was good enough to read the entire script and make valuable suggestions for improvement. Any views expressed are, of course, entirely my own.

Although this book is intended primarily for law students both in England and Wales and overseas, I hope that others will find it a useful statement of the principal problems and areas of interest in family law today.

The law is given as at 20 August 1976, but some decisions reported to 22 October have been briefly noted.

22 October 1976   Olive M. Stone

Table of Statutes

(1) UNITED KINGDOM STATUTES

(2) EUROPEAN COMMUNITIES STATUTES

(3) OVERSEAS STATUTES

Table of Statutory Instruments

Table of Cases

*Indicates a temporary reference.

AUSTRALIAN CASES

CHAPTER I

Introduction

A. MARRIAGE, FAMILY AND HOUSEHOLD AT DIFFERENT TIMES AND PLACES

Humanity survives by reproduction, which involves sexual relations[1] between a man and a woman, followed by conception, gestation and the birth of a helpless infant. It is therefore a simple physical or biological truism that family relationships (whether they are strictly kinship groupings or socially sanctioned by marriage or not) underlie all societies and that the family (variously defined) is their basic unit. This does not mean that the traditional legal and social rules which the particular society has evolved to regulate these relationships are equally basic. Many of these social and legal rules are in fact habitually retained long after the conditions that were thought to justify them have disappeared.

Recent research has now established that, at least in England, 'the large joint or extended family seems never to have existed as a common form of the domestic group at any point in time covered by known numerical records'.[2] But everywhere 'the nuclear family predominates ... in fact the classic nuclear family of man, wife and children formed the household, with or without servants, in more than half of the Western European cases (examined) and in a third of the others'.[3] Certainly extended household groups have existed in the past, in England probably particularly among the upper classes, thus Laslett: 'high social status led to large households in the traditional English social order, along with and because of the presence of large numbers of servants which high social status – and also large-scale economic activity –

---

1. Except for artificial insemination of a woman or a human ovum with the semen of a man, as to which see *Law and Ethics of A.I.D. and Embryo Transfer* (CIBA Foundation Symposium, 1973).
2. E.g. Peter Laslett (ed.), *Household and Family in Past Time* (1972), p. 126.
3. Ibid. pp. 59–60.

made imperative'.[4] Usually those of lower social status have tried to identify with their understanding of the *mores* of those higher in the social scale. The part played by fantasy and ideology in imagining the mating rules and household arrangements of the past is stressed by many writers,[5] but the bachelor Earl of Lonsdale existed in 1787, heading a household of fifty persons, consisting of himself and forty-nine servants.[6]

Some writers have argued that the irreducibly basic unit of family and household is that between mother and child,[7] and Robin Fox concludes[8] that 'A tendency of all societies to strain towards (the) hunting pattern of adult males together, relatively separate from females-with-young, with adolescent males as a third unit, seems universal.' The commuter syndrome from suburbs to male-dominated factories and commercial city centres, and the gangs of adolescent youths in many city centres and at commercially-organised sports events, such as football matches, demonstrate the same tendency.

It seems now to be established that all societies have rules regulating sexual relations. Thus Robin Fox:[9] 'In all societies there is some form of more or less regularised mating. Often a female has only one mate. Very often circumstances are such that the female and her mate form a domestic unit – living under one roof and raising their children together. But this is a highly variable arrangement.' The days when political thinkers[10] and lawyers[11] alike could imagine a kind of 'golden age' in which there was complete promiscuity between the sexes have passed. Indeed, there is evidence that the progression from the primitive to the more advanced societies traces a simplification rather than elaboration of the rules.[12]

The incest taboo, if not universal[13] as was until recently thought, is certainly

---

4. E.g. Peter Laslett (ed.), *Household and Family in Past Time* (1972), p. 156.
5. E.g. Laslett, ibid. p. 3, for the widespread conviction that most girls in England married in their teens in earlier times. Also P. Laslett; *The World we have lost* (1965). M. R. Paulsen, in 'Support rights and duties between husband and wife', 9 *Vanderbilt Law Rev.*, (1956) 709, emphasises the importance in American mythology of the idealised agricultural household.
6. Laslett, ibid. p. 135.
7. E.g. Robin Fox, *Kinship and Marriage* (1967), p. 39: 'The basic unit is the mother and her child, however the mother came to be impregnated.' He therefore prefers the term 'conjugal unit' for both parents and their children. See also the same author in *The Family and its Future* (CIBA Foundation Symposium, 1970), p. 2. Also Jack Goody (ed.), *Kinship* (1971) and John Bowlby, *Child Care and the Growth of Love*, 2nd ed. (Penguin 1965) and *Attachment and Loss* (1969).
8. *The Family and its Future*, p. 5.
9. *Kinship and Marriage*, p. 39.
10. E.g. F. Engels, *The Origin of the Family, Private Property and the State*, in the light of the researches of Lewis H. Morgan, with an introduction by Eleanor Burke Leacock (1972) pp. 97–101.
11. E.g. T. James, 'The English law of marriage', in *A Century of Family Law*, ed. R. H. Graveson and F. R. Crane (1957), p. 20.
12. See e.g. *Kinship and Marriage in African Society*, ed. Radcliffe-Brown and Ford (1950), and the complex variations there illustrated, less of prohibitions than of mating arrangements preferred for the royal family, and therefore cited as ideal, but rarely adopted, by the people generally.

general, and should be distinguished from the exogamous rule for socially recognised marriages. Robin Fox succinctly points the contrast:[14] 'we must distinguish sharply between: (*a*) incest – which pertains to sexual relations and (*b*) exogamy – which pertains to conjugal relations'. In English law the distinction is that whereas incestuous sexual relations constitute a criminal offence[15] the rules of exogamy, or the prohibited degrees of marriage, range more widely, include affinal[16] as well as consanguinous relationships, and simply render any purported marriage of no effect. The incest taboo is not based wholly or even primarily on biological reasons, since primitive societies in which the biological relationship between father and child is imperfectly understood usually have prohibitions on sexual relations, at least between those in the first degree of relationship.[17] A far stronger reason seems to be that of social discipline. Sexual relations between members of a family other than the nuclear pair or pairs around whom the household is grouped would be disruptive, and the informality and 'familiarity' normally existing between members of a family would quickly disappear if sexual or conjugal relations between its members were permissible.[18]

On the other hand, the exogamous marriage preferences, whether enforced or not, have a far more important expansionist than restrictive aspect. They are a primary means of making friends and influencing people. For the ambitious or fearful, arrangements will long precede possible performance. Hence child betrothal, even child marriage. Hence also the importance of taking account of the financial aspects of marriage and family relations.

Most societies usually enforce also, by custom rather than by law,[19] certain

---

13. Certain exceptions were always recognised, usually for royalty represented as divine or quasi-divine, thus emphasising the generality of the rule for humans. The most famous of the exceptions were the Ptolemys of Egypt, and the ancient Kings of Hawaii, who must marry incestuously and also a non-subject woman.

14. *Kinship and Marriage*, p. 55.

15. Under the Sexual Offences Act 1956, s. 10(1), it is a criminal offence for a man to have sexual intercourse with a woman whom he knows to be his grand-daughter, daughter, sister or mother, and s. 11(1) of the Act provides for corresponding offences by a woman who knowingly has sexual intercourse with her grandfather, father, brother or son.

16. That is, relationship by marriage only, where biological considerations are by definition irrelevant.

17. Even classical Greece, as interpreted by Sophocles, suggests no biological abnormality in the children of Oedipus and Jocasta. The view of the Teutonic and Norse sagas is discussed by Engels, *The Origin of the Family*, 4th edn.

18. Robin Fox's chapter on 'The incest problem' in *Kinship and Marriage* reviews much of the recent thinking on the subject. His conclusion, that general avoidance of incest is part of our cultural heritage, is probably as near the truth as we are likely to get. But he may be in error when, with regard to the most common exception, relations between father and daughter, he doubts if 'mothers have much of a say in it when it occurs'.

19. But for example in the United States at the end of 1964 nineteen of the fifty States still had in their legislation some prohibition on so-called 'miscegenous' marriages. In *Loving* v. *Virginia* (1969) U.S. 1, 87 S.Ct. 1817, the U.S. Supreme Court declared such prohibitions unconstitutional, but the decision did not wipe the State legislation from the statute book. See W. Wadlington, 'The Loving case: Virginia's anti-miscegenation statute in historical perspective', 52 *Virginia Law Rev.*, (1966) 1189, and for results of exogamous breeding in the United States see *Science* (22 August 1969).

endogamous rules, prohibiting marriage, and sometimes also sexual relations, between those allegedly of different 'races'.[20] Prohibitions on sexual relations *per se* between members of different groups are, of course, enforceable only in a situation in which all social relations between those groups are circumscribed. They are rarely invoked to deter the casual abuse of the poor and helpless by those whose right to authority over them is assumed.

There are at least three main characteristics of marriage, as compared with sexual relations *per se*; these are: (1) social approval of the union, usually after the performance in public of some prescribed ritual ceremony; (2) the intention to form a continuing relationship; and (3) the presumption that the man is the father of children born to the woman. In monogamous societies, there is also a general presumption that the couple and their minor children will live together, enjoying a shared standard of living and status in society, and that, on the death of the principal property-owner (normally the man) some part of that property will be available for the maintenance of the woman and their minor children, if necessary, while the rest devolves on the children. A definition of marriage of 1933[21] is: 'Unequivocally sanctioned unions which persist and thus come to underlie family life', while a slightly more elaborate one of 1964[22] defines marriage as denoting 'mating arrangements approved in society with special reference to the institutionalized relationships of husband and wife; also the ceremonies which establish such relationship. In ordinary usage marriage includes two distinct ideas: (*a*) that a man and a woman cohabit, generally with the intention of founding a family, and (*b*) that some distinction can be drawn between marriage and other forms of sexual union, qualifiable as pre-marital, extra-marital, adulterous etc.'

The fact that the wedding ceremony is so often called a marriage (with or without the addition of the word 'ceremony') emphasises the fact that the word 'marriage' is used not only with two, but with three or more different meanings.[23] The use of the word 'marriage' for the wedding ceremony has resulted in endless fruitless discussions and at least one absurdly worded statute. Argument has raged round the question whether wilful refusal to consummate a marriage should be a ground for divorce, rather than of nullity, as at present in English law.[24] The argument for making it a ground for divorce rather than nullity is that it is something that occurs after the wedding ceremony, always called the marriage by those who so argue.[25] On the other hand,

20. E.g. South Africa.
21. Robert H. Lowie in the *Encyclopaedia of the Social Sciences*, vol. X.
22. Gould and Kolb (eds), *A Dictionary of the Social Sciences*.
23. See Peter Schofield in his article 'Reforming the Law of Family Property' (Comments and some counter-proposals in relation to Working Paper No. 42): vol. 2 *Family Law* (1972), p. 117.
24. Matrimonial Causes Act 1973, s. 12(*b*). Since the Matrimonial Causes Act 1937 came into operation in 1938 this has been a ground rendering a marriage voidable. The distinction between void and voidable marriages is discussed in Chapter II.
25. Thus Warrington L.J. in *Napier* v. *Napier* [1915] P. 184, 192–3 in the Court of Appeal said: 'nullity, in its very nature, presupposes a cause existing at the date of the marriage. Wilful and persistent refusal, unless it results from incapacity, necessarily arises after the marriage'. See *The Church and the Law of Nullity of Marriage* (S.P.C.K., 1955), pp. 38

Lord Denning M.R. has said that: 'No-one can call a marriage a real marriage when it has not been consummated.'[26] The question is: Is the wedding ceremony the final act of marriage, or does it mark an earlier stage? Parliament has not lagged in the confusion of terminology, and has provided against bigamous wedding ceremonies in England, and made them a criminal offence[27] in the following terms: 'Whosoever, being married, shall marry any other person during the life of the former husband or wife ... shall be guilty of ...',[28] and the Matrimonial Causes Act 1973, s. 11 provides that 'a marriage celebrated after 31st July 1971 shall be void on the ... grounds ... (b) that at the time of the marriage either party was already lawfully married.' What these statutes mean is that if anybody is married he (or she) is by law incapable of marrying another in England, and that if he purports to do so, or goes through any wedding ceremony with another person, that ceremony is of no effect, and he has committed a criminal offence. If the term 'wedding' or 'ceremony' were used instead of 'marriage' in this context, confusion might be reduced.

Confusion has not been lessened by the fact that English law now provides[29] as the alleged[30] sole ground for divorce 'that the marriage has broken down irretrievably'. What has broken down is clearly not the wedding ceremony. Nor is it the legal relationship between husband and wife, of which dissolution is sought. It is the personal relationship between the parties, albeit following a valid wedding ceremony.

That there must be some prescribed ceremony, sanctioned by the particular society, and that this should be publicly performed, seems inevitable. Marriage carries important public rights, of nationality, citizenship or patriality; it is the primary method of conferring legitimacy on the children, and confers on them similar public rights. It should also carry certain private rights of close association, and property rights. These are not referred to in the two definitions of marriage cited[31] from the Social Science Dictionaries, but property rights are inherent in the marriage and family relationship, and are absent only by legal aberration. While natural resources remain scarce, human relationships will be called in aid of claims to them. Thus in the questions of kingship or chieftainship, public recognition of the sexual relationship is crucial, except when overborne by force of arms. The close relationship

and 48, and *Putting Asunder* (Report of a group appointed by the Archbishop of Canterbury) (S.P.C.K., 1966), pp. 67 and 124–5, and the Royal Commission on Marriage and Divorce (Cmd 9678, 1956) paras 88, 89 and 283. These arguments (but not the terminology) were exhaustively considered by the Law Commission in Law Com. 33 (1970), paras 26–8.

26. *Ramsay-Fairfax* v. *Ramsay Fairfax* [1956] P. 115, 133.
27. Since 29 June 1972 Parliament has recognised for purposes of matrimonial relief the validity of polygamous marriages contracted overseas by people not domiciled in the British Islands.
28. Offences Against The Person Act 1861, s. 57.
29. Matrimonial Causes Act 1973, s. 1(1), originally introduced by the Divorce Reform Act 1969, s. 1, which came into operation on 1 January 1971.
30. The word 'sole' appeared in the Act of 1969, but has been omitted in the consolidation of 1973. The interactions between this ground and the 'fact situations', one at least of which must be proved before the marriage is found to have broken down irretrievably, is considered *post* in Chapter V.
31. *Ante*, nn. 21 and 22.

between marriage rules and property transactions is generally admitted, and the property transfers associated with the marriage ceremony itself are almost infinite in their variety, reflecting different organisations of society, distribution of property, economic activities, the status of women, and population pressures.

The payment by the man or his kindred of a bride-price is frequently regarded as the purchase of authority over the woman's children. It helps to ensure the stability of the marriage. It is now generally accepted that the Christian missionaries did many of their converts a dis-service when they set their faces so strongly against the bride-price in Africa,[32] but the commercialisation of the institution did much social harm there.[33]

On the other hand, in Western Europe and among many other communities,[34] the payment of a dowry by the bride's family to the bridegroom was usual, and although its incidence has steeply declined in Western Europe in the last fifty years, it is still usual, for example, in Greece. But although transferred to the husband it is generally inalienable by him, except under certain conditions. The payment of a dowry should not be confused with the widow's dower at English common law,[35] the essential points about which were: (1) it inhered only in the widow, not in the wife; (2) it was eventually set at her right to receive after her husband's death the income from one-third of the land of which he had been seised in fee simple[36] at any time during the marriage, and (3) it carried no rights to administer or control the land itself. Thus as Lord Simon of Glaisdale has said,[37] the widow at common law 'looked like a pensioner of the heir rather than a partner of the ancestor'.[38]

In two fairly recent cases before the English courts[39] the wife in a Moslem marriage has succeeded in enforcing an agreement made before the marriage that, should the husband predecease or divorce her, he or his personal representative would pay her a prearranged sum. In the first case the agreed sum

---

32. See e.g. *A Survey of African Marriage and Family Life*, ed. A. Phillips (1953), especially the introductory essay by the editor, and *African Marriage and Social Change* by L. P. Mair (1969).

33. Particularly when the traditional payments in cattle were superseded by cash payments, eventually payable in instalments. The young men of the family might be unable to obtain brides because the family was still paying off the instalments on their mother.

34. In English law there have been a few cases arising from payment of a dowry on a Jewish marriage, e.g. *Bomzee and Ledermann* v. *Bomzee* [1931] 1 Ch. 289 where it was held that one-quarter of the dowry was recoverable when the parties separated soon after the marriage, and *Kelner* v. *Kelner* [1939] P. 411, where on divorce each former spouse was held entitled to one-half the balance remaining.

35. Dower was abolished in England after 1925 by the Administration of Estates Act 1925, s. 45.

36. Ownership, in lay terms.

37. In his Presidential lecture (as Sir Jocelyn Simon, President of the Probate, Divorce and Admiralty Division of the High Court) to the Holdsworth Club of the Faculty of Law at the University of Birmingham, 'With all my Worldly Goods' (1964), p. 8.

38. The widow's right to dower at common law had its counterpart in the husband's right to curtesy over her lands (also abolished in England in 1925). The great differences were that the husband's right of curtesy took effect at the marriage, included the right to possession of the land itself, and included also the right to manage, control and draw the income from it; the rights normally associated with ownership.

39. *Shahnaz* v. *Rizwan* [1965] 1 Q.B. 390, and *Qureshi* v. *Qureshi* [1972] Fam. 173.

was described as 'deferred *mehar* or dower', and in the second as *'sadaqa,* a type of dower', but as Sir Jocelyn Simon P. pointed out:[40] 'it does not correspond to the concept of dower in former English law'. Neither did these sums correspond with the payment of a dowry, as normally understood in Western Europe and elsewhere. It was a form of bride-price, payable only in certain contingencies.[41]

The equivalent in English law to dowry elsewhere is the marriage settlement, which is deeply rooted in the customs of the propertied classes. From the latter part of the seventeenth century it became usual, on the wedding of any woman belonging to a landed family, for property to be settled 'to her separate use'. This removed the property from the jurisdiction of the common law.[42] The common law purported to give the wife a right to be maintained during the marriage (unless she committed adultery), but this right could not be effectively enforced.[43] When after 1882 the concept of a married woman's separate property was extended by legislation to all married women, a more general type of marriage settlement became customary among the propertied classes, which usually makes it impossible for either husband or wife to touch the capital during their lifetime; often the husband may draw the income produced during his lifetime. The survivor is usually entitled to all the income. Only on the death of the survivor does the capital become divisible, usually among the children. This inveterate habit among propertied families of making a marriage settlement accounts for several curious survivals amongst our property law, including the provision that, if the children become entitled to property on the death intestate of one of their parents[44] or other relatives, they are entitled to be paid this sum on reaching the age of 18 or marriage under that age.[45]

This is one illustration of how deeply English family law in the latter part of the twentieth century is marked by the relics of history, and particularly by feudalism and the influence of the Church, which have themselves profoundly interacted. The doctrine of *laissez-faire* has left some but fewer scars. There are many other examples of the influence the feudal law of property still exercised on property relations within the family. It is even more curious that, whereas in 1925 England abolished some relics of feudalism such as dower, curtesy, the right of primogeniture, and in general the superior rights to property of men compared with women, some feudal rights such as dower still persist in

---

40. [1972] Fam. 173, 184B.
41. It was nevertheless misleadingly translated as dower in the *Muslim Family Laws Ordinance* (VIII of 1961), which governed the marriage.
42. See *ante* n. 38.
43. The only method of enforcement was for the wife to 'pledge her husband's credit'. This assumed that: (1) he was credit-worthy, (2) a tradesman was prepared to supply goods or services to a woman and assume the task of collecting payment from her husband.
44. After June 1972 if the deceased parent leaves a surviving spouse (whether the parent of the children or not), this will happen only if the parent dying leaves more than about £20,000. Since July 1972 the surviving spouse of anyone dying intestate is entitled to (1) all the deceased's personal chattels, (2) the first £15,000 of the estate, and (3) a life interest in half the remainder, before any child of the deceased is entitled to anything at all.
45. Administration of Estates Act 1925, ss 46 and 47, as amended by the Family Law Reform Act 1969, s. 3(2).

other parts of the world which have taken over English common law, but never lived under a full feudal system, such as many of the United States of America and most of Canada.

The influence of the Church and its doctrines over large parts of English family law arose because from before the Conquest until 1857 all matters of family law[46] and the right to succeed to personal property were matters for the Church, which from about 1072 until 1857 administered canon law to them in a separate series of church courts.

On one aspect of family law, however, the influence of the Church is normally exaggerated, and that is the monogamous nature of marriage throughout Western Europe from time immemorial. In many former colonies which practised polygamy, the introduction of a system of monogamous marriage, usually under a special ordinance, was characterised as a 'Christian' marriage. Christianity did not invent monogamy. In fact, there is no trace of polygamy in Western Europe for centuries before the advent of Christianity. Julius Caesar has a fantastic account of the marriage customs of the Celts in Britain amounting to a kind of group marriage[47] but it appears to be accepted by no historian of repute,[48] corresponds to no known custom, and is almost certainly pure fantasy. Tacitus is emphatic about the monogamous nature of marriage and the high status of women among the Germanic tribes who were later to conquer Britain,[49] and classical Greece and Rome, although admitting both concubinage and slavery, were monogamous. Even the Christian contribution of the indissoluble marriage (possibly based on the Roman patrician marriage by *confarreatio*), was riddled with grounds for nullity, until these were drastically reduced by the Protestant reformers in the sixteenth century.

It is true that far more people in the world today live under a system of potentially polygamous than of monogamous marriage, but doctrine and practice do not coincide, and probably more people live in monogamous than in polygamous unions. Except in Africa, polygyny has always been predominantly rich man's or very poor man's law. Even the theory of polygamy is in decline. Its abolition for Hindus in India in 1955[50] was a decisive step.

---

46. But from about the end of the thirteenth century the common law courts ousted the church courts from any matters pertaining to the ownership of real property, and in particular the widow's right to dower and the rights as heir of the eldest surviving son.
47. *De Bello Gallico*, Book V, Ch. 14. Polygyny may have been known among the Celts, but the Irish evidence shows that there was a single principal wife: T. G. E. Powell, *The Celts* (1958), p. 84.
48. E.g. C. W. C. Oman, *History of England*, vol. I, p. 35; Rhys, *Celtic Britain*, 3rd edn (1904) p. 55. There is no evidence that Julius Caesar met many Britons in their homes.
49. *Germania*, Ch. 18. In his *Life of Agricola* he does not mention the marriage customs of the British Celts, but in chapter 16 he refers to Boudicca 'a woman of royal descent (for they make no distinction between the sexes in succession to the throne)'. This would be unusual in a polygynous society.
50. By the Hindu Marriage Act 1955. Polygamy was abolished in Singapore by the Women's Charter in 1961, and its abolition in Malaysia for non-Muslims was proposed late in 1975. In the People's Republic of mainland China, the most populous country in the world, the Marriage Law of 1950 is reported to have effectively abolished arranged marriages, wife purchase, polygamy, concubinage, child brides and interference in the remarriage of widows. Time will show how far the changes go beyond name and form. An English translation of the

Some early theories of the strict correlation between economic activity, the status of women and the incidence of polygyny[51] are no longer accepted, but polyandry appears to be confined to small areas and to be associated with inhospitable territory, in which it is difficult or impossible for one man to provide sufficient sustenance for himself, a woman and their children.

B. MARRIAGE AND FAMILY TODAY

It is now more important than ever to stop 'acting out' in law reform our fantasies of restoring a highly idealised golden age. There is no alternative to rethinking our domestic structures, rules and customs, to correspond with present and future needs, however inconvenient and even painful that may be.

There is first the regional and world population situation. The Hebrew blessing upon Jacob, that God should make him fruitful and increase his descendants until they became a host of nations[52] has been over-fulfilled.[53] Population pressures throughout the world have become intense although some areas may be under-populated, e.g. parts of Canada or the U.S.S.R.[54] Rising standards of living have increased the life expectancy of children born, and prolonged the adult active and sexual life of both sexes, while the age of marriage and parenthood has fallen.

The second great change is the contraction of distance by improved communications; of people and things by aeroplanes and motored vehicles; of information by radio and telecommunications aided by orbiting satellites. The rise in the level of knowledge and awareness of others has considerably loosened the old hierarchical monopolies of government and property. The monopoly of power in its various aspects by certain groups and individuals is no longer accepted as part of a divinely appointed order.

On the macrocosmic scale, new and larger regional groups are sought by nation-states as the old connections break down or assume new forms. Some

---

law is appended to Maurice Freedman's *Colonial Law and Chinese Society* 80, Royal Anthropological Institute Journal (1950) 97.

51. E.g. L. T. Hobhouse, C. C. Wheeler and M. Ginsberg, *The Material Culture and Social Institutions of the Simpler Peoples* (1930).

52. *Genesis* i, 28 (New English Translation 1970).

53. *The United Nations Demographic Yearbook* published February 1975 showed that in mid-1973 world population was 3860 million, an increase of 78 million compared with a year previously. If maintained, this rate of increase would double world population by the year 2007. Figures later published by the United Nations gave the population in mid-1974 of the world's twenty-five most populous countries. The seven whose population exceeds 100 million are (figures in millions): China: 827·8; India: 586; Soviet Union (mid-1973): 249·7; U.S.A.: 211·9; Indonesia: 124·6; Japan: 109·7; Brazil: 104·2. *Keesing's Contemporary Archives*, 9–15 (June 1975).

54. Hungary, with its low and declining birth-rate, may have been justified in legislating against abortion (apparently still its principal method of contraception) in January 1974. In 1972 the number of legally-induced abortions exceeded the number of live births. The annual divorce rate was, in the same year, running at nearly 25 per cent the rate of marriages contracted.

form of world order approaches more closely, however fierce and recurrent the pre-birth pangs may be. At the microcosmic extreme, nuclear families, compulsorily segregated in uniform dwellings, and classified to conform with simplified computerised formulae, find themselves more isolated than before from kindred, neighbourhood and understanding.

Twice within living memory the West has engaged in internecine warfare on a vast scale, producing only common injury. Minor sectarian and national differences, often misnamed religious or racial struggles, are still made the excuse for atrocities against mere passers-by. But increasingly these aberrations are seen as the death-throes of an old order, to be contained and reduced, but no longer accepted as inevitable. Today also the victims of war and atrocities are found increasingly among all ages and both sexes. The segregation of women and children from male warriors and decision-makers no longer applies, if it ever really did so.

We have the beginnings of a new understanding of human mental and emotional processes. Our knowledge in this field is still rudimentary; witness the inadequacy of provisions for dealing with children deprived of the healthy home background in which they still develop and flourish best. But we have the means, if we choose to use them, of removing some of the encrusted prejudices that still infect the laws and practices applied to domestic relation-ships.

Whereas, in England a hundred years ago, adults usually died in their early forties – a woman after she had given birth to anything up to (sometimes exceeding) twenty children – today people who marry in their early twenties have a life expectation of a further fifty to sixty years. Women in England today give birth on average to just over two children, both of whom will be born and at school by the time the mother has reached the age of 30. She can then expect a further forty to fifty years of life, and is likely to outlive her husband, even if they are of the same age. The *Finer Report on One-Parent Familes* points out[55] that 'The fall in the age of marriage is a demographic development of pervasive social importance yet it has not attracted extensive study and is not fully understood. The trend has gone much further amongst manual workers than amongst non-manual, professional and managerial workers.'[56] The proportion of those married has been described[57] as 'as near an approach to practically universal marriage as has been achieved in this country', and the *Finer Report* points out that 'given what is known about such factors as the distribution of homosexuality and chronic ill-health, psychological as well as physical, among the population at large, it is obvious

55. Cmnd 5629, para. 3.11.
56. 'The difference between the marriage patterns of different socio-economic groups has widened since the 1930s', in the words of the Commentary on the Registrar General's *Statistical Review of England and Wales for the Year 1965*, Part III, pp. 40–1, quoted *supra*.
57. By E. Grebenik and Griselda Rowntree, 'Factors associated with the age at marriage in Britain', in *Proceedings of the Royal Society*, Series B, 159 (1964) 180, quoted ibid. para. 3.8. *The Population Projections of the Government Actuary*, Nos 2 and 3, 1971–2012 (1972–3) assume a decline in the unmarried population. The proportion of women aged up to 29 years who are married is expected to rise from 0·877 in mid-1971 to 0·881 by 1986.

that the present popularity of marriage must be drawing into the institution large numbers who lack any evident vocation for it. From this point of view, a very high marriage rate will lead to a disproportionately high rate of breakdown'.[58]

Women, as a legacy of their former inferior education and compulsion to comply with the male-dominated social order, are still the main bulwarks of tradition. It is still principally women who fear change. But this conservatism may not continue indefinitely. Other occupations have opened to women during the last hundred years, although admittedly they are still illogically restricted, and in England they are still paid on average just over half of men's earnings.[59] This level of male/female earnings is clearly linked with the 'one-third rule' for financial provision on divorce, inherited from the church courts in 1857, and recently reintroduced by the Court of Appeal 'not as a rule, but as a starting-point', which emerged also as the finishing point.[60] But whether the age of first marriage continues to decline or not, and whether the pattern of 'marriage-divorce-remarriage-divorce' (and so on) proves as popular as is frequently suggested,[61] the pressure of population must inevitably lead to a decline in the birth-rate and an extension of the average female lifespan after the birth of her last child.

Recently there has been further advance in the range of occupations open to women. The higher ranks of commerce, finance and banking are still virtually closed to them.[62] They are totally excluded from authority in the Church, which uses its inherited wealth and its link with the State to reaffirm the serfdom of one sex in marriage by insisting that when the traditional Church-controlled buildings are used for wedding ceremonies, the woman must publicly vow to obey and serve the man.[63]

The British House of Commons elected on 10 October 1974 contains 635 members, of whom only 27 are women. No woman has ever yet sat on the Judicial Committee of the House of Lords, or in the Court of Appeal. In 1965 the first woman ever was appointed among the seventy-two High Court judges, and she was joined by a second in 1974. Women are still about 1 per cent of County Court and Circuit judges, about 8 per cent of practising barristers

---

58. Cmnd 5629, para. 3.9.
59. See 'The status of women in Great Britain', XX *American Journal of Comparative Law*, (1972) 592. More than two million full-time women workers earned less than £20 a week, including overtime. See also *The Times* 14.3.73.
60. *Wachtel* v. *Wachtel* [1973] Fam. 72 C.A., discussed further in Chapter VII. Ormrod J. had held husband and wife equally entitled on divorce to the sole substantial asset, the matrimonial home. A decision of the Court of Appeal cutting the wife's share from £10,000 to £6000 and maintenance for the daughter from £500 to £300 a year was reported under such headlines as 'Great Women's Lib. Breakthrough' in the popular press. Only *The Guardian* correctly assessed the decision. Bagnall J. commented in *Harnett* v. *Harnett* [1973] Fam. 156, 162C: 'If, therefore, it was a triumph, it was at least tinged with Pyrrhic characteristics.'
61. E.g. O. R. McGregor, *Divorce in England* (1957).
62. The London Stock Exchange opened to them on 2 May 1972. The Baltic Exchange still refuses them membership. In 1974 the City of London vetoed the appointment of a woman alderman, but in 1975 one was elected.
63. An alternative wording is available for use in church weddings at the priest's option but is never used on publicised occasions.

and about 3 per cent of practising solicitors. On the other hand, more than one-third of the unpaid lay magistracy is female; another example of conservative clinging to unpaid status.[64] In the medical profession, in 1970 women constituted 14 per cent of hospital medical staff and about 12·2 per cent of general practitioners in England and Wales;[65] in dentistry they were only 8·5 per cent of qualified dentists in hospitals and 7·32 per cent of those in private practice.[66]

A few professions have traditionally been considered particularly appropriate to women, and women predominate in them. Examples are nursing,[67] teaching, and the social and welfare services. All represent extensions of the duties which women have been expected to perform domestically. All are notoriously underpaid, overworked, and generally exploited, and in all but nursing, in the higher managerial positions men predominate. Thus at the beginning of 1970, women represented 58 per cent of teachers but 40 per cent of head teachers at schools, and only 11 per cent of teachers at universities.[68] In June 1971 of a total of 3281 full professors in universities in Great Britain, 3237 were men and only 44 women.[69] Of these half were at the University of London. The local authority welfare services were reorganised after 1970,[70] and Directors of Social Services were newly appointed. By June 1972, of 173 such Directors only 16 were women.[71] The Sex Discrimination Act 1975 came into operation in part on 29 December 1975, establishing an Equal Opportunities Commission. Much will depend on its energy and wisdom. The Equal Pay Act 1970 was due to be fully implemented by 29 December 1975, but it is now widely accepted that, without legislation against discrimination in employment on grounds of sex, the Equal Pay Act would merely have intensified the segregation of the sexes in employment and accentuated the tendency to illogical classification: e.g. man's job if the wheel is turned right; woman's job if it is turned left.[72] Even after 1975,

---

64. There is probably a social element in the number of women practising members of the Bar, but no figures are available for those who intend to earn a reasonable living. Of 3881 practising members of the bar 313 were women according to 73 *Guardian Gazette* 29.9.76.
65. Memorandum to the Select Committee of the House of Lords on the Anti-Discrimination (No. 2) Bill by the Department of Health and Social Security: 13 June 1972; *Minutes of Evidence and Proceedings of the Select Committee on the Anti-Discrimination (No. 2) Bill,* Session 1971–2, ref. 160, p. 35.
66. Ibid., In reply to questions from Baroness Summerskill. See also Mr Salter, Under-Secretary of the D.H.S.S.. at p. 43.
67. Memorandum to the Select Committee of the House of Lords on the Anti-Discrimination (No. 2) Bill from the D.H.S.S. on 13 June 1972: 'Traditionally nursing the physically ill has been regarded as a female occupation but nursing the mentally ill and mentally handicapped has been regarded as a job for either sex.'
68. Memorandum submitted by the Department of Education and Science to the Select Committee of the House of Lords on 13 June 1972. Ibid. p. 26.
69. Reply by Secretary of State for Education and Science to a question from Mr Edward Bishop, M.P. on 23 June 1971. H.C. Deb. vol. 819, cols 301–2.
70. Under the Local Authority Social Services Act 1970, ss 2 and 6, in operation from 1 January 1971.
71. *Minutes of Evidence and Proceedings of the Select Committee on the Anti-Discrimination (No. 2) Bill,* H.L., ibid., p. 41, para. 48.
72. Discrimination on grounds of sex within the six original member States of the European Communities was considered in a report by Mme Evelyne Sullerot (undated. about 1970): *L'Emploi des Femmes et ses problèmes dans les États Membres de la Communauté*

however, it will probably be some decades before the idea is laid to rest that it is for men alone to say what work women will be allowed to do. [73]

If the broad lines of developments in the status of women within and outside the domestic sphere over the next few decades are now reasonably clear, the same cannot be said for developments in relation to children. Apart from some attenuated rights to property, always subject to rights of management by a parent, guardian, trustee or personal representative, those under the age of sixteen years have no rights in English law, and they have few below the age of eighteen. The whole of our law relating to minors is derived from the rights of guardianship over the heir to land by feudal tenure, the most important of which were the guardian's right to waste the heir's land, and his right to 'give' the heir in marriage at a profit the guardian considered appropriate. [74] Parental rights were exclusively paternal rights until 1886, [75] although from about 1660 the Court of Chancery might, in very rare cases, intervene between a father and his children, acting under the prerogative of the Crown as *parens patriae*. From 1839 by statute, [76] the same court might, if it saw fit, grant a mother custody of her young children, and the right of access to all her children until they reached full age. [77] The Guardianship Act 1973 [78] provides that in relation to the custody or upbringing of a minor, or the administration of a minor's property, and the application of income of his property, a mother shall have the same rights and authority as the law allows to a father, and the rights and authority of mother and father shall be equal and exercisable by either without the other.

Even a child's most basic requirement, that of maintenance by the parents

---

Européenne, of which a summary in English (also undated) is entitled: *The Employment of Women and the Problems it Raises in the Member States of the European Community.*

73. The Chairman of the Employment Development Policy Committee of the Trades Union Congress: 'There are still some old-fashioned men who do not believe in their wives going out to work and I am one of them.' *Sixth Report from the Expenditure Committee*, Session 1972–3, printed 8 March 1973, ref. 182, p. 36, para. 2102.

74. In *The Queen's Wards*, Joel Hurstfield (1958) gives a graphic account of unscrupulous trading in these rights. The Court of Wards was abolished under the Restoration settlement in 1660, and the Tenures Abolition Act 1660, s. 8 (repealed only by the Statute Law Repeals Act 1969) gave the father the right to custody of all his children (not only of the heir as previously) and the right to appoint by deed or will a guardian in whom his powers of custody of the person and management of the property of any of his children would vest after the father's death. The right to refuse consent to the marriage of any child other than the heir was not granted until the first Marriage Act of 1753.

75. The Guardianship of Infants Act 1886 replaced the Infants Custody Act 1873, extending the discretion of the courts under the 1839 Act, *post*, Chapter III. It followed the decision in *Re Agar-Ellis* (1883) 24 Ch.D. 49.

76. The Infants Custody Act 1839, commonly called Talfourd's Act, as promoted by counsel for the father, who had, in *R. v. Greenhill* (1836) 4 Ad. & E. 624, won the father's absolute right to custody of his three children aged $5\frac{1}{2}$, $4\frac{1}{2}$ and 2 years. In *R. v. de Manneville* (1804) 5 East 221 the Lord Chancellor held a French father entitled to enter by force a house in which his British born wife had sought shelter from his cruelty, and forcibly remove the child of 8 months whom she was suckling.

77. Then 21 years, but from 1970 reduced to 18 years by the Family Law Reform Act 1969, s. 1.

78. By S.I. No. 695 of 1974, Parts I and III of the Act and Schedules 1 to 3 were brought into operation from 8 May 1974. See Chapter VIII.

who brought him helpless into the world, in law is still not the child's right. It is a duty owed by the parent only to the other parent, or a third party including a public authority, and enforceable only by that parent, person or authority. Whether it is enforced or not will depend less on the child's welfare than on the emotional relationships between the parents or the attitude of the authority. And it is still usual for one order to be made for the maintenance of the wife and children that is manifestly insufficient to maintain the child or children alone.

The first intervention of the public authorities in relation to children was at the parish level under the Poor Law. In the nature of things, a high proportion of the children who became a charge on parish funds were born outside marriage. The medieval approach was that such a child was *filius nullius* or nobody's child. If such a child was born to a woman who was a villein (or serf), the child was a free man, since his unknown putative father might have been free, and a free man could not beget a serf. This 'free' child would be unable to claim unfree land which could be held only by those bound to it. It was decided in 1326 that, if a lord was claiming the return of an escaped villein, 'a plea that he or any of his male ancestors was a bastard was a peremptory answer to the lord, because a bastard is a *filius nullius*, and it cannot be presumed that this unknown person was a villein'. The canon law on the other hand said that whenever one of the parties was servile, so was the child. But from the twelfth century the canon law recognised that the child was legitimated by the subsequent marriage of his parents, whereas the common lawyers rejected this view at the Council of Merton in 1235–6. At common law bastardy remained indelible until 1927. The common law position that the child born outside marriage was 'nobody's child' is greatly misunderstood. Its only real effect was that he could not succeed to property as the heir of either his mother or his putative father. The passage in Blackstone's *Commentaries* on the question is usually quoted out of context; it is a particularly humane and sympathetic one.

One of the first statutes we have dealing with children is the Poor Law Act of 1576, of Elizabeth I, with its preamble reading: 'Concerning bastards begotten and born out of lawful matrimony (an offence against God's law and man's law), the said bastards being now left to be kept at the charges of the parish where they be born, to the great burden of the same parish, and in defrauding of the relief of the impotent and aged true poor of the same parish, and to the evil example and encouragement of the lewd life.' Two justices of the peace could both punish the mother and the reputed father of the child and charge both of them with the costs of the child's maintenance. Not until the passage of the Poor Law Act 1844[79] was the mother of a child born outside marriage enabled in her own right to obtain an affiliation order against the putative father for the child's maintenance. The maximum amount was then set at two shillings and sixpence (or twelve and a half new pence) per week. The power of the Poor Law Authorities to charge the putative father for the child's maintenance was repealed at

---

79. By s. 2.

the same time. Today only the mother may try to recover maintenance for her child from the putative father unless someone else has a custodianship order for the child, or the child has become a charge on the Supplementary Benefits Commission, in which cases the custodian or the Commission also has a right of action. If the court has appointed a guardian, the guardian may also apply. Action is still possible only in quasi-criminal affiliation proceedings in the magistrates courts, unless by a marriage the child has become a child of the family of the mother and her husband, and the number of affiliation actions is small.

There were attempts by statute from 1802 onwards to regulate the conditions in factories of apprentices, who were young children, many of them in the care of the Poor Law Authorities, but all were ineffective until the Factories Act of 1833 provided for a salaried inspectorate to enforce the law. The Act of 1833 provided that children under the age of 13 in factories must attend a school for two hours a day, six days out of seven. The same year saw also the provision (by Order in Council) for Grants in Aid for education administered by the Treasury. A general system of public education was introduced by the Elementary Education Act 1870.

The law relating to those children we still call 'illegitimate' is considered in Chapter VIII. No British Parliament would today adopt the wording the Elizabethan Parliament chose four hundred years ago, but in 1959 it legislated and in 1971 repeated the legislation concerning the 'natural' father of an 'illegitimate' child. The problem of children born outside marriage has always concerned mainly the poor. The woman of property could and can buy herself either a marriage or an abortion.

With hindsight it seems incredible that in 1967 the Abortion Act, legalising termination of pregnancy in certain conditions, should have been passed before any educational campaign dealing with improved methods of contraception had been undertaken, but only an Act[80] enabling such local authorities as were prepared to do so to make arrangements for providing advice on contraception, medical examination, and the supply of contraceptive substances and appliances. Not until 1975[81] were contraceptive substances and appliances made generally available free of charge under the National Health Service, and staff and supplies were not always adequate.

The rate of illegitimate births has nevertheless not fallen, but has risen by over 50 per cent in the period 1950–71, from 51 to 83 per thousand live births.[82] The incidence of illegitimate births to mothers under 20 years of age has increased sixfold over the period 1938 to 1971.[83] In 1971 there were 25,490 legally induced abortions performed on girls under 20 years of age.

---

80. The National Health Service (Family Planning) Act 1967. The National Health Service (Family Planning) Amendment Act 1972 added voluntary vasectomy to the services available under the Act of 1967.

81. The National Health Service was reorganised from 1 April 1974. Free family planning services by medical practitioners were introduced on 1 July 1975. See H. C. Deb., *Written Answers* vol. 892 cols. 115–6, vol. 896 col. 426, 14 May and 29 July 1975.

82. Written reply by the Under-Secretary of State for Social Services, 22 September 1971, H.C. Deb. vol. 823, col. 9.

83. From 2·80 live births per 1000 women under 20 in 1938 to 14·27 in 1971: Registrar

A girl under 16 years of age cannot lawfully consent to sexual inter-course, and a man who has intercourse with her commits a criminal offence. If the girl is over 13 years of age the man may have a defence if he reasonably believed she was his wife; or provided he is under 24 years of age and has not previously been charged with such an offence, if he reasonably believed that she was over 16 years of age.[84] In 1971 there were 1624 live births to girls under 16, representing 2·2 per cent of illegiti-mate live births, and 2436 abortions were also performed on girls under 16, making a total of 4060 pregnancies recorded amongst under-age girls.[85] In 1972 the corresponding figures were 1490 live births and 2804 abortions, making a total number of recorded pregnancies of 4294 among this under-age group,[86] thus maintaining the 'steady increase' in the number of preg-nancies and abortions in this group, which the Lane Committee found.[87] In May 1974 a Department of Health circular on the Family Planning Service[86] advised medical practitioners that they are not acting unlawfully if, in good faith, and for the protection of their patients, they do not tell the parents of girls under 16 that their daughters are being supplied with contraceptives. Doctors are, however, advised that it is prudent to seek the girl's consent to their being informed.

The Lane Committee Report has drawn attention to the differences shown by the Registrar General's *Supplement on Abortion* 1971, in proportions of pregnant women who obtain abortions in different areas of the country under the National Health Service (not necessarily free of charge) and at private clinics.[88] Although finding that much adverse criticism of the private sector was justified, and that a small number of members of the medical profession and their associates 'have brought considerable reproach on this country', the Committee found that the more reputable parts of the private sector had performed valuable service,[89] and that while illegal abortions had not been eliminated they had probably been reduced. It was, however, unable

---

General's *Statistical Review* (1971), table EE(b). Births to mothers aged under 15 have been included in the age-group 15–19.

84. Sexual Offences Act 1956, ss 5 and 6.
85. Registrar General's *Supplement on Abortion 1971*, Table 1A: *Lane Committee Report on the Working of the Abortion Act*, Cmnd 5579, para. 221. Table 11 gives the age breakdown for abortions, showing that three were carried out on girls of 11. In para. 231 the Report gives a figure of 2296 resident girls under 16 having abortions of whom twenty-five had previously had an abortion.
86. *The Times* 15.5.74 on a Department of Health circular to doctors on the Family Planning Service.
87. Cmnd 5579, vol. I, para. 216 et seq.
88. Cmnd 5579, vol. I, para. 43 and figs. CIII–CVII. Only Newcastle recorded over 80 per cent of patients terminated under the N.H.S. in their home region. Figures for the Metropolitan regions are distorted by the high mobility of patients between them. In vol. III of the Report, the study by the Institute for Studies in Medical Care suggests at p. 21 that of women resident in England and Wales and having abortions in 1971, 48 per cent paid for them. In 1971 nearly a half of the women having abortions were treated in the private sector: vol. I, paras 400–1. See also vol. II, paras 161–74.
89. Cmnd 5579, vol. I, para. 443. A further report by a Select Committee of the House of Commons was published on 28 July 1976.

either to accept suggested estimates of the annual number of such abortions, or to make any estimates of its own as to their level.[90] The cost of abortions under the less scrupulous areas of the private sector are so high as to send women away into the cheaper back streets.

As from 1970[91] the position of children born outside marriage was greatly improved by statute. For the first time they were given the same rights of succession on the death intestate of either of their parents as if they had been born legitimate. This is not likely to affect many people, since 'illegitimacy' and riches rarely coincide. Much more important were provisions sweeping away the common law rule of judicial interpretation and establishing that after 1969 all words of relationship such as 'child', 'son', 'daughter' and so on should include illegitimate as well as legitimate relationship. The old rule, that a child born outside marriage was not a 'child' unless, exceptionally, he was clearly included in the description, came very close to saying that a person born outside marriage was not a person. Also important was the provision that such children could apply to the court, like their legitimate counterparts,[92] for provision to be made for them from the estate left by a deceased parent, however his will or the law of intestate succession might dispose of it. After 1 April 1976 all children of any age and whether married or not, may apply.[93]

The major recommendation of the Latey Committee,[94] also implemented as from 1970, was that reducing the age of majority from 21 to 18 years.[95] One reason was that this would enable young people to marry at that age without parental consent, which was not the strongest argument for reducing the age of majority. Our minimum age of marriage at 16 years for both sexes (which is also the age below which sexual intercourse with a girl is normally a criminal offence), is lower than that in the majority of western countries. Even in the U.S.S.R. the minimum age is 18 years for both sexes, with power to individual Republics to reduce the age by not more than two years. In theory Islamic Central Asian Republics in the U.S.S.R. have therefore the same minimum age of marriage as this country.[96]

After 1969 it is also now provided[97] that any person aged 16 may give consent to any surgical, medical or dental treatment to himself as effectively as if he were of full age. This of course includes contraceptive advice, drugs, and appliances. The same Act also enabled the term 'minor' to be applied to anyone under full age, instead of the former term 'infant', and many have found this a relief.

From the beginning of 1974 anybody who attains the age of 16 years

---

90. Cmnd 5579, vol. I, paras 502–9.
91. Family Law Reform Act 1969, ss 14–19.
92. Under the Inheritance (Family Provision) Act 1938, as amended in 1952 and 1966.
93. Inheritance (Provision for Family and Dependants) Act 1975, s. 1(1) (c).
94. *Report of the Committee on the Age of Majority*, Cmnd 3342 (1967).
95. Family Law Reform Act 1969, s. 1 and 1st Schedule.
96. How far theory corresponds with practice is a question to which no honest and impartial answer is obtainable.
97. Family Law Reform Act 1969, s. 8.

or marries under that age[98] may acquire an independent domicile.[99] This is important, as it is the law of the domicile that governs personal questions such as capacity to marry and grounds for, and other relief[100] obtainable on divorce.

Education is now governed by the Education Act 1944, as amended, and from 1 September 1972 the minimum school-leaving age was compulsorily raised for all children from 15 to 16 years.[101]

Adoption of children was introduced by statute after 1926 and the number of adoptions rose from under 3000 in 1927 to a peak of 24,831 in 1968, and dropped back to 21,495 by 1971. In 1971 children adopted who were born outside marriage numbered 14,907, compared with 6588 legitimate children. Another feature of adoption in recent years is that parents, alone or with a step-parent, have constituted nearly half of adopters; they numbered 10,751 in 1971 out of a total of 21,495 adopters. Some 90 per cent of non-parental adoptions involve children born outside marriage, but the percentage has fallen in recent years, and today unwed mothers are less likely than they were a few years ago to place their children for adoption. In part this may be due to improved financial provision for such children by the welfare agencies; probably more to increased knowledge of the financial provision available and to the greater tolerance, especially in the large conurbations, shown to the unmarried mother and her child.

Since 1948 the local authority has had primary responsibility to provide for the accommodation and care of children in their area whose parents are unable to do so, and since 1958 local authorities have been empowered to act as adoption agencies. After 1970 the major way in which the juvenile courts can deal with children and young people who infringe the law is to place them in the care of the local authority. The local authorities are therefore increasingly involved in all aspects of child care.

Cases of children battered or starved to death by their parents have recently thrown a spotlight on the assumption generally held by welfare workers both of local authorities and voluntary bodies, and persisted in despite evidence to the contrary, that those who procreate a child are in all cases best fitted to handle the child's upbringing. Where parents are obliged to place their children in the care of the local authority the local authorities try to place the children in foster homes, which are not only preferable to institutions for the children, but are generally far cheaper for the local authorities (that is to say, for their ratepayers).[102]

---

98. Since 16 is the minimum age of marriage in England and Wales, the exception can apply only to those married overseas while domiciled abroad.
99. Domicile and Matrimonial Proceedings Act 1973, s. 3.
100. Viz. property transfer, financial provision by way of a lump sum and/or periodical payments, and orders for the custody and maintenance of children of the family.
101. S.I. No. 444 of 1972.
102. According to *Children in Care in England and Wales, March 1975*, of 99,120 children then in care 31,930 or 32 per cent were boarded out at an average cost of £7 per child per week; 34,582 were in local authority community homes at an average cost of £50 per week; 4,335 were in voluntary homes at an average cost of £22 per week.

Some limited recognition of the claims of those who have provided a reasonable home for the child, perhaps for years, and guided his steps into the world, as distinct from those who physically produced him and left his upbringing to others, have now been introduced by the Children Act 1975, considered in Chapter X.

The Church of England Board of Social Responsibility reported in 1966[103] in favour of a putative father's right to acknowledge his illegitimate children and have the same rights and authority in respect of them as if they had been born following his lawful marriage to the mother. This system of recognition of non-marital children is usual in civil law systems derived from the Roman Law, and is of course based on the Father as Head of the Family, even if illicit. It gives the putative father a right to accept or reject his children born outside marriage, which he does not have for children born to his wife. Parental rights in respect of the child give him a powerful lever of control over the mother throughout the child's minority. It is, of course, unnecessary to declare any such 'right' if the mother agrees. If she does not agree, she could be subjected, throughout her child's minority, to having her child kept against her will under the influence of a man to whom she was not married, who had no liabilities towards her, and whom she may have met only in peculiar circumstances. Her chances of marriage with another man would be correspondingly reduced. Her only alternative (to which European women are often driven by the system) is to deny the true paternity and exonerate the father from any contribution to the maintenance of the child for whose existence he was responsible equally with herself.

A more balanced view was expressed by Wilberforce J. (now Lord Wilberforce) in 1964:[104] 'The tie (if such is shown to exist) between the child and his natural father (or any other relative) may properly be regarded in this connection, not on the basis that the person concerned has a claim which he has a right to have satisfied, but, if at all, and to the extent that, the conclusion can be drawn that the child will benefit from the recognition of this tie.' It is hoped that this wiser approach will soon be preferred to the ancient lore of the 'blood-tie'. Psychiatric writers have long stressed the possible divergence between biological and psychological parenthood, and recent studies have strengthened the value of the distinction.[105]

Perhaps the most beneficial provision with regard to the custody and education of children of the family whose parents are petitioning for divorce, or nullity or judicial separation, is that[106] providing that the petitioner must set

---

103. *Fatherless by Law?* Professor D. Lasok advances a similar theory in 'The Legal status of the putative father' 17 *ICLQ* (1968) 634.

104. In *Re Adoption Application 41/61* (No. 2) |1964| Ch. 48, 53, cited with approval by Lord MacDermott in *J.* v. *C.* |1970| A.C. 668, 713, and by Baker P. in *Re D.* |1973| Fam. 209, 216.

105. E.g. *Beyond the Best Interests of the Child* by Joseph Goldstein, Anna Freud and Albert J. Solnit (New York: The Free Press, 1973). Although written from an American standpoint, this book draws lessons from the English decision in *Re W.* [1971] A.C. 682.

106. First introduced in 1958, and now embodied in the Matrimonial Causes Act 1973, s. 41, and Form 2 of the Matrimonial Causes Rules 1973.

out on the divorce petition full details of all the children of the family, and that the decree cannot be made absolute until the court has declared itself satisfied with the arrangements proposed for the care of the children or that no more satisfactory arrangements can be made. This concentrates the parents' minds before the proceedings begin on the fact that the children's lives will be profoundly affected by the divorce, nullity, or judicial separation. But there is no requirement that parents applying for custody of a child shall give any account of the extent to which they have in the past involved themselves in the child's upbringing. This would seem reasonable and necessary.

There is room for improvement in family law relating to husband and wife, but the direction of the changes needed are reasonably clear, at least in their broad outlines. In regard to children, on the other hand, perhaps we have advanced only to the stage of realising that we may not be asking the right questions, and have almost certainly not yet formulated the right answers. If, indeed, our law is to be improved and not allowed to stagnate it is reasonable to prophesy that it is in the law relating to children that advances will be most notable over the next twenty years or so.

PART I

Legal Family Relationships

CHAPTER II

Before the Ceremony: The Wedding Ceremony: Void and Voidable Marriages and their Effects

A. BEFORE THE WEDDING CEREMONY

Today English law attaches minimal legal significance to the engagement to marry. In some European countries there are still remnants of the canon law of the Middle Ages.[1] In time of war similar provisions are frequently extended to the dependants of engaged men killed on active service. Such institutions and procedures have long been unknown in English law.

(i) DAMAGES FOR BREACH OF PROMISE OF MARRIAGE

Until it was abolished in England after 1970 by the Law Reform (Miscellaneous Provisions) Act, 1970, however, English law knew the action for damages for Breach of Promise of Marriage, a form of breach of contract. Once injury was proved, the sum recoverable might include exemplary or punitive damages, more akin to those normally awarded in an action of tort than one for breach of contract.

It was principally the measure of damages that marked off the common law action from its equivalents in civil law countries. Similar heads of recovery still exist, for example, in such countries as France,[2] Federal Germany,[3]

---

1. Notably the law of Switzerland, providing that on the application of one parent or of the child (or his issue) the child of an engaged couple may be declared legitimate by a judge if marriage between the engaged parents became impossible by the death or incapacity of one party. The legitimised child has the same rights in respect of his parents and their kindred as if born legitimate, and these rights are transmitted to his own descendants. *Code Civil Suisse*, Arts 260, 261, 263, and see Law Com. 26 (1969) Appendix C (iv).
2. *Code Civil (Francais)*, Art. 1382 imposes a general liability of compensation on all who cause loss or damage to another.
3. *B.G.B.*, Art. 1298, limited to expenses or losses reasonably incurred by the other or a third party and not if the breach were justified: Art. 1299.

Switzerland[4] and Greece.[5] But in all these countries there exists between spouses either a system of community of property, or community of gains, and they all retain the system of *legitim*, which existed in England throughout the Middle Ages, but after falling into disfavour in much of the southern part of the country, was abolished by legislation in the latter part of the seventeenth and the early eighteenth century.[6] Until 1883, when the Married Women's Property Act 1882 came into operation, the wedding ceremony conveyed to the husband all the wife's personal property, the right to manage, control and draw the income from her freehold land, the right to all her income, earned and unearned, from any source, and after the abolition of her *legitima portio* the absolute right to dispose of all 'his' property at his death as he chose, leaving his wife and children destitute. The contrast between the wife's lack of rights at common law and the right of the jilted fiancée to punitive damages was startling. Gold-digging actions for Breach of Promise of Marriage by women were clearly encouraged.

In 1954 the Court of Appeal had given a novel, if not bizarre, application to the breach of promise action in *Shaw* v. *Shaw*,[7] where a woman bigamously married who survived her purported husband was held entitled to damages from the estate equal to the share to which she would have been entitled on intestacy if she had been the deceased's widow. The promise to marry was thus interpreted as including a promise not only to predecease the plaintiff, but to do so intestate. The Law Commission recommended[8] that the party who had in good faith entered into any void marriage should be brought within the provisions of the Inheritance (Family Provision) Act 1938, enabling her or him to make application to the court for discretionary provision from the deceased's estate, and this was also done by the Law Reform (Miscellaneous Provisions) Act 1970.[9]

Hardship may now be caused by lack of any possibility of recovering expenses, representing a violent swing from the possibility of obtaining swingeing punitive damages to the impossibility of recovering any money when an intended marriage does not take place. This was linked not only with other reforms effected by the same statute, viz. the abolition of damages for adultery[10] and of actions for enticement, seduction or harbouring of a spouse or child,[11] but also with the curtailment of enquiries into matrimonial behaviour in divorce.[12]

---

4. *Code Civil Suisse*, Art. 92 provides for an equitable indemnity payable by the party who breaks an engagement without good cause, for expenses incurred in good faith with a view to marriage, and Art. 93 sanctions the award of 'moral damages' to the innocent party whose personal interests have been gravely damaged by the breach of the engagement.
5. See *Kremezi* v. *Ridgeway* [1949] 1 All E.R. 662.
6. See Chapter VI.
7. [1954] 2 Q.B. 429 C.A., Singleton, Denning and Morris L.JJ.
8. Law Com. 26.
9. Section 6, overruling previous decisions in *Re Peete* [1952] 2 All E.R. 599 and *Re Watkins* [1953] 1 W.L.R. 1323 that an applicant as surviving spouse under the Inheritance (Family Provision) Act 1938 (as amended) must adduce at least good evidence of the validity of her or his marriage to the deceased.
10. Law Reform (Miscellaneous Provisions) Act 1970, s. 4.
11. Ibid. s. 5.
12. Particularly the presumption that a marriage has broken down irretrievably if the parties

The Law Reform (Miscellaneous Provisions) Act 1970 provided that a party who gives property to the person he or she is engaged to marry may recover it if the engagement is terminated, provided the gift was made on condition, express or implied, that it should be so returned.[13] Where both parties have a beneficial interest in property, the illogical but practical solution has been adopted of extending to engaged couples the summary court procedure for determining their respective rights provided by the Married Women's Property Act 1882, s. 17,[14] and also for applying to them the rules applied to the property of married couples.[15] In a number of recent decisions,[16] the courts have sought to eliminate applications on divorce and other matrimonial causes under s. 17 of the Act of 1882, and bring all property rights of divorcing spouses so far as possible within their discretionary jurisdiction.[17] Such restriction as between spouses of claims to property under s. 17 of the Act of 1882 cannot extend to those engaged couples who resiled from the marriage.

(ii) THE PRESUMPTION OF UNDUE INFLUENCE

Until recently, where an engaged couple entered into any contract which appeared unduly advantageous to the man, it was for the man to prove that no undue influence was exercised. As late as 1931, in *Bomze and Lederman* v. *Bomze*,[18] the existence of the presumption was accepted, but the Court of Appeal in *Zamet* v. *Hyman*[19] thought that no presumption was any longer appropriate, but that in any transaction made between an engaged couple which upon its face appears much more favourable to one party than the other, the court may find a fiduciary relationship.

After 1882 it has been held that there is no presumption of undue influence as between husband and wife,[20] although undue influence may be proved as a fact.[21]

---

have lived apart continuously for two years and the respondent consents to a divorce, or if they have lived apart continuously for five years: now Matrimonial Causes Act 1973, s. 1(2)(*d*) and (*e*).

13. Law Reform (Miscellaneous Provisions) Act 1970, s. 3. But the gift of an 'engagement ring' (which is not defined) is presumed to be unconditional, and the ring need not therefore be returned unless the conditional nature of the gift can be proved.
14. On which see generally Chapters III, V and VII.
15. Including the Matrimonial Proceedings and Property Act 1970, s. 37, not incorporated in the Matrimonial Causes Act 1973.
16. E.g. *Gordon* v. *Gordon*, *The Times* 12.10.73 C.A., per Lord Denning M.R., but see *Glenn* v. *Glenn* |1973| 1 W.L.R. 1016.
17. Matrimonial Causes Act 1973, ss 21–33.
18. |1931| 1 Ch. 289, Maugham J. The pre-nuptial agreement was there upheld, but partial repayment was ordered of sums withdrawn by the prospective husband before the marriage.
19. |1961| 1 W.L.R. 1442 C.A., affirming Pennycuick J.
20. *Barron* v. *Willis* |1899| 2 Ch. 578; *Howes* v. *Bishop* |1909| 2 K.B. 390 C.A. (wife liable on a promissory note signed with her husband, although not independently advised); *Mackenzie* v. *Royal Bank of Canada* |1934| A.C. 468 P.C. from Ontario (but the deed was avoided for material misrepresentation).
21. *Bank of Montreal* v. *Stuart* |1911| A.C. 120 (P.C. from Canada); *Chaplin* v. *Brammall* |1908| 1 K.B. 233.

B. THE MARRIAGE CEREMONY (OR WEDDING)

(i) PRESENT BACKGROUND

In 1753 the legislature made its first major incursion into the ecclesiastical monopoly over family law in relation to the actual ceremony of marriage. [22] Paradoxically it is in this area that the influence of the Church remains most clearly visible today, retaining its old procedures and traditions in uneasy double harness with the secular procedures first introduced in 1836. In regard to the ceremony of marriage there is today one group of preliminary and celebratory requirements according to the rites of the Church of England, and another group for all other wedding ceremonies. These latter date only from 1836, when purely secular preliminaries were first introduced, to be followed for the first time by a secular ceremony, or a religious ceremony conducted by rites other than those of the Church of England, [23] and by a national system of civil registration of births, marriages and deaths.

In June 1971 a working party from the Law Commission and the Registrar-General published a Working Paper on the subject [24] which concluded that: 'the law falls woefully short of the optimum attainment' of desirable objectives 'particularly, perhaps, as regards simplicity and intelligibility'.

The Law Commission suggested that the simplest and most effective method of meeting the criticisms would be by making a civil ceremony compulsory, allowing it to be followed by a religious service if the parties wished. [25] If such a proposal proved unacceptable it was suggested that at the least uniform civil preliminaries should be made compulsory for all marriages, whether in the Church of England or elsewhere. [26] The Law Commission's Report, published almost two years later, [27] was considerably more restrained. The proposal for a compulsory civil ceremony had been abandoned *sub silentio*. But the Report supported uniform civil preliminaries for all marriages regardless of where they they were to be celebrated; the abolition of the legal requirement that banns should be published before Church of England marriages [28] and of common licence. By mid-1976 no action had been taken to implement this or any other of the Law Commission's recommendations in this area.

It must be anticipated that many even of the non-churchgoing population

---

22. By the Marriage Act 1753, commonly known as Lord Hardwicke's Act, see *post* nn. 41–5.
23. Including those of the Quakers or Jews, who had been exempt from the provisions of Lord Hardwicke's Act, which forced the much larger Roman Catholic and dissenting minorities into the Church of England for recognition of their marriages.
24. Law Commission Published Working Paper No. 35 (P.W.P.), probably the most comprehensive accurate account available in layman's language of this area of the law. It may advantageously be read together with the *Report of the Kilbrandon Committee on the Marriage Law of Scotland*, Cmnd 4011 of 1969.
25. Ibid. paras 70 and 142(2)(*a*).
26. Ibid. para. 16.
27. Law Com. 53: *Family Law: Report on Solemnisation of Marriage in England and Wales*, 8.5.73.
28. The *Kilbrandon Report (ante,* n. 24) made a similar recommendation for abolition of banns as a legal preliminary in Scotland in Cmnd 4011 para. 51.

will wish if possible to celebrate in our ancient and beautiful churches the crucial events in their lives: baptism to celebrate birth; the wedding ceremony to legitimate cohabitation and its offspring; and the funeral service to precede their burial. If a compulsory civil ceremony were introduced, the number of church ceremonies would, however, decline, both because those who now reluctantly submit themselves to 'that curious cabinet of antiquities, the marriage ritual of the English Church'[29] would be even more reluctant to do so if they were already legally married, and because the arguments within the Church for confining the church ceremony to regular churchgoers would be strengthened if this became merely a voluntary religious garnish to the legal ceremony. At present every incumbent is obliged to perform a marriage ceremony for any parishioner who wishes it, provided he or she has no divorced former spouse still alive.[30] The desire for ceremonial in a beautiful and preferably ancient building (even though not a church) exists not only in England and Wales, as demonstrated by the fact that 'in response to public demand', the U.S.S.R. was constrained to open in 1959 the first of many 'marriage palaces', and that the Fundamental Principles of Soviet Family Law of June 1968 provide in Art. 9 that 'Marriage is registered in a ceremonial atmosphere.'[31]

(ii) HISTORICAL EVOLUTION OF THE LAW[32]

Questions of marriage and succession to property on death were subject to canon law before the Norman Conquest. By an Edict of 1072 William decreed that canon law and common law should not be dispensed in the same court, thus necessitating the foundation of the church courts,[33] which retained jurisdiction over laymen in matters of marriage and succession to personal property at death (except for a brief period under the Protectorate) until this was transferred to secular courts in 1857.[34] By the beginning of the thirteenth century, however, the common law courts established their exclusive jurisdiction over all questions concerning title to English land.[35] On death, therefore, the church courts were confined to proof of the validity of wills and succession to personal property.

---

29. As Maitland found it in 1895: Pollock and Maitland, *History of English Law before the time of Edward I*, vol. II, ch. VII.
30. P.W.P. 35, para. 16.
31. See 'Fundamental principles of Soviet Family Law', 18 *ICLQ*. (1969) 397 and n. 17. The lessons to be derived from Soviet law should be viewed with reserve, but the reintroduction of wedding ceremonial seems to have been undertaken in response to genuine a-political public demand.
32. There can be no substitute for Maitland's incomparable account in Pollock and Maitland, *History of English Law before the time of Edward I*, vol. II, ch. VI, 'Inheritance' and ch. VII, 'Family Law'. For a more modern detailed study see J. Jackson, *The Formation and Annulment of Marriage*, 2nd edn (1969).
33. Commonly known as 'the bawdy courts' because of their concentration on offences in the sphere of sexual morality.
34. By the Matrimonial Causes Act and the Court of Probate Act respectively.
35. From the Restoration in 1660 onwards the common law courts in their turn increasingly forfeited jurisdiction over land to the Court of Chancery.

Differences over marriage arose between the common law and the canon law on two major matters, on both of which the common law eventually prevailed. These were: (i) the widow's right to dower and (ii) the right of the eldest son to claim freehold land as his father's heir.

By canon law, after the middle of the twelfth century, the only requirement for a valid marriage was the consent of both parties expressed in words of the present tense (*per verba de praesenti*) to take each other as husband and wife. Neither priest nor witness nor prior announcement of intention was necessary. The reason was that adultery was a deadly sin, the textual gloss: 'It is better to marry than to burn.' Thus the form of the wedding ceremony was reduced almost to vanishing point, and the 'error of formlessness' arose. The result was that the marriage celebrated in church, and of which children had been born, might be set aside years later in favour of a clandestine marriage *per verba de praesenti* shown to have preceded it.

If the words of consent used were expressed in the future tense: 'I will' instead of 'I do', only subsequent consummation would render the marriage binding. It is now accepted that the House of Lords was misinformed in its legal history when it decided in *Reg.* v. *Millis*[36] that the 'presence' of 'an episcopally ordained clergyman' was necessary in the Middle Ages for a valid marriage at common law (meaning canon law). The fact that the decision was historically wrong does not, of course, detract from its legal binding force, and it is in theory followed today, although the courts show some greater disposition to dispense with the need for episcopal ordination. As part of a general, though unsuccessful, attempt to make all dealings in English land public and notorious, the common lawyers insisted that whilst a woman might be legally married in the eyes of the Church, if she wished to claim dower[37] on her husband's death, she must prove that she had been publicly endowed *in facie ecclesiae,* literally 'in the face of the church', meaning at the church door.

Secondly, during the twelfth century canon law introduced in most of Christendom the concept of legitimation of a child by subsequent marriage of its parents. The English earls and barons repudiated this theory in 1236,[38] thus establishing the indelibility of bastardy in English law for almost a further seven hundred years.[39] On the death of a landowner, therefore, if there

---

36. (1844) 10 Cl. & Fin. 534 H.L., followed in *Beamish* v. *Beamish* (1861) 9 H.L. Cas. 274, despite a cogent criticism of it by Willes J. in the later case, which decided that a clergyman could not conduct his own marriage ceremony.

37. The right if she survived the husband to receive what was eventually agreed to be the rents and profits of one-third of the freehold land of which he had been seised during the marriage.

38. At the Council of Merton 1235–6, recorded in the famous words: '*Et omnes Comites et Barones una voce responderunt, quod nolunt leges Angliae mutare, que usitate sunt et approbate.*'

39. Until 1 January 1927, when the Legitimacy Act 1926 came into operation. There had always been two exceptions to indelibility at common law: (1) the Act of Parliament: John of Gaunt's children were legitimated by such an Act, but this method was exceedingly costly and rarely exercised; (2) the conflict of laws, by which the legitimacy of offspring might be governed by a foreign (including Scottish) law, both at the time of the child's birth and at the date of the subsequent marriage.

was dispute about whether the eldest son had been born before or after his parents' marriage, the common law courts would not consult the church courts, but a jury would be asked the question whether the child was born before or after his parents' marriage. If after – even minutes after – he was entitled to the lands as his father's heir; if before, he was indelibly a bastard without rights of succession.

For over two hundred years the error of formlessness haunted the English institution of marriage, until the legislature intervened in 1753 to end 'one of the strangest scandals of English life'.[40]

Lord Hardwicke's Act laid down the following requirements for all marriages celebrated in England and Wales:[41]

(1) The due publication of banns in the parish church or usual place of worship in the Church of England on three previous Sundays, seven days' advance notice being given to the clergyman, or the issue of a common[42] or special licence.[43] The sole exceptions were for marriages performed according to the usages of the Quakers or the Jews, where both parties were members of the community concerned. The Act did not apply to members of the Royal Family.

(2) The consent of the parent or guardian for the marriage of any infant under the age of 21 years. For this purpose the parent was defined as the father, or if he were dead the guardian of the person lawfully appointed,[44] or failing either, the mother if living and unmarried, or if none, the guardian appointed by the Court of Chancery.[45]

(3) The presence of two or more credible witnesses apart from the minister celebrating the marriage and

(4) registration of the marriage, the registers being in the sole control of the ecclesiastical authorities.

---

40. W. E. H. Lecky, *England in the Eighteenth Century*, vol. I, ch. III, has a colourful account of the 'atrocious abuses' at which the Act was aimed, e.g. 'A multitude of clergymen, usually prisoners for debt and almost always men of notoriously infamous lives, made it their business to celebrate clandestine marriages in or near the Fleet' (prison). 'Almost every tavern or brandy shop in the neighbourhood had a Fleet parson in its pay . . . (but) Divorce, except by a special Act of Parliament, was absolutely unattainable.'
41. The Act did not apply to Scotland or Ireland, hence *Reg* v. *Millis* (1844) 10 Cl. & Fin. 534, which concerned a marriage performed by a Presbyterian Minister (not episcopally ordained) in Ireland.
42. Issued by the Bishop of a diocese acting through his chancellor or a surrogate. It has been in use since the fourteenth century, and is now covered by the Marriage Act 1949, s. 16. The licence must specify the church in which the ceremony is to be performed. The ceremony may be performed immediately but unless it takes place within three months from the date of issue the licence is void.
43. Issued by the Archbishop of Canterbury acting through the Master of the Faculties. It enables the marriage to be celebrated at any time in any place. It costs about £25, its grant is entirely discretionary, and it is said to be granted only in exceptional circumstances or in emergencies. The Law Commission recommends its retention.
44. Viz. the guardian appointed by the deceased father by deed or will, although usually called the testamentary guardian.
45. Section 11 (relating to marriages of infants by common licence). This followed the priorities of parental authority until the Infants Custody Act 1839. The mother first received parental authority exercisable in her own right by the Guardianship of Infants Act 1886.

The Act provided that any purported marriages not celebrated in accordance with its provisions were absolutely null and void,[46] thus ending common law (that is canon law) marriage in England and Wales.

There is great confusion about the use of the terms 'common law marriage' and 'common law husband' or 'common law wife'. A combination of ignorance of history and 'well-meaning sloppiness of thought' sometimes applies these terms to the cohabitation of two people, at least one of whom is known to be legally married to another. This usage is indefensible. At common (canon) law such a cohabitation was not only meretricious; it was a deadly sin. The canon lawyers did not transform adultery into bigamy and sanctify it.

There is another meaning of the term in England, Scotland and most common law countries including Australia[47] and most of the United States of America, arising from a rule of evidence. If it is shown that a man and woman have been openly cohabiting as man and wife and were treated as married by those who knew them, in the absence of evidence to the contrary the law will presume by such cohabitation and repute that they were married, rather than presume an illicit cohabitation until a valid marriage between them is proved. This arises from the general presumption that anything done is lawfully done unless the contrary is shown.[48] It is part of the general presumption of innocence and right conduct. As compulsory centralised registration of marriages has been functioning in this country since 1836, there is now little scope for the application of the presumption. It was, however, applied as recently as 1961 where both parties were dead and the woman had been illiterate.[49] Where the common (canon) law marriage survives, by exchange of consents to present marriage or exchange of promises followed by cohabitation, as in Scotland until 1940,[50] and in certain States in the U.S.A.,[51] there is clearly much greater latitude to assume that those cohabiting as husband and wife have exchanged such consents since acquiring capacity to marry each other.

The provisions of Lord Hardwicke's Act were draconian. Even if the parties innocently failed to ensure that the banns were 'duly' published, which meant in their 'true' names,[52] or that the common licence they obtained was properly issued for the church in which the wedding was celebrated, or that the church

46. Section 8.
47. See *Jacombe* v. *Jacombe* [1960] N.S.W.R. 704 and 707 and (1960) 105 C.L.R. 355, and the discussion in Finlay and Bissett-Johnson: *Family Law in Australia* (1972) pp. 67–70.
48. *Omnia praesumuntur rite esse acta.*
49. *Re Taylor* [1961] 1 W.L.R. 9, 1 All E.R. 55 C.A.
50. See Kilbrandon Committee Cmnd 4011, ch. 9, paras 138–43.
51. In 1968, fourteen States of the Union and the District of Columbia still recognised the informal common law marriage: See Homer Clark, *Law of Domestic Relations* (1968) p. 45; Ploscowe, Foster and Freed; *Family Law: Cases and Materials* pp. 69, 79–83 and 125, and Foote, Levy and Sander, *Cases and Materials on Family Law* 2nd edn. (1976) pp. 685–6.
52. In English law this means the name by which one is generally known, provided that the name is not assumed for any fraudulent purpose. There is still confusion over the extent to which a married woman's 'true' name is necessarily the surname of her husband, discussed in Chapter III.

was licensed to celebrate marriages, or that the wedding was celebrated by someone in holy orders, their marriage was absolutely void. The requirement for 'due' publication of banns in particular was called in aid of the notorious Settlement Acts to deny poor law relief to women and children by attacking the validity of marriages.[53] Even today the provision for 'due' publication of banns may cause difficulty and hardship.[54]

The major vice of Lord Hardwicke's Act, however, was the monopoly it gave to the Church of England over all wedding ceremonies (excluding those of the Royal Family)[55] except those of Quakers or members of the Jewish community. This caused great hardship to Catholics and dissenters and it has been estimated that up to a third of all marriages between 1753 and 1836 were illegal and void. The rush north of the Scottish border to Gretna Green also set in.[56] In 1836, as part of the movement for religious toleration, the Marriage Act of that year provided that notice of marriage might be given to the Superintendent Registrar of Births, Deaths and Marriages,[57] who was empowered to issue a certificate, with or without a licence, enabling the parties to marry each other in the presence of the registrar, either in a purely secular ceremony in the register office, or in a 'registered building' (normally the parties' usual place of worship; a Roman Catholic church or Nonconformist chapel or meeting house).[58]

The two Acts of 1836 first inaugurated a centralised system of registration

---

53. As in *R. v. Tibshelf (Inhabitants of)* (1830) 1 B. & Ad. 190. See also *R. v. Wroxton* (1833) 4 B. & Ad. 640, discussing the change in the law effected in 1823. After that Act, before a marriage could be held void for misdescription, both parties must know that the 'true' name had not been used.

54. Now by the Marriage Act 1949, s. 25: 'If any persons knowingly and wilfully intermarry according to the rites of the Church of England (otherwise than by special licence) . . . (*b*) without banns having been duly published . . . the marriage shall be void.' See *Chipchase* v. *Chipchase* [1939] P. 391 and [1942] P. 37. It is thought that the decision must be wrong. It was 'explained' in *Dancer* v. *Dancer* [1949] P. 142. See also Sachs J. in *Chard* v. *Chard* [1956] P. 259, 271. The difficulties were not considered by the Law Commission in P.W.P. 35.

55. These are governed by the Royal Marriages Act 1772, reviewed by C. d'O Farran in 14 *MLR* (1951) 53. Briefly, the Act provides that no descendant of King George II, other than the issue of princesses who have married into foreign families, may marry without the previous consent of the Sovereign formally granted under the Great Seal and declared in Council. The Act raises questions of constitutional rather than marriage law, and is not further considered.

56. See Ploscowe, Foster and Freed, *Family Law: Cases and Materials.*, p. 80. The *Kilbrandon Report*, Cmnd 4011, in para. 11 draws attention to the scandals arising from the build-up of Gretna Green as a tourist attraction, leading to the abolition of informal marriages by the Marriage (Scotland) Act 1939. But the powerful attraction of runaway marriages is not yet spent.

57. Constituted at the same time by the Births and Deaths Registration Act (Ch. 86) of which the Marriage Act 1836 (Ch. 85), was declared to be part, 'as if incorporated therein', Marriage Act 1836, s. 44.

58. Members of the Society of Friends (Quakers) and persons professing the Jewish religion were covered by s. 2, as amended by the Act of 1860. See also The Places of Worship Registration Act 1855 and *Reg.* v. *Registrar General, Ex parte Segerdal* [1970] 1 Q.B. 430, for definition of religious worship.

of births, marriages and deaths and gave the first real facts about the country's population, birth rate, death rate and expectation of life. The Marriage Act 1898 finally provided that marriages might be solemnised in a building registered for the purpose (normally a Roman Catholic church or Nonconformist chapel or meeting house) in the presence of an 'authorised person', who is usually the priest or minister of the building. For the first time it was no longer necessary for the Registrar to attend such ceremonies held in places of worship other than churches and chapels of the established Church.

The law was eventually consolidated in the Marriage Act 1949, which as slightly amended,[59] and in part incorporated first in the Nullity of Marriage Act 1971, and later in the Matrimonial Causes Act 1973[60] gives the following situation until amended:[61]

(iii) PRELIMINARIES TO MARRIAGE

Marriages following civil preliminaries now account for more than 60 per cent of those celebrated in England and Wales, but religious ceremonies take place in more than 58 per cent of marriages.[62]

(a) Civil Preliminaries. There are three different types of authorisation to marry obtainable from the civil authorities: the superintendent registrar's certificate without a licence,[63] the superintendent registrar's certificate with a licence,[64] and the Registrar General's licence. The certificate without a licence was intended to be the normal civil preliminary, but the certificate with a licence is now chosen in about 30 per cent of civil marriages.[65]

Notice of marriage applying for a certificate with or without a licence must be given on a prescribed form, which bears a warning that marriage by the law of this country is the union of one man with one woman voluntarily entered into for life, to the exclusion of all others. The notice must state the name and surname, age, marital status, occupation, place of residence and period of such residence of each of the persons to be married and the church or other building in which the marriage is to be solemnised. It must

---

59. By the Marriage Act 1949 (Amendment) Act 1954, and as to fees and times of opening of Register Offices by the Registration Service Act 1953; by the Marriage Acts Amendment Act 1958, the Marriage (Secretaries of Synagogues) Act 1959, the Marriage (Wales and Monmouthshire) Act 1962 and the Marriage (Registrar General's Licence) Act 1970. The Marriage (Enabling) Act 1960 amended the prohibited degrees of marriage and is considered *post*.
60. Section 11 provides that: 'A marriage celebrated after 31 July 1971 shall be void on the following grounds only, that is to say (*a*) that it is not a valid marriage under the provisions of the Marriages [*sic*] Acts 1949 to 1970 (that is to say where . . . (iii) the parties have intermarried in disregard of certain requirements as to the formation of marriage).'
61. Law Com. 53, with or without some additional recommendations in P.W.P. 35.
62. Law Com. 53, p. 79.
63. Printed in black ink: Marriage Act 1949, ss 27 and 40.
64. Printed in red ink on paper bearing a 'licence' watermark: Ibid. s. 40.
65. P.W.P. 35, para. 7.

be accompanied by a solemn written and signed declaration.[66] A false statement made wilfully is an offence under the Perjury Act 1911.[67] Any person may enter a caveat against the issue of the certificate, after which none will be issued until inquiry has been made.[68] A parent or guardian whose consent is required for the marriage of a minor over 16 but under 18 years of age may forbid the marriage by writing 'forbidden' opposite the entry in the marriage notice book.[69] Even if no caveat is entered and no objection made by a parent, the registrar may not issue a certificate if any lawful impediment to the marriage is shown to his satisfaction[70] and in practice registrars seek to satisfy themselves that the marriage is in order. Registrars may require documentary evidence of consent to the marriage of those under 18, but have at present no power to require evidence of age, such as a birth certificate.[71] No corresponding certificate is required for those seeking to marry by Jewish rites.

Before he may issue a certificate without a licence the registrar must screen the notice of marriage (which must be given to the superintendent registrar of the district in which each party has resided for seven days), for twenty-one days after the notice has been entered in the marriage notice book, which is also open to public inspection. The ceremony may not in any event be celebrated until twenty-one days after notice has been given.[72] The certificate without a licence is the only form of civil preliminary after which the wedding may, with the consent of the incumbent, be celebrated in a church of the Church of England.[73] For a certificate with a licence, notice need be given only to the superintendent registrar of the district in which one party has resided, but this must have been for 15 days previously.[74] Charges are minimal, but the licence is slightly more expensive than the certificate alone. Both forms of certificate expire three months after issue, but the crucial difference between them is that, whereas the marriage after certificate alone may not be celebrated until at least 21 days after notice has been given and displayed, the marriage may be celebrated one full day after notice if a certificate with a licence is obtained.[75] Such speed clearly rules out any possibility of enquiry or publicity. Even though the notice is entered in the marriage notice book, it can be seen only during one day and need not be displayed.

The third present form of civil preliminary is the Registrar General's licence,

---

66. Marriage Act 1949, ss 3, 27(3) and 28.
67. But even the giving of a false name does not invalidate the marriage: *R.* v. *Lamb* (1934) 50 T.L.R. 310, *Plummer* v. *Plummer* [1917] P. 163.
68. Marriage Act 1949, s. 29. If the Registrar General certifies that the caveat is frivolous, the caveator may be liable for the cost of proceedings before the Registrar General and damages.
69. Ibid. ss 3 and 30.
70. Marriage Act 1949, s. 31(2)(*a*).
71. Family Law Reform Act 1969, s. 32(2) and see P.W.P. 35, para. 7.
72. Marriage Act 1949, s. 31 and P.W.P. 35, para. 7.
73. Including the Church in Wales., Ibid. ss 5(*d*), 17, 26(1)(*e*) and 26(2). In 1971 only 106 marriages were so celebrated out of a total of 160,165 Church of England weddings.
74. Ibid. s. 27(2).
75. Marriage Act 1949, ss 31, 32 and 27, P.W.P. 35, para. 8.

introduced for the first time in 1971[76] as the civil equivalent to the Archbishop of Canterbury's special licence. It had long been considered a hardship that for the urgent wedding not in a registered building and between the normal hours of 8 a.m. and 6 p.m., (of which the most usual is the deathbed marriage conducted in a hospital or private home) application could be made only to the principal ecclesiastical authority of the established Church, and was subject to that Church's own rules (including no marriage for divorced persons with a surviving former spouse). The Registrar General's licence may, however, be issued only for deathbed marriages[77], does not authorise any marriage according to the rites of the Church of England, must specify the place of marriage, and although it authorises an immediate wedding, expires one month after issue.

The penalty for non-compliance with any of the necessary civil formalities, is that the marriage is void.[78] However, lack of prior residence in the district of one or both parties, or of parental consent to the marriage of minors, or celebration in a building not authorised for the celebration of marriages, does not affect the validity of the marriage.[79]

(b) Ecclesiastical Preliminaries. These also are of three possible kinds: banns, common licence, and special licence. Publication of banns is overwhelmingly the most popular.[80] The special licence, issued by the Archbishop of Canterbury, was until 1971 the only possible preliminary for a marriage which could not take place in an authorised building between the normal hours of 8 a.m. and 6 p.m.

(1) *Due Publication of Banns.*[81] Banns must be called in each parish where either of the parties resides and, if desired or if the marriage is to take place there, also in the church where they usually worship. Seven days' notice may be required before banns are called, giving the names of the parties, their places of residence, and the period of their residence. These banns must then be called on three Sundays during morning service[82] by the officiating clergyman from the register book of banns and not from loose papers, using the form of words laid down by the Book of Common Prayer. Thereafter the clergyman must sign the book to confirm that publication has taken place.

No minimum period of prior residence in the parish is required, nor is any proof of the age of the parties, nor of parental consent to the marriage

---

76. By the Marriage (Registrar General's Licence) Act 1970.
77. Ibid. s. 3: The declaration accompanying the notice must declare that one of the persons to be married is seriously ill and is not expected to recover and cannot be moved to a place at which a normal marriage could be solemnised.
78. Marriage Act 1949, s. 49.
79. Ibid. s. 48.
80. Used for over 94 per cent of ecclesiastical preliminaries.
81. Marriage Act 1949, ss 6–14 and s. 25, and see *ante* n. 54 as to 'due' publication.
82. Ibid. s. 7. The Act does not specify that the banns be called on successive Sundays, except by s. 14 when they are published on board ship, one of the parties being an officer, seaman or marine. If there is no morning service, they may be published during evening service.

of a minor over 16 years of age. It is for anyone knowing of an impediment to the marriage to declare it publicly when the banns are read. If this is done, the reading of the banns becomes ineffective, and the wedding cannot be celebrated unless the objection is withdrawn. Like the common licence, the certificate of publication of banns is valid for three months only. Before solemnising the marriage in one of the churches or chapels in which banns were read the officiating clergyman must be satisfied that they have been called in all the churches necessary and see a certificate of banns.[83]

(2) *The Common or Surrogate's Licence.*[84] This must specify the building in which the marriage is to be celebrated. The wedding may take place immediately, but must be celebrated within three months. At least one of the parties must have been usually resident for 15 days in the parish in the church of which the marriage is to be solemnised, or one of them must usually worship there. One of the parties must also swear that there is no impediment to the marriage, that the residential qualifications have been fulfilled, and that if either party is a minor the necessary parental consent has been given or the need for it dispensed with, but the Church authorities are under no obligation to check these statements, and have no power to check that parental consent has been given. Any person with an interest may enter a caveat, in which event no licence may be issued until the caveat has been withdrawn or the ground on which it was entered has been removed.[85]

(3) *The Special Licence.*[86] This alone is valid for a marriage in any place at any time.[87]

If the Law Commission's recommendations are accepted, this welter of alternative civil and ecclesiastical preliminaries, with their different residential qualifications, waiting periods, applicabilities and expiry times, would be superseded by a civil authorisation of marriage issued by the superintendent registrar, normally 15 days after the notice of marriage was received, but with discretion to authorise its earlier issue if he were satisfied, (after making any enquiry he considered necessary,) that there was no lawful impediment to the marriage, that all necessary consents had been received or dispensed with, that the parties could not reasonably have been expected to have given earlier notice, and that hardship would be caused if the marriage had to be delayed until

---

83. Marriage Act 1949, s. 11. He must ensure that the banns were called in each of the parishes in which the parties reside, as well as in the church in which the marriage is to be celebrated, if not the parish church of either.
84. See *ante* n. 42; covered by the Marriage Act 1949, ss 15−16. Only 7766 such licences were issued in 1971, and the Law Commission suggests that the licence be abolished.
85. Ibid. s. 16(2).
86. Issued by the Archbishop of Canterbury, acting through the Master of the Faculties, and under the power granted to him by the Ecclesiastical Licences Act 1533, which transferred this part of the former papal power of dispensation. See also *ante* n. 43.
87. But members of the Jewish community and the Society of Friends are not bound to celebrate their marriages within the normal hours and they may do so in any place.

the expiry of the full waiting period. The existing certificate and licence would be abolished, but the new authority would be called a licence and not a certificate. The Archbishop of Canterbury would retain his power to grant a Special Licence for a wedding to be celebrated at any time and place, and the corresponding civil licence from the Registrar General would also be retained, but with wider discretion than at present as to place and hours of marriage.[88]

(iv) THE SOLEMNISATION OF MARRIAGE

The only form of marriage into which anybody may enter in England and Wales, and into which anybody domiciled in England and Wales may enter anywhere in the world[89] is the monogamous union for life of one man and one woman, to the exclusion of all others. In *Reg.* v. *Bham*[90] the Court of Criminal Appeal held that, since the monogamous marriage has alone been recognised in this country from time immemorial, the Marriage Act 1949, applies only to such marriages. Accordingly, where a Moslem performed a ceremony of potentially polygamous marriage by Islamic rites in a private house in England, he had not purported to solemnise a marriage, and had not therefore committed any offence under the Act.[91] The Law Commission finds 'a growing mischief – namely, the deliberate solemnisation of invalid marriages', and says there is little doubt that in many cases both parties, and probably the bride in nearly all of them, think that a proper marriage has been contracted and enter into cohabitation in that belief. The Law Commission recommends that the wording of the statute should be amended so as to make the celebration of such ceremonies a serious offence. It is hoped that reform in this part of the marriage law will not be much longer delayed.

The ceremony of marriage, that is monogamous marriage as understood in England, may take place either in the office of a superintendent registrar,[92] or in a parish church or authorised chapel[93] or in a registered building. Marriages

88. P.W.P. 35, paras 22–6 as modified by Law Com. 53, paras 13–19.
89. Matrimonial Causes Act 1973, s. 11 lists among the grounds on which a marriage is void: (*b*) that at the time of the marriage either party was already lawfully married and (*d*) in the case of a polygamous marriage entered into outside England and Wales, that either party was at the time of the marriage domiciled in England and Wales.
90. [1966] 1 Q.B. 159.
91. Marriage Act 1949, s. 75(2) 'Any person who knowingly and wilfully . . . (*c*) solemnises a marriage . . . in any place other than – (i) a church or other building in which marriages may be solemnised . . . shall be guilty of felony . . .' The bride was an English girl aged 16. The ceremony was performed in a private house. The bridegroom had been unable to obtain a registrar's certificate to marry, since he could not satisfy the registrar that he was a single man. A document, called a Marriage Certificate, partly in English and partly in Arabic, was issued after the ceremony. When questioned by the police the celebrant replied: 'under Islamic law we are allowed to marry in quadruped [*sic*] . . . it is legal . . .'
92. Marriage Act 1949, ss 26(*b*) and 45–6.
93. Ibid. ss 20–1.

may be solemnised only between the hours of 8 a.m. and 6 p.m.[94] But these rules do not apply, and marriages may be celebrated anywhere at any time, if in pursuance of a Special Licence from the Archbishop of Canterbury, or a Registrar General's licence, or according to the usages of the Quakers or Jews. The Law Commission recommends changes in the rules relating to registered buildings, and in particular that the parties need no longer marry within the parish or district in which one of them resides;[95] but is divided on whether Quakers and Jews should be obliged to celebrate marriages within the normal hours and in specified places.[96]

A marriage celebrated in a register office must be attended by the superintendent registrar, the registrar, and at least two witnesses, and must take place 'with open doors'.[97] Similarly in a registered building the authorised person and two witnesses must be present, and the doors must be open.[98] In some part of the ceremony each party must make, in the presence of the witnesses and the person officiating, a statutory declaration: 'I do solemnly declare that I know not of any lawful impediment why I, *AB*, may not be joined in matrimony to *CD*' and each must say to the other: 'I call upon these persons here present to witness that I, *AB*, do take thee, *CD*, to be my lawful wedded wife (or husband)' except that, where the marriage is solemnised in the presence of an authorised person with no registrar present, the address to the other party to the marriage may omit the calling on the persons present and take the form of: 'I, *AB*, do take thee, *CD*, to be my wedded wife (or husband).'[99] It is, however, not clear what, if any, effect infringement of any of these rules may have.[100] When the wedding is celebrated in the register office no religious service may be used,[101] but in a registered building, the marriage may be by 'such form and ceremony as the persons to be married see fit to adopt'.[102] However, since all registered buildings must be places of public religious worship, registered for the solemnisation of marriages by the Registrar General, and the marriage may be solemnised there only with the consent of the religious authorities[103] the form adopted will clearly be that required by the religious body concerned.

Church of England weddings must also be celebrated in the presence of two witnesses in addition to the officiating clergyman,[104] but the statute does not prescribe any formula to be used.

---

94. Marriage Act 1949, ss 4 and 75(1)(*a*).
95. P.W.P. 35, paras 73–80 especially para. 79.
96. Ibid. paras 81–2 and Law Com. 53, para. 22.
97. Marriage Act 1949, s. 45.
98. Ibid. s. 44(2).
99. Ibid. s. 44(3).
100. P.W.P. 35, paras 91–8 suggests some tightening-up, and that the sanction should be cancellation of the registration of the building. Greater control of authorised persons is also recommended.
101. Ibid. s. 45(2).
102. Ibid. ss 26(1)(*a*) and 44(1).
103. Ibid. s. 44(1) and P.W.P. 35, para. 66.
104. Ibid. s. 22.

C. VOID AND VOIDABLE MARRIAGES

Originally at canon law all marriages that were not valid and for which no valid papal dispensation was obtained were absolutely void and of no effect.[105] Gradually the common lawyers encroached upon the jurisdiction of the canon lawyers and after the Reformation refused to allow the church courts, after the death of both the parties, to declare a marriage void as within the prohibited degrees[106] or because of impotence.[107] The reason was that avoidance of the presumed marriage resulted in the bastardy of any children of the union.[108] It might be difficult or impossible for the issue to prove the validity of the marriage of their parents, both of whom were dead. There therefore arose the voidable marriage, which might be annulled, but until annulment was considered in all respects a valid marriage. Its validity could be attacked only by one of the parties to it during the lifetime of both. On the death of either party before the marriage had been avoided, its validity could no longer be impugned.

The Law Commission in 1970 summarised the distinction between valid, void and voidable marriages as follows:[109]

(*a*) A valid marriage is one which is in no sense defective and is, therefore, binding on the parties (and on everyone else); it can only be terminated by death or by a decree of divorce, which decree acknowledges the existence of a valid marriage and then proceeds to put an end to it.

(*b*) A void marriage is not really a marriage at all, in that it never came into existence because of a fundamental defect; the marriage is said to be void *ab initio*; no decree of nullity is necessary to make it void and parties can take the risk of treating the marriage as void without obtaining a decree.[110] But either of the spouses or any person having a sufficient interest[111] in obtaining a decree of nullity may petition for a decree at any time, whether during the lifetime of the spouses or after their death. In effect,

---

105. See D. Tolstoy, 'Void and voidable marriages', 27 *MLR*. (1964) 385.
106. There was considerable confusion after the reformation about the prohibited degrees of relationship, considered by Sir J. Simon P. in *Cheni* v. *Cheni* [1965] P. 85. The Marriage Act 1835 'for the avoidance of doubt' declared such marriages void, instead of voidable as previously.
107. Classically 'canonical disability'. This eventually became the sole ground on which a marriage was voidable at common (viz. canon) law, new statutory grounds being added by the Matrimonial Causes Act 1937. It was not included in any statute before the Nullity of Marriage Act 1971. All grounds of nullity are now statutory.
108. Bigamy was a criminal offence as well as rendering the marriage void at all times. Similarly, lack of age of either party made the marriage void.
109. Law Com. 33, para. 3.
110. See Lord Greene M.R. in *de Renneville* v. *de Renneville* [1948] P. 100, 115 C.A., but emphasising the risk of such a course. In para. 4 of its Report the Law Commission thinks it would 'add needlessly to the expense to the parties and to the public' if legal proceedings 'were necessary before parties could regard themselves as free from a marriage which was palpably invalid'. This probably means that legal aid will not be available for a decree of nullity, which would seem desirable for anyone involved in such an invalid ceremony.
111. This means, as always in English law, the possibility (however remote) of a pecuniary advantage (however slight).

the decree is a declaration that there is not and never has been a marriage.

(c) A voidable marriage is a valid marriage unless and until it is annulled; it can be annulled only at the instance of one of the spouses during the lifetime of both, so that if no decree of nullity is pronounced during the lifetime of both spouses the marriage becomes unimpeachable as soon as one of the spouses dies.

The report favoured the retention of the intermediate category of voidable marriages.[112] However, on its recommendation, after July 1971 the decree of nullity of the voidable marriage made it clear that the marriage was avoided from the date of the decree only, and was valid until that date.[113] It is difficult to argue that anything would now be lost by the total elimination of the voidable marriage, and the absorption of the grounds on which such a marriage can be avoided into the grounds for dissolution, although the bar to a decree within three years of the ceremony would of course be inappropriate.[114]

(i) VOID MARRIAGES

The grounds on which a marriage celebrated after July 1971 is void, now contained in the Matrimonial Causes Act 1973,[115] are:

'(a) that it is not a valid marriage under the provisions of the Marriages [sic] Acts 1949 to 1970 (that is to say where –
  (i)   the parties are within the prohibited degrees of relationship;
  (ii) either party is under the age of 16; or
  (iii) the parties have intermarried in disregard of certain requirements as to the formation of marriage);
(b) that at the time of the marriage either party was already lawfully married;
(c) that the parties are not respectively male and female;
(d) in the case of a polygamous marriage entered into outside England and Wales, that either party was at the time of the marriage domiciled in England and Wales.

For the purposes of paragraph (d) of this subsection a marriage may be polygamous although at its inception neither party has any spouse additional to the other.'

As to (i), the prohibited degrees of relationship are now set out in the

---

112. Law Com. 33, para. 25.
113. Now the Matrimonial Causes Act 1973, s. 16.
114. As the Law Commission points out in para. 24(d) of its report. In 1974 there were 785 decrees *nisi* granted in England and Wales, of which 68 were for void and 717 for voidable marriages: Cmnd 6361: *Civil Judicial Statistics Annual Report* 1974, Table B12(iii). The Australian Family Law Act 1975, s. 51 abolished from 6 January 1976 the voidable marriage and all prohibitions on marriages between persons related only by affinity.
115. Section 11.

Marriage Act 1949 Sched. 1, as amended by the Marriage (Enabling) Act 1960 and the Children Act 1975, Sched. 3 [116] They are:

for a man	*for a woman*
1. Mother or adoptive or former adoptive mother	Father or adoptive or former adoptive father
2. Daughter or adoptive or former adoptive daughter	Son or adoptive or former adoptive son
3. Grandmother	Grandfather
4. Granddaughter	Grandson
5. Sister	Brother
6. Aunt [117]	Uncle [117]
7. Niece	Nephew
8. Father's or son's or grandfather's or grandson's wife	Mother's or daughter's or grandmother's or daughter's husband
9. Wife's mother or daughter or grandmother or granddaughter	Husband's father or son or grandfather or grandson

The prohibited degrees include relationships by the half-blood and illegitimate relationships, [118] and apply to all marriages in England, and to those celebrated abroad by anybody domiciled in England. [119] Any person who has at any time adopted a minor is within the prohibited degrees of relationship to the adopted person. [120] This prohibition reflects the important social, as distinct from biological, reasons for the prohibition on marriage within closely related members of an existing family group.

The minimum age of marriage was raised from 12 for a girl and 14 for a boy to sixteen for both sexes in 1929, [121] and is low rather than

---

116. Marriage between a man and his deceased wife's sister was legalised in 1907 by the Deceased Wife's Sister's Marriage Act, but the clergy might refuse to celebrate any such marriage. Not until 1921 did the Deceased Brother's Widow's Marriage Act legalise marriage by a woman to her deceased husband's brother. See H. F. Morris, 'Marriage law in Uganda: sixty years of attempted reform', in *Family Law in Asia and Africa*, ed. J. N. D. Anderson (1968), for clerical opposition to such marriages in Africa. The Marriage (Enabling) Act 1960, which validated marriage by a man with his divorced wife's sister or aunt or niece or the former wife of a brother or uncle during the lifetime of the former spouse, raised different social problems, and hardened the perimeters of the nuclear family. See 23 *MLR* (1960) 538.
117. Marriage between a man and his niece by marriage only and between a woman and her nephew, similarly by affinity, was legalised by the Marriage (Prohibited Degrees of Relationship) Act 1931. As to the recognition by English law of marriages contracted under foreign law between uncle and niece or aunt and nephew by blood, see *Cheni* v. *Cheni* [1965] P. 85.
118. Marriage Act 1949, s. 78(1) and Marriage (Enabling) Act 1960, s. 1(2) for the half blood and *Restall* v. *Restall* (1929) 45 T.L.R. 518 for illegitimate relationship.
119. *Re de Wilton* [1900] 2 Ch. 481.
120. Children Act 1975, Sched. 3 para. 8 and see Sched. I, para. 7(1).
121. By the Age of Marriage Act, 1929. But the English courts will consider a marriage valid if contracted at a lower age permitted by the law of the place where the marriage was celebrated and by the personal law of the parties. See *Alhaji Mohamed* v. *Knott* [1969] 1 Q.B. 1, an extreme and disturbing case.

high.[122] Now that the age of majority has been lowered to eighteen[123] there is a case for raising the minimum age of marriage to eighteen. On the other hand, many countries permit marriage at a lower age with judicial permission, the most usual ground being the pregnancy of the girl. Marriages contracted for this reason, and particularly where the parties are young, are highly unstable and not to be encouraged. If the price of raising the minimum age in this country were the introduction of exceptions to the general rule, that price would be too high.

The Law Commission also considered,[124] and rightly rejected, the arguments frequently advanced for making marriages below the minimum age merely voidable and not void. The pressures for child marriage have all the forces of tradition and profit for others behind them. Such pressures for the exploitation of children generally and girls in particular must be consistently resisted.

It is a defence to the criminal charge of bigamy[125] that the spouses were living apart for seven years or more and that at the time that one of them went through the bigamous ceremony with a third party he or she reasonably believed the other spouse to be dead. But this defence does not validate the second ceremony, which is void if it subsequently transpires that the lawful spouse was alive when it took place. A decree of presumption of death and dissolution of marriage[126] is essential before remarriage. Sometimes the question of estoppel may arise. At the time of the ceremony either both parties know that one of them probably has a living husband or wife, or that party knows, and seeks later to plead the invalidity of the ceremony, usually to avoid making financial provision for the other.[127] It is frequently argued that nobody should be considered married by estoppel, and that knowing participation in what is believed to be a bogus ceremony should not bar subsequently pleading and profiting from its invalidity.[128] The citation and rigid application of precedents set in former centuries on such questions binds us to the traditional view of status as of overwhelming importance, irrespective of its effects, and it is thought that the courts should not permit knowing parties subsequently to plead their own wrong to their own advantage.

Since 1972[129] the English courts take jurisdiction in matrimonial causes and will make declarations of validity of marriages contracted abroad, even though actually or potentially polygamous, provided they are valid by the

---

122. See Law Com. 33, footnote 80, for age-limits in various countries.
123. Family Law Reform Act 1969, s. 1 and Sched. 1, in operation from the beginning of 1970.
124. Law Com. 33, ch. II, paras 16–20.
125. Established in *Reg.* v. *Tolson* (1889) 23 Q.B.D. 168. For bigamy in England after a potentially polygamous ceremony overseas see *Reg.* v. *Sagoo* [1975] 3 W.L.R. 267 C.A.
126. Now under the Matrimonial Causes Act 1973, s. 19.
127. See *Bullock* v. *Bullock* [1960] 1 W.L.R. 975 D.C.; *Hayward* v. *Hayward* [1961] P. 152, and *Chard* v. *Chard* [1956] P. 259.
128. See Phillimore J. in *Hayward* v. *Hayward supra*, p. 158. See further D. Tolstoy; 'Marriage by estoppel', 84 *LQR.* (1968) 245, and *contra* 24 *MLR* (1961) 371.
129. By the Matrimonial Proceedings (Polygamous Marriages) Act 1972, now the Matrimonial Causes Act 1973, s. 47.

personal law of the parties concerned. In its Report in 1970 the Law Commission considered[130] that a purported wedding ceremony between two persons of the same sex was not a void marriage, but a *matrimonium non existens,* an absolutely spurious ceremony. But s. 11(c) of the 1973 Act includes as a ground for nullity that the parties are not respectively male and female, so that the courts may make financial provision for one party to such a spurious union. The Law Commission's view is preferred to the legislation.[131]

(ii) VOIDABLE MARRIAGES

The six grounds on which a marriage is voidable in English domestic law are now enumerated in s. 12 of the Matrimonial Causes Act 1973,[132] which applies to marriages celebrated after 31 July 1971. They are as follows:

(*a*) that the marriage has not been consummated owing to the incapacity of either party to consummate it;

(*b*) that the marriage has not been consummated owing to the wilful refusal of the respondent to consummate it;

(*c*) that either party to the marriage did not validly consent to it, whether in consequence of duress, mistake, unsoundness of mind or otherwise;

(*d*) that at the time of the marriage either party, though capable of giving a valid consent, was suffering (whether continuously or intermittently) from mental disorder within the meaning of the Mental Health Act 1959 of such a kind or to such an extent as to be unfitted for marriage;

(*e*) that at the time of the marriage the respondent was suffering from venereal disease in a communicable form;

(*f*) that at the time of the marriage the respondent was pregnant by some person other than the petitioner.

Any decree of nullity granted after July 1971 in respect of a voidable marriage annuls the marriage only in respect of any time after the decree has been made absolute, and despite the decree, the marriage is treated as if it had existed up to that time.[133] In other words, it is equivalent to dissolution of a valid marriage.

(a) Incapacity to Consummate the Marriage. This is the old common (canon) law ground, sometimes designated 'canonical disability', but more commonly

---

130. Law Com. 33, paras 30–2.
131. Two cases have been reported in the last decade, *Talbot* v. *Talbot* (1967) 111 Sol. Jo. 213 (which concerned two women) and *Corbett* v. *Corbett* [1971] P. 83 (two men). In *Corbett* v. *Corbett* the petitioner pleaded a so-called 'sex change operation' about which he refused to disclose or to allow the surgeon to disclose any details. The clear inference was rightly drawn.
132. Formerly Nullity of Marriage Act 1971, s. 2.
133. Matrimonial Causes Act 1973, s. 16.

known as impotence. It first appeared in the statutes in 1971.[134] The incapacity is in relation to sexual intercourse, and infertility is not a ground for nullity.[135] The incapacity must exist both at the date of the wedding ceremony and that of the hearing of the petition; if it has been rectified before the date of the hearing, or if at the hearing there is evidence that the defect may without danger be rectified so as to permit sexual intercourse, and the respondent undertakes that the necessary measures will be taken, the marriage will not be annulled.[136] Supervening incapacity is not a ground of nullity.[137] Incapacity may arise from a mental condition such as invincible repugnance to sexual intercourse[138] and may exist only in relation to the other spouse, in which event there is incapacity *quoad hunc* or *quoad hanc*.[139] Now that most marriages are dissoluble after five years' delay, many of these old distinctions in nullity may be expected to become obsolete.

It appears always to have been the law that either party may petition, so that provided he or she did not know of the incapacity at the date of the wedding and has a justifiable sense of grievance, a petitioner may plead his or her own incapacity in applying for a decree.[140] However, the courts have emphasised that they will not necessarily grant a decree in such circumstances.[141] Many of the circumstances in which the courts would, before August 1971, have refused a decree, would now in any event be covered by the revised bar of approbation.[142]

(b) Wilful Refusal of the Respondent to Consummate the Marriage. The continued argument that this should be a ground for divorce and not for nullity since it arises after the 'marriage' is, as has already been shown, semantic, since it depends upon the preferred definition of 'marriage', and whether the speaker thinks it consists solely of the wedding ceremony. It was the principal new ground for nullity introduced by statute in 1937[143] and, in a beneficent judgement in 1948 the House of Lords overruled previous contrary decisions and held in *Baxter* v. *Baxter*[144] that insistence by one spouse on the use of contraceptive measures does not amount to refusal to consummate the

---

134. Nullity of Marriage Act 1971, s. 2(9).
135. *L.* v. *L.* (1922) 38 T.L.R. 697, approved in *Baxter* v. *Baxter* [1948] A.C. 288 H.L. In *L.* v. *L.* the wife was incapable of childbearing, but as inability to consummate the marriage was not proved, the husband's petition was refused.
136. See *S.* v. *S.* (*Orse C.*) [1956] P. 11; *S.Y.* v. *S.Y.* [1963] P. 37 C.A.
137. *Brown* v. *Brown* (1828) 1 Hag. Ecc. 523.
138. *G.* v. *G.* (1871) 2 P. & D. 287 (excessive sensibility); *P.* v. *L.* (1873) 3 P. & D. 73n. *G.* v. *G.* [1924] A.C. 349 (invincible repugnance).
139. *G.* v. *G.* [1924] A.C. 349 *supra*.
140. In *Harthan* v. *Harthan* [1949] P. 115 C.A. the husband was allowed to avoid the marriage because of his own psychological incapacity twenty-two years after the wedding, but the parties had lived apart for at least twelve years.
141. *Pettit* v. *Pettit* [1963] P. 177 C.A., where husband was not granted a decree, although he proved his own incapacity.
142. Now the Matrimonial Causes Act 1973, s. 13(1), formerly Nullity of Marriage Act 1971, s. 3(1), considered *post*.
143. By the Matrimonial Causes Act 1937, s. 7.
144. [1948] A.C. 274.

marriage. An advantage of this ground is that, if a marriage has not been consummated, the petitioner may plead this fact and allege that it is due either to the incapacity of the other party or, in the alternative, to the other party's wilful refusal to consummate it. No petitioner may plead his own wilful refusal. In *Horton* v. *Horton*,[145] Lord Jowitt L.C., while declining to define the expression, considered that, 'in determining whether there has been a refusal without just excuse, the judge should have regard to the whole history of the marriage.'[146] The need for 'just excuse' was applied by Hewson J. in *Jodla* v. *Jodla*,[147] which concerned Roman Catholic parties of Polish origin. Being unable to arrange a church ceremony in the time available, they married by licence in a register office, intending to arrange a subsequent church ceremony. This did not take place and there was no cohabitation. When both parties petitioned for a decree of nullity it was held that, since the husband knew that the wife would not contemplate cohabitation until a church ceremony had been performed, his failure to proceed with the church ceremony constituted a just excuse for her to refuse sexual intercourse, and it was the wife who was entitled to a decree of nullity on the ground of the husband's wilful refusal to consummate the marriage. The decision was approved and applied by the Court of Appeal in *Kaur* v. *Singh*.[148]

(c) Lack of Valid Consent in Consequence of Duress, Mistake, Unsoundness of Mind, or Otherwise. A major change in the law was effected in respect of marriages after July 1971, on the recommendation of the Law Commission,[149] as to lack of consent of either party. Before August 1971 a marriage to which either party had not validly consented, because of fundamental mistake as to the identity of the other party, or the nature of the ceremony, or unsoundness of mind, was void, although the position in respect of duress was the subject of controversy.[150] However, by an anomalous rule of the canon law, a marriage void for lack of consent might subsequently be ratified[151] by free consent, in which event the consent was deemed to relate back to the time of the original ceremony. After July 1971, lack of consent for any reason no longer renders a marriage void but only voidable, and then only if proceedings for nullity are instituted within three years of the ceremony.[152] The Law Commission considered an alteration in the law desirable not only because of the confusion caused by the canonical doctrine of ratification, but also because investigation by a court is always necessary before lack of consent can be

---

145. (1948) 64 T.L.R. 62; [1947] 2 All E.R. 871 H.L.
146. Ibid. p. 874 at B.
147. [1960] 1 W.L.R. 236.
148. [1972] 1 W.L.R. 105 C.A.
149. Law Com. 33, paras 11–15, introduced by the Nullity of Marriage Act 1971, s. 2(*c*), operative August 1971.
150. See Tolstoy in 27 *MLR* (1964) 385. Such marriages were void and not voidable, and recent judicial doubts arose from erroneous views of textwriters during the eighteenth and nineteenth centuries.
151. Tolstoy ibid. and Law Com. 33, para. 11.
152. Matrimonial Causes Act 1973, s. 13(2), formerly Nullity of Marriage Act 1971, s. 3(2).

shown, and the ceremony cannot simply be disregarded by either party. Confusion was also caused because of the various degrees of unsoundness of mind that might render a marriage either void, voidable or dissoluble.

(1) *Duress.* Duress may arise from force, fear or fraud. The fear must be sufficiently grave, but the standard is 'subjective', in so far as it need not be shown that a normally tough-minded person would have been afraid, provided the individual concerned was in genuine fear. Duress must arise from external circumstances for which the petitioner is not himself responsible, but it need not be induced by the other party to the ceremony. The older cases arose largely from the financial gains consequent upon marriage.[153] After years of few reported cases, there has recently been an upsurge of litigation.

In *Buckland* v. *Buckland*[154] the petitioner was employed as a policeman in the dockyard area in Malta. He was falsely charged by the Maltese police with defiling a 15-year-old Maltese girl and legal advice, confirmed by his dockyard superintendent, was that he would have no chance of acquittal on the charge before a Maltese court, and would probably be imprisoned for up to two years. He agreed to marry the girl and the ceremony took place that evening. His petition for nullity was granted. Other cases have arisen from attempts to escape political oppression.

A doubtful decision was that reached in *H.* v. *H.*,[155] which concerned a woman aged 18 resident in Hungary in 1949 who, because she was anxious to leave the country, went through a ceremony of marriage with a relative of French nationality. She obtained a French passport, left Hungary, and never cohabited with her husband. A decree of nullity was granted. The choice here was between continuing to live under a Government she feared and entering into an unwanted marriage so that she could emigrate. Having chosen the unwanted marriage and achieved her exodus, why should she also be relieved of the marriage? There was no evidence of threats to her.

The line between the marriage induced by political fear and the sham marriage may sometimes be fine. *Silver* v. *Silver*[156] illustrates the sham marriage. The woman's petition for nullity was dismissed, but she was granted a divorce.

A very different case from a background similar to that of *H.* v. *H.* is *Szechter* v. *Szechter,*[157] where the woman concerned was not only directly threatened, but imprisoned in conditions calculated to cause her maximum physical pain and probably shorten her life. Convinced that she could not survive her sentence, she consented to go through a ceremony of marriage with the respondent, whose wife had divorced him for the purpose, and they left Poland. The marriage was held void for duress.

---

153. Typical is *Scott* v. *Sebright* (1886) 12 P.D. 21. Contrast *Cooper* v. *Crane* [1891] P. 369, where the threat was to blow his own brains out, and that was held not to constitute duress.
154. [1968] P. 296.
155. [1954] P. 258.
156. [1955] 1 W.L.R. 728.
157. [1971] P. 286.

Duress in this country was found to exist in a Yugoslav family in *Parojcic* v. *Parojcic*[158] where a father terrified his daughter with threats to send her back to Yugoslavia, and struck her when she refused to marry the man of his choice. The marriage ceremony eventually took place in a register office but the bride never again saw or communicated with the respondent. A decree of nullity was granted on the ground of duress exerted by the bride's father. In the rather similar case of *Singh* v. *Singh*[159] however, a decree of nullity was refused. There was no evidence of any force or fear or threat.

(2) *Mistake.* In order to avoid a marriage, the mistake must be as to the nature of the ceremony or the identity (not the characteristics) of the other party. Most of the cases arise in respect of register office ceremonies, which were first introduced in 1836. Young women who have led sheltered lives, and foreigners accustomed to a church ceremony, have been allowed to plead that they did not realise the ceremony was one of marriage. In *Hall* v. *Hall*[160] Gorell-Barnes J. summarised the dilemma: 'The difficulty is to decide whether the petitioner is really married or is devoid of intelligence.' He decided against her intelligence and granted her a decree of nullity. Similarly in *Kelly* v. *Kelly*[161] a young woman brought up in an orthodox Jewish family was found to be unaware as late as 1933 that a marriage could be celebrated in a register office, and was allowed to avoid it. In *Valier* v. *Valier*[162] an Italian 'not quick on the uptake' when spoken to in English was able to avoid a register office ceremony for mistake. Similarly in *Mehta* v. *Mehta*[163] an Englishwoman was able to avoid a ceremony conducted in Hindustani, which she did not understand. But a mistake as to the effects of the marriage, e.g., mistakenly thinking it was a polygamous ceremony, is not a ground for nullity.[164]. So also in *Kenward* v. *Kenward*[165] where Englishmen who had contracted marriages in the Soviet Union during the war of 1939–45 were held unable to avoid those marriages because the Soviet authorities refused to grant exit permits to the Soviet wives.

(3) *Unsoundness of Mind.* Before August 1971 the rule was that if either party was so mentally infirm that he could not understand the nature of the ceremony the marriage was absolutely void. In *Re Park,*[166] although

---

158. [1958] 1 W.L.R. 1280.
159. [1971] P. 226 C.A.
160. (1908) 24 T.L.R. 756.
161. (1933) 49 T.L.R. 99.
162. (1925) 133 L.T. 830.
163. [1945] 2 All E.R. 690.
164. *Kassim* v. *Kassim* [1962] P. 224.
165. [1951] P. 124 C.A.; the form in which *Way* v. *Way* [1950] P. 71 reached the Court of Appeal. It was found that certain formal requirements of the Soviet Code relating to the wedding ceremony had not been complied with. The marriages concerned were therefore void for defect of form.
166. [1954] P. 112 C.A. The man died 17 days after the ceremony. On the afternoon after the ceremony of marriage he executed a new will in the same complicated terms as an earlier will, but with additional provision for the second wife. The widow was successful

the 78-year-old (and very rich) man concerned was in a confused state following two heart attacks, there was no doubt that he intended to marry a second time. Before leaving his home for the ceremony he looked at a portrait of his first wife and said aloud that whatever happened, nobody would ever take place her place. It was held that he knew that the ceremony was one of marriage, that the marriage was valid, and therefore that it revoked his earlier will.

(d) Mental Disorder. One of the statutory grounds on which a marriage might be voidable, introduced in 1937, was then worded: 'that either party to the marriage was at the time of the marriage of unsound mind or a mental defective within the meaning of the Mental Deficiency Acts 1913 to 1938, or subject to recurrent fits of insanity or epilepsy'. The wording was amended by the Mental Health Act, 1959,[167] but was criticised by Ormrod J. in *Bennett* v. *Bennett,* [168] and considered in detail by the Law Commission, which recommended the present phraseology. Here again, proceedings for annulment must be taken within three years of the marriage.[169] The party mentally affected may petition.[170]

(e) Communicable Venereal Disease. This was also a ground of nullity introduced for the first time in 1937. Proceedings must not only be taken within three years of the marriage, but the petitioner must satisfy the court that at the time of the wedding he was ignorant of the facts alleged.[171]

(f) Pregnancy *per alium*. The same comments apply as to communicable venereal disease above. The great difference between this ground and the others is that the child by whom the wife is pregnant is by definition not the husband's child, nor has he been treated by both parties as a child of their family, and therefore he is not a 'child of the family'[172] for the purposes of the jurisdiction of the court.

---

in showing that he was incapable of understanding the will when he executed it, and had it set aside. The marriage effectively revoked the earlier will under the Wills Act 1837, s. 18, and the widow was therefore entitled to the whole of the estate on intestacy.
167. Reproduced in the Matrimonial Causes Act 1965, s. 9(*b*)(ii).
168. [1969] 1 W.L.R. 430, . . . 435A: 'this is about the most awkwardly drafted provision that it is possible to imagine'. Ormrod J. (now Ormrod L.J.) is also a qualified medical practitioner.
169. Matrimonial Causes Act 1973, s. 13(2). Before August 1971 the time limit was one year. It is now no longer necessary to show that the petitioner was unaware of the facts at the date of the ceremony. The old requirement that there must have been no marital intercourse since the petitioner discovered the facts has been abolished for this and the two following grounds of venereal disease and pregnancy *per alium*. The newly worded bar of approbation in s. 13(1) is thought to cover the situation adequately.
170. *Iddenden* v. *Iddenden* [1958] 1 W.L.R. 1041.
171. Ibid. s. 13(3) and see n. 169 *supra*.
172. As defined by the Matrimonial Causes Act 1973, s. 52(10).

D. BARS TO AVOIDANCE OF VOIDABLE MARRIAGES

The grounds on which a decree of nullity may be refused for a voidable marriage were considerably revised for proceedings after July 1971.[173] Proceedings must be instituted within three years from the date of the ceremony for a petition based on lack of consent to the marriage;[174] mental disorder; communicable venereal disease or pregnancy *per alium*; and for petitions based on communicable disease or pregnancy *per alium*, the petitioner must also satisfy the court that at the time of the ceremony he was ignorant of the facts alleged.

In proceedings after 1971 the doctrine of approbation of the voidable marriage has been amended. This had been inherited from the church courts and was far from clear. The new bar to relief comprises two aspects: (*a*) conduct by the petitioner, knowing that he could avoid the marriage, such as to lead the other party reasonably to believe that he would not do so, and (*b*) injustice to the other party if the petitioner were allowed to avoid the marriage.[175] It is too soon to know what the effects of the revised bar will be, but it will of course be affected by the fact that annulment of a voidable marriage takes effect after July 1971 only as from the date of the decree absolute.[176]

E. PRIVATE INTERNATIONAL LAW[177]

(i) JURISDICTION OF THE ENGLISH COURTS

After 1973,[178] the English High Court and Divorce County Courts now have jurisdiction in proceedings for nullity of marriage[179] if and only if, either of the parties:

(*a*) is domiciled in England and Wales on the date when the proceedings are begun, or

(*b*) was habitually resident[180] in England and Wales throughout the period of one year ending with that date, or

---

173. By the Nullity of Marriage Act 1971, s. 3(1), now the Matrimonial Causes Act 1973, s.13. The reforms were based on the recommendations of the Law Commission in Law Com. 33.
174. Whether arising from duress, mistake, unsoundness of mind or otherwise: Matrimonial Causes Act 1973, s. 12(*c*).
175. Matrimonial Causes Act 1973, s. 13(1)(*a*) and (*b*).
176. Ibid. s. 16.
177. Private International Law (or the Conflict of Laws) is a large subject, and it is possible here only to draw attention to some of its main features in relation to family law. Further information will be found in the standard works on the subject, viz.: Dicey and Morris, *Conflict of Laws*; (the classic); or more manageable textbooks; viz. J. H. C. Morris, *Conflict of Laws*; R. H. Graveson, *Conflict of Laws*; or G. C. Cheshire, *Private International Law*, ed. P. M. North. See also Chapter VI.
178. By the Domicile and Matrimonial Proceedings Act 1973, which came into force on 1 January 1974 and repealed ss 19(2)(5) and 46 of the Matrimonial Causes Act 1973. See also T. C. Hartley and I. G. F. Karsten, 37 *MLR* (1974) 179.
179. Heads (*a*) and (*b*) apply to divorce and judicial separation; head (*c*) is confined to nullity.
180. Distinguished from ordinary residence in *Cruse* v. *Chittum* [1974] 2 All E.R. 940 by Lane

(*c*) died before the proceedings were begun, and at the date of death that party was either domiciled in England and Wales or had been habitually resident in England and Wales throughout one year ending with the date of death.[181]

On the basis of comity, in *Law* v. *Gustin*[182] Bagnall J. recognised on the man's petition, a decree of nullity obtained in Kansas by the woman with whom he had been through a ceremony of marriage. Her connection with Kansas was held to be sufficiently real.

After 1973 it is also no longer conclusively presumed that a married woman is domiciled where her husband is domiciled, but instead, a married woman's domicile is to 'be ascertained by reference to the same factors as in the case of any other individual capable of having an independent domicile'.[183] Anybody may acquire his or her own domicile on attaining the age of 16 years or marriage under that age.[184]

(ii) CHOICE OF LAW

(a) Form. It is a rule of the conflict of laws that the form of any contract is primarily governed by the law of the place where the contract is made. Therefore anybody making a contract knows that, if the local form is complied

---

J., who held that an acknowledgement from a court in the U.S.A., that the wife petitioner for divorce there was 'an actual *bona fide* resident . . . and had been for more than one year before the filing of the bill' was sufficient evidence of habitual residence. 'Habitual residence' was held to indicate quality rather than duration of residence, and to imply an intention to reside in the country rather than residence of a temporary or secondary nature. The divorce decree granted in Mississippi was accordingly recognised under the Recognition of Divorces and Legal Separations Act 1971, s. 3(1)(*a*).

181. This provision can apply only to the void marriage which some third person seeks to annul after the death of one of the parties.

182. [1976] Fam. 155.

183. Domicile and Matrimonial Proceedings Act 1973, s. 1(1). The root concept is that a person is domiciled in the place where he has his permanent home. It is reasonable that the law of that place should be his personal law. Unfortunately, 'the once simple concept has been so overloaded by a multitude of cases that it has been transmuted into something further and further removed from the practical realities of life' (per Morris, *Conflict of Laws*, p. 13). The Domicile and Matrimonial Proceedings Act 1973 has remedied only two of a host of difficulties, and in particular has done nothing to remedy the unreasonable survival and revival qualities of the domicile of origin.

Nobody can have more than one domicile operative at one time, but a domicile may be of three kinds: (*a*) the domicile of origin, dependent on the domicile of the father at the time of birth (or of the mother if the birth was ex-nuptial); (*b*) the domicile of dependence (which until 1974 domiciled every married woman wherever her husband was domiciled, although she had at no time set foot in, far less lived in, the country concerned). After 1973 only minors of less than 16 years and those of unsound mind have a domicile dependent on that of another person. (*c*) The domicile of choice, which any independent person may acquire. After 1973 independent persons include all those of sound mind over 16 years of age and women even if married. See further Morris, *Conflict of Laws*, ch. 2; Dicey and Morris, *Conflict of Laws*, ch. 8; Graveson, *Conflict of Laws*, ch. 6.

184. Domicile and Matrimonial Proceedings Act 1973, s. 3. Marriage can apply only to those domiciled abroad who marry abroad.

with, the contract will be formally valid. It does not necessarily follow that if the local form is not followed, the contract must be formally invalid. Failing conformity with the primary law governing the appropriate form, viz. the place where the contract is made, the form of some other law may be used, such as that of the place with which the contract has the closest connection.

This general rule applies also to the form of a marriage. It is clear that if two people marry each other in accordance with the formal requirements of the law of the place where the marriage is celebrated, their marriage will be valid as to form.[185] The general rule is that, if they do not comply with local forms, the marriage will be invalid,[186] but to this negative rule English law has always made certain exceptions, viz:

(1) *Where it is impossible or would be repugnant to expect the parties to comply with the local form.* For example, Christians cannot be expected to conform with the local forms appropriate to a polygamous marriage with a bride-price, or applicable only to persons professing some other religion.[187]

(2) *Marriages under the Foreign Marriages Acts 1892 and 1947.* These fall into two groups:

(*a*) *Under the Foreign Marriages Act 1892:* This statute provides that if one of the parties is a British subject, a marriage ceremony may be celebrated abroad before certain officials, designated 'marriage officers' (who include the British Ambassador, Governor, High Commissioner, Resident or Consul), provided the official holds a marriage warrant from the Secretary of State. The official may refuse to perform such a ceremony if there are likely to be difficulties about recognition of its validity by other countries.[188]

(*b*) *Marriages of members of H.M. armed forces abroad:* The Act of 1892 (as amended in 1947) provides that a wedding may be solemnised in any foreign territory by a chaplain serving with any part of the naval, military, or air forces of Her Majesty serving in that territory, or by a person duly authorised by the commanding officer to celebrate such marriages, provided that at least one of the parties is a member of the British forces serving in that territory or is employed in the territory in certain other capacities to be prescribed by Order in Council.

Difficulties arose after the Second World War, during the course of which large numbers of people had been forcibly transported into enemy territory. With the advance of the Allied forces they were released from their former concentration camps or private forced labour. There were also members

---

185. *Scrimshire* v. *Scrimshire* (1752) 2 Hagg. Con. 395, *Dalrymple* v. *Dalrymple* (1811) 2 Hagg. Con. 54, *Apt* v. *Apt* [1948] P. 83. See D. Mendes da Costa, 'The formalities of Marriage in the Conflict of Laws' 7 *ICLQ* (1958) 217.
186. *Berthiaume* v. *Dastous* [1930] A.C. 79, especially Lord Dunedin at p. 83.
187. *Wolfenden* v. *Wolfenden* [1946] P. 61, and generally in those countries in which status is determined by the personal religious law of the parties.
188. Contrast *Collett* v. *Collett* [1968] P. 482, with *Hooper* v. *Hooper* [1959] 1 W.L.R. 1021. See also the Marriage with Foreigners Act 1906.

of Allied forces fighting with the British, but who did not come within the definition of His Majesty's Forces abroad. Many such people celebrated their liberation or victorious advance by contracting marriages, which did not comply as to form with the local (enemy) law. In some cases the parties went through the form of marriage traditional to those of their nationality which, unknown to them, had recently been changed by new governments in their homeland. In a series of cases, the English courts sought to uphold the validity of such marriages by a strained and extended application of the first exception. They held that, where the form of marriage complied neither with the local law nor with the law of the parties' nationality, it was nevertheless a valid marriage at English common law. These decisions have been attacked, particularly by writers in the United States, [189] as an attempt to extend outmoded English law to the marriages in foreign countries of persons who had at the time no connection with this country. The extension of the doctrine of common law marriage in England before 1753 [190] to such marriages was certainly strained, but these were beneficent attempts to uphold the validity of the marriages concerned when the parties subsequently became involved before the English courts in litigation about them.

The leading case is *Taczanowska* v. *Taczanowski*, [191] which concerned an officer of the Polish forces then occupying Italy with the Allied forces, who in 1946 went through a wedding ceremony in Rome with a woman of Polish nationality living in Rome as a civilian refugee. The ceremony was performed by a Polish army chaplain. There had been no attempt to comply with the Italian forms, but by Italian law the marriage would be valid if the parties had complied with the form laid down by the law of their nationality. Unknown to the parties, the power of Polish army chaplains to solemnise the marriages of Polish armed forces had been withdrawn by the provisional Polish government after 1945, and from the beginning of 1946 only marriages celebrated before a civilian official were valid. A mere two days before the wedding, the Polish authorities had issued an order that Polish forces abroad would no longer be considered units of the Polish army. When the woman applied to the English courts in 1956 for a declaration of nullity of the marriage by reason of defect of form, the Court of Appeal held the marriage valid at English common (canon) law, as found (wrongly) in *Reg.* v. *Millis* [192] as an exchange of consents to marry in the presence of an episcopally ordained clergyman, viz. the Roman Catholic priest. The decision was followed in *Kochanski* v. *Kochanska*, [193] and *Preston* v. *Preston*. [194] In none of these cases had any attempt been made to comply with the local form of marriage. But in *Lazarewicz* v. *Lazarewicz* [195] the parties had

---

189. E.g. Ploscowe, Foster and Freed, *Family Law: Cases and Materials*, 2nd edn, p. 57. See also 20 *MLR* (1957) 505.
190. When Lord Hardwicke's Act abolished common law marriage in England and Wales (but not Scotland or Ireland).
191. [1957] P. 301 C.A., together with *Holdanowski* v. *Holdanowska*.
192. (1844) 10 Cl. & Fin. 534.
193. [1958] P. 147.
194. [1963] P. 411 C.A.
195. [1962] P. 171.

attempted but failed to comply with the local Italian law, and the marriage was held void.[196] An even more remarkable extension of the common law marriage was applied in *Penhas* v. *Tan Soo Eng*.[197]

(b) Capacity to Marry (or Essential Validity). The classic and preferable view is that the capacity of each party to marry, either generally or to the particular spouse concerned, is governed by the law of that party's domicile before the marriage.[198] A contrary view, first put forward by Professor Cheshire,[199] is that such matters should be governed by the law of the place where the couple intend to establish their permanent home after the marriage, and this view has received some judicial support. This is a gloss on the original view that all such matters in respect of both parties should be governed by the law of the husband's domicile at the time of the marriage. The law of the intended matrimonial domicile raises great difficulties of definition. In most cases it will be the law of the husband's pre-nuptial domicile. The theory is, in fact, a fairly transparent attempt to subject the wife, in respect of her capacity to marry, to the law of her husband's domicile, and thus to extend back to a time before the marriage a wife's subjection to that law. The law of the intended matrimonial home is less fashionable today than it was. One may hope soon to see it entirely discarded.

(iii) THE RECOGNITION OF POLYGAMOUS MARRIAGES IN ENGLISH LAW

Before 29 July 1972, English law would grant no matrimonial relief in respect of a marriage celebrated according to the law of a country that recognised polygamy. This followed from the decision in *Hyde* v. *Hyde and Woodmansee*.[200] Increasing hardship was caused in England after 1945 when large numbers of immigrants arrived from countries which permitted polygamy. The courts refused to enforce the duty of the man (not recognised as a husband 'as understood in Christendom') to maintain the woman (not recognised as a wife), and there were difficulties about maintenance of the children. The dependants of such marriages were therefore forced to seek relief from the public purse by way of national assistance or supplementary benefit,[201] whilst the wage-earner could escape all his financial obligations to them.

The rule had been eroded from various directions, and the Law Commission belatedly recommended its abolition.[202] Accordingly the Matrimonial Pro-

---

196. There was a similar decision in *Merker* v. *Merker* [1963] P. 283.
197. [1953] A.C. 304 P.C. The decision is explicable on the ground that since Singapore was formerly a British settled colony, English law applied to British subjects there as part of the local law. See Morris, *Conflict of Laws*, p. 93.
198. Dicey and Morris, *Conflict of Laws*, Rule 31, p. 254, and Morris, *Conflict of Laws*, p. 98.
199. Cheshire, *Private International Law*.
200. (1866) L.R. 1 P. & M. 30.
201. E.g. *Sowa* v. *Sowa* [1961] P. 70 C.A., and cf. *Imam Din* v. *N.A.B.* [1967] 2 Q.B. 213.
202. Law Com. 42 (1971), *Family Law: Report on Polygamous Marriages*.

ceedings (Polygamous Marriages) Act 1972 provided by s. 1[203] that no court in England and Wales should be precluded from granting matrimonial relief or making a declaration concerning the validity of a marriage by reason only that the marriage in question was entered into under a law which permits polygamy.

Section 4 of the Act[204] amended s. 1 of the Nullity of Marriage Act 1971 to provide that a marriage should be void if it was a polygamous marriage celebrated outside England and Wales and either party was at the time domiciled in England and Wales. The decision in *Radwan* v. *Radwan (No. 2),*[205] reached in defiance of the statute, sought nevertheless to apply the law of the intended matrimonial home to the capacity of both spouses to enter into a polygamous marriage. Now that the Matrimonial Causes Act 1973, s. 11(*d*) has re-enacted s. 1 of the 1971 Act as amended in 1972, it is hoped that the decision will be treated as plainly wrong, being both based on a false and mischievous principle and contrary to enacted law.

---

203. Now Matrimonial Causes Act 1973, s. 47. See *Chaudhry* v. *Chaudhry* (Note) [1976] 1 W.L.R. 221 C.A. for the jurisdiction of the courts to deal with property of spouses married by polygamous ceremony, and *Reg.* v. *Sagoo* [1975] 3 W.L.R. 267 C.A. for bigamy by subsequent ceremony in England.
204. Based on the 'dual domicile' theory, *ante* n. 198.
205. [1973] Fam. 35. See I. G. F. Karsten, 'Capacity to contract a polygamous marriage', 36 *MLR* (1973) 291.

CHAPTER III

Personal Legal Relations in the Functioning Family

Words such as 'marriage' or 'family' readily import the static idea of an object represented graphically by the space inside an outline. Such an approach was typical of nineteenth-century thinking. Witness Lord Dunedin's oft-quoted and much-approved declaration: 'A metaphysical idea, which is what the status of marriage is, is not strictly a *res*, but it, to borrow a phrase, savours of a *res*, and has all along been treated as such.'[1] The married state is, on the contrary, a series of complex and ever-changing relationships between two individuals of opposite sexes. A family is a more varied complex of different relationships, and exists in fact in so far as those individuals who form it consider themselves to be continuously related to each other either biologically or socially or (more usually), both. The exact nature of their various relationships will be in a continual state of flux. In seeking to add stability to the family, therefore, the law should select with care the relationships it seeks to buttress. Too little law here may well be preferable to too much. Legal sanctions attached to personal relationships may petrify those relationships in their existing form and prevent their development.

At common law, in <u>Blackstone's words,</u> 'the very being or legal existence of the woman is suspended during the marriage, or at least is incorporated and consolidated into that of the husband, under whose wing, protection and *cover* she performs everything'.[2] As late as 1843 the court handed back to her husband the wife he was holding a prisoner under guard in his home[3] for what was recognised as perpetual imprisonment by him there. In 1852,

---

1. *Salveson* v. *Administrator of Austrian Property* [1927] A.C. 641, 662. The phrase is cited with approval by Cheshire, *Private International Law*, e.g. 9th edn p. 85, and is linked with the unity of domicile, finally abolished after 1973 by the Domicile and Matrimonial Proceedings Act 1973. It is also linked with the concept of a judgement *in rem* as one in respect of a *res*, which no longer commands universal acceptance.
2. *Commentaries*, Kerr edn (1857) vol. 1, p. 468.
3. *In re Cochrane* (1843) 8 Dowl. 630.

the court would not go further and grant the husband a writ of *habeas corpus* so that the law could capture the wife for him and hand her over,[4] and in 1891 the Court of Appeal at last reversed the decision of a Divisional Court of two judges and overruled the common law by ordering the husband to produce his wife in court, where she was released.[5] The court also denied the proposition that a husband had the right to beat his wife 'but not in a violent or cruel manner'.[6]

The authority of the husband and father over his minor children excluded any claim by the mother.[7] By the common law (and equity) of England parental rights were exclusively paternal rights.[8] But paternal rights in English law never approached the *patria potestas* of the Roman Law; their diminution when the child reached the age of discretion (14 years for a boy and 16 years for a girl)[9] and their extinction when the child reached majority (or, if a girl, married and came under the authority of her husband) are two of the differences between the two concepts.

The erosion of the common law, which sought to ensure the stability of families by subjugating the will of wife and minor children entirely to that of the husband, and the present legal relationships within the functioning family, may be considered under two main aspects: (1) personal relations, and (2) financial and proprietary relations. So far as possible, relations between husband

---

4. *Reg.* v. *Leggatt* (1852) 18 Q.B. 781.
5. *Reg.* v. *Jackson* [1891] 1 Q.B. 671, the famous Clitheroe case. Having obtained a decree of restitution of conjugal rights, the husband appeared with two young men outside a church on Sunday afternoon and carried off the wife by force 'in the face of the whole congregation', thereafter imprisoning her under guard in his home.
6. [1891] 1 Q.B. 671, 679, per Lord Halsbury L.C.: 'such quaint and absurd dicta as are to be found in the books as to the right of a husband over his wife in respect of personal chastisement are not, I think, now capable of being cited as authorities in a court of justice in this or any civilised country'; per Esher M.R. at p. 682: 'I do not believe this ever was the law'. But Fry L.J. dissociated himself from these dicta.
7. '. . . this Court, whatever be its authority or jurisdiction, has no right to interfere with the sacred right of a father over his own children,' per Bacon V.C. in *Re Plomley* (1882) 47 L.T. (N.S.) 283, 284, cited with approval by Brett M.R. in *Re Agar-Ellis* (1883) 24 Ch. Div. 317, 329. See also Bowen L.J. ibid. 335, 'the Court must not be tempted to interfere with the natural order and course of family life, the very basis of which is the authority of the father . . .'
8. In *R.* v. *de Manneville* (1804) 5 East 221, the mother left her husband because of ill-treatment, taking with her the child eight months old whom she was still nursing. When the father 'found means, by force and stratagem, to get into the house where she was, and had forcibly taken the child then at the breast, and carried it away almost naked in an open carriage in inclement weather' the court refused to interfere. In *R.* v. *Greenhill* (1836) 4 Ad. & E. 624, the mother returned to her parents' house while her husband was openly living in adultery and frequenting brothels. Her three daughters aged $5\frac{1}{2}$, $4\frac{1}{2}$ and $2\frac{1}{2}$ were brought to join her the following day. The court held the husband and father absolutely entitled to recover their custody, although he was demanding it primarily to exert pressure on his wife to withdraw her proceedings for divorce *a mensa* before the church courts. Littledale J. declared at p. 641: 'If . . . each of the parents . . . claimed custody, there is no doubt that the Court would give it to the father; the mother's application would not be attended to.'
9. Per Brett M.R. in *Re Agar-Ellis* (1883) 24 Ch.D. 317, 326, per Cotton L.J. ibid. p. 330, per Bowen L.J. ibid. p. 335.

and wife will be distinguished from those between parent and child, but the law tends to group wife and minor children together. Witness the judicial tendency to classify as wife maintenance what is really maintenance for the children; the whole concept of a wife as her husband's 'dependant'; the failure of the Matrimonial Homes Act 1967 to accord to minor children any security of residence as against the father in the absence of the mother[10] and many other difficulties.

The law's views of relationships within the functioning family are usually clarified only when those relationships are disrupted. Hence most of the illustrations of the functioning position are taken from the family already out of joint. Personal relations will first be considered.

A. SURNAME

(i) MARRIED WOMAN

The custom once generally considered to be a rule of law, that on marriage a woman acquires her husband's surname, has been described by a recent American commentator[11] as: 'In a very real sense . . . the destruction of an important part of her personality and its submersion in that of her husband.' In the United States, the courts of Illinois held in 1944[12] that a woman licensed to practise as a member of the Bar in that State, with her own law office in her maiden name, was not entitled to vote under that name after her marriage in 1944, even with her husband's active support. But in Ohio in 1961, where there was a written ante-nuptial agreement between the spouses that the wife should retain her maiden name, the contrary decision was reached.[13] In 1972 the U.S. Supreme Court upheld the right of a state to require married women to bear their husbands' surnames on their drivers' licenses.[14] Two conflicting views circulated by the General Council of the Bar in England and Wales on the need for married women practising at the English Bar in their maiden names to register under the Registration of Business Names Act 1916,[15] testify to a conflict of view in England on whether a woman is compelled to adopt her husband's surname on marriage and whether her maiden name ceases to be her 'real' name.

---

10. Considered *post* Chapter IV: Financial and proprietary relations.
11. Leo Kanowitz, *Women and the Law: The Unfinished Revolution* (1969) p. 41.
12. *People ex rel. Rago* v. *Lipsky* (1945) 327 Ill. App. 63, 63 N.E. 2d 642.
13. *State ex rel. Krupa* v. *Green* (1961) 114 Ohio App. 497, 177 N.E. 2d 616.
14. *Forbush* v. *Wallace* (1972) U.S. 92 S.Ct. 1197. See further Kanowitz, *Women and the Law*, pp. 41–6, and *Sex Roles in Law and Society* (1973), pp. 185–92; M. M. Hughes, 'And there were two', *Hastings Law Jo.* 23 (1971) 233.
15. The first circular was sent to all women practising at the Bar in England in 1971, citing the opinion of a recently-called male barrister. The contrary view of a senior woman barrister was circulated nearly two years later.

The preferable view is that of the editors of *Halsbury's Laws of England*,[16] that

When a woman on her marriage assumes, as she usually does in England, the surname of her husband in substitution for her father's name, it may be said that she acquires a new name by repute. The change of name is in fact, rather than in law, a consequence of marriage. Having assumed her husband's name, she retains it, notwithstanding the dissolution of the marriage by decree of divorce or nullity, unless she chooses . . . or acquires another name by reputation. On her second marriage there is nothing in point of law to prevent her from retaining her first husband's name. [17]

The general rule of English law is that there are no rules about surnames. In the words of Buckley J. [18]

. . . a person's surname is a conventional name and forms no part of his true legal name. An adult can change his or her surname at any time by assuming a new name by any means as a result of which he or she becomes customarily addressed by the new name. There is no magic in a deed poll . . . But a change of name on the part of an adult must, in my judgment, involve a conscious decision on the part of the adult that he wishes to change his name and be generally known by his new name.

It is thought that married women are entitled to inclusion under the general heading of adults by whom a conscious decision is required before their surname is changed. [19]

Elsewhere the surnames of married women have provided widespread stimulus to legislators. [20] Absence of regulation appears to have caused no difficulty with the other adult population of England and Wales, or of Australia, which shares the lack of rules. There seems no reason why married women (other than life peeresses) should cause problems by the exercise of their conscious decision as to the surname by which they wish to be known. [21]

---

16. Third edn vol. 19 (1957) p. 829
17. *Earl of Cowley* v. *Countess of Cowley* [1901] A.C. 450 H.L.
18. In *Re T. (Orse H.) (An Infant)* [1963] Ch. 238, 240.
19. There are two precedents among life peeresses. The Baronesses Wootton and Summerskill were accorded life peerages respectively in 1958 and 1961 in surnames other than those of the husbands to whom they were at that time married; the Baroness Wootton in the name of her first husband who died in 1917, and the Baroness Summerskill in the maiden name she used throughout her Parliamentary career, and which is used also by her daughter, Dr Shirley Summerskill M.P.
20. Including those in the United States, see nn. 12–14 *supra.* The law is frequently complex. For example, in the French *Code Civil* art. 57; arts 299 and 310.1; art. 334; and arts 357 and 363. *The Encyclopedie Dalloz, Droit Civil*, Tome III (1953) devotes 413 paragraphs to the subject of *Non-Prenoms*. In Federal Germany, arts 1355 and 1616–18 are the principal provisions. In the D.D.R. (Eastern Germany) parties have been able since 1965 to choose the surname each will use after marriage, but before 1968 the choice was rarely exercised. On 16 December 1970, however, a growing fashion was reported for bridegrooms to assume on marriage the surname of their brides. Erfurt was said to have seen seventy-six such recent elections, and other towns showed a similar trend.
21. Under the Enrolment of Deeds (Change of Name) Regulations 1949, No. 316 (heading:

The custom of a wife adopting the same surname as her husband is responsible for the decision of the House of Lords in 1933[22] that when a woman seeks to open a bank account a banker is negligent if he fails to enquire: (i) whether she is married or single, and (ii) if she is married, the name of her husband's employer.

(ii) MINOR CHILD

The paramountcy of the legitimate father of course meant that at common law his children were both obliged and entitled to bear his surname during minority.[23] The spread of divorce and remarriage of those with minor children from an earlier marriage, who normally live with one of the parents (usually the mother), has caused problems about the children's surnames. English judicial opinion is that the father retains the paramount right to have children born to his wife bear his name throughout their minority.[24] In 1969 a *Practice Direction*[25] provided that before a deed poll could be registered in respect of a minor's change of name, there must be supporting evidence that the change of name was for the minor's benefit; that both parents consented (unless special reasons were shown); and that the deed poll was executed by a parent or guardian if the minor were under 16 years of age, or bear the minor's consent if over that age.

The actual change in the child's surname usually takes place on entry to a new school. In one case,[26] where a divorced and remarried mother had so changed the children's name, it was some four years before the father discovered the fact and took legal action. In view of the lapse of time it was held not in the children's best interests to order another change to the former name. In *Re D. (Minors)*[27] the children were enrolled at their new school in the surname of their mother and stepfather, who then jointly applied to adopt[28] them on the ground that their mother wished their surname to be the same as hers. The father objected. Although he had deserted his former wife and

---

'Supreme Court' among the statutory instruments) as amended by Regn. 1951, No. 377 para. 3(2) the applicant to change her name by deed poll must, if a married woman, produce her certificate of marriage and, unless good cause is shown to the contrary, obtain the written consent of her husband. But she has the alternative of executing a statutory declaration, for which she needs the consent neither of her husband nor of any functionary.

22. *Lloyds Bank* v. *Savory* [1933] A.C. 201. The husband stole cheques payable to his employers and paid them into his wife's account. The bankers were held liable to the husband's employers.

23. The ex-nuptial child usually bore his mother's surname, but with the putative father's consent it was not unknown for the child to bear his name.

24. In *re T* (supra) [1963] Ch. 238 at p. 241.

25. *Practice Direction (Deed Poll) (Minors)* [1969] 1 W.L.R. 1330.

26. *Y.* v. *Y. (Child: Surname)* [1973] Fam. 147 (decided 1969).

27. *(Minors) (Adoption by Parent)* [1973] Fam. 209.

28. The change of name is subsumed under the provision in the Adoption Act 1976 s. 39 that an adopted child shall be treated as the child of the marriage of a married couple, and if adopted by a sole adopter, as if born to the adopter in wedlock. See also s. 50.

children and left them dependent on social security benefits for two years[29] until the mother remarried after a divorce, the Divisional Court held that the magistrates had been wrong to dispense with his consent, and disallowed the adoption.[30]

All the children concerned in the 'change of name' cases were by chance girls. Since the courts have denied the right of anyone to change their surname during minority without the consent of the guardian, the agreement of both parents, proof of benefit to the child, and the minor's consent when over 16 years, it would seem difficult on their majority to deny their right to retain their former name on marriage or remarriage in the face of a clear pre-nuptial declaration of intent.

The Children Act 1975 has in effect outlawed adoption by a natural parent and step-parent after 1975 in all but the rarest cases by providing[31] that application for such an adoption shall be dismissed if the court considers the matter would be better dealt with under s. 42 of the Matrimonial Causes Act 1973, and that a custodianship order may not be made in favour of a physical parent, nor in favour of a step-parent if the child were named in an order made on a petition for divorce or nullity, as a child about whose welfare the court was required to satisfy itself before making a decree absolute.[32]

B. NATIONALITY, CITIZENSHIP AND PATRIALITY[33]

According to Clive Parry[34] 'It is usually said that at common law marriage had no effect on nationality. It would be more correct to say that the common law never developed any particular rules as to the nationality of married women.' Nineteenth and twentieth-century statutes, however, starting with the Aliens Act 1844, culminating in the British Nationality and Status of Aliens Act 1914,[35] clearly subjected every married woman by force of British law[36] to the nationality laws of her husband. The provisions applied even though

---

29. Apart from some Christmas, Easter and birthday presents for the children, which appear to have been pleaded as mitigation rather than compounding his two-year denial to them of the necessities of life.
30. A desire to change the surname of minor children to correspond with the mother's change of name on remarriage must be an inadequate reason for so drastic a step as adoption. But the male partner in a failed marriage, not being affected by the customary change of name, is not confronted with the need for such disguises.
31. Children Act 1975, s. 10(3); now Adoption Act 1976, ss. 14, 15.
32. Ibid. s. 33(4)(5).
33. Defined in the Immigration Act 1971, c. 77, s. 2(6) as having a right of abode in the United Kingdom, as distinct from citizenship of the United Kingdom and Colonies, which is one of the qualifications for British nationality.
34. Clive Parry, *Nationality and Citizenship Laws of the Commonwealth and of the Republic of Ireland* (1957) vol. I, p. 71.
35. Section. 10.
36. Nationality is governed by British Law, unlike private law which is governed by the law of England and Wales, or of Scotland, or of Northern Ireland.

the law governing the husband might withhold protection from his wife, and render stateless a woman of British origin who might live throughout her life in Great Britain.

These statutes denying separate national personality to the married woman were enacted when both statute law[37] and – more rarely – judicial decisions[38] were at least loosening the shackles that bound every wife to her husband in domestic English law. The provision in the Act of 1914, that the wife of a British subject should be deemed to be a British subject and the wife of an alien be deemed to be an alien, and that the dissolution of her marriage by death or divorce should not affect her national status, lasted until 1933.

The reforms of 1933 provided that

(*a*) a British subject who married an alien husband did not lose her British nationality automatically unless the law of her husband's nationality recognised her as a national by reason of her marriage;

(*b*) the wife of a man who ceased to be British should not automatically lose her British nationality unless she acquired some other nationality by virtue of its acquisition by her husband.[39]

British nationality is now derived from the possession of citizenship of either the United Kingdom and Colonies[40] or of one of the self-governing countries of the Commonwealth.[41] There is no provision in the British Nationality Act 1948 imposing the law of the husband's nationality upon his wife. In recent years, however, the concept of citizenship has assumed increasing importance as one condition of patriality under the Immigration Acts.[42] Under the Act of 1971 the patrial, who has a right of abode in the United Kingdom, is alone entitled to enter or re-enter the United Kingdom subject to routine production of a passport. The adherence of the United Kingdom to the Treaty of Rome,[43] however, involves the duty of progressively establishing the free movement of workers between member States, and the Immigration Act 1971, will require amendment.[44]

A recent attempt by an illegal immigrant awaiting deportation to pray in

---

37. E.g. the Married Women's Property Acts 1870, 1874, 1882, 1893 and 1907.
38. E.g. *Reg.* v. *Jackson* [1891] 1 Q.B. 671 C.A. *ante.*
39. British Nationality and Status of Aliens Act 1933, s. 1(1).
40. British Nationality Act 1948, s. 1.
41. These are enumerated in s. 1(3) of the Act, which has been much amended since 1948.
42. The Immigration Act 1971 came into operation on 1 January 1973 by S.I. No. 1514 of 1972. It repealed previous legislation. See J. M. Evans, 35 *MLR* (1972) 508.
43. Particularly arts 48−9 dealing with the free movement of workers and arts 52 et seq. dealing with the right of establishment and to engage in and carry on self-employment. *The European Convention on Establishment* (European Treaty Series No. 19) concluded in 1955, is also relevant. Regulation 1612 of 1968, provides *inter alia* by art. 10 that the spouse of a migrant E.E.C. worker, children under the age of 21 or dependent on him; dependent relatives in the ascending line of himself and his spouse, and other dependants, including those 'living under his roof in the country from which he comes' are all entitled to join him. See also Regulation No. 1251 of 1971 and Directive 68/360.
44. On 16 May 1975, the Minister of State, Home Office, stated that the Government did not intend to introduce new immigration legislation until the law of nationality had been brought up to date: H.C. Deb., vol. 892, col. 197.

aid Art. 12 of the European Convention on the Protection of Human Rights to enable him to marry before deportation was unsuccessful.[45] Nationality, citizenship, patriality and the right of free movement across frontiers are complex questions,[46] but most of these rights are derived from family relationships. They are an important part of family law. Here it is possible only to indicate the broad outlines.

(i) HUSBAND AND WIFE

A woman who has married a citizen of the United Kingdom and Colonies[47] is entitled[48] to be registered as a citizen on application and, if an alien or British protected person, on taking the oath of allegiance. The market in marriages to a man of United Kingdom citizenship therefore continues, and advertisements offering such unions with the cash price demanded are sometimes published.[49] But a man who marries a citizen of the United Kingdom and Colonies has no right to be registered as a citizen, although the rules concerning immigrants have recently been relaxed.

A woman has patriality and a right of abode in the United Kingdom *inter alia* if she is a Commonwealth citizen and is or has at any time been the wife of a citizen of the United Kingdom and Colonies or a Commonwealth citizen who has a right of abode under s. 2(1) of the Immigration Act 1971,[50] or has at any time been the wife of a British national who, but for his death, would (broadly) have been entitled to a right of abode.[51] But difficulties may arise for women married to patrials who are not citizens.

Under the Immigration Rules,[52] the wives of non-patrials granted temporary

---

45. *Reg.* v. *Sec. of State for Home Dept. ex parte Bhajan Singh* [1976] Q.B. 198 C.A.
46. For further details see, e.g. Clive Parry, *op. cit.*, Ian A. Macdonald, *The New Immigration Law* (1972).
47. Including a naturalised citizen.
48. Only if she has previously renounced or been deprived of citizenship of the U.K. and Colonies is her registration subject to executive approval. By the British Nationality Act 1965, a married woman is entitled to registration as a British subject without citizenship under ss 13 or 16 of the 1948 Act if her husband would have been a British subject without citizenship but for his death. See also the 1948 Act s. 12(5), and s. 19 as amended by the British Nationality Act 1964, s. 1(1)(*b*). But the alien wife of a patrial citizen may be refused entry to the country if she does not apply for registration: *Reg.* v. *Secretary of State for Home Dept., ex parte Akhtar* [1975] 1 W.L.R. 1717.
49. See also, e.g. *Silver* v. *Silver* [1955] 1 W.L.R. 728; *Jodla* v. *Jodla* [1960] 1 W.L.R. 236 for sham marriages contracted to obtain a right of abode or, as in *H.* v. *H.* [1954] P. 258 and *Szechter* v. *Szechter* [1971] P. 286, the right to quit a country whose nationals are bound to its soil.
50. In *Reg.* v. *Secretary of State for Home Dept., ex parte Phansopkar*, [1976] Q.B. 606 C.A. the Court of Appeal held that the Home Office cannot refuse to consider an application by a patrial's wife to obtain a certificate of patriality and enter the United Kingdom, on the ground that the application could be more satisfactorily dealt with in the patrial's homeland, at least where this was likely to result in delay and inconvenience to her.
51. Immigration Act 1971, s. 2(2).
52. (1971) *Control on Entry*: Cmnd 4606 amended by Cmnd 5715 (1974) for Commonwealth Citizens and Cmnd 5717 for E.E.C. and other non-Commonwealth nationals; *Control after*

admission to the United Kingdom as workers, businessmen, self-employed, or with their own source of income are normally admitted for the same period as their husbands but not allowed to take employment.[53] If the initial leave of a work-permit holder is extended, his wife and minor children normally receive a corresponding extension, but there appears to be no rule about the wife and minor children of other categories of men granted temporary admission.

The wife and minor children of a non-patrial with entry clearance for permanent settlement in the United Kingdom are normally admitted, but if they arrive later, for admittance as the dependant of someone already resident in the United Kingdom, they require a current visa (or entry certificate if a Commonwealth citizen). Such dependants will in any event need to satisfy the immigration officer of their relationship, and this may be difficult.[54] By amendments of the rules in 1974, the husbands and fiancés of women already settled or being admitted for settlement in the United Kingdom are to be admitted if holding a current entry clearance, and a man admitted for a limited period who marries a woman already settled in the United Kingdom may be granted indefinite settlement. On the other hand, if a deportation order is made, the deportee's family may also be deported.[55]

(ii) PARENT AND CHILD

The general requirements for acquisition at birth of citizenship of the United Kingdom and Colonies are: (i) birth within the United Kingdom and Colonies, under the *jus soli,* or (ii) descent from a citizen by birth or, in certain additional circumstances, from a citizen by descent,[56] under the *jus sanguinis.* Citizenship may be acquired after birth by either (i) registration,[57] (ii) naturalisation, or (iii) adoption.

The general rule is that citizenship by descent is transmissible only through

---

Entry: Cmnd 4610, amended by Cmnd 5716 (1974) for Commonwealth citizens and Cmnd 5718 for E.E.C. and other non-Commonwealth nationals.

53. Cmnd 4606, r. 35; See also *Immigration Law* by Lawrence A. Grant and John Constable, VII 'Admission of dependants for Settlement: wives', *New Law Jo.,* vol 125, No. 5716 of 11.9.75, p. 897.
54. See *Reg.* v. *Chief Immigration Officer* ex parte *Salamat Bibi* [1976] 1 W.L.R. 979 C.A. It may be difficult to prove a marriage, particularly one by polygamous form, where written registers are not compulsory or are defective. For example, the Pakistan Muslim Family Laws Ordinance 1961 requires a Muslim husband to register his marriage or, in the case of a second marriage, to obtain permission before marrying, but non-compliance with these provisions does not invalidate the marriage. In August 1976 the Home Secretary appointed a Parliamentary group under the chairmanship of Lord Franks to examine the feasibility and usefulness of a register of dependants of those settled here, who may claim to join them. Other members are Mr. Mark Carlisle Q.C. and Mr. Stanley Irving M.P. There is no woman member.
55. A man's family includes his wife or wives and minor children: Immigration Act 1971, ss 3(5)(6) and 6, and s. 5(4). A woman's illegitimate children belong to her family for this purpose.
56. British Nationality Act 1948, ss 5 and 6.

males. Thus the British Nationality Act 1948 provided[58] that a person is a citizen if his father [*sic*] is a citizen. But an amendment adds[59] that a person is entitled to be registered as a citizen on satisfying the Secretary of State that he is and always has been stateless and that his mother was a citizen when he was born. Under the Act of 1948 the Secretary of State has also a discretion, in special circumstances,[60] to register as a citizen any infant of any nationality. Children legitimated by the subsequent marriage of their parents and posthumous children are, for the purposes of British nationality and citizenship of the United Kingdom and Colonies, treated as having been born legitimate.[61]

Immigration law recognises that children are born not of one, but of two parents. Patriality and the right of abode in the United Kingdom are conferred[62] *inter alia* on (i) a citizen of the United Kingdom and Colonies born to or legally adopted by a parent [*sic*] who had such citizenship at the time of the birth or adoption, if the parent either then had such citizenship or had been born to or adopted by a parent who then so had it; and (ii) a Commonwealth citizen born to or legally adopted by a parent who at the time of the birth or adoption had citizenship of the United Kingdom and Colonies.

The Adoption Act 1976 provides[63] that where an adoption order is made in relation to a child who is not a citizen of the United Kingdom and Colonies, if the adopter or, in the case of a joint adoption, the adoptive father, is a citizen of the United Kingdom and Colonies, the child shall also be such a citizen from the date of the order. Section 70(2) provides for the order of precedence of deemed nationality if the adopted person had more than one nationality.[64] Section 17 of the Act now provides for Convention Adoption Orders. These will not be applicable where the prospective adopters and the child to be adopted are all United Kingdom nationals living in British territory. Applicants for such orders must, if a married couple, either (*a*) each be a United Kingdom national or a national of a Convention country, and both habitually reside in Great Britain, or (*b*) both be United Kingdom nationals and each habitually resident in British territory or a Convention country. The child to be adopted must be either a national of the United Kingdom or of a Convention country, and habitually reside in British territory or a Convention country.[65]

---

57. This additional requirement is discussed only in the context of a wife's right to registration. It is also needed in some cases of citizenship by descent.
58. Section 5(1).
59. British Nationality (No. 2) Act 1964, s. 1(1)(*a*), enacted in consequence of the United Nations Convention on the Reduction of Statelessness. (Cmnd 1825), and extended by the British Nationality Act 1965, s. 4 to the children of mothers entitled to registration as British nationals without citizenship under the 1965 Act, s. 1(1).
60. British Nationality Act 1948, s. 7(2).
61. Ibid. ss 23 and 24.
62. By the Immigration Act 1971 s. 2(1)(*b*).
63. Section 40, substantively re-enacting the Adoption Act 1958, s. 19.
64. Formerly Adoption Act 1968, s. 9.
65. The Adoption Rules are not available at the time of writing. They may be expected to clarify details of Convention Adoption Orders.

C. DOMICILE

During the nineteenth century the common law rule imposing on a wife and all minor children a domicile of dependence on the husband and father became established.[66] Only after many efforts was the unity of domicile of wife and minor children with that of the husband shattered after 1973 by the Domicile and Matrimonial Proceedings Act 1973.[67] Section 1 of this Act now provides that the domicile of a married woman shall be ascertained 'by reference to the same factors as in the case of any other individual capable of having an independent domicile', except that a woman having a domicile of dependence on her husband when the provision comes into operation is to be treated as retaining it until it is changed by subsequent acquisition or revival of another domicile.[68]

The law of the domicile has always been accorded predominance in the regulation of matters of personal status, and the courts of the domicile are similarly predominant in jurisdiction in matrimonial causes.[69] For a long time the English courts would not accept jurisdiction in divorce unless the parties (meaning the husband) were domiciled in England. Since the legislature could not, until 1973, bring itself to adopt the obvious remedy, it had given the courts special jurisdiction to hear matrimonial proceedings on a wife's petition, even though she (meaning her husband) was not domiciled in England. These special provisions for wives have therefore now been repealed.[70]

As regards minors the Domicile and Matrimonial Proceedings Act 1973 provides[71] that on attaining the age of 16 years or marriage under that age[72] a person shall become capable of having an independent domicile. For unmarried minors below the age of sixteen whose parents are alive but living apart,[73] the child's domicile will depend on that of his mother and not that of his father while the child has a home with his mother and none with his father or, having had such a domicile dependent on his mother, has not since had a home with his father.[74] The Act therefore affirms the paramountcy of the father's domicile, but permits exceptions.

---

66. Finally by *Lord Advocate* v. *Jaffrey* [1921] 1 A.C. 146, in which the House of Lords, on an appeal from Scotland, decided that even though a woman had instituted divorce proceedings for desertion and adultery against her husband, she died domiciled in Queensland, Australia, which she had never visited but which was the place to which her family had paid to send her husband because of his dissolute habits. He committed bigamy there.
67. By s. 17(5) the Act came into force on 1 January 1974.
68. Ibid. s. 1(2).
69. See now the Domicile and Matrimonial Proceedings Act 1973, s. 5.
70. Originally by the Matrimonial Causes Act 1937, s. 13, and by the Law Reform (Miscellaneous Provisions) Act 1949, s. 1(1). Both were consolidated in the Matrimonial Causes Act 1973, s. 46, now repealed by the Domicile and Matrimonial Proceedings Act 1973, s. 5 and Sched. 6.
71. Section 3.
72. Since the minimum age of marriage in England is 16 the provision can apply only to marriages celebrated abroad.
73. Section 4(1); by s. 4(5) references to an adopted child's father and mother are to be construed as references to his adoptive father and mother.
74. Domicile and Matrimonial Proceedings Act 1973, s. 4(2)(*b*). There is no express provision

D. ACTIONS IN TORT BETWEEN HUSBAND AND WIFE

It followed from the common law rule that husband and wife were one that neither could sue the other, since no one may sue himself. The rule persisted despite the establishment of judicial divorce in 1857 and was expressed in s. 12 of the Married Women's Property Act 1882, although various recommendations were made for its abolition.[75] However, following the Ninth Report of the Law Reform Committee[76] in 1961, the Law Reform (Husband and Wife) Act 1962 eventually abolished the prohibition, from which in recent years the motor-car insurance companies had been the principal beneficiaries. This reform, so long delayed and so fiercely resisted, appears to have produced no unfortunate results so far; nor has there been any noticeable need for the courts to stay or dismiss such actions as likely to produce no substantial benefit for either party, or as more conveniently dealt with under the Married Women's Property Act 1882, s. 17.[77]

E. CRIMINAL INJURIES COMPENSATION

The schemes operated under the Royal Prerogative by the Criminal Injuries Compensation Board for compensating the victims of criminal injuries, provide[78] that no compensation will be payable where the victim and the offender were 'living together at the time as members of the same family'. It was held in *Reg.* v. *Criminal Injuries Compensation Board*[79] that this rule applied where the husband and wife were living in separate households under the same roof, the matrimonial concept of desertion being inapplicable. Where in those circumstances the husband inflicted grievous bodily harm on his wife she was, therefore, denied compensation.

F. A HUSBAND'S ACTION FOR DAMAGES AGAINST THOSE DE- PRIVING HIM OF HIS WIFE'S SOCIETY OR SERVICES: *PER QUOD CONSORTIUM AMISIT OR PER QUOD SERVITIUM AMISIT*

At the end of 1976 it is still a tort actionable at the suit of a husband, to take away, imprison or do physical harm to his wife provided that: (i) the

---

in respect of the 'illegitimate' child whose custody may be awarded by the court to the 'natural' father under the Guardianship of Minors Act 1971, s. 14(1). But by s. 14(3) of that Act the 'natural' father entitled to his custody is treated as if he were the lawful father of the minor. It is thought that except in the rare case where the child does not have his home with the custodial father, the child's domicile will depend on that of the custodial father.

75. See Glanville Williams, 24 *MLR*. (1961) 101.
76. Cmnd 1268 of 19.1.61. See 24 *MLR*. 481 and O. Kahn-Freund, 25 *MLR*. 695.
77. As permitted by ss 1(2) or 2(2) of the 1962 Act.
78. Cmnd 2323 (announced in Parliament 24.6.64), para. 7. The scheme was amended on 3.8.65 and 21.5.69.
79. [1972] 1 W.L.R. 569; 1 All E.R. 1034.

act is wrongful as against the wife, and (ii) the husband is thereby deprived of her society or services. The action is quite separate from any action the wife may have on her own behalf, and the husband is therefore not affected by any contributory negligence of the wife.[80] It is also now clear that the husband may recover damages for partial impairment of the wife's consortium.[81]

The action is an anomalous survival from the days when a husband was regarded as his wife's feudal Lord, entitled by his status to her services, both marital and in the household. In *Best* v. *Samuel Fox*[82] a misguided attempt to proclaim women's improved status by extending the action to a wife for injury to her husband's sexual capacity was rightly rejected by the House of Lords, which said that the survival of the husband's action was an anomaly which should not be extended. As Professor Glanville Williams wrote nine years later:[83] 'matters cannot be left like this: either the action should be abolished, or it should be made available to both spouses on equal terms. What is to be done?' Since then the Law Reform Committee[84] and the Law Commission[85] have both recommended abolition of the action in its present form. No legislation has yet appeared, even in draft form, and it can only be hoped that the Royal Commission on Damages for Personal Injuries[86] will soon make recommendations leading to legislation.

G. EVIDENCE BETWEEN HUSBAND AND WIFE

Most of the rules excluding a spouse's evidence of marital communications in civil cases were repealed by the Civil Evidence Act 1968.[87] In particular it is now established[88] that interrogatories to the spouses may now ask the direct question whether that party has committed adultery or not, and if asked such questions must be answered. But the court will not always permit such interrogatories, particularly if the interests of other persons might be jeopardised.[89] Since 1949 either husband or wife may give evidence that

---

80. The Australian decision *Curran* v. *Young* 112 (1965) C.L.R. 99 is generally accepted.
81. *Cutts* v. *Chumley* [1967] 1 W.L.R. 742, C.A. The House of Lords refused leave to appeal: [1968] 1 W.L.R. 668.
82. [1952] A.C. 716 H.L.
83. 'Some Reforms in the Law of Tort', 24 *MLR*. (1961) 101, 103.
84. 11th Report Cmnd 2017 (1963) para. 19.
85. Working Paper No. 19 (1968) paras 46–87, and Law Com. 56.
86. Under the Chairmanship of Lord Pearson.
87. Section 14 allowed marital privilege only in respect of criminal proceedings under the law of some part of the United Kingdom; ss 16(3) and 16(4) repealed specific provisions making a spouse not compellable in civil proceedings; s. 16(5) revoked the privilege in respect of evidence of adultery.
88. *Nast* v. *Nast* [1972] Fam. 142 C.A. (petition to appeal to the House of Lords dismissed), following the Civil Evidence Act 1968, s. 16(5).
89. As in *C.* v. *C.* (*Divorce: Interrogatories*) [1973] 1 W.L.R. 568, where the husband, a pensioner without means, accused his wife of adultery with three men. It was held the wife must not answer in the absence of the three other persons concerned.

marital intercourse did or did not take place between them at any time.[90]

In criminal cases, the general rule is that the accused's spouse is neither compellable nor competent[91] to give evidence for the prosecution, but there are the following exceptions:

(i) On a charge of violence to the spouse, the spouse against whom the violence was directed has always been both competent and compellable. Otherwise few men would be convicted of brutal treatment of their wives, (or vice versa) since it is not usually indulged in in public. By similar reasoning it seems probable that the accused's spouse is a competent and compellable witness in respect of violence to minor children of the family.

(ii) Under the Criminal Evidence Act 1898, s. 4 and the Sexual Offences Act 1956, s. 39, a spouse is a competent witness against the accused spouse but not compellable (that is to say, may voluntarily give such evidence but may not be compelled to do so).[92]

(iii) By the Theft Act 1968, s. 30(3), a spouse is competent in proceedings brought by a third party 'with reference to that person's wife or husband or to property belonging to the wife or husband'.[93]

(iv) A spouse is probably both competent and compellable to give evidence in cases of treason and abduction.

Some questions between husband and wife relate particularly to children. The law is involved in such matters as contraception, abortion, and pre-natal injury to children.

H. CONTRACEPTION

The decision of the House of Lords in *Baxter* v. *Baxter*[94] that a marriage was consummated even although contraceptive measures were taken, accords with the more enlightened approach of the post-1945 era to family planning. The massive publicity generated by the debate about legalising abortion has in recent years focussed attention on the need for wider dissemination of

---

90. Law Reform (Miscellaneous Provisions) Act 1949, s. 7, now the Matrimonial Causes Acts 1965 s. 43 and 1973 s. 48(1). Great hardship was caused to husbands of unfaithful wives by the former prudish rule.
91. That is, not only is not obliged to give such evidence, but cannot be permitted to do so voluntarily. In *Reg.* v. *Deacon* [1973] 1 W.L.R. 696, a man was charged with the murder of *X* and the attempted murder of his own wife. The wife gave evidence on both counts, *X* having been her brother. The accused was convicted of murdering *X*, but the Court of Appeal quashed the conviction because the accused's wife had been allowed to give evidence.
92. These offences include wilful neglect to maintain wife and children; sexual offences against children; child destruction; bigamy; and offences under the National Insurance Act and similar provisions. See R. Cross, *Evidence*, 3rd edn, (1974) pp. 147–9; 154–62, with proposed reforms.
93. See *Reg.* v. *Noble* [1974] 1 W.L.R. 894, 2 All E.R. 811 C.A. The provision probably disposes of the troublesome decision in *Reg.* v. *Algar* [1954] 1 Q.B. 279.
94. [1948] A.C. 274. The decision overruled two contrary decisions in *Cowen* v. *Cowen* [1946] P. 36 and *J.* v. *J.* [1947] P. 158, and was controversial for some years.

contraceptive information. The National Health Service (Family Planning) Act 1967 enabled local authorities, with the approval of the Minister of Health, to make arrangements for providing advice on contraception, medical examination of persons seeking advice, and supply of contraceptive substances and appliances. In 1973 the National Health Service Reorganisation Act[95] declared it to be the duty of the Secretary of State to make arrangements for advice and examination and treatment of those seeking contraception, and supplies of contraceptive substances and appliances were included in the National Health Scheme. Since 1970 those over the age of 16 are entitled to obtain contraceptive advice or undergo sterilisation if they wish without the consent of parent or guardian.[96]

J. ABORTION

The Abortion Act 1967 came into operation on 27 April 1968,[97] and provides that pregnancy may lawfully be terminated by a registered medical practitioner if two registered medical practitioners are of the opinion, formed in good faith:

(a) that the continuance of the pregnancy would involve risk to the life of the pregnant woman, or of injury to the physical and mental health of the pregnant woman or any existing children of her family greater than if the pregnancy were terminated, or

(b) that there is a substantial risk that if the child were born it would suffer from such physical or mental abnormalities as to be seriously handicapped.

The Act provides that in determining whether the continuance of a pregnancy would involve risk of injury to health, account may be taken of the pregnant woman's actual or reasonably foreseeable environment. There is no need for anyone other than the woman herself to consent to the abortion. Following continued controversy, the Lane Committee was appointed in 1971 and reported in 1974[98] on the functioning of the Act, making some recommendations for amendment.[99]

---

95. Section 4.
96. Family Law Reform Act 1969, s. 8, which provides that anyone over 16 may validly consent as if of full age to any surgical, medical or dental treatment.
97. Viz. six months after receiving the Royal Assent: s. 7(2).
98. Cmnd 5579.
99. In particular, for an upper time limit of twenty-four weeks' gestation before abortion, and for the licensing and control of all medical referral agencies. Ibid. paras 520–3. See also J. Temkin, William M. Rees and Paul M. White 37 *MLR*. (1974) 657, 663. The House of Commons Select Committee on the Abortion (Amendment) Bill, the first report of which was published on 28 July 1976, recommended an upper time limit of twenty weeks.

K. DAMAGES FOR INJURY TO UNBORN CHILDREN

Starting in 1962 in England (following previous proceedings in Federal Germany[100]) the horrifying story has unfolded of unforeseen injuries caused to the foetus as a result of the administration of the drug thalidomide[101] to a woman during pregnancy. The drug had been advertised by the distributors as a safe sedative for pregnant women. It is not possible here to enter into all the ramifications of the ensuing litigation both in England and elsewhere.[102] The Law Commission, having considered what the nature and extent of civil liability for ante-natal injury should be, reported in August 1974[103] with a draft Bill, and the Congenital Disabilities (Civil Liability) Act came into force on 22 July 1976.[104] It provides in brief that, if a child is born disabled because the wrongful act of another person resulted in an occurrence before the birth that either affected the ability of either parent to have a normal healthy child, or affected the mother during her pregnancy, or affected her or the child in the course of its birth, the disabilities are to be regarded as damage resulting from the wrongful act, and will be actionable at the suit of the child. The Act does not affect the operation of the Nuclear Installations Act 1965 as regards injuries arising from radiation. Damages for loss of expectation of life are recoverable only if the child survives for 48 hours. The child's mother is exempted from liability to her child for such pre-natal injuries,[105] unless she drives a motor-car while pregnant and fails to take the same care for the child's safety as she has a duty to take for the safety of others under the general law. The Act has no retroactive effect.[106]

---

100. The number of deformed children born there following thalidomide is more than ten times the number in England and Wales.
101. The Law Commission declared in Law Com. 60, Cmnd 5709 that the terrible teratogenic effect of thalidomide 'is no longer in doubt', thus ending a long and costly controversy. About 450 children were born in England and Wales with gross deformities. But the Law Commission pointed out that 'There are known to be about 1500 drugs having teratogenic effects (i.e. capable of causing damage to the foetus)'.
102. They include (i) assessment of damages for such deformities; (ii) an attempt, successful at first instance but fortunately overruled on appeal, to replace a father by the Official Solicitor, since he would not agree to conditions the distributors insisted must be accepted unanimously: see *Re Taylor's Application* [1972] 2 Q.B. 369 C.A., and (iii) contempt of court in the publication, while long drawn out negotiations continued, of newspaper articles outlining the history of the manufacture and marketing of the drug. See *Att.-Gen.* v. *Times Newspapers* [1974] A.C. 273. On 29 November 1973 the House of Commons debated the matter, and the substance of some of the newspaper articles was revealed and reported. See H. C. Deb., vol. 847, cols. 431–500, and *The Sunday Times* 27 June 1976.
103. Law Com. 60, *Report on Injuries to Unborn Children*, Cmnd 5709, considerably departing from recommendations in Published Working Paper No. 47, published 19.1.73.
104. The Act extends to Northern Ireland but not to Scotland.
105. Sir G. Baker, President of the Family Division of the High Court, opposed granting the child a cause of action against his mother or father because 'it would give a new weapon to the unscrupulous spouse – and there are many'. Law Com. 60 para. 56.
106. S. 4(5). The Law Commission considered it important to make clear that in its view and that of the Scottish Law Commission, liability for pre-natal injury caused by another's fault (including negligence), already existed under the common law, and that therefore no legislation should have retrospective effect or prejudice claims made in respect of causes of action arising before the legislation became effective: Law Com. 60, para. 8.

L. MARITAL CONSORTIUM

Since *Reg.* v. *Jackson*[107] the old lore that every man had a common law right to beat his wife, to imprison her and to force his sexual attentions upon her at will has been discredited. In *Reg.* v. *Reid*[108] a man was convicted of the criminal offence of kidnapping his wife because he forced her at knife-point to leave her separate residence and return to live with him. In *Reg.* v. *Davies (Peter)*[109] the Court of Appeal affirmed a husband's conviction for murdering his wife; although the acts of a third party (in this case the wife's lover) may amount to provocation to reduce the charge to manslaughter, they were held not to do so in that case.

In recent years there has been considerable publicity about the number of battered wives and children, and the failure of the law to protect them or afford them relief. There are two major difficulties:

Firstly, usually the woman of the lower socio-economic groups, particularly if she has young children, does not have the finance to enable her to find, move to and cover the outgoings for separate accommodation. Most housing for the poor is provided by local authorities and the shortage is acute. Few local authorities are likely to encourage a woman with young children, living in such housing with the husband and father, to move out and occupy another housing unit for which other applicants are clamouring after a wait of several years. That would be so even if the woman were reasonably certain of being able to find the rent for the new accommodation.

Local authorities have been slow either to constitute husband and wife joint tenants[110] or to rehouse a wife and children unless a separation order is first obtained from the courts.[111] Much hardship results for the woman below normal intelligence, physical fitness, or determination.[112] On the other

---

107. [1891] 1 Q.B. 671.
108. [1973] Q.B. 299 C.A. The Court at p. 302 expressly left open the question whether the decision in *Reg.* v. *Miller* [1954] 2 Q.B. 282 was still good law. There the Court found no case for a husband to answer on a charge of raping his wife when there was no separation order in operation.
109. [1975] Q.B. 691, C.A.
110. The *Finer Report on One-Parent Families*, Cmnd 5629, at pp. 357–404, found the arguments for and against joint tenancies somewhat evenly balanced in the private sector: Ibid. para. 6.46. In paras 6.81–6.84 the Report found that local authorities might well relax some of their rigid rules, and in particular show greater willingness to assist the husband who must leave the home to find other accommodation, so that his wife and children can remain. Some authorities were said to refuse all assistance to such 'single men' seeking accommodation.
111. Ibid. para. 6.80. When President of the P.D.A. Division of the High Court, Sir J. Simon (now Lord Simon of Glaisdale) gave an interview to *The Times* on 31 January 1964 about the difficulties arising. See also *Montgomery* v. *Montgomery* [1965] P. 46.
112. See Interim Report from the House of Commons Select Committee on *Violence in Marriage*: H. C. 553–i (1975). In *Bradley* v. *Bradley* [1973] 1 W.L.R. 1291 C.A., a County Court judge refused to dissolve a marriage although violent cruelty by the husband to the wife and children was proved, because the woman and her nine children (of whom six were from a previous marriage) continued to live with him in the local authority accommodation, having nowhere else to go. The Court of Appeal, however, ordered a full hearing of her petition. See also Chapter V.

hand the courts do not seek to encroach on the local authority's statutory duties. As Dunn J. said in *Brent* v. *Brent*:[113] 'the court should not lend itself to any extension of attempts to influence the housing priorities of the local authority by itself creating priorities'. In that case, the court declined to order the chronically sick husband to leave the local authority flat occupied also by the wife in full employment, and by two adult employed children.

Secondly, although the High Court and the Divorce County Courts may issue injunctions to prevent a husband assaulting his wife, there may be difficulties even here.[114] Moreover the magistrates' court—which is the court most likely to be known to married women who are poor, and the most available for one who must trail young children with her,—has no power to enjoin parties against molestation. The Law Commission's recommendation for such a power to be given to these courts[115] will, it is to be hoped, soon be implemented, and include power to prohibit entry on any premises where the wife or children are.

The courts are today showing greater sensitivity to such problems. A Practice Direction has provided[116] that the Registrar may direct the omission of the petitioner's address from a divorce petition where necessary for the petitioner's protection. Another Direction[117] that from October 1974 the hearing of applications for injunctions (not necessarily about violence) should take place in Chambers has come under attack on grounds of undue secrecy.[118]

M. PARENTAL CUSTODY OF MINORS

After the Guardianship of Infants Act 1886[119] for the first time gave legal rights to the mother of legitimate children in the presence of her husband, the Act was

---

113. [1975] Fam. 1 at 8 F. and H. See also *Hale* v. *Hale* [1975] 1 W.L.R. 931 C.A.
114. In *McGibbon* v. *McGibbon* [1973] Fam. 170, the High Court had evidence of extreme physical violence by the husband to the wife sufficient for leave to be granted for the wife to petition for divorce within three years of the marriage. The court also granted an injunction against further molestation by the husband, but doubted whether it had power to enjoin the husband from entering the matrimonial home on such an application: see [1973] Fam. 170 at 175–8. In *McLeod*, v. *McLeod*, *The Times* 3.7.73, and [1973] C.L. 1621, two months after the wedding a High Court judge granted an injunction against molestation of the wife by the husband and against the husband re-entering the home. But in that case the wife was the sole tenant. See also *Vaughan* v. *Vaughan* [1973] 1 W.L.R. 1159, C.A., and Domestic Violence and Matrimonial Proceedings Act, 1976.
115. P.W.P., No. 53, para. 70. It is recommended that such an order should be enforceable under the Magistrates' Courts Act 1952. s. 54, providing for a monetary sanction or committal to custody.
116. *Practice Direction* (*Petition: petitioner's address*) [1975] 1 W.L.R. 787.
117. *Practice Direction* (*Matrimonial Causes: Injunction*) [1974] 1 W.L.R. 936.
118. See the *New Law Journal* of 9 July 1974; *The Times* 28 June and 10 July 1974. The difficult question of publicity in matrimonial matters is considered in Chapter V.
119. Passed as a result of the 'strong' decision in *Re Agar-Ellis* (1883) 24 Ch.D. 317, that the father of a daughter over 16 years of age had an absolute right until her majority to decide with whom she should live (the families of Church of England clergymen), and to

amended, principally by the Act of 1925, and the legislation was consolidated[120] in the Guardianship of Minors Act 1971. Until 8 May 1974,[121] however, paternal rights were superior. What the Acts from 1886 onwards had done was to provide increasingly that, if the mother did not agree with decisions made by the father of children born in marriage, she might apply to a court, and that the father could not by *inter vivos* or testamentary acts oust her authority, except on the order of a court. Once the question came before the Court, under the Act of 1925[122] it was under a duty to regard the welfare of the infant (or minor as he is now called) as the first and paramount consideration, and not take into consideration whether the claim of the father or any right at common law possessed by the father was superior to that of the mother.[123]

The situation has now been radically changed by the Guardianship Act 1973, which provides[124] that 'In relation to the custody or upbringing of a minor, and in relation to the administration of any property belonging to or held in trust for a minor or the application of income of any such property, a mother shall have the same rights and authority as the law allows to a father, and the rights and authority of mother and father shall be equal and be exercisable by either without the other.' The Act declares unenforceable any agreement by a parent to surrender any part of the parental rights and authority[125] except as part of a separation agreement, in which event the

---

prohibit any uncensored correspondence or conversation between the girl and her mother or other relatives. Coming a year after the legislature had effectively given a married woman the right to manage and control her own property, the decision that she had no rights in respect of her children born in marriage could not long stand. The unwed mother, on the other hand, was held in the same year, in *Reg.* v. *Nash* (1883) 10 Q.B.D. 454 C.A. to have a right to claim custody of her illegitimate child by *habeas corpus*, a complete reversal of the common-law position in *Re Ann Lloyd* (1841) 3 M. & G. 547.

120. Except for s. 9 of the Tenures Abolition Act 1660, which by s. 8 of the Guardianship of Minors Act 1971 was expressly left unaffected. This ancient relic was eventually repealed by the Guardianship Act 1973, s. 7 of which makes new provisions for the powers of a minor's guardian to receive and recover in his own name for the minor's benefit any property to which the minor is entitled.

121. The Guardianship Act 1973 came into force from 8 May 1974 by S.I. 695 of 1974.

122. Guardianship of Infants Act 1925, s. 1(1).

123. The section also added the meaningless phrase: 'or the claim of the mother is superior to that of the father'. No such superior claim of the mother existed.

124. Section 1(1). The provision is based on similar provisions in certain jurisdictions of the United States, and is still flawed by the concept of each parent having a bundle of rights, now to be exactly equal.

125. This has always been the common law position. Some religious sects are known to exert pressure on members (i) not to marry outside the sect, and (ii) if unable to refrain from doing so at least to insist on a pre-nuptial agreement that all children (or all sons) will be raised in the tenets of the sect. The agreement was always held unenforceable unless the husband and father had, over a considerable period, acted upon it and allowed others not only to maintain his children but to settle property on them. Until the Custody of Infants Act 1873, even on separation any agreement by the father to allow another (usually the mother), custody of his children, was void and so inherently contrary to public policy that it rendered void the whole agreement of which it formed part. By s. 2 of the Act of 1873 such agreements were not necessarily void, but the courts would not enforce them unless for the benefit of the child. See *Re Besant* (1879) 11 Ch.D. 508; *Besant* v. *Wood* (1879) 12 Ch.D. 605. The Guardianship Bill, as originally introduced in the House of

agreement will not be enforced if the court is of the opinion that it will not be for the benefit of the child to give effect to it.

If the parents disagree on any question affecting the child's welfare, either of them may apply to the court, which may make such order as it thinks proper. But the court order on such an application may not include provisions for custody of the minor or the right of access to him of the father or mother.[126] This provision is apparently designed to deal with differences of opinion between the parents not amounting to disruptive disputes. Where they are in real dispute, however, it is difficult to envisage the two parents, each with the absolutely equal right, exercisable separately, to the sole custody of the child. This difficulty seems to have been appreciated and s. 85(3) of the Children Act 1975 provides that 'Where two or more persons have a parental right or duty jointly, any one of them may exercise or perform it in any manner without the other or others unless the other or one or more of the others has signified disapproval of its exercise or performance in that manner.'

THE REDUCTION AND TERMINATION OF PARENTAL AUTHORITY

By the Family Law Reform Act 1969, s. 1 and Sched. 1 the age of majority was reduced from 21 to 18 years.[127] There has also recently been increasing recognition of the child's need for a graduated progression rather than a traumatic leap from dependence to autonomy, and provisions have been made that those over 16 years may give their own consent to any surgical, medical or dental treatment;[128] may establish their own domicile,[129] and should not be the subject of supervision orders.[130] Magistrates may make custody or maintenance orders in respect of them only if they are physically or mentally incapable of self-support.[131] There are difficulties about fixed age limits, and a flexible approach is preferable in some circumstances.[132] A graduated approach was inherent in the common law, which would not compel an unwilling child

---

Lords in 1973, would have rendered pre-nuptial agreements of this kind absolutely binding and enforceable. See 339 H.L. Deb., col. 39–40 per Lord Simon of Glaisdale; vol. 340, cols 643–58.

126. Section 1(3) and (4).
127. From 1 January 1970. The Act followed the recommendation of the *Latey Report on the Age of Majority*, Cmnd 3342. The ancient rule that a particular age was attained on the first moment of the day before the relevant birthday was also abolished by s. 9(1), which provided that a particular age is attained at the commencement of the relevant anniversary.
128. Family Law Reform Act 1969, s. 8.
129. Domicile and Matrimonial Proceedings Act 1973, s. 3.
130. Guardianship Act 1973, s. 2(2).
131. Guardianship of Minors Act 1971, s. 15(2), re-enacting in slightly amended form the provisions of the Guardianship of Infants Act 1925, s. 7(1), which first gave magistrates jurisdiction under the statutes.
132. See S.I. No. 444 of 1972 raising the universal compulsory minimum school-leaving age from 15 to 16 years from 1 September 1972. Some discretion might have been preferable.

above the age of discretion [133] to the custody of the father. The rule that time runs against a person under a disability (including minority) in the custody of a parent was repealed by the Limitation Act 1975. [134]

---

133. Sixteen years for a girl and 14 for a boy. But equity would intervene for the child's welfare until majority.
134. See Chapter IV, notes 169–70.

CHAPTER IV

Legal Property and Financial Relations in the Functioning Family

A. AREAS OF UNITY

There still remain some areas of financial or property relationship in which not only husband and wife but minor children also are regarded as a unit, headed as a matter of law by the husband and father. The principal areas are:

(i) *Maintenance.* The husband's common law duty to maintain his wife and minor children, which survived the introduction in 1870 of a partial system of separate property between husband and wife, and the more thoroughgoing separation introduced in 1882 which is still operative.[1]

(ii) *Taxation.* For purposes of income tax, capital gains tax, capital transfer tax, and the proposed wealth tax husband and wife are treated as one and the legislation spells out that the husband is that one.[2] The incorporation of the income and property of minor children into the unit for tax purposes is less complete, and has varied in recent years on political grounds.

(iii) *Social security and welfare:* including National Health Insurance, retirement benefit and unemployment insurance; supplementary benefit and family income supplement. Exceptionally, under the Family Allowances Act 1965 and the Child Benefit Act 1975[3] family allowances[4] and child benefit which will

---

1. Until the Law Reform (Married Women and Tortfeasors) Act 1935, a married woman's property was her 'separate' property, held 'to her separate use'.
2. The Government of 1971 reintroduced in s. 23(1) of the Finance Act of that year the principle that, before a married woman could be separately assessed to tax on her earnings, husband and wife must *jointly so elect*. In other words, the husband's permission was a prerequisite to the wife's application in respect of her earnings outside the home.
3. In partial operation from 7 August 1975 although child benefit will be brought into operation fully only after April 1979.
4. First introduced in 1945 by the Family Allowances Act, and payable for the second and subsequent children. Child benefit is now payable for the first child. The allegation sometimes

replace them, are normally sent by post to the mother, reaching her on Tuesday. When Government proposals for a tax credit system were published in 1972,[5] the representations made about the importance of a woman with young children receiving at least such minimum amounts direct and in the middle of the week resulted in a government assurance early in 1973 that family allowances would not be absorbed into the combined tax and social security scheme, but would continue to be paid direct to the mother without deduction.[6]

These three areas of unity will be considered before the general rule of separation of property between members of the family.

(i) MAINTENANCE

The fact that a husband still has the common law duty of maintaining his wife unless she has committed some matrimonial offence[7] has the most profound effects on the whole of family law. In the first place, such a duty is general, and legislation has greatly reduced the ambit of the sole common law exception, viz. the matrimonial offence. The fact that the wife has property or a separate income greater than the husband's is irrelevant.[8] So is the question whether the wife performs any duties, or has any minor children. On the other hand the duty is in the last analysis unenforceable. The husband who refuses to support his wife may be imprisoned. This ensures not only that he will not be in a position to maintain anyone else, but that he must on the other hand himself be maintained in secure conditions at great expense to the community. Whilst the family is still functioning as such, the duty appears to lie for the bare necessities of life, since the courts have no jurisdiction to make maintenance orders whilst the husband and wife are living together, and in general it is for the husband to decide the living standard of the family.

Maintenance for minor children was also a common law duty, but it was always considered an appendage to the duty to maintain the wife. When

---

made in the United States that the allowances were introduced as a means of increasing the population is demonstrably false. They were introduced primarily for the relief of poverty amongst young children and their mothers: See H.C. Deb. vol. 408, cols 2260–3.

5. Cmnd 5116 of October 1972.
6. The tax credit scheme seems to have been shelved. It would necessarily involve simplifications. It was the shift from man's pay packet to woman's purse at a time of pay restraint that primarily caused the postponement of the child benefit scheme. See H. C. Debs. 27.5.76 Vol. 912 *Written Answers* col. 331, 30.7.76 Vol. 916 cols. 1088–1160.
7. At common law a man's duty was to maintain his wife, but not if she had committed adultery, and in *National Assistance Board* v. *Wilkinson* [1952] 2 Q.B. 648, the Divisional Court extended the exception to the woman in desertion. Even when she became a public charge on the predecessors to the Supplementary Benefits Commission, the husband was not a 'liable relative', answerable to the public purse for the maintenance of a wife in desertion. It is assumed that a husband is similarly exonerated from his common law duty in respect of a woman who has given the husband good grounds for leaving her. The fact that the husband is paying agreed but inadequate maintenance does not exonerate him, either from claims by his wife: *Tulip* v. *Tulip* [1951] P. 378 C.A., *Dowell* v. *Dowell* [1952] 2 All E.R. 141 D.C., or from claims by the public authorities: *N.A.B.* v. *Prisk* [1954] 1 W.L.R. 443; *N.A.B.* v. *Parkes* [1955] 2 Q.B. 506 C.A.

maintenance orders were first introduced in the magistrates courts[9] they were for the wife only, and not until 1920 was a wife entitled to make a separate application for the maintenance of the children. The children have no direct and separate right to claim maintenance from their parents. Indeed, since a married woman has no right to any part of her husband's income or property, the duty to maintain her children is unenforceable against her unless she has separate income or earnings.[10] Orders are still normally made allegedly for the maintenance of wife and children for sums which are patently inadequate to maintain the children, even if the cost of supervising them to the extent their infancy requires is assumed to be paid from public funds. In *S.* v. *S.* (*Note*)[11] a man earning £25 a week was ordered to pay £1 a week for the maintenance of his (former) wife and £3 a week for their child, aged 12, who had kidney trouble, so that the mother could work only part-time. The reasons why this former husband should be told that by such a token contribution he is maintaining or even contributing towards the maintenance of his former wife might merit careful examination. Surely any sum below £200 a year cannot maintain a child. In its Published Working Paper on Matrimonial Proceedings in Magistrates Courts[12] the Law Commission Working Party declared in one paragraph[13] the duty of both parents to maintain their minor children, and in the next the duty of each spouse to support the other.[14] There was no attempt to say which duty should take priority when, as with the majority of those who resort to the magistrates' courts, it is impossible to do both.[15]

Any duty at public law for an adult child to maintain his or her parent was revoked by the National Assistance Act 1948, and in *Reg.* v. *West London Supplementary Benefits Appeal Tribunal, ex parte Clarke*,[16] it was held that a son-in-law had no duty to support his mother-in-law in order to relieve the Supplementary Benefits Commission, even though he gave an undertaking to do so to secure her entry into this country.

---

8. In *Samson* v. *Samson* [1960] 1 W.L.R. 190 C.A., the wife who claimed half the value of wedding presents made to her and her husband by her husband's relatives contended that the expense of setting up home was payable exclusively by the husband from his half share. Fortunately she failed on the first point.

9. By the Matrimonial Causes Act 1878, s. 4.

10. See, e.g. *Kirke* v. *Kirke* [1961] 1 W.L.R. 1411. which seems to decide that a wife is not entitled to a bus or train fare for her own, as distinct from her husband's, purposes.

11. [1976] Fam. 18.

12. No. 53, published 30 November 1973 (and not as stated on its face).

13. Para. 33.

14. Para. 34.

15. Much later in its paper, in para. 154, the Working Party points out that an applicant for maintenance may 'not infrequently' not be in the position to obtain financial relief for herself 'because the sum she is likely to receive by way of maintenance for her children is as much as it is feasible for her husband to pay altogether for the whole of the family'. Would this statement not be more logical if the six words after 'altogether' were deleted? The Working Party appear to have overlooked the fact that in the magistrates' courts both law and practice have always been clear. A woman without young children has always been required to produce evidence of unfitness to work before she can claim to be maintained entirely by her husband.

16. [1975] 1 W.L.R. 1396; 3 All E.R. 513.

The research team from Bedford College London, led by Professor O. R. McGregor, has since 1966 produced mounting evidence (i) that the maintenance orders made in the county courts and even in the High Court on divorce are little higher than those made in the magistrates' courts; (ii) that the amount ordered to be paid in the magistrates' court is usually less than the level of supplementary benefit the woman could obtain for herself and her children and (iii) that some 40 per cent of orders examined were in arrear for payment, and only 28 per cent of those ordered to pay maintenance did so regularly. In 1970 the Supplementary Benefits Commission paid some £93·25 million to separated or divorced wives and mothers of ex-nuptial children, and a further £8 million (or less than 10 per cent of that provided from public funds) was paid by husbands and fathers.[17]

The higher courts have no hesitation in enforcing the rights of parents who have failed to maintain their children, as in *Re D. (Minors)*.[18] The Divisional Court commented: 'In all too many cases there is a temporary drifting apart and a withdrawal by the husband father,[19] when a marriage is breaking up, especially when he has another woman to keep (the father is now remarried and has two children).'[20]

If a man did not provide for his wife and minor children the bare necessities of life, the only way in which his duty could be enforced at common law was by the wife 'pledging his credit'. This assumed two things: (i) that the husband was considered creditworthy by tradesmen. No credit was extended to the day labourer, to whose wife the remedy was therefore useless. Hence the fact that maintenance orders were first introduced in the magistrates' courts in 1878, and not until 1949 could a wife apply to the High Court for maintenance without what the law chose to call some substantive cause of action.[21] (ii) The second assumption was that the wife could find a tradesman gullible enough to supply her with goods or services and take upon himself the obligation of collecting the value from a husband who, by definition, was refusing to maintain his wife. Only a tradesman who did not know the law would do so. The charitable tradesman would find it cheaper to give the wife the goods or services free than to attempt to collect the value from the husband. Hence

---

17. Such figures were first produced in the Report of the Graham Hall Committee on Statutory Maintenance Limits, Cmnd 3587 (1968). In 1970 they were supplemented by *Separated Spouses*, by O. R. McGregor, C. Gibson and L. Blom-Cooper, and the latest publication is in the *Finer Report on One-Parent Families*, Cmnd 5629, pp. 88 et seq. and appendix 7, pp. 260 et seq.

18. [1973] Fam. 209.

19. In 1969 the father sent Christmas presents to the children; he sent £5 to each child for her birthday and Easter eggs and clothes at Easter 1971, thus ensuring that he would be associated with 'treats', whilst others must provide the daily bread.

20. [1973] Fam. 209, 215 at F. Adoption by the mother and stepfather was not appropriate here, but access for the biological father must have caused difficulties for them and for his second wife.

21. Law Reform (Miscellaneous Provisions) Act 1949, s. 5, now the Matrimonial Causes Act 1973, s. 27, as amended by the Domicile and Matrimonial Proceedings Act 1973, s. 6(1). 'Wilful neglect' to maintain or provide for the spouse or children must be shown.

the agency of necessity had long fallen into disrepute before it was abolished in 1970.[22]

It is because the law still places on a husband a duty to maintain his wife (or former wife) and children that the Court of Appeal justified in *Wachtel* v. *Wachtel*[23] its reduction of the wife's share in the value of the matrimonial home from one-half (as decided by the judge at first instance) to one-third. Even if the husband was fully maintaining his former wife in that case (as distinct from one of their children who lived with her) it is almost certain that she would have been better off with a larger lump sum than a continuing obligation. This must be even more clearly the situation where, as in the vast majority of the cases, the husband is not ordered to pay sufficient to maintain the wife, does not pay regularly what he is ordered and cannot be made to pay.

(ii) TAXATION

It is possible here only to indicate the major points at which family law and taxation lock into each other. The basis of personal direct taxation remains for the most part the family unit, and in no branch of the law does the legislation spell out so clearly as in tax and social welfare law that not only are husband and wife one, but that the husband is the one. The law applicable is that of the United Kingdom. Residence in the United Kingdom is the predominant criterion of taxability, and such factors as domicile in England and Wales are of relatively minor importance.

Income tax is now levied at the basic rate and at higher rates on higher incomes. There is also an investment income surcharge payable on investment income exceeding a certain figure.[24] By s. 37 of the Income and Corporation Taxes Act 1970,[25] consolidating the rule applicable ever since income tax was introduced in 1799, the income of a married woman living with her husband[26] is 'deemed to be the husband's income and not to be her income'. The same rules apply to capital gains tax.[27]

There are two ways in which separate assessment of a married woman's

---

22. By the Matrimonial Proceedings and Property Act 1970, s. 41.

23. [1973] Fam. 72 C.A.

24. The basic rate is currently 35 per cent: Finance (No 2) Act 1975 s. 25; Finance Act 1976 s. 24. The higher rates start at £5000: Finance Act 1976 s. 24. An investment income surcharge becomes payable at 10 per cent on investment income exceeding £1000 p.a., rising to 15 per cent over £2000. For those (including the wife of a taxpayer) over 65 years of age the starting point for the 10 per cent surcharge is £1500. Finance Act 1976, s. 24.

25. Hereafter the Taxes Act 1970.

26. By s. 42(1) of the Taxes Act 1970, 'a married woman shall be treated for income tax purposes as living with her husband unless: (*a*) they are separated under an order of a court of competent jurisdiction, or by deed of separation, or (*b*) they are in fact separated in such circumstances that the separation is likely to be permanent.' But see s. 42(2).

27. Finance Act 1965, s. 45 and Sched. 10, para. 3(1). See also s. 20(5) on allowable losses, and generally G. S. A. Wheatcroft and A. Park, Capital Gains Tax (1967) esp. pp. 4–12 et seq.

income can be obtained: (i) What may be called the old rule,[28] under which either spouse may apply for separate assessment. This makes no difference to the method of assessment, which is to aggregate the income of husband and wife, allow each the allowances he or she may claim and send each a note of the proportionate tax payable. (ii) A new rule introduced after 1972[29] provided that, if husband and wife *jointly so elect,* the wife's earned income only may be separately assessed and charged to income tax as if she were a single woman with no other income. The husband's 'other' income is charged as if the wife's earnings were nil. Personal reliefs are given as if the husband and wife were not married, and the husband is entitled to the child relief for any children 'as if the children were his and not hers'.[30] A joint tax return signed by the husband is still required.

The aggregation of income of husband and wife has been considered by both Royal Commissions on taxation; the Colwyn Commission on the Income Tax, which reported in 1920[31] and the Royal Commission on the Taxation of Profits and Income in its second report of 1953.[32] Both were firmly in favour of aggregation on the simple principle of progressive taxation based on ability to pay.[33] Both denied that aggregation was based on any conception of the wife's surbordination to the husband.[34] This latter contention has been refuted by the enactment of the Finance Act 1971, which for the first time since 1882 required the husband's consent to any application for separate assessment of the wife's earnings after 1972. From the opposite position the Carter Commission in Canada, where the incomes of husband and wife were not aggregated, found that there were many undesirable consequences

---

28. Taxes Act 1970 s. 38 as amended by the Finance Act 1971, s. 37 and Sched. 6.
29. By the Finance Act 1971, s. 23, under which Sched. 4 applies.
30. Ibid. Sched. 4, para. 3.
31. Cmd 615. This and other material on the taxation of the family unit is helpfully collected by A. J. Easson, *Cases and Materials on Revenue Law* (1973) pp. 351 et seq.
32. *Second Report,* Cmd. 9105 (1953).
33. Thus the Colwyn Commission (1920) in para. 259: 'The incomes are aggregated because the law of taxable capacity is the supreme law in matters of taxation, and taxable capacity is in fact found to depend upon the amount of the income that accrues to the married pair, and not upon the way in which that income happens fortuitously to be owned by the members of the union.' The *1953 Report* concluded: (Cmd 9105, para. 119): 'Taxation of the combined incomes of husband and wife as one unit is to be preferred to their separate taxation as separate units because the aggregate income provides a unit of taxation that is fairer to those concerned.' This Commission concluded that if the French quotient system were to be introduced in the United Kingdom: 'its immediate effect would be a marked improvement in the relative position of most married couples, especially those with children, in the upper income ranges'. (Ibid. para. 114.) The incomes of husband and wife are aggregated in Belgium, Holland, Denmark, Norway and Sweden as well as France and some countries outside Europe. Of the system in the United States the 1953 Report said: 'while nominally one of separate assessment, it tends to produce some of the effects of aggregation under the quotient system. Prima facie, assessment of husband and wife is made separately, but they have a right to choose aggregation, in which event the tax charged is twice the tax on half the joint income. The resulting liability therefore can never be heavier than if the joint income was equally divided between them'.
34. See the *Colwyn Commission,* Cmd. 615, para. 259; the *1953 Report* Cmd. 9105, para. 117.

and anomalies and recommended that the family and not the individual should be regarded as the tax unit.[35]

Such unanimity of expert opinion cannot be ignored. Aggregation of income between husband, wife, and minor children is probably the best available tax basis. Opposition to aggregation as such might be more profitably concentrated on the second limb of the present proposition, namely, that the aggregated income belongs to the husband. The Finance Act 1971 may suggest a precedent. Since the legislation now requires the husband's consent because his interests are affected by the taxation of his wife's earnings, the wife's consent and joinder in all returns and statements of income to the Revenue should *a fortiori* be required. Her interest is undeniable. Those spouses who were content to leave matters involving the joint incomes and taxation of them to the other spouse could, if they so wished and the Revenue was satisfied that a free choice had in fact been made, appoint the other as agent for both, such appointment being revocable on reasonable notice.

The two assumptions: (i) that the income of husband and wife is aggregated for tax purposes, and (ii) that the income so aggregated is deemed to belong solely to the husband, are reinforced by other tax rules. For example, an adult living alone is entitled to deduct a single person's allowance from his income before tax, whereas a married man living with his wife receives a 'married man's allowance'.[36] If the wife is earning he is entitled to a further single person's allowance,[37] the net result being to make the position more favourable for those couples whose joint earnings fall in the lower income groups, and less favourable where they reach the higher groups.[38]

In respect of children, the father (or mother if she satisfies the Revenue that she lives separately from the father and that she alone supports the child) is entitled to relief depending on the age of the child:[39] other reliefs are available for the widow with children;[40] child minder where the wife is totally incapacitated,[41] dependent relatives supported by the taxpayer;[42] or widower's or widow's housekeeper.[43] The child allowance will end when child benefit becomes payable.

---

35. *Report of the Royal Commission on Taxation, Canada, 1966*: 'We . . . recommend in this Report that the income of families should be aggregated and taxed as a unit on a separate rate schedule.'
36. Viz. a man is entitled to an allowance for 'keeping' a wife. That is, providing her with the bare necessities of life is assumed to be bounty on his part. By the Finance Act 1976, s. 29 the married man's allowance is £1085 p.a. and the single person's allowance £735. The wife's earned income relief is also £735 or 7/9 of her earnings, whichever is the less.
37. Wife's 'earned income relief', *supra* n. 36. In practice this will be deducted under the P.A.Y.E. scheme from the tax on salary paid to her, and credit allowed to the husband on his liability.
38. Income tax at the higher rate over £5000 (aggregated) soon absorbs the additional earned income allowance.
39. From April 1976 the range is from £300 p.a. for a child not over 11 to £365 for one over 16 (Taxes Act 1970, ss 10–11; Finance Act 1976, s. 29(2)).
40. Taxes Act 1970, s. 14(1)(*a*) as amended by Finance Act 1971, s. 37(1) and Sched. 6, para. 9.
41. Taxes Act 1970, s. 14(1)(*b*) as amended by Finance Act 1971, s. 37(1) and Sched. 6, para. 9.
42. Taxes Act 1970, s. 16 as amended by Finance Act 1971, s. 37(1) and Sched. 6, para. 10.
43. Taxes Act 1970, s. 12 as amended by Finance Act 1971, s. 37(1) and Sched. 6, para. 7.

There is also a 'clawback' of family allowances for those paying higher rate tax.[44] The child allowance may be claimed if a child is over 21 years of age but receiving full-time education or training, but if the child is entitled to his own income subject to tax within the United Kingdom over a low figure[45] the child relief is reduced by the excess.[46]

After separation or divorce any periodical payments made to the wife or former wife by the husband or former husband, or vice versa, were formerly called 'unearned income'. Under the new terminology, after the financial year 1973–4[47] the first £1000 of such income in the recipient's hands is not deemed to be investment income, but anything over this figure bears the investment income surcharge. It is important that any maintenance order should state clearly which party is liable for tax on the payment.

A mass of provisions has accumulated to prevent avoidance of taxation by settlements on adult children or more remote issue.[48] The aggregation of income between husband and wife is too well established to require bolstering by such measures, but the settlement, and in particular the discretionary settlement, was at one time a favoured method of avoiding both income taxes and estate duty.[49]

Similarly, in respect of corporation tax, there are special rules about close companies,[50] that is companies controlled by not more than five persons or owned solely by directors. These rules include not only participants in such companies but also their associates who include[51] a partner or relative, viz. a husband or wife, parent or remoter forebear, child or remoter issue, or brother or sister.

The Capital Transfer Tax, which is a cumulative tax on transfers of capital *inter vivos* or on death, has been in operation since 25 March 1974, and since 13 March 1975[52] has superseded estate duty. There is total exemption from the tax for all transfers between husband and wife[53] unless the recipient

---

44. Taxes Act 1970, s. 24.
45. Currently £350 p.a. excluding scholarships etc. But if an unmarried child under 18 has an earned income of less than £235 the limit is £115 investment income. Taxes Act 1970 s. 10(5) as amended by Finance Act 1976 s. 29(3).
46. See *Mapp* v. *Oram* [1970] A.C. 362; *Murphy* v. *Ingram* [1974] Ch. 363 C.A.
47. By Finance Act 1974, s. 15.
48. See Taxes Act 1970, ss 437, 438 et seq. as amended by Finance Act 1971, s. 16; *Crossland* v. *Hawkins* [1961] Ch. 537. Sections 43–8 of the Taxes Act 1970, aggregating the income of minor children with that of the parent, were introduced by the Finance Act 1968, s. 15 et seq. and repealed after 1971–2 by the Finance Act 1971, s. 16(1).
49. The Finance Act 1969, s. 36 brought many such discretionary settlements within the ambit of estate duty, at the same time as the former proportional rate of duty was replaced by the 'slice' system applicable to income tax.
50. Taxes Act 1970, ss 282 et seq. as amended by Finance Act 1972, s. 94(2); Finance Act 1971, s. 69(7); Finance Act 1971, s. 37(1) and Sched. 6 and s. 25. See also Finance Act 1975, s. 39.
51. Taxes Act 1970, s. 303.
52. Finance Act 1975, ss 19–52 and Scheds 4, 5, 6 and 7 esp. ss 22 and 48–50.
53. Ibid. s. 29 and Sched. 6, para. 1.

spouse is not domiciled in the United Kingdom, in which event the exemption is limited to £15,000.[54]

The proposed wealth tax is still at the consultative stage,[55] but will be an annual tax starting at 1 per cent on capital exceeding £100,000, and rising to either $2\frac{1}{2}$ per cent or 5 per cent on capital exceeding £5 million. The question of aggregation between spouses has not yet been decided.

(iii) SOCIAL SECURITY

Here also it is possible only to isolate the main principles. The system was considerably amended in 1975 by seven statutes.[56]

One of the basic assumptions of the post-war social security legislation was that a married woman is a dependant of her husband and will not normally be gainfully employed. Sir William Beveridge said in his famous *Report on Social Insurance and Allied Services*:[57] 'During marriage most women will not be gainfully occupied.' The *Finer Report on One-Parent Families* considers Sir William Beveridge's various attempts to deal with the special problems posed by the married woman, and the effects of the survival of the old principle.[58]

The Social Security Act 1973 made all contributions earnings-related[59] and brought together the financial bases for national health and industrial injuries insurance. Existing provisions were consolidated in the Social Security Act 1975. The Social Security Pensions Act 1975[60] will, when in force, provide

---

54. No capital transfer tax is incurred on transfers whose aggregate value is less than £15,000, which was formerly the threshold for estate duty. But the cumulative character of the new tax will considerably affect its incidence, and since the transferor is responsible for payment of the tax, the tax is added to the cumulative capital.
55. Cmnd 5704 was issued in August 1974 as a consultative 'green paper'.
56. Excluding those applying only to Northern Ireland. Three of the seven, viz. the Social Security Act, the Industrial Injuries and Diseases (Old Cases) Act and the Social Security (Consequential Provisions) Act, were consolidations of existing law, and the last-mentioned repealed much of the previous legislation. All three came into force on 6 April 1975. The Social Security Benefits Act increased the benefits payable and came into force on 13 March 1975. Large parts of the remaining three statutes are not yet operative, although ss 25 and 61–8 and parts of Scheds 4 and 5 of the Social Security Pensions Act came into force on 7 August 1975. The Child Benefit Act became operative on the same date, but child benefit at differential rates will replace family allowances and child allowances against income tax only from 1979. For the Employment Protection Act please see note 71 post. See further Sir R. Micklethwait's Hamlyn Lectures 1976, *The National Insurance Commissioners*, and Harry Calvert. *Social Security Law* (1974).
57. Cmd 6404 (1942), para. 111.
58. Cmnd 5629–1, Appendix 5, Part 3, pp. 136 *et seq*. A Civil Service memorandum of 1944 is cited reiterating the principle of 'the husband as head of the house and principal insured person.'
59. Now the Social Security Act 1975 ss 4–11. Class 1 contributions are for employed earners; class 2 are flat rates for the self-employed; class 4 are for profits or gains of a trade or profession or equivalent earnings. Class 3 contributions are intended only to allow a contributor, by making additional contributions, to satisfy conditions of entitlement to basic scheme benefits: Social Security Act 1975 s. 1(2).
60. s. 3 and Sched. 5, repealing ss 5–6 of the Social Security Act 1975, were not in force by July 1976.

an increasingly earnings-related pension, but employed married women will no longer be able to opt not to pay or to pay reduced contributions, and the reductions for wives who have already exercised the option will be gradually phased out. On the other hand, widows may receive pensions in right of contributions by their deceased husbands.

The benefits available may be either contributory or non-contributory,[61] and increases are granted for adult and child dependants[62] to unemployment benefit, sickness benefit, invalidity pension, maternity allowance[63] and category A retirement pension.[64] Increases for child dependants are granted to the widow's allowance, the widowed mother's allowance[65] and category B retirement pension,[66] and these increased benefits may be payable to a married woman residing with her husband provided the husband is incapable of self-support.[67] Other benefits obtainable include an invalidity allowance, a maternity grant, and a child's special allowance,[68] as well as industrial injuries benefits.

Agreements for reciprocity as regards some social security benefits have been made or are proposed with: Austria, Belgium, Bermuda, Canada, Cyprus, Denmark, Finland, France, Federal Germany, Gibraltar, the Republic of Ireland, Israel, Italy, the Isle of Man, Jamaica, Jersey and Guernsey, Luxembourg, Malta, the Netherlands, New Zealand, Norway, Spain, Sweden, Switzerland, Turkey, the United States of America and Yugoslavia. These have now been modified to take account of the Social Security Act 1975.[69]

By the Employment Protection Act 1975, an employee is unfairly dismissed[70] if the reason for her dismissal is that she is pregnant, or is any other reason connected with her pregnancy, unless that renders her incapable of doing her work adequately, or it would contravene the law for her to continue that work. Even then the dismissal is unfair unless the employer can prove either that the woman employed has been offered suitable and appropriate alternative work starting immediately, on terms no less favourable than those enjoyed previously, or that there is no suitable vacancy for her.[71] If a woman has been continuously

---

61. Social Security Act 1975 ss 12−33 and 34−40 respectively. Ch. IV, ss 50−75 of the Act covers industrial injuries benefits.
62. Ibid. ss 41−9 and Sched. 4 Part IV.
63. With earnings-related supplement.
64. Payable to a person by virtue of his own contributions: Social Security Act 1975 s. 28.
65. Both the widow's allowance and the widowed mother's allowance, as well as the widow's pension, cease on remarriage or cohabitation with a man as his wife: ss 24(2), 25(3) and 26(3).
66. Payable to a woman by virtue of her husband's contributions: Ibid. s. 29. Retirement pensions category C were granted to those above the age for participation when the scheme was introduced in 1948, and are also increased for dependants. Category D pension is payable to those over 80 years of age.
67. Social Security Act 1975 s. 41(6).
68. Payable in respect of a child to a divorced woman who neither remarries nor cohabits, where the former husband and father satisfied the contribution conditions and has since died.
69. See Social Security (Reciprocal Agreements) Order No. 225 of 1976.
70. Under the Trade Union and Labour Relations Act 1974, Sched. 1.
71. Employment Protection Act 1975 s. 34. Sections 34, 35, 48, 49 and 50 of the Act were brought into operation from 1 June 1976 by S.I. No. 530 of 1976.

employed for at least two years and gives reasonable notice that she will be absent from work wholly or partly because of pregnancy or confinement, she is entitled to maternity pay from her employer[72] for a maximum of six weeks within eleven weeks before her expected confinement. A woman employee absent from work because of pregnancy or confinement is also entitled under the Act[73] to return to work with her employer at any time within twenty-nine weeks after her confinement. She is entitled to the job she left, on terms and conditions not less favourable than those that would have applied if she had not been absent. Her pre-absence and post-absence employment is regarded as continuous for purposes of pension and other rights. If her former work is not available because of redundancy she is entitled to suitable alternative employment. These provisions must militate against the employment of women of child-bearing age, especially in key positions requiring qualities of intelligence, decision and personality.[74] There seems no good reason why employers should be taxed to finance employees' child-bearing activities. The requirement of two years' employment as a qualification for maternity pay is the only limit placed on the provisions which are not, for example, limited to two or three children.

By law the pensionable age for a man is still 65 and for a woman is 60,[75] which is rigid and directly opposed to the vital statistics.[76] A married woman is not entitled to a category A pension unless she married after attaining the age of 55 or complies with some complicated provisions about the rate and period of her earnings-related contributions.[77]

The Child Benefit Act 1975 provides for a cash benefit payable primarily to the mother in respect of all children, including the first. This benefit is wider in scope than the family allowances it will replace when it comes fully into operation.[78]

In 1971 a new Family Income Supplement was introduced, designed to

---

72. Maternity pay will be nine-tenths of a week's pay less the maternity allowance payable under the Social Security Act, whether the employee is entitled to any part of that allowance or not. A maternity pay fund is to be established under s. 39 of the Act and maintained together with the Redundancy Fund under the Redundancy Payments Act 1965 s. 26, to provide for payments to the employee in case of the employer's default or insolvency.

73. Employment Protection Act ss 35, 48–50 and Sched. 3.

74. Modelled on I.L.O. recommendations, they owe more to the ancient equation of women of all ages and in all circumstances as persons about to give birth or having recently produced children, (or perhaps who ought to be in one of those situations) than to any correlation with women in advanced industrial societies today.

75. Social Security Act 1975 s. 27. By s. 27(5) a person not retired from regular employment is deemed so to retire five years after attaining pensionable age, and by s. 30(1) earnings exceeding a normal wage reduce his pension for these five years.

76. According to *Social Trends*, No. 5 (1974), Table 28, in 1971 a man aged 60 years had an expectation of a further 15.1 years of life, and a woman of a further 19.7 years. At 65 years their respective expectations were 12 and 15.9 years.

77. Social Security Act 1975 s. 28(2). If she is a widow, by s. 28(3) Sched. 7 of the Act may apply, enabling a deceased husband's contributions to be treated as those of his widow.

78. Interim child benefit is already paid to the sole parent of a family (viz., divorced, separated or unmarried) for the first child, under the Child Benefit Act 1975 s. 16, and payment of £1 a week will be made for first and only children from April 1977.

provide additional funds to those heads of households in employment, but at exceptionally low wages. The Family Income Supplements Act[79] and subsidiary legislation[80] define a family as consisting of a household comprising (*a*) one man or one single woman engaged and normally engaged in remunerative work for not less than thirty hours a week, (*b*) if (*a*) is a man, the woman to whom he is married or who lives with him as his wife, and (*c*) children whose requirements are provided, in whole or in part, by either (*a*) or (*b*). It is the presence of children in the household that enables supplement to be claimed, but the right to claim it is in the wage earner, who must work a minimum of thirty hours a week. Only exceptionally can it be a woman, and never a woman living with a man, even if he is incapacitated. The feudal doctrine is preserved that the man in the household must of necessity be its head, and that even if he cannot support himself without State assistance he is entitled to have an adult able-bodied woman as his dependant.

The doctrine appears most clearly, however, in the law applicable to the very poor. Under the Supplementary Benefits Act 1966:[81] 'Where a husband and wife are members of the same household their requirements and resources shall be aggregated *and shall be treated as the husband's,* and similarly, unless there are exceptional circumstances, as regards two persons cohabiting as man and wife.'[82] The following comments seem relevant:[83]

(i) Here as under the tax legislation, aggregation is probably justified; attribution of all income to the husband, and even to the male cohabitee, cannot be justified and is unnecessary. If the man and woman do not want each to collect his or her several benefit, either may appoint the other as his or her agent. It is not for the legislature to decree that even by marriage and certainly not by illicit cohabitation, a man acquires the right to receive a woman's income from public funds.

(ii) At public law, since 1948[84] a man is liable to maintain his wife and his children and a woman to maintain her husband and her children. There seems to be no legislative sanction other than the Supplementary Benefits Act for the practice of bringing pressure on a man to persuade him to support not only his wife or cohabitee, but her children by another man. The knowledge

---

79. Brought into operation on 3 May 1971 by Commencement Order S.I. 225 of 1971.
80. Family Income Supplements (General) Regulations 1971 No. 226, as amended and expanded by S.I. Nos. 227, 622 and 702 of 1971; Nos. 14, 135 and 1282 of 1972; Nos. 177 and 1362 of 1973; emergency provisions by Nos. 59 and 905 of 1974, No. 1360 of 1975 and Nos. 289 and 806 of 1976.
81. Formerly the Ministry of Social Security Act, Sched. 2, para. 3(1). By S.I. 1699 of 1968, para. 2 all the functions *inter alios* of the Minister of Social Security were transferred to the Secretary of State for Social Services, and the Ministry of Social Security was dissolved. See also Social Security Act 1973 s. 99(18).
82. For children see ibid. para. 3(2), and *Supplementary Benefits Handbook* (1970), para. 16, p. 9, presumably referring to the Supplementary Benefits Act 1966, s. 13, which gives overriding discretion.
83. See also Tony Lynes, *The Penguin Guide to Supplementary Benefits*, 2nd edn (1974).
84. Supplementary Benefits Act 1966, s. 22, repeating the National Assistance Act 1948, s. 42, which is still in operation.

that such pressure is exerted among the very poor is likely to deter marriage or cohabitation with a woman who has minor children.

B. SEPARATION OF PROPERTY – THE GENERAL RULE AND ITS MITIGATION

Apart from these exceptional hangovers from the feudal concept of the family as a unit consisting of Lord and vassals, coloured possibly by the Roman Law concept that the law deals only with Heads of Families,[85] the general rule introduced by legislation in the nineteenth century is that of separation of property between husband and wife, with no independent rights for minor children. What a man owns before marriage and subsequently acquires is his alone; what a woman owns before marriage and subsequently acquires is hers alone; but (by the retention of the common law) the man has a duty to maintain his wife and minor children, and by recent legislation the woman with means has also a duty to maintain her minor children. In other words, we have no system of family property. The nineteenth-century legislation simply replaced the common law system giving all control to the husband by one in which the husband and wife are treated exactly as if they were strangers; individuals at arm's length, always except for the (unenforceable) duty of maintenance, primarily of the wife and only by extension of the children.[86]

Such a system, although not based on the common law, has all the 'stern and rugged simplicity' that Maitland found characteristic of the English common law. The importance of simplicity cannot be denied. By common consent each of the many different systems of community of property, or of gains, or accountability, can lead to great complications probably soluble only by 'guesstimates'. These complications are greatly exacerbated by inflation, and the systems can sometimes produce hardship, especially when the courts have little discretion to deal with exceptional cases.[87] With a separate property system there is rarely difficulty in deciding which property belongs to whom.

Another great advantage of the system is that it usually involves a woman, even after marriage, in routine administration of her property, however small. A major disadvantage of any system (such as that at common law, or total community of property or community of gains) in which the husband has

---

85. W. Müller-Freienfels in *Ehe und Recht* advances this explanation for the refusal of the English Court of Appeal to enforce in *Balfour* v. *Balfour* [1919] 2 K.B. 57 C.A., a maintenance agreement made between husband and wife.

86. In *Bazeley* v. *Forder* (1868) L.R. 3 K.B. 559 C.A., Lord Cockburn L.C.J. dissented from the seminal decision that, when a wife was living apart from her husband through his fault, she could pledge his credit for necessaries (clothes) for their child, as well as for herself. The child was under 7 years old and the mother had obtained a custody order for him. A theme running all through our law of maintenance is that, because the wife is regarded as the primary dependant, maintenance for the children is a mere afterthought and invariably pitched at an unrealistically low level.

87. See, e.g. B. Bodenheimer, 'The community without community property', *Calif. Western L. Rev.* 8 (1971) 381.

the right and duty of administration, is that when the marriage is dissolved, perhaps by accidental death, the woman who throughout her adult life has never paid a bill, run a bank account, or signed a cheque, will find herself confronted with such unaccustomed duties, apart from that of wise administration on behalf not only of herself, but probably of minor children also.

The separate property system can, however, give rise to major injustices both between husband and wife and as regards creditors.

As recently as 1968 the Court of Appeal held that it was perfectly legal for a man to give away secretly in his old age the house in which he and his wife lived, that the recipient of the house had a right to evict the widow,[88] and that it showed 'extraordinary ingratitude' for the widow to resist his claim on the ground of limitation of time, 'the testator being her husband, and having lived under somebody else's roof for 15 or 20 years.'[89]

(i) TRANSFERS OF PROPERTY BETWEEN SPOUSES TO DEFEAT CREDITORS' CLAIMS

By a series of decisions since 1888[90] the courts have held that a husband may be able to place personal property beyond the reach of his creditors by transferring the ownership to his wife, or probably his mistress,[91] despite the provisions of the Bills of Sale Acts[92] and the Married Women's Property Act 1882[93] designed to avoid unregistered transfers of ownership where the goods remained in the apparent possession or on the premises of the transferor.[94] In *French* v. *Gething*,[95] where the husband had made a deed of gift to his wife of the furniture

---

88. *Hughes* v. *Griffin* [1969] 1 W.L.R. 23 C.A. *T*, aged 74, owned a freehold bungalow and smallholding when in 1947 he married a woman of 50. In 1951 *T* secretly conveyed the house and land to *N*, who agreed that *T* and his wife would continue living in the house so long as *T* wished. The wife knew nothing of the transaction until *T* died in 1965, aged 95, and *N* sought (successfully) to evict her.

89. Ibid. pp. 28–29.

90. *Shepherd* v. *Pullbrook* (1888) 4 T.L.R. 642, where the husband about to become insolvent 'sold' the furniture to his brothers, who constituted themselves trustees of it for the wife. In *Ramsey* v. *Margrett* [1894] 2 Q.B. 18 the 'sale' was direct by the husband to the wife, who was given a receipt for her money, which was held not to be a Bill of Sale. In *Antoniadi* v. *Smith* [1901] 2 K.B. 589 the husband 'sold' the furniture to his mother-in-law.

91. The attempt failed in *Youngs* v. *Youngs* [1940] 1 K.B. 760 C.A., because the mistress, as a paid servant, could not be in apparent possession of the furniture in her master's house, but Goddard L.J. pointed out that the decision might be otherwise if there were no employment nexus. But such an attempt failed in *Hislop* v. *Hislop* [1950] W.N. 124 because the owner failed to make a valid gift to his mistress. In this case the former wife appeared as creditor for unpaid maintenance. Even where the transfer is defeasible, a third party may acquire a good title to the goods before it is defeated: *Harrods* v. *Stanton* [1923] 1 K.B. 516 D.C.

92. Of 1878, 1882, 1890 and 1891.

93. Section 10.

94. The best account of this line of decisions is still that by O. Kahn-Freund in 15 *MLR* (1952) 133 and 16 *MLR* (1953) 148. This aspect of separate property is not considered by the Law

in the matrimonial home, Atkin L.J. clearly considered it part of the movement for the emancipation of married women to establish that the furniture in the matrimonial home could both be and appear to be in the possession of the wife and not in the possession or apparent possession of the husband as soon as ownership was effectively transferred to her,[96] although the furniture remained in the same position as when it belonged to the husband, and it would be impossible for a third party to ascertain which of the spouses owned it. In the two most recent cases, it was held in *Re Cole*[97] that the husband had not effectively transferred possession of valuable fittings and furniture to his wife when he showed her for the first time the expensively equipped house and said: 'It's all yours'. But in *Koppel* v. *Koppel*[98] the gift was upheld where negotiations about the furniture had been carried out when the parties were at arm's length, and the transfer to her was a condition on which the woman insisted before she would give up her flat and return to live with the husband and look after his children.

Judicious handling of bank accounts between the spouses may also enable them to defeat the claims of creditors. Thus a joint account of both spouses cannot be attached by the husband's creditors,[99] and a wife's creditor was held unable to garnishee an account in the wife's name fed solely by money provided by her husband.[100] In 1918 the Court of Appeal even upheld as against the wife's creditors[101] a fantastic agreement between the husband and wife under which 'all articles of wearing apparel used or worn by the wife' were to be purchased by the husband in his own name and on his credit and were to be the absolute property of the husband, that he was to be 'entitled to dispose of them as and when and how he pleased, his wife having no right or title in them except to wear them during his pleasure'.

Such transactions in real property are not possible, because of the need for claims to land in law or equity to be evidenced either by writing or by deed.[102]

However, it is not unusual for spouses to have real property, usually the matrimonial home, conveyed into their joint names as trustees holding on trust for sale for themselves as beneficial joint tenants under the Law of Property Act 1925, ss 23–33. It has recently been held[103] to be misrepresentation under the Misrepresentation Act 1967 for one joint owner spouse to represent himself as entitled solely to sell the property and damages were awarded against him when his wife refused to complete.

Commission either in P.W.P. 42 (1971) on *Family Property Law* or in Law Com. 52 (1973): *First Report on Family Property: A New Approach.*
95. [1922] 1 K.B. 236 C.A.
96. Ibid. pp. 246–7.
97. [1964] Ch. 175 C.A. In *Re Eichholz* [1959] Ch. 708, s. 172 of the Law of Property Act 1925 was brought into operation where a solicitor had misused clients' money, and valuable gifts to his wife and others were recovered after he had died hopelessly insolvent.
98. [1966] 1 W.L.R. 802; 2 All E.R. 187 C.A.
99. *Hirschhorn* v. *Evans* [1938] 2 K.B. 801.
100. *Harrods* v. *Tester* [1937] 2 All E.R. 236 C.A.
101. *Rondeau, Le Grand* v. *Marks* [1918] 1 K.B. 75 C.A.
102. Law of Property Act 1925, ss 40, 52 and 53.
103. *Watts* v. *Spence* [1976] Ch. 165.

In *Re Solomon, A Bankrupt*,[104] the husband had deserted the wife, who subsequently obtained a court order for maintenance and an undertaking from the husband not to dispose of the house *inter vivos* or by will or charge it by way of security. Five years later he became bankrupt, and the trustee in bankruptcy obtained a court order for sale of the house under the Law of Property Act 1925, s. 30 and the Bankruptcy Act 1914, and a declaration that he was entitled to half the proceeds of sale. The marriage was in this case at an end in fact if not in law.[105] The Matrimonial Causes Act 1973, s. 39 confirms this decision. More recent cases have arisen when the marriages were continuing in fact and in law. In *Re Turner*[106] the husband and wife purchased a property in August 1971 as registered joint owners. Six months later the husband became bankrupt, with no other realisable assets, and an order for sale of the house with vacant possession was made but suspended for two months or such longer time as the parties might agree. In *Re McCarthy*,[107] also the bankrupt husband had no other assets, but he and his wife had undertaken to co-operate with the trustee to effect a sale if one were ordered. The wording of s. 30 of the Law of Property Act 1925 enables the court, on the application of any person interested, to 'make such order as it thinks fit'. Dunn J. held that this gave the court the widest possible discretion[108] and therefore entitled him not only to make an order for sale, but also to order that possession be delivered up to the trustee in bankruptcy.

A recent decision has affirmed[109] that on the bankruptcy of a married woman her husband is not by reason only of his matrimonial relationship, 'a person interested' within the meaning of s. 29(1) of the Bankruptcy Act 1914, so as to give him *locus standi* to have the bankruptcy annulled.

(ii) SAVINGS FROM HOUSEKEEPING ALLOWANCE

There had been an unfortunate series of decisions under which as late as 1949[110] the Court of Appeal by a majority held that if a husband made an allowance to his wife for housekeeping and the like, from which she was able to save, the savings and anything bought with them belonged exclusively to the husband. Some of these decisions and the circumstances in which they were made

---

104. [1967] 1 Ch. 573.
105. The case is further considered in Chapter VII. It is discussed here as the precedent for the more recent decisions where the marriage was continuing in law and in fact.
106. [1974] 1 W.L.R. 1556. Goff J. here considered the decision of Plowman J. in *Boydell* v. *Gillespie*, reported only in (1970) 216 E.G. 1505, where the circumstances were similar.
107. [1975] 1 W.L.R. 807. See also *Re Bailey* (a bankrupt), *The Times*, 12.10.76.
108. This wording is identical with that used in s. 17 of the Married Women's Property Act 1882, but it has never been held (or *semble* seriously argued) that this empowered the court, under the Law of Property Act, to vary existing proprietary rights as it had been held the courts might do under the same wording in the Married Women's Property Act 1882, s. 17. The House of Lords killed the heresy in *Pettitt* v. *Pettitt* [1970] A.C. 777.
109. *Re Beesley (A.) (A Bankrupt)* [1975] 1 W.L.R. 568; 1 All E.R. 385, D.C.
110. *Hoddinott* v. *Hoddinott* [1949] 2 K.B. 406.

were so intolerable that in 1964 a very short Married Women's Property Act was passed,[111] containing only one substantive provision. This reads:

> If any question arises as to the right of a husband or wife to money derived from any allowance made by the husband for the expenses of the matrimonial home or for similar purposes, or to any property acquired out of such money, the money or property shall, in the absence of any agreement between them to the contrary, be treated as belonging to the husband and the wife in equal shares.

Sometimes the choice is between such isolated provisions or no legislative reform at all. It is unfortunate that the statute should be expressly limited to the case (albeit the more usual one) in which the husband makes a house-keeping allowance to his wife. There is no reason why a similar provision should not apply where the wife has property and makes an allowance to the husband. The expression 'the expenses of the matrimonial home or ... similar purposes' also lacks clarity and has caused problems of interpretation.[112] But the general principle that money provided for the joint purposes of spouses living in amity should be equally divisible on dissension and separation would be sound, if the law gave the priority to the maintenance of minor children over the claims of their parents that it has so far withheld.

(iii) THE WIFE'S AGENCY FOR HER HUSBAND

The common law agency of necessity, which could be used only where a tradesman was unwary and did not know the law, has been abolished after July 1970.[113] However, a wife, like anybody else, may always be appointed an agent, by her husband or any other person. Or the husband may represent her as his agent, as by paying debts she incurs. In that event her agency will be revocable only if the husband advises the individual creditor of the revocation of the agency.[114]

There is, however, another agency presumed by law, which is untouched by the abolition of the agency of necessity. Where one person has a household and another runs that household for him or her, the housekeeper has implied authority to pledge the householder's credit for the kind of goods normally supplied to a person running a household. For this purpose marriage is neither necessary[115] nor sufficient.[116] This implied agency is, however, merely a

---

111. Reviewed 27 *MLR* (1964) 576.
112. *Tymoszczuk* v. *Tymoszczuk* (1964) 108 S.J. 676, *The Times* 30.6.64. The date at which the provision applies is also not clear; see *Re Johns' Assignment Trusts* [1970] 1 W.L.R. 955, Goff J.
113. By the Matrimonial Proceedings and Property Act 1970, s. 41.
114. *Spiro* v. *Lintern* [1973] 1 W.L.R. 1002 C.A.: attempted gazumping on the sale of a house.
115. A mother, sister or mistress could all exercise the agency.
116. *Debenham* v. *Mellon* (1880) 6 App. Cas. 24 H.L. The wife was not a housekeeper, since she and her husband were both employed to manage an hotel and had no separate house-hold for her to run. The husband also made her a sufficient allowance.

presumption, and the presumed agency may be rebutted in a number of ways,[117] namely: (i) if the householder warns individual tradesmen that he is not liable for supplies to the housekeeper; (ii) if the housekeeper is sufficiently supplied with the particular goods or services; (iii) if the housekeeper has a sufficient allowance or means to obtain for cash what is required; (iv) if the householder has forbidden the housekeeper to pledge his credit; or (v) if the order is extravagant or excessive, having regard to the householder's standard of living. The creditor has normally no means of knowing whether exceptions (ii) to (v) exist, and anyone giving credit on such a presumed agency does so at his peril. As with the agency of necessity, it is only the small tradesman who does not know the law who is likely to be trapped.

(iv) OTHER ATTEMPTS TO MITIGATE SEPARATE PROPERTY

There have been several recent attempts to mitigate the sternness of the system of separate property. In so far as they are successful, they of course replace simplicity by some degree of complication. An obvious area for mitigation is in the law of succession, where one spouse has died. An important asset meriting special consideration is the matrimonial home, which may be dealt with in one of two ways or a mixture of both, viz: (i) by declaring some possessory right in the spouse, irrespective of property rights, or (ii) by finding or declaring some property right in the owner's spouse. Both these possibilities are covered by s. 17 of the Married Women's Property Act 1882,[118] the relevant parts of which provide that: 'in any question between husband and wife as to the *title to* or *possession of* property, either party may apply . . . in a summary way to any judge . . . and the judge may make such order . . . as he thinks fit'. Most questions concerning either property or possessory right of course arise for adjudication when one of the parties has died or the spouses are in dispute, and are therefore considered in detail in Chapters VI and VII. But the knowledge not only of both the spouses, but of the whole community, of what would be decided if there were a death or a dispute of course affects the relations between the spouses from their first acquaintance, and both before and during the marriage. It also affects the standing of each man and woman in the community. The Law Commission rightly pointed out in its Working Paper on Family Property Law[119] that property rights and support rights are complementary, but it went on to say that: 'During a stable marriage the distinction has no importance: each spouse shares the use and enjoyment of the other's property and income and each helps to support the family.' And again in respect

---

117. See *Gray* v. *Cathcart* (1922) 38 T.L.R. 562, where McCardie J. considered the law at length. The historical accuracy of this approach has been doubted, e.g. by T. Plucknett, who considered the wife's agency for the husband derived from the monk's agency for his abbot.

118. Only ss 11 and 17 of the Act now remain in operation; italics supplied.

119. P.W.P. 42: *Family Property Law*, 26.10.71, paras 0.20 and 1.2. The Working Paper is now replaced by Law Com. 52: *First Report on Family Property: A New Approach*, published 22.5.73.

of the matrimonial home: 'While a marriage is happy, the home will normally be used for the benefit of the family irrespective of who owns it. But when a marriage breaks down, it becomes important to the spouses to know the extent of their rights in relation to the home.' This is too rosy. It suggests there is never a 'pecking order' between spouses, and that the attitude of married people is in no way affected by their rights *vis-à-vis* the other. Neither proposition is credible, and the history of the subjection of women disproves both.

(v) THE MATRIMONIAL HOME

The duty at common law of the spouses to live together and the common law duty of the husband to maintain his wife were seized upon by the Court of Appeal in *Bendal* v. *McWhirter*[120] to spell out for the wife whose husband deserted her, leaving her in possession of the matrimonial home, the right to remain in possession even as against the husband's trustee in bankruptcy. After the Second World War the housing situation was particularly acute. If the spouse who owned the house (usually the husband) sold the house with vacant possession, his wife and minor children had nowhere else to go. But it was anomalous that this particular right of occupation of the home should be given to the woman who had been deserted and not to the woman whose husband had committted adultery or treated her or the children with violence, nor to the woman who, because of such treatment, found other accommodation for herself and her children. To establish such a right in a wife as against the husband's creditors also offended against the fundamental principle of the common law that 'debts must be paid before gifts can be made'.[121] After the newly invented 'deserted wife's equity' was finally declared non-existent by the House of Lords in 1965,[122] the Matrimonial Homes Act was passed in 1967.[123] This Act gives the spouse without a right of property in the home the right to occupy it; this occupation right may be valid against third parties but not against the trustee in bankruptcy of the owning spouse.[124]

---

120. [1952] 2 Q.B. 466 C.A. There had been a contrary decision by a Chancery judge, Roxburgh J., in *Thompson* v. *Earthy* [1951] 2 K.B. 598, which was eventually vindicated by the House of Lords.
121. The Homestead Acts in the United States have spread north and east from the community property States in the South-West. They are not directly linked with community of property between the spouses, but are based on a different view of creditors' rights, viz. that the needs of the family should be met before debts are paid. This is contrary to the common law approach.
122. In *National Provincial Bank* v. *Ainsworth* [1965] A.C. 1175. Here the husband and father had conveyed the home occupied by his wife and four minor children to a company, which charged it to the plaintiffs who, it was held, had a right to vacant possession. The decision did not affect a spouse's occupation under a statutory tenancy, established in *Brown* v. *Draper* [1944] 1 K.B. 309 C.A., *Old Gate Estates* v. *Alexander* [1950] 1 K.B. 311 C.A. *Middleton* v. *Baldock* [1950] 1 K.B. 657, so that the tenant spouse has still no power to contract out of his or her statutory rights under the Rent Acts to the detriment of the other spouse.
123. Since amended by the Matrimonial Proceedings and Property Act 1970, s. 38.
124. Section 2(5).

Unfortunately, although the Act gives either spouse the right to possession, it gives no right as such to minor children, so that for example if the spouse without a property right were dead or in desertion, the owning parent could dispossess his or her minor children occupying the house with some other guardian.[125] The right of occupation of the childless spouse is, on the other hand, fully covered. In order to protect her or his occupation right, the spouse must either (*a*) register a Land Charge Class F[126] or a notice or caution against the title[127] or, (*b*) while the marriage is in existence,[128] or during the course of proceedings for divorce or nullity,[129] obtain an order for possession from the court.[130] The Act is further considered in Chapter VII.

As regards property rights for the spouse of the apparent owner, the courts could call upon two well-established equitable presumptions: (*a*) the presumption of advancement, and (*b*) the presumption in favour of the purchaser. The presumption of advancement applies only where a husband provides the means to buy property which is bought in the wife's name as apparent purchaser. The law may then presume that the husband intended to make a gift of the property to the wife, and he may not be heard to say that she was to hold it as trustee for him, or for them both. The reason for the presumption is that otherwise any married man could place property beyond the reach of his creditors by buying it in his wife's name, but then claim the property for himself should he be in dispute with his wife. Where property is clearly bought in the wife's name to put it beyond the reach of creditors the presumption is still applied,[131] but except in such a clear case the courts have said[132] the presumption will rarely be applied today.

It is a general presumption of equity that if *A* provides the purchase money for property bought in *B*'s name, *B* will hold the property on trust for *A*. Similarly, if *A* and *B* both provide part of the purchase money for property in *B*'s name, *B* will hold as trustee for them both in the proportions in which they provided the purchase money. This presumption had been applied to

125. Children are mentioned only incidentally in s. 1(3). If the wife and mother had died or deserted in a case like *National Provincial Bank* v. *Ainsworth* and the children were being cared for by an aunt or other relative, the father could sell the house with vacant possession.
126. Under the Matrimonial Homes Act s. 2(6).
127. Under s. 2(7).
128. That is, before a decree of nullity or divorce, under s. 1(1)(*b*) or 1(2) or, in respect of statutory tenancies, under s. 7.
129. Under s. 2(2).
130. Once obtained, such an order can of course be enforced and entry made by an officer of the court. Less satisfactory is the fact that, if the owning spouse locks the other out, illegal as the act may be it is effective until the other spouse obtains a court order, probably after a delay of several weeks. This does not provide a roof over the head of the spouse or children that night.
131. As in *Tinker* v. *Tinker* [1970] P. 136 C.A. In respect of banking accounts, the presumption was applied in *In re Figgis* [1969] 1 Ch. 123 and *Re Bishop* [1965] Ch. 450. In both cases the decision in *Marshal* v. *Crutwell* (1875) L.R. 20 Eq. 328 was again not only cited but once distinguished and once followed, although it should have been buried in 1882.
132. See *Falconer* v. *Falconer* [1970] 1 W.L.R. 1333 C.A., at 1335–6; *Pettitt* v. *Pettitt* [1970] A.C. 777, pp. 793F, 811G, 874–5F and 824A and *Gissing* v. *Gissing* [1971] A.C. 886 at 907D.

husband and wife as to strangers. If the wife could prove that she had provided part of the price of a particular asset (usually the matrimonial home) bought in the husband's sole name, the courts would hold that the husband held that asset as a trustee for them both in the proportions in which they contributed to its cost. This presumption still applies.[133] However, following an unreported decision of the Court of Appeal in 1950,[134] little noticed at the time, the presumption was expanded in *Rimmer* v. *Rimmer*[135] to one that if both husband and wife had subscribed, however unequally, to the purchase of an asset[136] in the name of one only of them, the legal owner would hold the asset on trust for them both in equal shares. The principle was undoubtedly pushed too far, so that the spouse who had subscribed to only a small degree might be in a better position than the full joint owner,[137] and in *Gissing* v. *Gissing*[138] Lord Reid[139] and Lord Pearson[140] both condemned this approach. In the words of Lord Reid: 'the high-sounding brocard equity is equality has been misused'.

Since 1970 by statute,[141] if one spouse contributes substantially, in money or money's worth, to the improvement of property belonging to the other spouse, subject to any agreement to the contrary express or implied, the spouse who has so improved the property of the other is entitled to a beneficial interest in the whole property to the extent agreed, or failing agreement, as may seem in all the circumstances just to any court before which the question arises.[142]

Also since 1970 on or after divorce, judicial separation, nullity or action for wilful neglect to maintain, the court has had wide discretionary powers not only to order the payment of periodical amounts or lump sums[143] by one spouse

---

133. See *Cowcher* v. *Cowcher* [1972] 1 W.L.R. 425, Bagnall J. The decision has been criticised by Lord Denning M.R. in *Kowalczuk* v. *Kowalczuk* [1973] 1 W.L.R. 930 at 933D, and in *Earley* v. *Earley*, *The Times* 20.6.75 C.A., but the presumption is undoubted.
134. *Newgrosh* v. *Newgrosh* [1950] 100 L. Jo. 525 C.A.
135. [1953] 1 Q.B. 63 C.A. This was the first reported case in which the application of the usual presumption would have given the wife the major share in the home, and the registrar so held at first instance. She had acquired the major part in that asset, including the windfall increase in value. On appeal the county court judge changed the basis of calculation to frustrate such female wiles, and gave the husband the major share on the ground of his potential liability. Only then did the Court of Appeal invoke the judgement of Solomon.
136. Not invariably the matrimonial home. *Jones* v. *Maynard* [1951] Ch. 572 concerned a bank account, *Spellman* v. *Spellman* [1961] 1 W.L.R. 921 C.A., the ownership of a motor-car.
137. The woman married for a short time who had made a small contribution would automatically be better placed than the woman married for some thirty years who had brought up several children and, by entertaining and the like, substantially contributed to the husband's financial success.
138. [1971] A.C. 886.
139. Ibid. p. 897B.
140. Ibid. p. 903A.
141. Matrimonial Proceedings and Property Act 1970, s. 37 (not incorporated in the Matrimonial Causes Act 1973).
142. This may confirm the decision in *Jansen* v. *Jansen* [1965] P. 478 and was applied in *Davis* v. *Vale* [1971] 1 W.L.R. 1022 C.A. The inclusion of references to 'substantial' improvement and 'implied' agreements to the contrary indicates the survival of considerable judicial discretion.
143. Now under the Matrimonial Causes Act 1973, ss 23 and 27. The term 'financial provision'

or former spouse to the other, but except in cases of wilful neglect to maintain may also order one spouse to transfer property to the other, to a child of the family or to a third person for the benefit of such a child; to settle such property for the benefit of the other spouse or of children of the family; to vary ante-nuptial or post-nuptial settlements and to extinguish or reduce the interest of either party under such settlements.[144] The use of these powers is considered in Chapter VII.

The Law Commission recommended[145] that (*a*) co-ownership of the matrimonial home be introduced, so that in the absence of agreement to the contrary, a matrimonial home would be shared equally between husband and wife;[146] (*b*) the claim of a surviving spouse on the family assets should be at least equal to that of a divorced spouse. The second recommendation has been followed by more detailed proposals in Law Com. 61 and the Inheritance (Provision for Family and Dependants) Act 1975. These are considered in Chapter VI.

The proposal that the matrimonial home, alone of all the assets owned by either spouse, should be owned equally by both, is supported by the findings of the national survey carried out[147] among married couples and formerly married people. Of those asked whether the home and its contents should legally be jointly owned by the husband and wife irrespective of who paid for it, 91 per cent of husbands and 94 per cent of wives assented. Among those who had bought their homes since 1964—5 the percentage of spouses who owned the home jointly had been continuously increasing.[148] To single out one particular asset or group of assets and provide that it or they alone shall be owned equally by the spouses will of course produce anomalies and distort questions of family property.[149] Consider for example a marriage between a man and a woman each of whom owns a house. The decision as to which

---

has now replaced the former bewildering plethora of terms, such as maintenance, alimony and periodical payments. But such orders are still described as 'ancillary relief', which is a hangover from the ecclesiastical viewpoint. Most contests about divorce have long been disguised disputes about money or property.

144. Matrimonial Causes Act 1973, s. 24. The power to vary nuptial settlements is not new, deriving in part from the Matrimonial Causes Act 1859. It has been expanded from time to time.

145. Law Com. 52: *Family Law: First Report on Family Property: A New Approach*, published May 1973. For comments see Tim Sharp, 7 *The Law Teacher* (1973) 147, and Ian F. G. Baxter, 37 *MLR* (1974) 175.

146. P.W.P. 42 referred to a 'matrimonial home trust' in paras 1.106, 1.116 and 1.128(ii). The term is not used in Law Com. 52, but the Law Commission has clearly been at pains not to use such terms as 'joint ownership' and ownership 'in common' which are technical terms of art.

147. By the Social Survey Division of the Office of Population Censuses and Surveys, the results of which were published in May 1972 as *Matrimonial Property*, by Jean Elizabeth Todd and L. M. Jones (H.M.S.O.).

148. The percentage of joint ownership dropped from 51 per cent on purchases in 1960—1 to 47 per cent in 1962—3, then rose to 52 per cent in 1964—5, 57 per cent in 1966—7, 69 per cent in 1968—9 and 74 per cent in 1970—1. Ibid. para. 12.1, p. 80.

149. It may also serve to screen a determination not to allow women a greater share in property as a whole. The biases of those responsible for the Social Survey (see n. 147 *supra*) are

house shall be retained for their joint use and which sold will have far-reaching effects. Of course the parties may otherwise agree, but this in effect means that those who own sufficient property to be constantly in touch with their solicitors, or who have experienced property complications in a previous marriage will have the advantage of a legal anomaly of which they know.

Both the courts and the Law Commission have declined to make the general distinction between property owned by either spouse before marriage and property acquired during the marriage, which is considered crucial in most systems of community.[150] With the spread of divorce and remarriage this distinction will assume greater importance. The Law Commission's hope that a Report with draft legislation covering co-ownership of the matrimonial home and occupation rights would be published in 1973 was not fulfilled, and no draft legislation on the Matrimonial Home Trust had appeared by the middle of 1976. Nor has anything apparently been done about extending s. 7 of the Matrimonial Homes Act 1967 to council tenancies, which would affect a large number of women and minor children now at physical, as well as financial, risk.

(vi) PROPERTY OF MINOR CHILDREN

The legal position in respect of the property of minor children in England and Wales is not clear, probably because the situation rarely comes before a court. If real[151] or personal property is given to a minor *inter vivos* it will normally be under a settlement, the adult trustees being the legal owners holding on trust for the minor. If the gift is by will the executors have power to appoint trustees, or may constitute themselves trustees.[152] Trustees have discretionary power under the Trustee Act 1925,[153] when holding property in trust for any person 'for any interest whatsoever', during his minority to 'pay to his parent or guardian, if any, or otherwise apply for or towards his maintenance, education or benefit, the whole or such part, if any, of the income of that property as may, in all the circumstances, be reasonable,

---

revealed by their division of employed wives into two groups; employment mainly as an employee, or mainly self-employed working *for* the husband in *his* business. Ibid. para. 13, pp. 84–5 and accompanying tables. Why such a woman is not working *with* her husband in *their* business might merit explanation.

150. This is the distinction between total community, from which married women have striven to escape, and community of gains, which is generally acceptable, though complex. In the 'deferred community', which is an accounting procedure, the Danish system does not and the Federal German system does distinguish between pre-nuptial and post-nuptial gains.

151. A minor cannot hold the legal estate in land: Law of Property Act 1925, s. 1(6). A gift of the legal estate will suffice to pass the equitable interest only.

152. Administration of Estates Act 1925, ss 42 and 36, and see *Re Yerburgh* [1928] W.N. 208. For the position and possible developments where the sole beneficiary and executrix was a married minor see *Harvell* v. *Foster* [1954] 2 Q.B. 367, C.A.

153. Section 31. The provision has considerable possible tax implications; see the Taxes Act 1970, ss 437–44. If the interest is contingent, this applies only if the contingent interest carries the intermediate income, as to which see the Law of Property Act 1925, s. 175: *Re Geering* [1964] Ch. 136 and *Re McGeorge* [1963] Ch. 544.

whether or not there is (*a*) any other fund applicable to the same purpose, or (*b*) any person bound by law to provide for his maintenance or education'. Trustees have also discretionary power to advance up to one-half of the presumptive share of capital money.[154]

A provision applying only to adults, but clearly envisaging the principal beneficiary, his or her spouse and minor children as a unit benefiting under a trust, is that concerning protective trusts.[155] If the principal beneficiary under such a trust forfeits his interest in the income, the trust in his favour determines, and the income is held on a discretionary trust for the maintenance, support or benefit of the principal beneficiary, his or her spouse if any, and his or her children or remote issue, if any. Failing them, the interest is held on trust for those who, if the beneficiary were dead, would be entitled to the property.

The discretionary power to pay income for the maintenance of a minor beneficiary to his parent or guardian seems to confirm that the parent or guardian has a right to receive income from a minor's property and apply it towards his maintenance. The Guardianship Act 1973, s. 7[156] also provides that a guardian under the Guardianship of Minors Act 1971 shall have 'all the rights, powers and duties of a guardian of the minor's estate, including in particular the right to receive and recover in his own name for the benefit of the minor property of whatever description and wherever situated which the minor is entitled to receive or recover'. The power does not apply where there is a separate guardian of the minor's estate.

Under the Administration of Estates Act 1925,[157] executors have power to pay capital to which a minor is entitled on intestacy when the minor reaches majority or marries under that age,[158] and it has been held that where a will directs payment on majority or marriage under that age, the married minor can give the executor a good discharge for capital.[159]

It is ancient law that a parent[160] is entitled to his minor children's services,[161]

---

154. Viz. money or securities for money, or property held on trust for sale and not by law considered as land: Trustee Act 1925, s. 32. As to land see *Re Collard's Will Trusts* [1961] Ch. 293. *Re Pilkington* [1964] A.C. 612 indicates desirable limits on the exercise of the power; *Re Clore's Settlement Trusts* [1966] 1 W.L.R. 955; *Re Pauling's Settlement Trusts* [1964] Ch. 303, C.A. (No. 2) [1963] Ch. 576. The court has additional powers under the Trustee Act 1925, s. 53.

155. Trustee Act 1925, s. 33.

156. Replacing the Tenures Abolition Act 1660, s. 9, now at last repealed and replaced by the Act of 1973, s. 7 and Sched. 3.

157. Section 47(1) as amended by the Family Law Reform Act 1969, s. 3(2). Executors may also, by s. 41(i)(ii) of the Act, appropriate property for minors.

158. This seems to derive from the habit of the propertied classes of making settlements before marriage of all the property of both spouses. Since marriage abroad is possible below the age of 16 years, it may be that the provision requires reconsideration in respect of the very young married person: see e.g. *Alhaji Mohamed* v. *Knott* [1969] 1 Q.B. 1.

159. *Re Someçh* [1957] Ch. 165.

160. At common law this meant the father and never the mother in his presence. The Guardianship Act 1973 s. 1(1) may now entitle the mother in her own right to the child's services, even in the presence of the father.

161. Improved communications have done more than the law to end exploitation of the children's

which implies that if they work for others the parent is entitled to their wages or salary. Legislation has considerably restricted parental rights in this area,[162] but it seems indisputable that, if the minor has an income, earned or unearned, the parent is entitled to recover from him the cost of his maintenance,[163] which in most cases will produce much the same result as taking the wages as a whole. The entertainment industry is a special case, since rewards for young entertainers can be substantial, and there have been scandals, especially in the United States.[164] In England there are special rules governing the employment of minors in the entertainment field and the manner of payment of their remuneration is frequently regulated.[165]

In 1967 the Latey Committee on the Age of Majority[166] did not consider the entitlement of the parent to his minor child's services, and therefore to his wages, which was probably outside its terms of reference. The implementation by the Family Law Reform Act 1969[167] of the Committee's recommendation that the age of majority for purposes of contracts and otherwise should be lowered from 21 to 18 years has reduced both the size and the malignancy of the problem.

Scattered throughout the statutes[168] are restrictions on the ages at and

---

labour by their parents, e.g. on the remote smallholding. But see, e.g. *Re Cummins* [1972] Ch. 62 C.A. See also H. L. Deb. 245, col. 502 10 September 1962, where peers expressed disquiet at the exploitation of teenage entertainers by specialist entrepeneurs.

162. The right of the parent or person *in loco parentis* to an action in tort for deprivation of the child's services by raping, seducing, or enticing, or for harbouring the child has been abolished after 1970 by the Law Reform (Miscellaneous Provisions) Act 1970, s. 5(*b*) and (*c*). The provision in the Sexual Offences Act 1956 s. 18, prohibiting fraudulent abduction of an heiress from her parent or guardian was repealed by the Family Law Reform Act 1969, s. 11(*c*) on the recommendation of the *Latey Report*, Cmnd 3342 (1967).

163. Cf. Trustee Act 1925, s. 31, *ante*, n. 153.

164. The squandering by parents of fortunes earned by some child film stars sparked off remedial State legislation. Now, e.g. under the California Civil Code, ss 36 and 37, contracts approved by the county court, under which minors work in the entertainment industry, may not be 'disaffirmed' (repudiated) by the minor either during minority or on attaining full age. Employers thus have an incentive to seek judicial approval of minors' contracts, and provisions about parental entitlement to the remuneration are normally included. In *Morgan* v. *Morgan* (1963) 34 Cal. Rptr. 82, a mother was held trustee of her minor son's earnings which she had reduced into her possession after relinquishing to him her right to receive them.

165. By the Children and Young Persons Act 1933, ss 22–4 as amended by the Education (Miscellaneous Provisions) Act 1948, s. 11, Sched. I, Part II and the Children and Young Persons Act 1963, ss 34–44 and 64–5. See also 27 *MLR* (1964) 61, 69; the Bateson Departmental Committee on the *Employment of Children as Film Actors, in Theatrical Work and in Ballet*, Cmd 8005 (1950), and *The Law on Performances by Children*, a Home Office Guide to the Children (Performances) Regulations 1968 and related statutory provisions (1968).

166. Cmnd 3342 (1967).

167. Section 1 and Sched. 1.

168. The Employment of Women, Young Persons and Children Act 1920 (as amended); the Young Persons (Employment) Acts 1938 and 1964; the Mines and Quarries Act 1954 Part VIII; the Shops Act 1950; the Factories Act 1961, Part VI; The Children and Young Persons Act 1933 ss 18–30, as amended by the Education Act 1944, ss 120–1, the Education (Miscellaneous Provisions) Act 1948, s. 11; the Children and Young Persons

the conditions in which minors may be employed, and local authorities have also power to issue byelaws regulating the employment of young people in their area.

Before September 1975 if a minor was injured, his right of action in tort for damages for the injuries received was lost if he did not sue within three years of the injury, provided he was in the custody of a parent when his cause of action accrued, viz. when he was injured. This rule was repealed by the Limitation Act 1975.[169] Now time does not begin to run until the injured minor attains his majority, and action must be started within three years of that date.

Equity raised two presumptions to protect the interests of the minor child from parental depredations: (a) the presumption of advancement, and (b) the presumption of undue influence. Unlike the presumption of advancement of a wife, that of a child appears still to be in full vigour. If a parent or person *in loco parentis* buys property in a child's name, there is a presumption that he intended to make a gift of it, and the parent must rebut this presumption before he can claim the property as his own.[170] This presumption seems not to extend to the minor's mother.[171] Similarly, if a child who has recently reached the age of majority executes a settlement, it will be presumed that he or she was under the influence of a parent or person *in loco parentis* who advised him, even if the settlement is not in favour of the parent, and the parent was actuated by unselfish motives.[172]

Apart from these presumptions of equity, which until the nineteenth century applied to the very rich, neither the law nor equity was in past centuries astute to support the minor or newly-adult child against his father, or to hold the parent or guardian accountable as a fiduciary.[173] In two recent decisions, however, the High Court has emphasised the duty of guardians *ad litem*, and in one case that of lawyers responsible for advising them, to apply themselves seriously to the interests of the minors they are appointed to represent. In *Re Whittall*[174] there was an application under the Variation of Trusts Act 1958 for the court to approve on behalf of minors variations in the terms of settlements. Brightman J. pointed out that the duties of guardians *ad litem* had never been explained to those appointed, who had merely lent their names to the proceedings, and relevant information had not been supplied to them. Only because of other exceptional circumstances was the court pre-

---

Act, 1963, ss 33−6, 44, 64−5 and Scheds III and V and 1969, ss 28 and 72; the Children Act 1972, s. 1 and the Employment of Children Act 1973, s. 1 and Scheds 1 and 2.

169. S. 2 and Sched. 2. The Act came into force on 1 September 1975: Ibid. s. 4(b).
170. *Crabb* v. *Crabb* (1834) 1 My. & K. 511; *Shepherd* v. *Cartwright* [1955] A.C. 431 H.L.
171. *Bennett* v. *Bennett* (1879) 10 Ch.D. 474.
172. *Bullock* v. *Lloyds Bank Ltd* [1955] Ch. 317 C.A. Here the father did not even exercise his influence directly, but through trustees, and influenced his daughter only to settle on herself the property she had inherited under her mother's will. The decision thus asserts that adult women should not be unduly persuaded to transfer the management of their property to trustees.
173. E.g. *Re Timmis* [1902] 1 Ch. 176.
174. [1973] 1 W.L.R. 1027, and see *Practice Direction (Variation of Trusts: Counsel's Opinion)* [1976] 1 W.L.R. 884.

pared, in that case, to approve the variation sought. In *Re Barbour's Settlement Trusts*[175] the court was asked to approve a compromise of a genuine dispute, but the trustees took the opportunity of inserting a clause applying for an increase in their remuneration. This request was refused. The court pointed out again that the guardians *ad litem* had not done their duty, and that those who had a duty to advise them had not done so in terms comprehensible to laymen, who 'ought not to have to unravel lawyers' nods and becks and wreathed smiles'.[176] The law must be vigilant to assert the interests of those incapable of protecting them themselves.

Since 1970, when the age of majority was reduced from twenty-one to eighteen years, those aged 18 have been able to make a valid will,[177] and the rule has been reaffirmed that minors who come within the description of 'soldiers on actual military service and sailors or seamen at sea' may make valid informal wills during their minority.[178]

---

175. [1974] 1 W.L.R. 1198.
176. Ibid. p. 1202 at C-D.
177. Wills Act 1837, s. 9, as amended by the Family Law Reform Act 1969, s. 3(1)(a).
178. Ibid. s. 11, as amended by the Wills (Soldiers and Sailors Act) 1918, s. 3(1) and the Family Law Reform Acy 1969, s. 3(1)(b). See also *Re Wernher* [1918] 2 Ch. 82 C.A.

PART II

The Disjointed Family

CHAPTER V

Services, Institutions, Courts and their Jurisdictions

A. MARITAL COUNSELLING: CONCILIATION AND RECONCILIATION PROCEDURES

The office of Censuses and Surveys found in 1972[1] that, even when buying their matrimonial home, between 24 per cent and 34 per cent of those interviewed had received advice on joint ownership from relatives and friends. When joy turns to misery among the married they are usually among the first to be consulted, and they still play a major role in either harmonising or exacerbating relations between spouses.

Most of the Churches have counselling provisions for their adherents. In the United States there has been a powerful movement to have the roles of marital counselling and conciliation closely linked with if not taken over by the courts, and many experiments were carried out in the 1960s.[2] The Conciliation Court of Los Angeles County in California received widespread publicity. A model Conciliation Agreement, modified by the couple concerned to suit their own needs, is still in use in the court which has a staff of trained and experienced conciliators. In England, however, it is not only the judges who might find difficulty about invoking the authority of the court to enforce an agreement that, *inter alia*, may specify how many times per week or month the husband shall take the wife out in the car, and lays down as

---

1. *Matrimonial Property*, by Jean E. Todd and L. M. Jones (Office of Population Censuses and Surveys) p. 11.
2. See, e.g. B. Bodenheimer, 'The Utah marriage counselling experiment', 7 *Utah LR* (1961) 443; Henry J. Foster Jr, 'Conciliation and counselling in the courts in family law cases', 41 *NYU L. Rev.* (1966) 353; B. Bodenheimer: 'New approaches of psychiatry: implications for divorce reform' 16 *Utah L. Rev.* (1970) 191. The most up-to-date summary of developments is that by A. H. Manchester and J. M. Whetton, 'Marital conciliation in England and Wales', 23 *ICLQ* (1974) 339. This covers a wider field than its title indicates.

axiomatic highly controversial propositions.[3] There is unease about the under-lying philosophy of provisions that, for example, the parties will 'strengthen our marriage through the making of mutual friends, new ones if necessary, among happily-married couples with responsibilities and problems similar to our own' and which specifically ban from the home unhappily married people.

The *Finer Report on One Parent Families*[4] concentrated on conciliation as contrasted with reconciliation and defined conciliation as:

> assisting the parties to deal with the consequences of the established break-down of their marriage, whether resulting in a divorce or separation, by reaching agreements or giving consents or reducing the area of conflict upon custody, support, access to and education of the children, financial provision, the disposition of the matrimonial home, lawyers' fees and every other matter arising from the breakdown which calls for a decision on future arrangements.

This seems to be the type of activity most appropriate to agencies connected with the courts, and that on which, for example, Conciliation Commissioners in New York State,[5] have tended to concentrate.

Under its Family Law Act 1975,[6] Australia has continued the provision in its Matrimonial Causes Act 1959 for financial assistance to approved marriage counselling organisations which must make annual reports. In some Australian universities, lectures from members of the counselling service are included in the undergraduate course on Family Law. Further developments in this area merit attention.

In England and Wales, marital counselling[7] was until recently largely a matter for voluntary organisations, although the Probation Service has long

---

3. E.g. (*a*) that women who refuse to accept a dependent role are robbed of their dignity; (*b*) that the married woman 'soon finds she lives in her own little world, entirely different from that of her single friends', and (*c*) that neither spouse has the right to refuse sexual intercourse, except for serious reasons (unspecified).
4. Cmnd. 5629, paras 4.288, pp. 176 et seq.
5. When new grounds for divorce in New York State were added to adultery in 1966 the Domestic Relations Law was amended to provide also that those commencing an action for separation, divorce or nullity must so notify the local conciliation bureau, which may summon them for at least one conciliation conference. There is a conciliation commissioner within the jurisdiction of each Supreme Court. See Jon M. A. McLaughlin, 'Court-connected marriage counselling and divorce: the New York experience', 11 *Jo. of Family Law* (1972) 517; Freda S. Nisnewitz, 'Matrimonial conciliation: theory and practice', 37 *Brooklyn L. Rev.* (1971) 366.
6. No. 53 of 1975, in operation from 6 January 1976, ss 11–13. See also *Divorce, Society and the Law*, ed. H. A. Finlay (1969).
7. See Manchester and Whetton, 23 *ICLQ*, (1974).
8. The Magistrates' Courts Act 1952, s. 59, provides for a report to be made to the court by the probation officer or other person requested by the court to attempt to effect a conciliation [*sic*] between the parties. The *Finer Report* in para. 4.296, p. 179 sets out the normal procedure. See also Table 4.16 on p. 180 of the *Finer Report* from Cmnd 5158 (1972), *Report on the work of the Probation and After-Care Department 1969–71*, Appendix E.

been concerned with it, both in the magistrates' courts[8] and the divorce (County and High) courts.[9] When the grounds for divorce were amended in 1969, it was thought desirable to write reconciliation provisions into the new law, derived from the Australian legislation. The Matrinonial Causes Act 1973 s. 6, now provides for the solicitor acting for a petitioner for divorce to certify whether he has discussed with the petitioner the possibility of a reconciliation and given him the names and addresses of persons qualified to help effect reconciliation between estranged spouses,[10] and s. 6(2) allows the court to adjourn the proceedings at any stage if a reconciliation between the parties seems a reasonable possibility. It has been suggested[11] that the need for the solicitor's certification may in fact have reduced the amount of genuine reconciliation activity. A Practice Direction issued in 1972[12] supersedes previous lists of organisations and persons considered qualified to attempt reconciliation[13] and emphasises that counselling is not to be regarded as a formal step to be taken in all cases. So far we have not grappled in this country, as some American courts have at least attempted to do, with the fact that a legal adviser who counsels or facilitates conciliation may greatly expand the time and trouble expended on his client, while depriving himself of at least part of his fee.

Now that legal aid is available not only for litigation, but also for advice,[14] the public image of solicitors could probably be improved to increase legal advice and even representation in the magistrates' courts. An increase in the proportion of women solicitors from the 3 per cent with practising certificates in 1971[15] might ease the problem as far as women complainants were concerned.

---

9. The Welfare Officers attached to certain divorce courts when requested investigate and report on matters arising in matrimonial proceedings, principally concerning the welfare of children. They are drawn from the Probation Service. See Cmnd 5158 (1972), paras 77–8.

10. Rule 12(3) of the Matrimonial Causes Rules 1973 (S.I. 2016), requires the solicitor to complete Form 3, a simple yes/no declaration. *Practice Note (Divorce: Conciliation)* [1971] 1 W.L.R. 223, issued by the President of the Probate, etc. Division on 27 January 1971, supplements the provisions by establishing machinery for conciliation by court welfare officers once the petition is before the court.

11. Manchester and Whetton, 23 *ICLQ*, at 350 et seq. On Legal Advice Services generally see Rosalind Brooke, *Information and Advice Services* (1972) ch. 5.

12. *Practice Direction (Divorce: Reconciliation) (No. 2)* [1972] 1 W.L.R. 1309.

13. The list, which is not exclusive, comprises: 'any marriage guidance council affiliated to the National Marriage Guidance Council; any centre of the Catholic Marriage Advisory Council; the Jewish Marriage Education Council; any probation officer; any Church of England clergyman nominated by the diocesan bishop; Ministers of the Free Church denominations nominated by the General Superintendent of the Baptist Union or chairmen of the Methodist Districts or by moderators of the United Reformed Church (Congregational and Presbyterian).

14. Legal Aid Act 1974 (a consolidating Act).

15. According to the Law Society, 25,366 practising certificates were issued to solicitors for the year ending October 1971, of which 803 were for women. The Select Committee on *Violence in Marriage* found many solicitors' offices intimidating to women, inaccessible, and usually only receiving clients on appointments days and sometimes weeks ahead. H.C. 553–i (1975), para. 53.

The establishment of the new Law Centres, which began in 1970, may point another path to advising the poor on the law.

Both solicitors and counsel have a long established practice in the formation of separation and maintenance agreements. When divorce was rare such an agreement was usual. The practice was important enough for the Bar Council to make a spirited defence of it to the Royal Commission on Marriage and Divorce of 1951–5,[16] resulting in the recognition of such agreements by statute, with power to the courts to enforce them and also to amend their financial terms[17] even after the death of the party liable. The Matrimonial Causes Act 1973 also provides for agreements which will operate after a divorce to be referred to the court for approval.[18]

The Matrimonial Causes Act 1963 first introduced provisions designed to encourage couples who had separated to resume cohabitation and attempt reconciliation[19] by providing for exceptions to the doctrine of condonation, under which sexual intercourse by a husband with his wife, knowing of her adultery, was an absolute bar to his subsequent petition based on that adultery,[20] and resumption of cohabitation similarly condoned cruelty and terminated desertion.[21] The provision enacted in 1963 caused difficulty in interpretation. When the divorce law was reformulated in the Divorce Reform Act 1969, the bars to matrimonial relief of connivance and collusion were abolished, together with the petitioner's discretion statement.[22] The opportunity was taken to reformulate the provisions so that at least they would not hinder reconciliation. They now appear in the Matrimonial Causes Act 1973, s. 2 and can more conveniently be discussed in connection with the jurisdiction for dissolution of marriage (post).

The *Finer Report on One-Parent Families* has now drawn attention to the extremely high proportion of married people in the general population, described as 'as near an approach to practically universal marriage as has been achieved in this country'.[23] Some resources might usefully be devoted towards lessening excessive social pressure to marry.[24]

---

16. This followed the decision in *Bennett* v. *Bennett* [1952] 1 K.B 249 C.A., that a deed by which the wife undertook not to apply to the court for maintenance for herself or the child was contrary to public policy and void. See 21 *MLR* (1968) 57.
17. Now the Matrimonial Causes Act 1973, ss 34–6, deriving from the Maintenance Agreements Act 1957. See *Pace* (formerly Doe) v. *Doe* [1976] 3 W.L.R. 865.
18. Section 7, the last remnant of the old bar of collusion.
19. See Matrimonial Causes Act 1963, s. 2; and 'The Matrimonial Causes and Reconciliation Bill 1963', 3 *Journal of Family Law* (1963) 87–8.
20. *Henderson* v. *Henderson and Crellin* [1944] A.C. 49. The rule was never so strictly applied to a wife, particularly one with young children, who might have nowhere to go apart from the place where her husband was living, and might be unable to refuse sexual intercourse with him there. See *Morley* v. *Morley* [1961] 1 W.L.R. 211.
21. *Morley* v. *Morley supra*, concerned persistent cruelty by the husband. *Abercrombie* v. *Abercrombie* [1943] 2 All E.R. 465 exemplifies termination of desertion by resumption of cohabitation. See also *Lowry* v. *Lowry* [1952] P. 252.
22. Compare Form 2: *General Form of Petition* in S.I. 219 of 1968 with the amendment by S.I. 1349 of 1970.
23. Per E. Grebenik and Griselda Rowntree: See ch. I, n. 57.
24. As for example by the provision of more low-cost housing for single people.

B. MARRIAGE CONTRACTS

A recent development has been the publication of model contracts the parties may sign before marriage, setting out the terms of their agreement on various matters that might otherwise cause friction between them. Such contracts are distinguishable from suggestions for so-called 'cohabitation agreements' in which the parties are sometimes referred to thereafter as husband and wife.[25] Cohabitation agreements would not constitute a marriage, since they do not comply with the essential forms laid down by the Marriage Act 1949, or the Marriage (Registrar General's Licence) Act 1970. Even their financial terms might be unenforceable as being contrary to good morals. Any reference to husband and wife in such a context is therefore unjustifiable, and likely to mislead.

The agreements designed for signature as ancillary to a genuine marriage[26] have the merit of directing the attention of intending spouses to potential points of disagreement so that they can work out their attitude to them in advance. Those intending to intermarry should of course discuss at length and in detail what kind of life they wish to lead together. There should be the greatest possible clarity about the number and timing of children and all aspects of money: capital, income and expenditure. No detail that could cause friction should be ignored. If the Australian federal provision for divorce on proof only of 12 months' separation[27] is likely to become the prevailing, or even a significant, mode for dissolution of marriage by legal action, those contemplating the birth of children (amongst others) may move to create some stability by contract. As sexual permissiveness is so much discussed, and probably to a lesser extent practised, those who expect marital relations to be exclusive may be wise to leave the intended partner in no doubt of this view. Any agreement reached before marriage should of course be variable by agreement, and the wisdom of signatures to a document is questionable. Ante-nuptial agreements about the upbringing of children should always be subject to variation when the children are in being. All pre-nuptial agreements about children's upbringing are and should remain totally void and unenforceable,[28] and all post-nuptial agreements are subject to the jurisdiction of the courts.

C. GOVERNMENT CONCILIATION SERVICES

In England the majority of the counselling services available have in the past

---

25. E.g. that published in the *New Law Journal* for 21.6.73, pp. 591 et seq.
26. E.g. that appended by Lenore J. Weitzman to, 'Legal regulation of marriage: tradition and change. A proposal for individual contracts and contracts in lieu of marriage', 62 *Calif. LR* (1974) 1169. Some fundamental matters, such as whether the parties expect sexual relations to be exclusive, are even there omitted.
27. Family Law Act 1975, s. 48(2): 'a decree of dissolution of the marriage shall be made if, and only if, the court is satisfied that the parties separated and thereafter lived separately and apart for a continuous period of not less than twelve months immediately preceding the date of the filing of the application for dissolution of marriage.'
28. See H. L. Deb. vol. 339, cols 39–40 of 20.2.73 and vol. 340, cols 646–58 of 20.3.73, Chapter III, n. 125 *ante*.

been manned by volunteers. In so far as they are funded from the public purse they should both be and appear impartial. They are open to the charge that they use their authority to reconcile spouses and keep families together at all costs, because not to do so would entail additional public expenditure. Because the local authorities are responsible for most low-income housing and for social services in their areas, they are particularly vulnerable to such charges. Many of them are known to insist upon a divorce decree or separation order from a court before they will consider rehousing separately some members of a family,[29] even when violence is habitually used against them. Maria Colwell and other maltreated children are recent evidence that some local authority social service officers do not question the right of a physical parent to custody of a minor child, are unmoved by the child's well-founded resistance, and are slow to examine charges of violence or parental neglect.

On the other hand where the local authority has statutory duties in spheres such as housing 'the court should not lend itself to any extension of attempts to influence the housing priorities of the local authority by itself creating priorities'.[30] In *Brent* v. *Brent* the court described such an application[31] as 'really an attempt to force the hand of the local authority, and in the absence of the authority'.

The role of the national probation service in marital conciliation is anomalous. Until recently probation officers received no training in it. The poor woman who goes to the magistrates' court to complain of wilful neglect to maintain, persistent cruelty or desertion, is first referred to a probation officer attached to the court, so that he can ascertain the facts and explore the possibilities of reconciliation. At least one member of the probation service will be in court during the hearing of all complaints under the Matrimonial Proceedings (Magistrates' Courts) Act 1960. On the other hand the petitioner for divorce does not undergo any compulsory attempts at reconciliation, and the duties of the welfare officers attached to the divorce courts are mainly concerned with the suitability of arrangements proposed for custody of children and with the supervision of children when ordered by the Court. The social services officers employed by the local authority have, however, largely displaced the probation officers in their supervision of children at risk.

D. MATRIMONIAL COMPLAINTS BEFORE MAGISTRATES

Although the statutes[32] provide that 'in so far as is consistent with the due despatch of business' matrimonial proceedings shall be heard separately from

---

29. See *ante* Chapter III *Marital Consortium*, notes 110–113, and the Report from the House of Commons Select Committee on *Violence in Marriage* H. C. 553–i (1975), paras 26–38.

30. *Brent* v. *Brent* [1975] Fam. 1 at 9.

31. Ibid. p. 8 F–H.

32. Magistrates' Courts Act 1952, s. 57, derived from the Summary Procedure (Domestic, Proceedings) Act 1937, s. 2, and governing the Matrimonial Proceedings (Magistrates Courts) Act 1960; see, e.g. ss 4(7)(8); 8(1)(3); 9(5); 10(2); 13(2)(3).

other proceedings of the magistrates' courts, the jurisdiction of magistrates is primarily criminal. It is an anomaly that their jurisdiction in matrimonial proceedings should as the result of an historical accident,[33] have endured so long. That the public prefers the atmosphere of the county courts for family proceedings is shown by their increasing popularity in adoption as compared with the cheaper magistrates' courts.

The magistrates' courts have no power to grant divorce decrees or, at the other extreme, injunctions against assault or entering the matrimonial home. Any married man or woman may apply to them alleging one or more of nine causes of complaint by the other spouse, viz.[34]

(a) desertion; or
(b) persistent cruelty to (i) the complainant, or (ii) to an infant child of the complainant, or (iii) to an infant child of the defendant, who was a child of the family at the relevant time; or
(c) a conviction either (i) on indictment of an offence involving an assault on the complainant, or (ii) by a magistrates' court of an offence against the complainant consisting of malicious wounding or inflicting grievous bodily harm; or common assault or battery for which the defendant was sentenced to at least one month's detention; or aggravated assault on a woman or a boy under 14 years; or assault causing bodily harm,[35] or (iii) of an attempted or actual sexual offence against an infant child either of the complainant or of the defendant if the child was a child of the family at the time of the offence; or
(d) adultery;[36] or
(e) insisting on or, without the complainant being aware of the disease, permitting sexual intercourse while knowingly suffering from venereal disease; or
(f) habitual drunkenness or drug addiction; or
(g) being the husband, compelling the wife to submit herself to prostitution or

---

33. In 1878 the Matrimonial Causes Act gave magistrates power to make a separation and maintenance order in favour of a wife whose husband had been convicted of an aggravated assault on her, and to grant her custody of children under the age of 10 years. This was the origin of the matrimonial jurisdiction of the magistrates courts, which has since continued. See Appendix 5 to the *Finer Report on One-Parent Families*, Cmnd 5629–I, paras 35–41.
34. Matrimonial Proceedings (Magistrates' Courts) Act 1960, s. 1(1) heads (a) to (i). For the improvements effected by this Act over previous legislation see 24 *MLR* (1961) 144.
35. The statute refers to the relevant sections of the Offences Against the Person Act 1861. The net effect is given here, and the wording used is not that of the statute.
36. It is indicative of the legislative approach that, whereas adultery was throughout the 150 years of legislative divorce and for the 80 years of judicial divorce from 1857 to 1937 the sole ground for divorce (although a woman petitioner had until 1923 to prove also some other matrimonial offence by her husband, such as cruelty or desertion), not until 1937 was the poor woman or man enabled to complain to the magistrates on this ground. By s. 2(3)(a)(b) of the 1960 Act the respondent's adultery is a valid ground for making a matrimonial order only if committed during the subsistence of the marriage and the court is satisfied that the complainant has not condoned or connived at or by wilful neglect or misconduct conduced to that act of adultery.

being guilty of conduct likely to result and resulting in her submitting herself to prostitution; or

(*h*) being the husband, wilfully neglecting to provide reasonable maintenance for the wife or any dependent child of the family; or

(*i*) being the wife, having wilfully neglected to make a proper contribution towards maintenance for the husband or for any dependent child of the family where the husband's earning capacity was impaired and it would have been reasonable in all the circumstances to expect her so to contribute.

On proof of any of these grounds of complaint, and provided the conduct complained of occurred within six months before the complaint was made,[37] the magistrates may make a matrimonial order[38] containing any one or more of the following provisions, viz:

(*a*) a provision for non-cohabitation, which has the same effect as a decree of judicial separation[39] in a divorce court except that it does not terminate the rights of succession of the survivor in the event of the death intestate of either spouse;[40]

(*b*) a provision for the payment of such weekly maintenance by the husband to the wife as the court considers reasonable in all the circumstances;[41]

(*c*) a provision for payment of maintenance by the wife to the husband where, because of impairment of the husband's earning capacity through age, illness or disability of mind or body, the court finds it reasonable so to order;

(*d*) a provision for legal custody[42] of any child of the family[43] under the age of 16;[44]

---

37. Magistrates Courts Act 1952, s. 104. If the complaint is of the defendant's adultery, it is sufficient if the complainant first became aware of the adultery within the preceding six months, and no time limit applies if the complainant was serving overseas in H.M. Forces or in a British ship; Matrimonial Proceedings (Magistrates' Courts) Act 1960, s. 12.

38. Matrimonial Proceedings (Magistrates' Courts) Act 1960, s. 2(1). The net effect only of the statutory words is summarised.

39. Ibid. s. 2(1)(*a*).

40. Matrimonial Causes Act 1973, s. 18(2)(3).

41. See *Lanitis* v. *Lanitis* [1970] 1 W.L.R. 503 condemning the practice of delaying payment of maintenance by requesting adjournments and then asking for the magistrates' proceedings to be withdrawn because divorce proceedings have been instituted. The upper limits of seven pounds ten shillings (or £7·50) for a wife and two pounds ten shillings (or £2·50) for a child were removed by the Maintenance Orders Act 1968, s. 1 and Schedule, but the tradition continues that a husband's primary duty is to 'maintain' his wife who does not have an independent income, and that when she has young children a derisory sum should be added for their maintenance. In the magistrates' courts a wife without dependent children cannot claim full maintenance unless she can produce evidence of her incapacity to support herself, and the one-third 'starting point' applies: *Gengler* v. *Gengler* [1976] 1 W.L.R. 275.

42. This term is unfortunate but is still used in this and other statutes in respect of care and upbringing of and visits to minor children.

43. This is defined in s. 16(1) of the 1960 Act to mean: (*a*) any child of both parties to a marriage and (*b*) any child of either party who has been *accepted* as one of the family by the other party. In the Matrimonial Causes Act 1973, s. 52(1) the same expression

(e) in exceptional circumstances a provision committing[42] the care of the child to the social services authority[45] for the area in which the child lives;

(f) in exceptional circumstances a provision for a child committed to the legal custody[42] of any person to be under the supervision of a probation officer or local social services authority;[45]

(g) a provision for access[42] to any child of the family by a parent who does not have legal custody[42] of the child;

(h) a provision for payment of reasonable maintenance for any child of the family by the complainant or the defendant or each of them, normally until the child is 16 but exceptionally until the age of twenty-one.

Although after 1937 it became possible for the first time for a man to complain to the magistrates because of his wife's conduct, the overwhelming majority of complainants are wives, and their complaints are most usually of wilful neglect to maintain, desertion, or persistent cruelty.[46] Adultery during the subsistence of the marriage is still an absolute bar to an order for maintenance of a spouse.[47] After 1882 the right of a married woman to her own property was not affected by her adultery or other matrimonial misconduct. Even the wife dependent for maintenance on her husband has not, on divorce, been denied maintenance because of her adultery, at least since 1943.[48] Only those

---

is defined in the same way as to (a) but includes in (b) any other child, not being a child who has been boarded out with those parties by a local authority or voluntary organisation who has been *treated* by both of those parties as a child of their family. It is incomprehensible that, when the term was redefined for divorce purposes in the Matrimonial Proceedings and Property Act 1970 and then incorporated in the Matrimonial Causes Act 1973, the amended definition was not extended to the magistrates' courts.

44. The Law Commission in P.W.P. 53, para. 125 recommends that the power should extend until the child reaches majority at the age of 18, and that the magistrates be given power to make 'split orders', viz. while leaving equal 'custody rights' with both parents to 'award' care and control to one only. It was held in *Wild* v. *Wild* [1969] P. 33 that the magistrates have no such power under the 1960 Act, although they possess it under what are now the Guardianship of Minors Acts 1971–3.

45. The wording of s. 2(1)(e) and (f) of the 1960 Act is amended by s. 195 and Sched. 23, para. 10 of the Local Government Act 1972.

46. Unfortunately there are no official figures, but this is thought to be the situation. The latest figures, contained in Table M of *Civil Judicial Statistics for 1973*, Cmnd 5756, give no information on grounds for complaint, but simply divide the applications for maintenance orders according to the statute under which they were brought. These are statistics at their most unenlightening. The *Civil Judicial Statistics for 1974*, Cmnd 6361, give no figures for magistrates' proceedings.

47. Matrimonial Proceedings (Magistrates' Courts) Act 1960, s. 2(3)(b), unless condoned, connived at or by wilful neglect or misconduct conduced to by the respondent.

48. When the House of Lords in *Blunt* v. *Blunt* [1943] A.C. 517 set out the considerations to be borne in mind when deciding whether to grant a divorce where both parties had committed adultery. *Miller* v. *Miller* [1961] P. 1 demonstrates that it is the court in which the maintenance order is made that decides the pecuniary cost of adultery. The decision is not applicable today since under the Act of 1960 the adultery must be committed during the subsistence of the marriage to compel termination of maintenance. But in *Gray* v. *Gray* [1976] 3 W.L.R. 181 it has been held that a wife is precluded by her uncondoned adultery from seeking financial provision in the divorce court on the ground of her husband's wilful neglect to maintain her. See also Cmnd 5629 (*Finer*), para. 4.65.

who use the magistrates' courts on bad legal advice or who apply in the divorce courts only for financial provision are deprived of maintenance on proof of adultery during the marriage.

The research conducted by Professor O. R. McGregor and his colleagues,[49] however, shows that those who cannot for one reason or another obtain a maintenance order from magistrates may be better off than those who do. Most of the maintenance orders are for the payment of sums below the level of supplementary benefit[50] and few are paid with any regularity.[51] The orders for the maintenance of children have always been derisory and never borne any relation to the cost of maintaining and bringing up a young child. The object of the present jurisdiction is said to be preventing the burial of dead marriages. The *Finer Report* would replace the magistrates' courts by a Family Court.

The Law Commission Working Party on Matrimonial Proceedings in the Magistrates' Courts has recommended, *inter alia*,[52] that (i) The present list of matrimonial offences should be replaced by the three grounds of complaint: (a) wilful neglect to provide reasonable maintenance for spouse or children; (b) such behaviour by the other spouse that the complainant cannot reasonably be expected to live with him or her;[53] and (c) desertion. (ii) The rule that adultery bars financial relief should be abolished. The Working Party also canvasses opinion on the extent to which the obligation to maintain should be dependent on matrimonial conduct.

The crucial question is: When there is insufficient income to maintain both, who takes precedence, spouse or minor children? The Working Party in para. 154 admits that under the Guardianship of Minors Act 1971 the sum the wife is likely to receive by way of maintenance for her children is as much as the husband can pay altogether 'for the whole of the family'. If it is not enough for the whole of the family or even for one member of it this

---

49. Published in the Report of the *Committee on Statutory Maintenance Limits*, Cmnd 3587 (1968); *Separated Spouses* (1970) and the *Report of the Finer Committee on One-Parent Families*, Cmnd 5629 (1974) esp. paras 4.72 to 4.101 and Table 4.10; also Cmnd 5629–I, Appendices 5 and 7.

50. Cmnd 5629: Table 4.10, p. 104 shows this clearly, and also that the discrepancy is greater in orders for the maintenance of children only than in those for maintenance of wife or former wife and children.

51. Ibid. Table 4.9, p. 100 shows that 55 per cent of orders for maintenance of wives or former wives and only 35 per cent of orders for such women and dependent legitimate children were complied with to the extent of 75 per cent or more; 37 per cent of orders for wives and former wives and 46 per cent of those for wives and legitimate children were complied with to the extent of less than 10 per cent of the amount ordered, many of them not at all.

52. Law Commission Working Paper No. 53: *Family Law: Matrimonial Proceedings in Magistrates' Courts* (1973). A total of 45 recommendations, of which 29 relate to husband and wife and 16 to children, is summarised in para. 167 of the Working Paper.

53. Viz., one of the fact situations on which the divorce court may conclude that the marriage has irretrievably broken down and grant a divorce under the Matrimonial Causes Act 1973, s. 1(2)(b). For divorce this head does not include adultery by the other spouse, a separate situation for which it must be shown that the petitioner finds it intolerable to live with the respondent. Will the poor, who resort to magistrates, have to show for separation or maintenance a higher standard, viz. that other people would think continued cohabitation intolerable?

fact should be made clear to all concerned. The myths that most men maintain their wives or former wives when they are living apart and that wives are their husbands' 'dependants' are perhaps the biggest obstacles to realistic financial provisions for the family.

Other recommendations included those that: (iii) Magistrates should have jurisdiction to issue a non-molestation order or one preventing a violent spouse from re-entering the matrimonial home (which would be preferable). This has now been strongly supported by the House of Commons Select Committee on *Violence in Marriage*. (iv) Magistrates should be able to make and enforce maintenance orders during cohabitation (unfortunately limited to a period of six months). (v) They should be empowered to order payment of a lump sum (unfortunately limited as to amount). (vi) They should be enabled to make consent orders. (vii) A simple form of pleadings should be introduced and the magistrates be required to record the factors taken into account when determining the amount of maintenance ordered. (viii) The jurisdiction over minor children in the divorce county courts, the county courts under the Guardianship of Minors Acts 1971–3 and the magistrates' courts under the Matrimonial Proceedings (Magistrates' Courts) Acts and the Guardianship of Minors Acts should be rationalised.[54]

It is now accepted that the abolition, root and branch, of the magistrates' jurisdiction, and the provision of a guaranteed maintenance allowance (G.M.A.) by administrative order for all who look after young children, as recommended in the *Finer Report*,[55] are not practicable in the present financial climate.[56] Both the Law Commission Working Paper and the *Finer Report* are, in their several ways, insufficiently child-centred. The first requirement is surely a recognition that, whenever there is marital disharmony, the first interest of society and the paramount function of the law is so far as possible to safeguard the interests of minor children, to which the interests of their parents should if necessary be subordinated.

For all their inadequacies the magistrates' courts have certain merits, of which the principal are:

(i) Their jurisdiction is based on residence,[57] which everyone can understand, and not on esoteric notions of domicile. They are the local courts, easily available to those who resort to them.

(ii) Except in London and some other large towns, the magistrates are unpaid, and the courts are cheaper to run than any other type of court, although the clerk is legally qualified and paid.

(iii) About one-third of the lay magistrates are women, and for matrimonial proceedings the bench is required to consist of not more than three magistrates, including so far as practicable, both a man and a woman.[58]

---

54. The anomalies of the several jurisdictions are charted at pp. 119–21 of the Working Paper.
55. The major recommendation in Part 5, s. 6, paras 5.111–5.319 of Cmnd 5629.
56. See H.C. Deb. vol. 896–7, col. 221, 5.8.75.
57. Matrimonial Proceedings (Magistrates' Courts) Act 1960, s. 1(2) and (3) and *Lowry* v. *Lowry* [1952] P. 252.
58. Magistrates' Courts Act 1952, s. 56(2).

Women are virtually excluded from judicial office[59] and even from the legal profession,[60] but they perform (frequently to bolster their husband's status rather than their own) unpaid judicial functions in unsatisfactory conditions. Many of them work with intelligence and sympathy among poverty-stricken litigants. The law they administer should soon be improved and there may be better procedures and records of what they do.[61] The Law Commission's Report No. 77 on Matrimonial Proceedings in Magistrates' Courts, with a Draft Domestic Proceedings and Magistrates' Courts Bill, was published on 21 October 1976.

E. MATRIMONIAL CAUSES

Until 1967 the fiction was maintained that jurisdiction was only in the High Court in matrimonial causes, viz. nullity, judicial separation, divorce, presumption of death and dissolution of marriage; and for applications to petition for divorce within three years of marriage.[62] For many years some two-thirds of such petitions had in fact been heard by specially appointed Divorce Commissioners, most of whom were county court judges, although some were practising barristers. Over 90 per cent of divorce petitions have long been undefended.

The fiction was abolished by the Matrimonial Causes Act 1967,[63] which provided that all petitions in matrimonial causes should be launched in a divorce county court (including the Registry of the Family Division of the High Court in London, which is a divorce county court for this purpose.)[64]

---

59. Since 1 October 1974, there have been two women judges of the High Court, from a total of 75. Both are in the Family Division. There are still no women among the 19 Lords Justices in the Court of Appeal and none in the Judicial Committee of the House of Lords. There are about 4 women county court and circuit judges out of some 240; 48 men and 1 woman were stipendiary magistrates in 1971. Of the 19,250 lay magistrates at the beginning of 1971, 12,550 were men and 6700 women.

60. The Bar Council's Report for 1970−1 gave the number of women in practice at the Bar as 147 out of a total of 2584. For Solicitors, see *ante* (A) note 15.

61. See the *Finer Committee*, Cmnd 5629, paras 4.412−4.423. In 1973 20,993 married women maintenance orders were applied for and 13,657 granted; 5787 guardianship of minors orders were applied for and 4865 granted and 5016 affiliation orders were applied for and 4331 granted. It is not known how many of the guardianship of minors orders were for custody and how many for maintenance. These statistics are from Cmnd 5756, *Civil Judicial Statistics* for 1973. Cmnd 6361, *Civil Judicial Statistics Annual Report 1974* includes no figures for magistrates' courts.

62. See Matrimonial Causes Act 1967, s. 10. The action for jactitation of marriage (to prohibit false claims of marriage where none exists) has not been abolished as it has been in Australia under the Family Law Act 1975, s. 8(2), together with proceedings for restitution of conjugal rights and judicial separation. In England the petition for restitution of conjugal rights was abolished by the Matrimonial Proceedings and Property Act 1970, s. 20, after the embarrassment caused by *Nanda* v. *Nanda* [1968] P. 35. Damages for a wife's adultery, for enticement of a spouse or child, and for breach of promise of marriage were abolished by the Law Reform (Miscellaneous Provisions) Act 1970, ss 4, 5 and 1, respectively.

63. In operation from 11 April 1968 by S.I. No. 228 of 1968.

64. Matrimonial Causes Act 1967, s. 4.

Undefended petitions were then to be heard and determined in the divorce county court, and defended petitions transferred to the High Court. However, as regards hearings at the Royal Courts of Justice in London, an amendment was made from the beginning of the Easter term 1973.[65] High Court judges of the Family Division now hear the longer and more substantial applications in county court matrimonial causes, and circuit judges hear the shorter High Court applications and 'short' High Court (defended) matrimonial causes.

The first order designating divorce county courts was made in 1968,[66] and existing orders were revoked and replaced in 1971.[67] There are now over ninety divorce county courts in which undefended petitions may be heard and determined, and twenty-six other courts in which ancillary matters may be dealt with. Every petition in which the only relief sought is a declaration as to anybody's matrimonial status must, however, be begun in the Family Division Registry and assigned to the Family Division of the High Court.[68]

Tables I and II from the *Civil Judicial Statistics* for 1974, which are here reproduced, show that of the 131,662 petitions filed during that year, the vast majority, viz. 129,993 were for dissolution of marriage, 696 were for judicial separation and 949 for nullity of marriage. The comparative table E.5 shows that more petitions for nullity and even for judicial separation have been presented in recent years, probably as a result of legal aid and greater knowledge of legal rights. The considerable increase in the annual number of petitions for divorce is therefore not all due to change in the divorce law effected by the Divorce Reform Act 1969, which came into operation at the beginning of 1971. But the change in the law was accompanied by a 50 per cent increase in the number of divorce petitions, which jumped from 70,575 in 1970 to 110,017 in 1971.

The ground for divorce is now set out in the Matrimonial Causes Act 1973 (hereafter referred to as the Act) s. 1(1), viz.: 'that the marriage has broken down irretrievably'. However, by s. 1(2), the court shall not hold the marriage to have broken down irretrievably unless the petitioner satisfies the court of one or more of the following facts, viz:

(*a*) that the respondent has committed adultery and the petitioner finds it intolerable to live with the respondent;

(*b*) that the respondent has behaved in such a way that the petitioner cannot reasonably be expected to live with the respondent;

(*c*) that the respondent has deserted the petitioner for a continuous period of at least two years immediately preceding the presentation of the petition;

---

65. *Practice Direction (Matrimonial Causes: R.C.J.)* [1973] 1 W.L.R. 554. This complicates appearances about rights of audience. A solicitor has no right of audience before a circuit judge hearing a High Court case but has a right of audience before a High Court judge hearing a county court case.

66. S.I. 314 of 1968.

67. Now S.I. 1954 of 1971, as amended by S.I.s No. 1746 of 1972, 1278 of 1973 and 1004 of 1974.

68. *Practice Direction (Petition for Declaration)* [1971] 1 W.L.R. 29, 1970 3 All E.R. 1024 and Rule 109.

TABLE I

Extract from Civil Judicial Statistics: Annual Report 1974, Cmnd 6361

[TABLES B.12. Family matters – Divorce – High Court, Family Division and county courts

TABLE B.12(i). Family matters – Divorce. Number of petitions filed during 1974, showing the nature of the relief sought, the allegations, whether by husband or wife petitioners and the numbers filed in the Principal Registry of the Family Division and in county courts]

Nature of relief sought and allegations	Total filed	By husbands	By wives	Principal Registry	County Courts
ALL PETITIONS TOTAL	131,662	41,442	90,220	16,957	114,705
DISSOLUTION:a					
Total	129,993	41,002	88,991	16,461	113,532
2(1) (a) Adultery	35,736	15,629	20,107	2,796	32,940
2(1) (b) Behaviour	37,012	3,348	33,664	4,712	32,300
2(1) (c) Desertion	6,712	1,888	4,824	598	6,114
2(1) (d) Separation (2 years and Consent)	30,201	11,516	18,685	5,003	25,198
2(1) (e) Separation (5 years)	16,445	7,801	8,644	2,662	13,783
2(1) (a and b) Adultery and Behaviour	2,367	443	1,924	462	1,905
2(1) (a and c) Adultery and Desertion	414	139	275	54	360
2(1) (b and c) Behaviour and Desertion	740	109	631	112	628
2(1) (a and b and c) Adultery, Behaviour and Desertion	93	26	67	17	76
2(1) (d and e) Separation (Consent and 5 years)	259	98	161	43	216
Presumed Deceased (Only ground)	14	5	9	2	12
JUDICIAL SEPARATION:					
Total	696	48	648	275	421
2(1) (a) Adultery	118	12	106	23	95
2(1) (b) Behaviour	464	27	437	208	256
2(1) (c) Desertion	22	3	19	6	16
2(1) (d) Separation (2 years and Consent)	6	–	6	5	1
2(1) (e) Separation (5 years)	6	1	5	3	3
2(1) (a and b) Adultery and Behaviour	66	5	61	27	39
2(1) (a and c) Adultery and Desertion	10	–	10	3	7
2(1) (b and c) Behaviour and Desertion	3	–	3	–	3
2(1) (a and b and c) Adultery, Behaviour and Desertion	1	–	1	–	1
2(1) (d and e) Separation (Consent and 5 years)	–	–	–	–	–

NULLITY:

	949	382	567	197	752
Total					
Grounds on which a marriage is void:					
Total	104	25	79	36	68
11 (a)(i) Prohibited Degrees	9	5	4	1	8
11 (a)(ii) Under 16 either party	4	2	2	2	2
11 (a)(iii) Disregard of formalities	1	–	1	1	–
11 (b) Bigamy	87	15	72	31	56
11 (c) Parties not of opposite sex	2	1	1	1	1
11 (d) Polygamy	1	1	–	–	1
Grounds on which a marriage is voidable:					
Total	845	357	488	161	684
12 (a) Incapacity	306	106	200	30	276
12 (b) Wilful refusal	438	199	239	56	382
12 (c) No valid consent	4	1	3	1	3
12 (d) Mental disorder	6	3	3	1	5
12 (e) Venereal disease	1	–	1	–	1
12 (f) Pregnancy	19	19	–	2	17
12 (a) and (b) Incapacity and Wilful Refusal	71	29	42	71	–
Other Proceedings[b]	24	10	14	24	–

a Excludes petitions in which divorce is asked for in the alternative to nullity.

b Petitions for declaration of validity of foreign decree of divorce.

Figures for individual courts are available on application to the Lord Chancellor's Department.

Further information may also be obtained from the Registrar-General's Statistical Review, published by H.M. Stationery Office.

TABLE II

Extract from Civil Judicial Statistics: Annual Report 1974, Cmnd 6361

[TABLE E.5. Divorce. Number of petitions filed, grounds and numbers of decrees granted for the year]

	1938	1963	1968	1969	1970	1971	1972	1973	1974
DISSOLUTION OF MARRIAGE:									
Petitions filed	9,970	36,385	54,036	60,134	70,575	110,017	109,822	115,048	129,993
On grounds of:									
Adultery	4,989	16,972	26,011	29,891	36,474	27,284	30,920	32,261	35,736
Desertion	3,909	9,179	11,147	11,490	12,266	11,277	8,650	7,626	6,712
Behaviour a	699	6,475	12,753	14,538	17,534	20,604	25,424	30,468	37,012
Separation (2 years and consent)	—	—	—	—	—	16,057	20,187	24,203	30,201
Separation (5 years)	—	—	—	—	—	29,911	19,270	16,593	16,445
Adultery and desertion	—	1,540	1,478	1,397	1,376	989	756	594	414
Adultery and behaviour a	—	902	1,212	1,397	1,563	1,722	1,977	2,113	2,367
Desertion and behaviour a	—	894	1,046	1,064	988	1,382	1,615	830	740
Adultery, desertion and behaviour a	—	85	100	92	95	148	565	104	93
Separation (consent and 5 years)	—	—	—	—	—	549	433	242	257
Unsound mind	326	101	63	56	63	—	—	—	—
Presumed decease	47	120	109	75	82	94	25	14	14
Rape, etc.	—	15	8	15	39	—	—	—	—
Cruelty and rape, etc.	—	102	109	119	95	—	—	—	—
By husbands	4,649	15,203	20,130	22,270	25,543	43,792	38,745	38,792	41,002
By wives	5,321	21,182	33,906	37,864	45,032	66,225	71,077	76,256	88,991
Decrees nisi granted	7,621	32,304	47,959	54,151	61,090	88,460	109,944	106,522	117,150
Decrees absolute	6,092	31,405	45,036	50,063	57,421	73,666	118,253	105,199	110,753
NULLITY OF MARRIAGE:									
Petitions filed	263	919	971	1,082	1,086	878	900	898	949
On grounds of:									
Incapacity	147	145	148	163	180	159	—	—	—
Wilful refusal	82	207	190	266	255	241	—	—	—
Incapacity and wilful refusal	—	471	497	516	495	367	—	—	—
Invalidity	2	63	94	98	95	76	—	—	—
Unsound mind or epilepsy	19	13	14	19	21	19	—	—	—
Incapacity, wilful refusal and pregnancy	—	—	—	—	—	—	—	—	—
Pregnancy	9	17	24	12	26	15	—	—	—
Venereal disease	4	3	4	8	14	1	—	—	—
By husbands	167	478	466	492	494	405	385	424	382
By wives	96	441	505	590	592	473	515	474	567
Decrees nisi granted	170	741	819	843	906	822	800	759	785
Decrees absolute	158	647	758	1,247	818	771	772	804	685

Grounds on which a marriage is void:									
Totals	104	77	100	–	–	–	–	–	–
11(a)(i) Prohibited degree	9	17	7	–	–	–	–	–	–
11(a)(ii) Under 16 (either party)	4	1	5	–	–	–	–	–	–
11(a)(iii) Disregard of formalities	1	3	11	–	–	–	–	–	–
11(b) Bigamy	87	52	76	–	–	–	–	–	–
11(c) Parties not of opposite sex	2	4	1	–	–	–	–	–	–
11(d) Polygamy	1	–	–	–	–	–	–	–	–
Grounds on which a marriage is voidable:									
Totals	845	798	800	–	–	–	–	–	–
12(a) Incapacity	306	260	382	–	–	–	–	–	–
12(b) Wilful refusal	438	416	382	–	–	–	–	–	–
12(c) No valid consent	4	5	15	–	–	–	–	–	–
12(d) Mental disorder	6	7	12	–	–	–	–	–	–
12(e) Venereal disease	1	2	2	–	–	–	–	–	–
12(f) Pregnancy	19	15	7	–	–	–	–	–	–
12(a) and (b) Incapacity and wilful refusal	71	93	–	–	–	–	–	–	–
JUDICIAL SEPARATION:									
Petitions filed	696	430	330	211	231	229	233	206	71
By husbands	48	20	23	10	15	19	14	16	10
By wives	648	410	307	201	216	210	219	190	61
Decrees granted	246	190	133	90	89	116	105	116	25
RESTITUTION OF CONJUGAL RIGHTS[b]									
Petitions filed	–	–	–	–	15	24	16	38	46
Decrees granted	–	–	–	–	3	9	6	18	27

a Grounds of behaviour were introduced from 1 January 1971 to replace grounds of cruelty.

b Under the Divorce Reform Act 1969, with effect from 1 January 1971, Restitution of Conjugal Rights is no longer a cause of action.

    (*d*) that the parties to the marriage have lived apart for a continuous period of at least two years immediately preceding the presentation of the petition (thereafter in the Act referred to as 'two years' separation') and the respondent consents to a decree being granted;

    (*e*) that the parties to the marriage have lived apart for a continuous period of at least five years immediately preceding the presentation of the petition (thereafter in the Act referred to as 'five years' separation').

On the presentation of the petition the court has the duty to inquire, so far as it reasonably can, into the facts alleged by the petitioner and into any facts alleged by the respondent. By s. 1(4) of the Act, if it is satisfied that any of the above five fact situations exists, then unless it is satisfied on all the evidence that the marriage has not broken down irretrievably, it shall, (subject to two minor conditions to be discussed later)[69] grant a decree of divorce.

Section 17 of the Act provides that any of the five fact situations is also a ground on which a petition for judicial separation may be presented to the court.

❧ THE FACT SITUATIONS

(i) ADULTERY AND COHABITATION INTOLERABLE

Adultery was, in the days of divorce by Private Act of Parliament, and for eighty years of judicial divorce from 1857 to 1937, the sole ground for divorce, although until 1923 a wife had to prove some matrimonial offence such as desertion[70] or cruelty by her husband, in addition to his adultery, before she could divorce him. When the grounds for divorce were reformulated in the Divorce Reform Act 1969, the Church insisted, as part of the price for withdrawing its opposition to the Bill as a whole, that in addition to proving the respondent's adultery, the petitioner must prove also that he or she found it intolerable to live with the respondent. Why anyone who did not find it intolerable to continue cohabitation should subject himself to the trauma and expense of petitioning for divorce is not clear. Moreover the Matrimonial Causes Act 1973, s. 2(1) provides that one party may not rely on adultery committed by the other if, after it became known to him that the other had committed that adultery, the parties have lived with each other for a period exceeding, or periods together exceeding, six months. By s. 2(2) of the Act, where the parties have lived with each other after it became known to one party that the other had

---

69. See *post.* nn. 111 and 136.

70. This accounted for the comparative popularity of the decree of restitution of conjugal rights before 1923. Failure to comply with it constituted desertion. See *The Forsyte Saga* by John Galsworthy, Book II, *In Chancery*, Chapters VII: *Dartie* v. *Dartie*, and XIII: *Here we are again.* Winifred Dartie's attempt to rid herself of an expensively embarrassing husband foundered when he obeyed the order for restitution of conjugal rights and returned to her six months after absconding with her pearls and the last in a long line of dancing girls.

committed adultery but s. 2(1) does not apply (that is, if cohabitation was for less than six months) then in any proceedings for divorce in which the petitioner relies on that adultery, the fact that the parties have lived with each other after that time shall be disregarded in determining whether the petitioner finds it intolerable to live with the respondent.[71] Such distinctions in the civil law may prove less than appealing to lawyers and their lay clients alike.

The Court of Appeal has now determined[72] that the petitioner need not show that he finds it intolerable to live with the respondent because of the respondent's adultery. This is probably a first step towards curtailing the mischievous possibilities of the additional requirement.

If adultery is proved, it has been held that the court should not withhold a decree nisi because it was not consulted about the financial terms agreed between the parties.[73]

Since the Civil Evidence Act 1968, s. 16(5) abolished the former privilege and required questions about adultery to be answered in proceedings instituted in consequence of adultery, interrogatories may be administered asking the direct question whether adultery has been committed or not,[74] and if asked, such questions must be answered. But the court has a discretion, and will not always allow interrogatories.[75]

A Practice Direction issued in 1973[76] provided that a signed statement by the respondent that he has committed adultery is admissible in evidence, the petitioner identifying the respondent's signature. Thus evidence from an inquiry agent is usually unnecessary, and where needed for some special reason, it should be given by affidavit. This demonstrates an endeavour to clear away some of the unsavoury aura formerly surrounding divorce proceedings. The tendency has of course been taken further by the provision[77] for all the evidence to be taken by affidavit from 1 December 1975, in uncontested cases where there are no minor or dependent children of the family, except where the petition is based on the respondent's unreasonable behaviour.

It has, however, been emphasised that if a respondent can prove the petitioner's adultery an answer to this effect may still be important even though no direct financial advantage to the respondent is likely[78] and *a fortiori* where

---

71. In *Carr (M)* v. *Carr (A.K.)* [1974] 1 W.L.R. 1534 it was held that the petitioner may rely on adultery committed after the spouses separated, although this was only the continuance of a former relationship. But see *Biggs* v. *Biggs and Wheatley* [1976] 2 W.L.R. 942: cohabitation for more than six months after decree nisi was held to bar decree absolute.
72. *Carr* v. *Carr (supra)* and *Cleary* v. *Cleary* [1974] 1 W.L.R. 73 C.A. confirming *Goodrich* v. *Goodrich* [1971] 1 W.L.R. 1142 and overruling *Roper* v. *Roper* [1972] 1 W.L.R. 1314, Faulks J.
73. *Thomas* v. *Thomas, The Times* 13.12.72 C.A.
74. *Nast* v. *Nast* [1972] Fam. 142 C.A. (a petition for leave to appeal to House of Lords was dismissed).
75. As in *C.* v. *C. (Divorce: Interrogatories)* [1973] 1 W.L.R. 568, where the husband, a pensioner without means, accused his wife of adultery with three men. The Court refused to allow the wife to answer in the absence of the men concerned.
76. *Practice Direction (Divorce: Proof of Adultery) (No. 2)* [1973] 1 W.L.R. 1052.
77. S.I. 1359 of 1975 and *Practice Direction (Matrimonial Causes: Special Procedure Extension)* [1975] 1 W.L.R. 1594, and see n. 165 *post*.
78. *Huxford* v. *Huxford* [1972] 1 W.L.R. 210; costs were involved there.

it might be directly material to the financial provision (or 'ancillary relief') to be made.[79]

(ii) UNREASONABLE BEHAVIOUR

It is for the court to decide whether the respondent's behaviour is such that the petitioner cannot reasonably be expected to live with her or him and that the marriage has broken down irretrievably. In *Katz* v. *Katz*[80] and *Ash* v. *Ash*[81] it was found that the marriage had irretrievably broken down. In *Richards* v. *Richards*[82] the wife's petition was dismissed because although the marriage had irretrievably broken down, she had failed to show that she could not reasonably be expected to live with the husband. A humane decision in *Bradley* v. *Bradley*[83] held that even though a poor woman was, despite separation orders for persistent cruelty, living with her husband from fear of violence if she refused sexual intercourse, and lack of any place to go with her nine children other than the council house in their joint names, it did not follow that she could reasonably be expected to continue living with him, nor make the continuance of such a situation reasonable. The county court judge's refusal to entertain the wife's petition was overruled, and it was sent back for a full hearing.

The Act provides in s. 2(3) that cohabitation for a period or periods (not exceeding a total of six months) after the behaviour complained of shall not preclude divorce.

The question of what behaviour makes it unreasonable to expect one party to continue living with the other is of course a matter of judgement on which differing views must be expected. On the one hand, a husband's petition was dismissed in *Pheasant* v. *Pheasant*[84] because he was found egocentric and obsessed with his grievances, whilst nothing in his wife's behaviour amounted to a breach of the obligations of marriage. The decision was not followed in *Livingstone-Stallard* v. *Livingstone-Stallard*,[85] where it was found unreasonable to expect the wife to continue living with a husband who was 'self-opinionated, didactic and critical', and whose approach was 'to educate the wife to conform entirely to his standards'. Dunn J. in that case also thought it preferable not to

---

79. *Rogers* v. *Rogers* [1974] 1 W.L.R. 709 C.A., and *Mustafa* v. *Mustafa* [1975] 1 W.L.R. 1277, where a contested suit was heard because of the importance of other relief.
80. [1972] 1 W.L.R. 955, Baker P. The respondent was mentally ill.
81. [1972] Fam. 135; The conduct admitted consisted of violence and drunkenness by the respondent who submitted that nevertheless the marriage had not broken down irretrievably. On the need for the respondent in a defended case to answer the charges made with sufficient particularity see *Andrews* v. *Andrews* [1974] 3 All E.R. 643 per Finer J.
82. [1972] 1 W.L.R. 1073, Rees J.
83. [1973] 1 W.L.R. 1291 C.A., dissenting on p. 1294 at C from the suggestion in *Katz* v. *Katz supra*, n. 80 at [1972] 1 W.L.R. 955, 961, that the continuance of cohabitation suggested it was not unreasonable. See also Chapter III note 112. *Carew-Hunt* v. *Carew-Hunt*, *The Times* 18.6.72 was another case in which the wife's petition was granted under this head.
84. [1972] Fam. 202.
85. [1974] Fam. 47. See especially p. 54C – F.

import into the new law notions of constructive desertion from the pre-1971 law as had been done in *Pheasant* v. *Pheasant*, or try to analyse the gravity of the conduct complained of. In *O'Neill* v. *O'Neill*[86] the county court judge found a wife's complaints trivial where the husband, who was without building experience, decided to improve the flat into which they had recently moved. The judge dismissed her petition on the ground that she was really complaining about her husband's character, which she was not entitled to do, since they had taken each other 'for better for worse'. The Court of Appeal did not agree and granted the wife a decree nisi, pointing out[87] that 'These matters are to be judged not by the language of the Book of Common Prayer but by the language of the statute'.[88]

There has also been difficulty about the interpretation of the word 'behaviour', particularly where the party whose conduct is complained of is mentally affected. Thus a county court judge held in *Smith* v. *Smith*[89] that pre-senile dementia in the wife, who at the time of the hearing was leading a 'cabbage-like' existence, quite unable to look after herself or make conversation and needing to be fed, did not constitute 'behaviour', since the wife's actions were involuntary and caused by the disease. Rees J., dissented from the decision in *Thurlow* v. *Thurlow*.[90] Here the wife had since infancy suffered from epilepsy, requiring hospital in-patient treatment from time to time, and her condition had deteriorated. All hope for a reversal had gone and she required continuing institutional care. The husband's petition for divorce was granted, the court holding that unreasonable behaviour could be constituted by negative behaviour and by behaviour caused by mental or physical illness. The husband's powers of endurance were exhausted and his health endangered. It is surely true that the institution of marriage is not served by compelling an unwilling partner to remain bound to one incapable of living outside an institution or of any reasonable communication, far less of a shared life.

In the leading case of *Wachtel* v. *Wachtel*[91] the husband petitioned for divorce on the ground of the wife's adultery but failed to satisfy the court that it had been committed. It was held at first instance, (and on this point there was no appeal,) that in such circumstances the court could find that, although adultery was not proved, the respondent had behaved in such a way that the petitioner could not reasonably be expected to live with the respondent. On the wife's answer, the court also found that the husband had behaved intolerably. As the marriage had broken down irretrievably, both spouses were granted a divorce based on the unreasonable behaviour of the other.

---

86. [1975] 1 W.L.R. 1118 C.A.
87. Ibid. per Cairns L.J. at 1121G.
88. Disputing paternity of the children without evidence was itself held good ground for divorce: Ibid. and per Roskill L.J. at p. 1125G of the husband's letter: 'to describe it as wicked is an understatement'.
89. *The Times* 15.12.73.
90. [1976] Fam. 32.
91. [1973] Fam. 72 C.A.

(iii) DESERTION CONTINUING FOR TWO YEARS IMMEDIATELY PRECEDING PRESENTATION OF THE PETITION

The continuous duration of desertion has been reduced from three years before 1971 to two years after 1970, but there has been no change in the legal content of desertion, which therefore still requires both the factum of separation without the consent of the party deserted and without good cause, and the *animus deserendi*, the intention to terminate the matrimonial consortium.[92] Desertion, it has been said and constantly repeated, is 'not the withdrawal from a place but from a state of things'.[93] Here again, although the statute still specifies in s. 1(2)(c) that the desertion must have been 'for a continuous period of at least two years immediately preceding the presentation of the petition', these words are heavily qualified by s. 2(5), which provides that in considering whether the period for which the respondent has deserted the petitioner 'has been continuous, no account shall be taken of any one period (not exceeding six months) or of any two or more periods (not exceeding six months in all) during which the parties resumed living with each other, but no period during which the parties lived with each other shall count as part of the period of desertion . . .' By s. 2(4), provided there was initially the necessary intention to abandon the other spouse, the fact that the deserter loses capacity to continue that intention does not terminate the desertion if the evidence before the court is such that, had the deserter not been so incapable, the court would have inferred that his desertion continued.

Now that unreasonable behaviour has supplanted cruelty as a fact that may lead to irretrievable breakdown of the marriage and hence permit divorce, the question arises how far it overlaps with or has displaced the former doctrine of constructive desertion which was, before 1971, defined as 'such grave and weighty matters as rendered the continuance of cohabitation virtually impossible'.[94] The difference between the two fact situations is a delay of two years in applying for divorce. The Court of Appeal held in *Stringfellow* v. *Stringfellow*[95] that unreasonable behaviour in s. 1(2)(b) of the Act means conduct other than desertion or behaviour leading up to desertion. Accordingly, where the petitioner's allegations were of conduct amounting to desertion and leading to desertion, her petition based on unreasonable behaviour had rightly been dismissed.

---

92. *Pulford* v. *Pulford* [1923] P. 18.
93. Ibid. at p. 21 per Sir Henry Duke P.
94. *Young* v. *Young* [1964] P. 152, *Timmins* v. *Timmins* [1953] 1 W.L.R. 757 C.A. In *Lang* v. *Lang* [1955] A.C. 402 P.C. the test applied was that: 'the appellant must have known that what he was doing would necessitate her withdrawal if she acted as any reasonable creature would'. Ibid. p. 430.
95. [1976] 1 W.L.R. 645 C.A. The court referred to its previous decision in *Evans* v. *Evans* 10 February 1976, Bar Library Transcript No. 56 of 1976, but no reference seems to have been made to the decision of Stirling J. in *Morgan* v. *Morgan The Times* 24.2.73, that the wife's sale of the matrimonial home she owned and her eviction of the husband from it amounted to constructive desertion and not to unreasonable behaviour.

(iv) TWO YEARS' SEPARATION AND THE RESPONDENT'S CONSENT TO A DIVORCE DECREE

Living apart for the purpose of both the two years' and five years' separation is defined in s. 2(6) as not living with each other in the same household.[96] By s. 2(5) the resumption of cohabitation for one or more periods not exceeding six months may be disregarded. It has been held[97] that not only separation of the parties, but also an intention never to return and ceasing to recognise the marriage as subsisting must be shown.

By s. 2(7), Rules of Court provide[98] that before consenting to a decree, the respondent shall be given such information as will enable him to understand the consequences to him of his consent and the steps which he must take to indicate that he consents to the grant of a decree. Section 10(1) of the Act provides that the respondent may apply at any time before the decree is made absolute and the court may rescind it if the petitioner has misled the respondent on any material fact.[99]

The respondent must actively consent to the divorce; in *McGill* v. *Robson*[100] the petition was adjourned until the consent of the husband was obtained from him in Rhodesia, and a petition has since been dismissed where only negative lack of objection could be shown.[101] But consent may be given by a person receiving mental treatment provided he can appreciate its meaning and results.[102]

It has also been held[103] that the respondent may consent to the divorce on condition, for example, that no order for costs will be made. In *Beales* v. *Beales*[103] the petitioner was a legally aided wife, so that the husband's condition to this effect meant that the legal aid fund and not the husband would be responsible for her costs. On the other hand the respondent's consent does not imply that no costs will be payable.[104] Spouses should not both launch cross-pleas for divorce on the ground of two years' separation with the consent of the other.[105]

---

96. This confirms the decision in *Mouncer* v. *Mouncer* [1972] 1 W.L.R. 321. The test was originally laid down in *Jackson* v. *Jackson* [1924] P. 19 and *Hopes* v. *Hopes* [1949] P. 277, 235. See *Fuller* v. *Fuller* [1973] 1 W.L.R. 730 C.A., a five years' separation case where the wife, having left the husband to cohabit with *X*, subsequently took the husband as a lodger in the house where she was living with *X*. It was held that the husband and wife were not 'living with each other as one household', since the wife was throughout cohabiting with *X*. For the computation of time see *Warr* v. *Warr* [1975] Fam. 25.
97. *Santos* v. *Santos* [1972] Fam. 247 C.A. The case was sent for re-hearing before a High Court judge because the provision now embodied in s. 2(5) of the Matrimonial Causes Act 1973 had not been considered.
98. Rule 16.
99. See *Parkes* v. *Parkes* [1971] 1 W.L.R. 1481 C.A.
100. [1972] 1 W.L.R. 237.
101. *Matcham* v. *Matcham, The Times* 30.6.76.
102. *Mason* v. *Mason* [1972] Fam. 302.
103. *Beales* v. *Beales* [1972] Fam. 210.
104. *Hymns* v. *Hymns (Practice Note)* [1971] 1 W.L.R. 1474.
105. *Darvill* v. *Darvill, The Times* 15.2.73, extended to five years' separation in *Parsons* v. *Parsons* [1975] 1 W.L.R. 1272; the respondent was, however, allowed to amend his answer to deny additional allegations.

The provisions in section 10(2)(3) and (4) of the Act apply after a decree *nisi* has been granted on the basis either of two years' separation and the respondent's consent, or of five years' separation, and there has been no finding that other facts exist from which the court might infer that the marriage has broken down irretrievably. On an application by the respondent after decree *nisi* for consideration of his (which usually means her) financial position after the divorce, the court shall consider all the circumstances, including the future prospects of the respondent should the petitioner die first, and not make the decree absolute unless satisfied either that the petitioner should not be required to make any financial provision for the respondent, or that the financial provision made is reasonable and fair or the best that can be made in the circumstances, or that circumstances make it desirable that the decree should be made absolute without delay. In this latter case the court must have obtained a satisfactory undertaking from the petitioner that he will make financial provision for the respondent which it has approved.[106]

In *West* v. *West*[107] Brandon J. adjourned a hearing on a husband's petition for divorce until he disclosed his financial situation, and the Court of Appeal said in *Grigson* v. *Grigson*[108] that, when this provision is invoked, the husband must outline his proposals for financial provision for his wife after the divorce. It is not sufficient that he undertakes to make some unspecified provision at some future date. The principal asset in *Wilson* v. *Wilson*[109] was the former matrimonial home worth about £17,000, held in the husband's name, and the Court of Appeal ordered that his decree should not be made absolute until the house had been sold and half the proceeds paid to the wife. Otherwise the husband could emigrate with the proceeds. It has been decided[110] however, that where by inadvertance the terms of the statute were not complied with and a decree nisi was made absolute without the judicial consideration of her financial position for which the wife had applied, the decree absolute so made was voidable and not void, and it was pronounced valid.

(v) FIVE YEARS' SEPARATION

In addition to the safeguards applying to divorce on separation either for two years with the respondent's consent or for five years, there is another defence available only after five years' separation. This is brought into action if the respondent opposes the grant of the decree on the ground that the dissolution of the marriage would result in grave financial or other hardship to him (which in all cases so far reported means to her) and that it would in all the circumstances

---

106. See *Rule* v. *Rule* [1972] 1 W.L.R. 218.
107. *The Times* 16.11.73.
108. *The Times* 6.11.73 C.A. The decision was reached on the Divorce Reform Act 1969. s. 6, now s. 10 of the Matrimonial Causes Act 1973.
109. [1973] 1 W.L.R. 555 C.A.
110. *Wright* v. *Wright* [1976] Fam. 114. See also the comments of Ormrod L.J. in *Cumbers* v. *Cumbers* [1974] 1 W.L.R. 1331, 1334H–1335A, casting doubt on the provisions.

be wrong to dissolve the marriage.[111] If the court finds that the petitioner is entitled to rely on the fact of five years' separation and makes no such finding as to any other fact from which irretrievable breakdown might be deduced, it must then 'consider all the circumstances, including the conduct of the parties to the marriage and the interests of those parties and of any children or other persons concerned, and if of opinion that the dissolution of the marriage will result in grave financial or other hardship to the respondent and that it would in all the circumstances be wrong to dissolve the marriage it shall dismiss the petition'.

(a) Grave financial hardship. Many of the cases in which this plea has been raised concerned the loss by divorce of the wife's rights under her husband's occupational pension scheme. *Julian* v. *Julian*[112] was reported as the first case in which a decree was refused because of financial hardship to the wife.[113] The husband, a retired assistant chief constable of police, had no means from which to compensate her for the loss of her pension, and could not therefore divorce her. In *Parker* v. *Parker*[114] on the other hand, the husband was in a position to compensate his wife for her loss of the police pension should she survive him, and obtained his decree. Other cases in which decrees were granted despite pleas of hardship by wives include *Talbot* v. *Talbot*,[115] *Mathias* v. *Mathias*,[116] and *Collins* v. *Collins*.[117] The Court of Appeal held[118] in *Brickell* v. *Brickell*[119] that 'conduct of the parties' in s. 5(2) of the Act includes but is not confined to matrimonial misconduct, and dissolved the marriage despite the fact that the wife would suffer financial hardship. She was in desertion and had behaved badly by disrupting the husband's business and causing distress to his elderly patients. The court pointed out that, despite this conduct, the wife was not precluded from financial provision after divorce, and could still invoke the provisions of s. 10 of the Act to obtain proper financial provision after decree *nisi* and before decree absolute.

Lower in the socio-economic scale, the Court of Appeal in *Reiterbund* v. *Reiterbund*[120] upheld Finer J.'s refusal to follow *Dorrell* v. *Dorrell*.[121] Here the wife was living on supplementary benefit of £7·75 a week, whilst the disabled husband was living on an invalidity benefit of £8·25 a week. The wife contended that if the husband died before she had reached the age of 60 she would lose her widow's pension. This was held not to amount to financial

---

111. Matrimonial Causes Act 1973, s. 5.
112. *The Times* 4.10.72.
113. But in *Dorrell* v. *Dorrell* [1972] 1 W.L.R. 1087 Sir G. Baker P. adjourned the suit to enable the husband to make proposals for financial provision for the wife.
114. [1972] Fam. 116.
115. *The Times* 19.10.71.
116. [1972] Fam. 287 C.A.
117. [1972] 1 W.L.R. 689 C.A. The wife was denied leave to defend out of time.
118. Overruling *Dorrell* v. *Dorrell* [1972] 1 W.L.R. 1087; and see n. 121 *post*.
119. [1974] Fam. 31 C.A.
120. [1975] Fam. 99 C.A.
121. [1972] 1 W.L.R. 1087, and see n. 119 *supra*.

hardship, since any pension she might receive would simply reduce her supplementary benefit. On a different point, it was held in *Burvill* v. *Burvill*[122] that the fact that the wife, who was earning £7 per week, would have to pay £1·67 per week for the next three years for national health insurance instead of 4p per week industrial injury insurance, before she could receive the State retirement pension, did not amount to grave financial hardship.

(b) Grave other hardship. So far this defence has not been pleaded by anybody living in England or Wales, and the plea had not been raised before 1973 in any reported case. However, the Court of Appeal allowed a Hindu woman living in India an adjournment to enable her to invoke this head of s. 5, on her plea that being divorced would make her a social outcast in India[123] But where a Hindu woman raised the defence in *Parghi* v. *Parghi*[124] her husband was granted his decree because the woman concerned moved in highly-educated circles in sophisticated Bombay, and would not be subject to the discrimination practised by less educated people living in more remote parts of India. Similarly, in *Rukat* v. *Rukat*[125] where the husband of Polish origin and his wife of Sicilian origin had been separated for twenty-five years, the Court of Appeal held that the adjective 'grave' applied to 'other hardship' as well as to 'financial hardship', and said that even if, as the wife alleged, she were to be ostracised in Sicily when she became a divorced woman, that did not amount to grave hardship.

Even so short a summary of cases coming before the courts in less than five years seems eloquent testimony to the fact that the overwhelming effect of divorce is financial hardship for the wife and minor children where they exist. It is not so much that 'divorce has become less about divorce and more about money'.[126] It is much more that divorce has always involved money and property, but that until recently the law camouflaged the real issues and compelled petitioners and respondents alike to indulge in shadow-boxing about such issues as sexual conduct, with which the church courts in earlier centuries had been so noticeably obsessed.

It was when much of the cost of such litigation began to fall for the first time on public funds under the Legal Aid Scheme that this obsessive litigation was effectively curtailed by granting legal aid only if contested allegations were not pursued,[127] and then progressively simplifying the procedure in undefended cases. The controversy concerning awards of costs or failure to award them is again testimony to the power of money and the passion it arouses. In *Chapman* v. *Chapman*[128] the Court of Appeal held that normally in the five-year separation situation no order for costs will be made. This

---

122. *The Times* 7.3.74.
123. *Banik* v. *Banik* [1973] 1 W.L.R. 860 C.A.
124. *The Times* 8.5.73.
125. [1975] Fam. 63 C.A.
126. Per Joseph Jackson Q.C. *Matrimonial Finance and Taxation*, p. v.
127. See, e.g. Finer J. in *Andrews* v. *Andrews* [1974] 3 All E.R. 643, at 645 *d–f*.
128. [1972] 1 W.L.R. 1544.

decision was attacked as providing not only divorce free of charge but in legally-aided cases at public expense. The principle was nevertheless extended by Latey J. to 'ancillary proceedings', viz. money, in *Wright* v. *Wright*.[129] On the other hand, where a legally-aided wife with a nil contribution had, over six days, raised numerous charges against her husband which were found to be totally false, an order for £5000 costs was made against the legal aid fund, and the husband was granted a decree based on her adultery and intolerable conduct, the court being satisfied that he was not the father of the child born to her in 1971.[130]

F. THE ROLE OF DIVORCE

It has been suggested[131] that a certain period of separation or estrangement, which would probably be for one year, might become the only ground for divorce in England, as the Family Law Act 1975 provides in Australia. The same writer suggests that the adjustive jurisdiction should not be limited to those who have been validly married according to law, but should be exercisable 'whenever parties to a relationship have been fulfilling roles equivalent to the marital roles'.[132]

It is hoped that before further experiments are made on these lines the legislature will wait to see the effect of recent changes in the divorce law in their own and other jurisdictions, and in particular their effect on the birth-rate, not only over the population as a whole, but in different strata of society. It will be interesting to see what effect, if any, the Family Law Act will have on the birth-rate in Australia. Many women may not consider giving birth to a child when their marital situation is at all times subject to twelve months' notice. Twelve months seems too short, and some evidence of real hardship would seem desirable before consideration is given to reducing the present periods of two years' and five years' separation respectively.

Moreover, there are some kinds of conduct of which the law is entitled to show its disapproval by releasing the other partner immediately from his or her obligations, Those who regard adultery or violence in this light are entitled to have their views considered. They are likely to be the same people who are primarily concerned with order and stability in their lives and those of their young children. They are interested in divorce only where it is less disruptive, to themselves and their children, than a continuance of the conduct of which they complain.

Our divorce courts inherited from the church courts an obsessive pre-occupation with sexual behaviour, and especially that of women. There are

---

129. [1973] 1 W.L.R. 1145.
130. *Stewart* v. *Stewart* [1974] 1 W.L.R. 877 C.A.
131. J. Eekelaar, 'The place of divorce in family law's new role', 38 *MLR* (1975) 241.
132. Unless 'marital roles' include the procreation of children, this would seem to bring homosexual relationships within the purview of the law. Clarification seems desirable. Would it not also be necessary to provide a minimum time for which the 'marital roles' should have been discharged?

practitioners specialising in 'breaking down' women in the witness box by cross-examination designed to create the impression that they are of loose moral character. The courts have rightly tried to limit this obsession, but in doing so have tended to speak of 'conduct' when what they mean is 'sexual conduct particularly by women'. In both *Wachtel* v. *Wachtel*[133] and *Trippas* v. *Trippas*[134] counsel overstressed the sexual behaviour of the woman concerned when it was of little relevance to what had to be decided. It would have been otherwise if the woman concerned had attacked her husband with a razor and injured him so that he could not continue with his profession, or habitually indulged in drugs or alcohol so that she was a menace to all with whom she came into contact.

G. NO DIVORCE WITHIN THREE YEARS OF WEDDING

By s. 3 of the Matrimonial Causes Act, no petition for divorce may be presented within three years of the date of the marriage unless application is first made to a judge, who may allow the petition on the ground that the case is one of exceptional hardship suffered by the petitioner or of exceptional depravity on the part of the respondent; 'but in determining the application the judge shall have regard to the interests of any child of the family and to the question whether there is reasonable probability of a reconciliation between the parties during the' three years.[135] If, on hearing the substantive petition, the court considers that leave to present it was obtained by misrepresentation or concealment of the nature of the case, it may either dismiss the petition,[136] or grant a decree nisi with a direction that it shall not be made absolute within the three years. The courts have wisely refrained from attempting to delineate the precise meaning of the word 'exceptional' in this context, although Denning L.J. (then) came near to doing so, under the pre-1971 law, in *Bowman* v. *Bowman*.[137] The three-year restriction was imposed in 1937, when grounds for divorce other than adultery were first introduced, and was at one time heavily criticised. These criticisms died away, but have recently been revived. It is hoped that the restriction will be retained, and that the exceptions to

---

133. [1973] Fam. 72 C.A.
134. [1973] Fam. 134 C.A.
135. Matrimonial Causes Act 1973 Section 3(2). Petitions may be presented in the normal way after 3 years of marriage based on events occurring within the 3 years: s. 3(4).
136. One of the two grounds on which a decree may be refused: *ante* n. 69. That leave must be granted assuming the facts alleged are true would seem obvious, but decisions may be cited in support.
137. [1949] P. 352 C.A. Some examples of exceptional depravity there advanced have given way before experience: e.g. in *Blackwell* v. *Blackwell, The Times* 13.11.73 C.A., the husband's adultery two months after the wedding did not constitute exceptional depravity in him or exceptional hardship to the wife who had cohabited with him for five years before the wedding. It was also suggested in *Bowman* v. *Bowman* that the petitioner should have sought reconciliation before most, if not all, applications. It is thought that the contrary is the case, and that in cases of exceptional depravity reconciliation should not be promoted.

it will not be too widely interpreted.[138] It is difficult to believe that the falling birth-rate in a country such as Hungary is not connected with the fact that parties who marry in April may obtain their divorce by mutual consent in the following September.[139] The open-ended exceptions to the two-year restriction introduced in Australia by the Family Law Act 1975 s. 14(6)[140] seem less satisfactory than the provisions under s. 3 of the English Act.

H. PROCEDURE IN DIVORCE COURTS

By s. 1(5) of the Act, every decree of divorce shall in the first instance be a decree *nisi*, and it may be followed by decree absolute, not to be declared less than six months after decree *nisi* unless a shorter period is fixed by general order of the High Court. The shorter period of six weeks was substituted from 1 September 1972;[141] a practice note[142] has pointed out that a special order further reducing the period between decree *nisi* and decree absolute was not generally desirable.[143] Until the decree absolute is pronounced, the parties remain husband and wife and are not free to marry another. By s. 15 of the Act, s. 1(5) applies in relation to proceedings for nullity of marriage. There is no decree *nisi* for judicial separation.

The general form of petition is in Form 2 of the Matrimonial Causes Rules 1973,[144] clause 4 of which requires the petitioner to state the number of children of the family now living; give the full name (including surname) of each, the date of birth if under 18, and state whether any child over 16 but under 18 years of age is receiving educational instruction or undergoing training. A wife petitioner must also give the name and date of birth of any other child born to her during the marriage. By s. 41 of the Act, the

---

138. Extreme physical violence should of course be an exception as in *McGibbon* v. *McGibbon* [1973] Fam. 170; unsuspected promiscuity or perversion should also fall within the exception.
139. I saw such a divorce in 1973.
140. (*a*) that the parties have considered a reconciliation with the assistance of a marriage counsellor, an approved marriage counselling organisation or some other suitable person or organisation nominated by the Director of Counselling and Welfare; or (*b*) that there are special circumstances by reason of which the hearing should proceed.
141. Matrimonial Causes (Decree Absolute) General Order dated 20 July 1972, as amended by the Matrimonial Causes (Decree Absolute) General Order 1973; published in the S.I.s (1972) Part II, s. 2, p. 4109 and (1973) Part I, s. 2, p. 2634 respectively.
142. *Practice Note* (*Divorce: Decree Absolute*) [1972] 1 W.L.R. 1261.
143. It may preclude defences on the five years' separation divorce, and the time for appeal may not have expired. Notice of any application for expedition of decree absolute must be given to all parties under Rules 65 and 66 of the Matrimonial Causes Rules. *Torok* v. *Torok* [1973] 1 W.L.R. 1066 exemplifies a case in which expedition was not only desirable, but imperative. *Dryden* v. *Dryden* [1973] Fam. 217, on the other hand, shows the hardship that can be caused by unnecessary expedition accompanied by both human and bureaucratic error.
144. S.I. No. 2016 of 1973, as amended by Nos. 1383 and 2168 of 1974, No. 1359 of 1975 and No. 607 of 1976, hereafter 'the Rules'.

Court shall not make absolute a decree of divorce or nullity, or grant a decree of judicial separation, unless it has first by order declared that it is satisfied either (*a*) that there are no children of the family, or (*b*) that the only such children are named in the order and that either (i) arrangements for the welfare of each such child have been made and are satisfactory or the best that can be devised in the circumstances; or (ii) it is impracticable for the parties before the court to make any such arrangements; or (*c*) that the court is unable to make any of the foregoing declarations; but it has obtained a satisfactory undertaking from the parties to bring the arrangements for the children before it within a specified time, and that circumstances make it desirable for the decree to be made absolute or granted without delay. By s. 41(3), if the declaration was made its validity cannot afterwards be challenged on the ground that the prescribed conditions were not met, but any decree absolute of divorce or nullity or any grant of judicial separation made without an order containing one of the above declarations is void. This is draconian since if, in reliance on the decree absolute, one or both of the parties should remarry, the second marriage is void. The hardship to the other party to the second marriage may be grave, and that party may be innocent and not even aware of the previous marriage. For these reasons, powerful judicial voices have contended that the decree absolute should be voidable only, and not be avoided to defeat the claims of innocent third parties.[145] The present rule that if no declaration is made the decree absolute is void, but that if made, its validity cannot later be questioned, seems an acceptable compromise. Strong measures are necessary to sharpen the memories of divorcing parents as regards their children.[146]

The general rule that details of all children of the family shall be given on the divorce petition is perhaps the most important result of the Royal Commission on Marriage and Divorce that sat from 1951 to 1955.[147] The effect of forcing adults obsessed with their marital problems to clarify at the earliest possible moment their intentions in regard to the minor children, who will probably be more profoundly affected than any adult, is wholly beneficial.

Before the Matrimonial Causes Act 1965 the provisions in the Matrimonial Causes Acts relating to children were grotesquely classified under the heading of 'ancillary relief'.[148] Although the statute then discarded this classification of questions concerning minor children, it has not disappeared completely.[149]

---

145. Sir J. Simon P. (as he then was) in *F.* v. *F.* [1971] P. 1, and *P.* v. *P. and J.* [1971] P. 217 C.A. See also *B.* v. *B.* (*Practice Note*) [1961] 1 W.L.R. 856 and the discussion by Rees J. in *Wright* v. *Wright* [1976] Fam. 114, 121–124D.
146. The wife who has given birth or is about to give birth during the marriage to a child by a man other than her husband is especially prone to amnesia on the subject: see, e.g. *N.* v. *N.* [1964] 108 S.J. 99, *F.* v. *F.* [1971] P. 1.
147. Its *Report*, Cmd 9678, was published in 1956.
148. Derivation: from *ancilla*, a female house-slave or maidservant.
149. For example, Rule 49 is headed: 'Right to be heard on ancillary questions', (*a*) to (*c*) of which refer to custody, care or supervision of and access to children. In the Recognition of Divorces and Legal Separations Act 1971, s. 8(3), there is reference to 'maintenance,

The principal rules relating to children are now classified as such.[150] There are complaints that the courts too readily accept at their face value the parties' descriptions of the arrangements made for the children, but viable alternatives are neither numerous nor apparent. It is probably for this reason, rather than exploded myths about the so-called 'blood tie', that the law must leave the upbringing of minor children to their physical parents in all but the grossest cases of abuse or neglect. The welfare of minor children still suffers, however, from being considered only after the relief to be granted to their parents or guardians has been decided.

By s. 26 of the Act, where a petition for divorce, nullity of marriage or judicial separation has been presented, proceedings for maintenance pending suit, for a financial provision order, or for a property adjustment order,[151] may be begun. But such applications should normally be included in the petition or answer if one is filed, and may only be presented later by leave of the court, or if the parties are agreed upon their terms. All such proceedings are still described as being for 'ancillary relief'. It is part of the legacy from the church courts before 1857 that the question of divorce and to a lesser extent nullity, is considered to be the substantive question in issue, sometimes justfied as involving a question of status. This overlooks the fact that the status of children is in no way affected by the divorce of their parents but financial hardship for them is a usual result. There has been belated recognition by some High Court judges in recent years that orders dealing with maintenance, financial provision or property are often the really substantial matters at issue between the parties,[152] but officially they are still classified as 'ancillary proceedings'. However, in case of wilful neglect to maintain dependants, an application for financial provision[153] is independent of any petition for divorce, nullity or judicial separation.

The Rules provide that, except for the special procedure considered later, the petition shall be heard by a judge,[154] and that applications for ancillary relief shall, with one exception, be heard and the order made by a registrar.[155] Thus only after the judge has already granted the decree *nisi* of divorce

---

custody or other ancillary order made in' proceedings abroad for divorce or judicial separation.

150. Rules 92–7, viz. following the rules about the 'substantive' cause between the spouses.

151. Respectively under ss 22, 23 and 24 of the Act, ss 23 and 24 being subject to the provisions of ss 21, 25 and 28–33. Under s. 23(2) the jurisdiction to order financial provision for children is wider than that to order it for a spouse.

152. *Porter* v. *Porter* [1969] 1 W.L.R. 1155 C.A., probably marks the watershed, with Sachs L.J. referring to some of the views of the county court judges on maintenance as 'decades if not generations out of date': Ibid. 1158H. See also 1160 D. and *Tumath* v. *Tumath* [1970] P. 78, 94C, per Sir G. Willmer.

153. Under s. 27 of the Act. *Gray* v. *Gray* [1976] 3 W.L.R. 181 confirms that this jurisdiction is merely an extension of that of magistrates, and therefore conditional on the applicant not having committed adultery.

154. Rule 43.

155. Rules 77–9. The exception is an application under s. 37 of the Act for the court to restrain intended dispositions or set aside dispositions already made with the intention of defeating or avoiding a claim for financial relief.

are the crucial questions about finance and property heard by a registrar in Chambers. Private hearings are of course essential when the details of the parties' income and obligations are under examination, but their dangers are obvious. No decisions below the level of the High Court are reported, and since the decisions of divorce county court judges at first instance are neither binding nor persuasive in future cases, nor even reported, it cannot be expected that those of the county court registrars will be. There have been suggestions that registrars be required to make a return showing the kinds of financial provision they have ordered and the financial and marital circumstances of the parties, but so far no action has resulted. At present only if there is an appeal from the registrar to a county court judge and then to the Court of Appeal is a report or any other form of accurate publicity probable. Hence the need for the superior courts to lay down guidelines and have them reported, as was done by the Court of Appeal in *Wachtel* v. *Wachtel*.[156] Unfortunate as the guidelines in that case may be,[157] the report ensured that those interested would know the kind of order likely to be upheld by the superior courts, and be able to judge whether a registrar's decision should be appealed.

Injunctions are another form of ancillary relief which have recently attracted increased attention. The power of the divorce county courts to grant them arises from the County Courts Act 1959, s. 74[158] which permits any county court to grant relief redress or remedies 'as regards any cause of action within its jurisdiction' as ought to be granted in like case by the High Court. It has been held[159] that the High Court's power[160] to grant injunctions is limited to matters ancillary to and comprised within the scope of the substantive relief sought in the proceedings, and that injunctions will be granted only to support a legal right[161] or for the welfare of children.[162] Unless there is some connected substantive cause of action, therefore, no injunction can be granted,[163]and when

---

156. [1973] Fam. 72 C.A.
157. They are discussed in Chapter VII. There was a great gulf between what the court said and what it did, and considerable differences between things said.
158. As amended by the Administration of Justice Act 1969, ss 6 and 35(2) and Sched. 2; and the Courts Act 1971, s. 45(6). See also *Practice Direction* (*Petition for Declaration*) [1971] 1 W.L.R. 29 or [1970] 3 All E.R. 1024.
159. *Des Salles d'Epinoix* v. *Des Salles d'Epinoix* [1967] 1 W.L.R. 554. See also *McGibbon* v. *McGibbon* [1973] Fam. 170.
160. Under the Supreme Court of Judicature (Consolidation) Act 1925, s. 45.
161. *Montgomery* v. *Montgomery* [1965] P. 46; *Des Salles d'Epinoix*, *supra* n. 159.
162. *Adams* v. *Adams* [1965] 109 Sol. Jo. 899; *Gurasz* v. *Gurasz* [1970] P. 11 C.A. and *Stewart* v. *Stewart* [1973] Fam. 21.
163. By contrast, the Australian Family Law Act 1975, s. 114 gives the courts power in matrimonial causes (which include child custody and ancillary proceedings and, by s. 4(1)(e), proceedings for an order or injunction in circumstances arising out of a marital relationship) to 'make such order or grant such injunction as it thinks proper with respect to the matter to which the proceedings relate, including an injunction for the personal protection of a party to the marriage or of a child of the marriage or for the protection of the marital relationship or in relation to the property of a party to the marriage or relating to the use or occupancy of the matrimonial home', and in other proceedings the court may grant an injunction . . . 'in any case in which it appears to the court to be just or convenient to do so . . .'

granted it can rarely be enforced with sufficient speed in cases of violence between husband and wife.[164]

As from 1 December 1973 a totally new procedure was introduced, and extended from 1 December 1975.[165] Until December 1975 it applied only where the sole fact alleged as showing that the marriage had broken down irretrievably was as under s. 1(2)(d) of the Act, viz. that the parties had lived apart continuously for at least two years immediately preceding the presentation of the petition, and the respondent consented to the grant of a decree. From December 1975, however, the special procedure has been extended to undefended petitions based on adultery or two years' desertion or five years' separation. There must be no children of the family under 16 years of age, or minor children undergoing full-time education or training. In such cases there need be no hearing of the petition in court; all the evidence may be supplied by affidavit. If the registrar certifies that he is satisfied that everything is in order, a day is fixed for the decree *nisi* to be pronounced in open court as one of a group, and the petitioner is not required to attend. If the financial terms have been agreed between the parties and a court order is required, the registrar may so certify. Application for an order may also be made after the decree, but if any substantial matter is involved, this would be, to say the least, unwise.[166]

J. JURISDICTION IN MATRIMONIAL CAUSES, CUSTODY OF CHILDREN AND ANCILLARY PROCEEDINGS

(i) DOMESTIC LAW

The Administration of Justice Act 1970[167] greatly clarified and simplified the jurisdiction of the High Court in matrimonial causes and connected matters by centering them all in the former Probate, Divorce and Admiralty Division, which was renamed the Family Division. This Division now has original jurisdiction:

(a) *as between husband and wife:* in matrimonial causes and matters arising out of or related to them; for decrees of presumption of death and dissolution of marriage; for proceedings under s. 17 of the Married

---

164. See Interim Report from the House of Commons Select Committee on *Violence in Marriage*, H.C. 553–i (1975) paras 45–52, recommending backing an injunction in cases of violence between spouses with a power of arrest, and notifying the police of all such injunctions. See now Domestic Violence and Matrimonial Proceedings Act 1976; and, for the magistrates' courts, the Bill included in Law Com. 77.
165. *Practice Direction (Matrimonial Causes: Special Procedure)* [1973] 1 W.L.R. 1442; *Practice Direction (Divorce Registry: Consent Summons)* [1974] 1 W.L.R. 937 and Rule 48, and *Practice Direction (Matrimonial Causes: Special Procedure Extension)* [1975] 1 W.L.R. 1594, and S.I. No. 1359 of 1975, and see *ante* n. 77.
166. The special procedure has led to a rash of lore on 'Do-it-yourself' divorces, likely to appeal only to the childless or ignorant and gullible.
167. Section 1 and Sched. 1.

Women's Property Act 1882[168] and the Matrimonial Homes Act 1967;[169] in applications for maintenance from the estate of a deceased spouse or former spouse;[170] or for alteration of the financial provision of separation and maintenance agreements either *inter vivos* or after the death of one party;[171]

(b) *in relation to children:* the Family Division has taken over from the Chancery Division of the High Court the prerogative jurisdiction in guardianship exercisable only in the High Court; from the Queen's Bench Division proceedings by way of *habeas corpus;* all questions coming before the High Court concerning custody, care, maintenance and supervision of and access to children under the Matrimonial Causes Act 1973 and the Guardianship of Minors Acts 1971 and 1973; adoption under the Adoption Act 1976.

Its appellate jurisdiction covers appeals from magistrates' courts under: the Matrimonial Proceedings (Magistrates' Courts) Act 1960, the Maintenance Orders Act 1958, or the enforcement of maintenance orders under the Maintenance Orders Act 1950, the Maintenance Orders (Reciprocal Enforcement) Act 1972, or the Attachment of Earnings Act 1971; the Guardianship of Minors Acts 1971 and 1973 and the Adoption Act; and on law by case stated in affiliation proceedings.

The inferior courts, however, were not affected by the Act of 1970. Thus the divorce county courts exercise jurisdiction in divorce, custody of children and ancillary matters under the Matrimonial Causes Act 1973, while the magistrates' courts may grant separation or maintenance orders and orders for the custody, maintenance and supervision of or access to children under the Matrimonial Proceedings (Magistrates' Courts) Act 1960. The other jurisdictions with regard to children are divided between the inferior courts as follows:

(i) Jurisdiction under the Guardianship of Minors Acts 1971 and 1973 is exercised by the county courts and the magistrates' courts.

(ii) In adoption under the consolidation Act of 1976 it is exercised by the county courts and the magistrates' courts.

(iii) In affiliation jurisdiction is in the magistrates' courts only.

(iv) In 'care' proceedings under the Children and Young Persons Acts 1933–69 and the Children Acts 1948–75 the juvenile courts only have jurisdiction.

(v) In prosecution of juvenile offenders under the Children and Young Persons Acts 1933–69 the juvenile courts only have jurisdiction.

Appeals under (v) on law by case stated lie to the Queen's Bench Division.

---

168. Determination of title to or possession of property in dispute between spouses; see Rules 104–6.

169. Right of occupation of a matrimonial home: Rule 107.

170. Under the Inheritance (Provision for Family and Dependants) Act 1975.

171. Under the Matrimonial Causes Act 1973, ss 34–6. In *Temple* v. *Temple* [1976] 1 W.L.R. 701 C.A., however, a wife was able to recover arrears of maintenance by summary judgement in the Queen's Bench Division.

On fact appeals under both (iv) and (v) lie to the Crown Courts under the Courts Act 1971, s. 8 and Scheds 1, 8 and 9.

(ii) PRIVATE INTERNATIONAL LAW

The Domicile and Matrimonial Proceedings Act 1973[172] allowed the domicile of a married women to be ascertained after 1973 in the same way as that of any other person of full capacity. This necessitated amendments to the basis of domicile, on which jurisdiction in matrimonial causes had been primarily founded. The Act therefore repealed and replaced those parts of the Matrimonial Causes Act 1973 concerned with jurisdiction.[173] The English High Court and a divorce county court now have jurisdiction[174] in proceedings for divorce, judicial separation, or nullity of marriage,[175] if and only if, either of the parties:

(*a*) is domiciled in England and Wales on the date when the proceedings are begun, or

(*b*) was habitually resident in England and Wales throughout the period of one year ending with that date.

For proceedings for presumption of death and dissolution of marriage, jurisdiction is based on the domicile or habitual one year's residence of the petitioner only.[176]

Once proceedings are pending in respect of which the court has jurisdiction as above, it acquires jurisdiction to entertain other proceedings in respect of the same marriage for divorce, judicial separation or nullity of marriage.[177]

Apart from the indignity and hardship of the law's former imposition of the domicile of her husband upon every wife irrespective of facts or intention, the whole concept of domicile in English law is now so technical that many people cannot know where they are domiciled until an English court tells them. Until the concept of domicile has been greatly simplified and clarified, the death of its exclusive authority in founding jurisdiction in matrimonial causes is a matter for celebration. Habitual residence was distinguished from ordinary residence in *Cruse* v. *Chittum*[178] and was said to indicate quality rather than duration of residence.

It is unfortunate that jurisdiction in judicial separation has been based on precisely the same grounds as in other matrimonial causes. This is not so much because judicial separation does not affect a change in status,[179] although that is the classic distinction. When matrimonial relief was available only to a tiny privileged elite, primarily concerned with the perpetuation of titles of honour and frequently with producing a male heir, status was all-important. It

---

172. See T. C. Hartley and I. G. F. Karsten, 37 *MLR* (1974) 179.
173. Viz. s. 19(2) and 19(5) and s. 46. The reference in s. 19(1) to subsect. (2) is also deleted.
174. Domicile and Matrimonial Proceedings Act 1973, s. 5.
175. *Ante*, Chapter II.
176. Domicile and Matrimonial Proceedings Act 1973, s. 5(4).
177. Ibid. s. 5(5).
178. [1974] 2 All E.R. 940, Lane J. See also Chapter II, n. 180.
179. See Hartley and Karsten, 37 *MLR* (1974) 184.

matters little today to the thousands of people who annually resort to the divorce county courts. The change in the basis of jurisdiction in judicial separation deprived a woman not only of her right to apply for judical separation when neither domiciled nor habitually resident here,[180] but to obtain remedies such as an injunction against violence, until the Domestic Violence and Matrimonial Proceedings Act 1976 came into operation.[181]

(iii) CONFLICTS OF JURISDICTION

Section 5(6) of the Domicile and Matrimonial Proceedings Act 1973 and Sched. 1 establishes the duty of every petitioner or of a respondent who is praying for relief, to furnish particulars of concurrent proceedings in another jurisdiction in respect of or capable of affecting the validity or subsistence of the same marriage. The English courts will be obliged to stay proceedings in England if such proceedings are continuing in a related jurisdiction in which either party was habitually resident for a year before both parties last resided together, and in which they were residing together when, or had last resided together before the proceedings were begun there. For these purposes a 'related jurisdiction' means Scotland, Northern Ireland, Jersey, Guernsey (including Alderney and Sark) and the Isle of Man. Possible conflicts of jurisdiction have been reduced by the enactment of the Divorce (Scotland) Act 1976, which from the beginning of 1977 will bring the Scottish divorce law closer to that applicable in England. In addition the English courts will have discretion to stay matrimonial proceedings in England where proceedings in respect of the same marriage, or capable of affecting its validity or subsistence, are continuing in another jurisdiction and the balance of fairness (including convenience) between the parties makes it appropriate for the proceedings in the other jurisdiction to be disposed of before further steps are taken in the English court.

In regard to applications to the court for financial provision only, where there has been wilful neglect to maintain dependants,[182] the basis of jurisdiction has been amended to apply where:

(a) the applicant or the respondent is domiciled in England and Wales on the date of the application; or

(b) the applicant has been habitually resident there throughout the period of one year ending with that date; or

(c) the respondent is resident there on that date.

When the English court has jurisdiction, English law will be applied.

Only brief reference is possible here to the general problem of conflicting jurisdictions and the conflict of laws, and reference should be made to specialist

---

180. In *Sim* v. *Sim* [1944] P. 87, jurisdiction was taken by the English courts at the suit of the wife when the parties were domiciled in Scotland and the wife was resident there, but the husband was resident in England. This would no longer be possible.

181. By s. 5(3) this must be by 1.4.77. The Act gives the county courts independent jurisdiction to grant injunctions.

182. Under the Matrimonial Causes Act 1973, s. 27.

works.[183] In the field of family law, it is undesirable that children should be considered legitimate in one jurisdiction and illegitimate in another, or that a husband and wife in one country should be considered strangers in another. A major complicating factor is that in many European countries the law of the nationality is regarded as governing such matters as capacity to marry, whereas in England the governing law has been the law of the domicile, now shared with the law of the country of habitual residence. The Recognition of Divorces and Legal Separations Act 1971 made major changes in the rules regarding recognition of decrees of divorce and judicial separation obtained overseas. The Act was passed to enable the United Kingdom to ratify the Hague Convention of 1968,[184] and came into operation at the beginning of 1972.[185] Briefly s. 1 provides that a decree granted under the law of any part of the British Isles shall be recognised throughout the United Kingdom. On the other hand s. 16 of the Act provides that throughout the British Isles, marriages may after 1973 be dissolved only by courts of law. The previous recognition of non-judicial divorces[186] in England is terminated. An anti-avoidance provision adds that, if non-judicial proceedings for dissolution of marriage are instituted overseas immediately after both parties had been habitually resident in the United Kingdom for one year, the proceedings will not be regarded as validly dissolving their marriage.

The validity of an overseas divorce or separation will be recognised in Great Britain if it was obtained by judicial or other proceedings,[187] and at the date of the institution of these proceedings either spouse was either (*a*) habitually resident in or (*b*) domiciled in[188] or (*c*) a national of that country. Recognition will, however, be withheld if the other spouse was not given reasonable notice of the proceedings or was in other ways denied reasonable opportunity to take part in them, or if recognition would manifestly be contrary to public policy. Any finding of fact, express or implied, on the basis of which jurisdiction was assumed in the overseas proceedings,[189] will be conclusive if both spouses took part in them, and in any other case will be

---

183. See Chapter II, n. 177.
184. But its terms are both simpler and wider than those of the Convention.
185. Section 10(5), except for s. 9, which empowered the government of Northern Ireland to enact similar legislation, and came into operation on 27 July 1971. The legislation followed the lines recommended by the Law Commission in Law Com. 34 (1970). See also I. G. F. Karsten, 35 *MLR* (1972) 299.
186. As by *gett for a Jewish divorce*: *Har-Shefi* v. *Har-Shefi (No. 2)* [1953] P. 220, or *talaq* for an Islamic divorce: *Reg.* v. *Registrar-General of Births, etc., ex parte Minhas*, [1976] 2 W.L.R. 473, confirms that *Qureshi* v. *Qureshi* [1972] Fam. 173, is no longer law. See also *Chaudhry* v. *Chaudhry* (Note) [1976] 1 W.L.R. 221 C.A.
187. The meaning of this phrase is far from clear, and there are other difficulties and gaps in the statute. See P. M. North, 'Recognition of extra-judicial divorces', 91 *LQR* (1975) 36 and addendum by A. J. E. Jaffrey, Ibid. p. 320.
188. Applicable only to a country the law of which grounds jurisdiction on domicile, as for example, the United States, where domicile is in a particular State. By s. 3(2) of the Act, the reference to habitual residence includes a reference to domicile in relation to such a country.
189. That is, as to domicile, residence or nationality of the parties. As to nationality, see *Torok* v. *Torok* [1973] 1 W.L.R. 1066, 1069.

sufficient proof unless the contrary is shown. The Act does not, however, require recognition in Great Britain of any finding of fault made in the proceedings overseas, or of any maintenance, custody or other ancillary order made in any such proceedings. By s. 6 of the Act[190] recognition is preserved of a divorce or legal separation obtained overseas if at the time when the proceedings were instituted there either the spouses were both domiciled in that country or the law of the country of their domicile or their several domiciles would recognise its validity.[191]

If the validity of a divorce is recognised under these rules, one party can no longer be prevented from remarrying in Great Britain because the divorce would not be recognised in some other jurisdiction.[192]

A gap so far unfilled is that the English courts have no power to make orders for ancillary relief, including financial provision or property transfer orders for one of the parties to a former marriage dissolved overseas. *A fortiori* the magistrates have no jurisdiction under the Matrimonial Proceedings (Magistrates' Courts) Act 1960 when there is no marriage. For example, in *Turczak* v. *Turczak*[193] the wife in Poland refused to institute divorce proceedings there. The husband from England instituted them in Poland and obtained a decree of dissolution, which was made final and absolute in October 1967. When the wife's application for maintenance came before the English court in March 1969, it was held that it had no jurisdiction, since the parties were no longer husband and wife. This appears still to be the position, notwithstanding the enlargement of the basis of the court's jurisdiction under s. 27 of the Matrimonial Causes Act 1973 by the Domicile and Matrimonial Proceedings Act 1973 s. 6(1).

Torok v. *Torok*[194] concerned two Hungarians who fled to England in 1956 at the time of the Hungarian uprising, married in Scotland, became British subjects and lived together, mainly in England, until 1967, when the husband went to live in Canada. Despite his British naturalisation, the husband was still of Hungarian nationality by Hungarian law. He instituted divorce proceedings in Hungary based on five years' separation. The wife entered an appearance. She then petitioned for divorce to the English court. The Hungarian courts had no power to deal with immovable property abroad, such as the house in England in which the wife and two children were living. The English courts alone could effectively enforce orders over English land, and they could exercise their matrimonial powers to deal with the property only if there were an existing marriage or one dissolved by the English court. The decree *nisi* was pronounced in the English proceedings, and the decree made absolute forthwith, so that the

---

190. Recognition of Divorces and Legal Separations Act 1971 as substituted by the Domicile and Matrimonial Proceedings Act 1973, s. 2(2).
191. Except for non-judicial proceedings instituted overseas immediately after one year's habitual residence in the United Kingdom, discussed *ante*.
192. Section 7, overruling *R*. v. *Brentwood Supt. Registrar of Marriages, ex parte Arias* [1968] 2 Q.B. 965 D.C.
193. [1970] P. 198.
194. [1973] 1 W.L.R. 1066.

court could exercise its powers to deal with the property and make financial provision before the marriage could be dissolved overseas.

Since a child remains the child of his parents after as before the parents' marriage has been terminated, under the Matrimonial Causes Act 1973, s. 23(3), there is jurisdiction to order financial provision for a child of the family (but not for a spouse) either before granting a decree of divorce, nullity or judicial separation, or where the proceedings are dismissed after the beginning of the trial. In *P. (L.E.)* v. *P. (J.M.)*[195] the court granted a declaration that a marriage had already been validly dissolved by the courts of Virginia, U.S.A., and dismissed a petition in the alternative for divorce.

The English and Scottish Law Commissions published in August 1976 their Working Paper No. 68 (resulting from the discussions of a joint Working Party of thirteen men) on *Custody of Children—Jurisdiction and Enforcement within the United Kingdom*. So difficult and complex are the problems even within the United Kingdom that the Law Commissions decided not to delay publication of their provisional proposals until they had considered even the problems in relation to the British Isles which are not part of the United Kingdom. A second consultative paper will consider the international aspects of these questions.

K. PRIVACY VERSUS PUBLICITY IN FAMILY PROCEEDINGS

The question of how far justice in domestic relations should be manifestly seen to be done, and how far the parties, or either of them, may be entitled to require privacy, is a difficult one to which no consistent solution has been found. The difficulties arising from financial provision orders made in Chambers have already been considered. The privacy of domestic proceedings was further safeguarded by the restrictions on publicity imposed by the Domestic and Appellate Proceedings Act 1968.[196]

The Rules still provide that the 'substantive causes' of divorce or judicial separation are heard not in Chambers but in open court,[197] both in the divorce county courts and in the High Court. However, the Judicial Proceedings (Regulation of Reports) Act 1926,[198] prohibits the publication:

(*a*) of any indecent matter or indecent medical, surgical or physiological details . . . the publication of which would be calculated to injure public morals,[199] and

(*b*) in relation to proceedings for divorce, nullity or judicial separation, anything other than the names, addresses and occupations of the parties

---

195. [1971] P. 318.
196. Section 2(1)(*a*).
197. Rule 37(1): examination of witnesses orally and in open court.
198. Section 1.
199. In *Argyll (Duchess)* v. *Argyll (Duke)* [1967] Ch. 302, an injunction was granted to prohibit publication by the Duke, after a divorce, of confidences made during the marriage.

and witnesses; a concise statement of charges and defences; submissions on points of law and the judgement.

The extension of the 'special procedure' by which evidence is received on affidavit in all undefended petitions where no minor and dependent children of the family are involved, unless the petition is based on unreasonable behaviour, has greatly reduced the oral examination of witnesses in open court, and now an order for the trial of an issue states whether it is to be tried in open court or in chambers.[200]

In nullity proceedings, evidence concerning sexual capacity must be heard *in camera* unless the judge is satisfied that in the interests of justice it should be heard in open court.[201]

In the magistrates' courts the statute[202] forbids the presence during the hearing of matrimonial proceedings of anyone other than officers of the court, the parties to the case before the court and their solicitors and counsel and others directly concerned or whom either party wishes to be present; solicitors and counsel attending for other cases; representatives of newspapers and news agencies, and other persons with the permission of the court. The court may, if it thinks it necessary for the administration of justice or public decency, direct the exclusion of all those other than officers of the court, the parties and their solicitors or counsel or others directly concerned. Restrictions on the publication of reports of proceedings are, *mutatis mutandis,* similar to those applying to matrimonial causes.[203] These provisions relating to domestic proceedings in the magistrates' courts extend also to enforcement of maintenance orders under the Maintenance Orders (Reciprocal Enforcement) Act 1972 or the Attachment of Earnings Act 1971; to proceedings under the Guardianship of Minors Acts 1971 and 1973; to maintenance for children of the family; and applications for the court's consent to the marriage of minors over 16 years whose parents have refused their consent.[204]

The Legitimacy Act 1959 provided that domestic proceedings for these purposes should include applications for the custody[205] or maintenance[206] of extra-marital children. Not until October 1972 were applications for the revival or revocation of an affiliation order included, and applications for variation of such orders are still classed as domestic proceedings only if the court so orders.[207] Any appeal on fact from the grant or refusal of an affiliation order is by way of rehearing in open criminal (Crown) court.[208]

---

200. *Practice Note (Matrimonial Causes: Issues)* [1975] 1 W.L.R. 1640. For the 'special procedure' see note 165 *ante*. See also the comments of Payne J. in *Biggs* v. *Biggs and Wheatley* [1976] 2 W.L.R. 942, 950 that applications for decree absolute made more than twelve months after decree nisi should be heard in open court.
201. Matrimonial Causes Act 1973, s. 48(2). Reports of nullity cases normally use initials only.
202. Magistrates' Courts Act 1952, s. 57.
203. Ibid. s. 58.
204. Marriage Act 1949, s. 3.
205. Section 3(1) and (3).
206. Ibid. s. 5(1).
207. Affiliation Proceedings (Amendment) Act, 1972, s. 3.
208. Courts Act 1971, s. 8 and Scheds 1, 8 and 9.

Under the Children and Young Persons Act 1933[209] the court may be cleared of all but members or officers of the court or parties to the case, their solicitors or counsel, others directly concerned with the case, or *bona fide* representatives of a newspaper or news agency, while a child or young person[210] is giving evidence in proceedings relating to an offence against or conduct contrary to, decency or morality. Unless the court or the Secretary of State otherwise orders, no newspaper report of any proceedings in a juvenile court may reveal the name, address or school, or include any particulars calculated to lead to the identification of any child or young person concerned in those proceedings, either as the person against or in respect of whom the proceedings are taken or as being a witness therein, nor may any picture be published in a newpaper as being or including a picture of any such child or young person.[211]

In the High Court, the county courts and divorce county courts applications for custody of children are normally heard in chambers.[212] Formerly the question whether a child was a child of the family had to be heard in open court,[213] and in *B. (L.A.)* v. *B. (C.H.)*[214] Payne J. suggested the discretion to hear such issues in chambers that has now been granted. In applications for a declaration of legitimacy connected with nationality under the Matrimonial Causes Act 1973 the court may direct that the whole or any part of the proceedings shall be heard *in camera,* and applications to this end are themselves heard *in camera* unless the court otherwise directs.[215] Under the Adoption Act 1976, jurisdiction in adoption is in the county court, the magistrates' court[216] or the High Court, and hearings are to take place in private.[217]

The Court of Appeal has recently held[218] that it is not a contempt of court under the Administration of Justice Act 1960 s. 12 to publish information

---

209. Section 37. Reports of cases concerning children normally use initials only.
210. A child is under 14 years; a young person is above 14 and below the age of 17 years; Ibid. s. 107(1). This special vocabulary is limited to the Children and Young Persons Acts 1933–69 and the Children Acts 1948–58. Under the Children Act 1975 s. 107, except where used to express a relationship, 'child' means a person who has not attained the age of 18.
211. Ibid. s. 49. The prohibition is not on publishing a picture of the child, but on representing any picture as being of the child.
212. By the county court rules 1936, Order. 46 r. 1, all proceedings under the Guardianship of Minors Acts shall be heard and determined in chambers unless the court otherwise directs. Rule 9 provides similarly for applications for consent to the marriage of a minor under the Marriage Act 1949, s. 3.
213. *Prior* v. *Prior* (1970) 114 Sol. Jo. 72.
214. *The Times* 18.2.75.
215. Section 45(9), and see *Barritt* v. *Attorney-General* [1971] 1 W.L.R. 1713.
216. Transferred from the juvenile court by the Children Act 1975, s. 21(3) and s. 100(2)(*d*) and classified as domestic proceedings. The courts are here listed in order of popularity.
217. Adoption Act 1976, s. 64. The adoption Rules 1976 specify proceedings in camera only in the magistrates' courts in S.I. 1768 r. 18, but in the county courts S.I. 1644 and in the High Court S. I. 1645 prescribe who may attend hearings and provide against disclosures. See further *In re R. (M.J.) (A Minor) (Publication of Transcript)* [1975] Fam. 89 on publication of the transcript of High Court proceedings to the male adopter's trustee in bankruptcy.
218. *In re F. (orse. A.) (A Minor) (Publication of Information)* [1976] 3 W.L.R. 813 C.A.

relating to a ward of court, unless the publishers knew that they were giving information about court proceedings in private concerning a ward. Guilty knowledge is essential to contempt of court.

The Domestic and Appellate Proceedings (Restriction of Publicity) Act 1968 [219] provides that where appeals are made from decisions in cases in which the court of first instance had power to sit in private, the appeal court shall also have power to hear the appeal in private, although the decision and the reasons for it shall be given in public unless there are good reasons to the contrary, in which case those reasons shall be stated in public.

---

219. Section 1.

CHAPTER VI

Dissolution of Marriage by Death[1]

The vast majority of marriages are still dissolved by the death of one of the spouses. In marriage it is divorce that is pathological and abnormal. Even today only some 15 per cent of English marriages are dissolved by orders made by men on the authority of the law. The law governing distribution of property on the death of a party to a marriage is therefore an important part of family law. In the words of T. Plucknett: 'The law of succession is an attempt to express the family in terms of property'.[2] By historical accident, resulting from the struggle for jurisdiction between the church courts and the courts of common law on the one hand, and then between the Court of Chancery and the common law courts (more narrowly defined) on the other, the law of succession to property on death became separated from rights to property and duties of maintenance between married people and parents and children *inter vivos*. It was this divided jurisdiction and the decline in the authority of the church courts from the sixteenth century that largely contributed to the final gross legal deformity; that (i) all a woman's personal property was conveyed to her husband by the wedding ceremony, which also transferred to him the right to manage, control and draw the income from her real property; (ii) a wife had an unenforceable 'right' to be maintained unless she committed adultery; and (iii) a husband had complete 'freedom' of testation, that is, to dispose of his (including most of her) property at his death, and leave his wife and children destitute, but (iv) after the mid-seventeenth century, all these rules could be avoided by settlements of property 'to the separate use' of a married woman. Among those with property it was then, as it is today, usual to make a will or testament. But the law must provide for the distribution of property when no will is left.

---

1. See 8 *Jo. SPTL* (1965) 188.
2. *A Concise History of the Common Law*, 5th edn (1956) Part 6, p. 711.

A. THE LAW OF INTESTATE SUCCESSION

This is now mostly contained in the Administration of Estates Act 1925, s. 46 as amended.[3] The general principles applicable are:

1. If the deceased left a surviving spouse and issue,[4] all the deceased's property is divided between the spouse and issue, who together exclude all other claimants, as do issue alone. The rights of the surviving spouse or issue are not affected by their sex. The law since 1925 has therefore been centred on the nuclear family which, if intact, excludes all others. This involves some incongruities with surviving remnants of the former legal approach, which was to consider property as destined to be handed down, intact if possible, from generation to generation of males or in their absence to females.[5]

2. If the deceased left no issue but a surviving spouse, that survivor alone excludes all claimants to the deceased's estate more remote than the deceased's parents or brothers or sisters of the full blood and their issue. This principle was established by the Intestates Estates Act 1952, following the Report of the Committee on the Law of Intestate Succession.[6] A census (conducted by the Probate Registries of all wills proved throughout England and Wales on two successive days in each week and for five successive weeks) showed that in wills executed from 1940 73 per cent of male testators leaving less than £2000 left the whole or most of their estate absolutely to their surviving spouse, as did 65 per cent of those leaving between £2000 and £5000 and 45 per cent of those leaving over £5000. The corresponding proportions of male testators who left a life interest in the whole or a major part of their estate to their widows were 11 per cent, 21 per cent and 45 per cent respectively. Women testators were less generous to surviving husbands, probably presuming the husband's capacity to support himself in the unlikely event of his surviving his (usually younger) wife. The committee therefore recommended an increase in the 'statutory legacy' given to the surviving spouse from £1000 to £5000 and

---

3. By the Intestates Estates Act 1952, the Family Provision Act 1966, s.1; the Family Law Reform Act 1969, s. 14; the Matrimonial Proceedings and Property Act 1970, s. 40(1); and the Family Provision (Intestate Succession) Order S.I. No. 916 of 1972.

4. In the context of the Law of Succession, this means descendants of all generations *ad infinitum*, as distinct from 'children', which means descendants of the first generation only, irrespective of their age. See Children Act 1975, s. 107.

5. Before 1926 the Rules of Inheritance excluded females if a male heir, however remote, could be traced. The Statute of Distributions 1670, as amended, laid down the rules for succession to personal property. The result was that until 1926, in Maitland's words: 'the law makes a will for intestates which no sane testator would make for himself': *The Law of Real Property, Collected Papers*, vol. I, p. 172. Remnants of the former theory of the devolution of property through the generations are found in the Wills Act 1837, ss 32 and 33. By s. 33 if a testator leaves property by his will to a child or other issue of his, who dies in the lifetime of the testator leaving issue alive when the testator dies, the gift does not lapse but subject to any contrary intention appearing in the will takes effect as if the beneficiary had died immediately after the testator. The effect is that the presence of the beneficiary's issue saves the gift, which falls into the principal beneficiary's residuary estate, and passes under his will or on his intestacy. After 1952 it is unlikely to pass on intestacy to the issue whose existence saved it for the estate. See, e.g. *Re Hurd* [1941] Ch. 196, *Re Basioli* [1953] Ch. 367.

6. Cmd 8310 of June 1951, especially para. 18.

this was effected by the Intestates Estates Act 1952.[7] Subsequent increases in the surviving spouse's 'statutory legacy' have been based on the fall in the value of money, and the assumption that it should cover the value of the 'average' matrimonial home. The Intestates Estates Act 1952 also considerably increased the interest of the surviving spouse in the matrimonial home, and allowed her (usually) or him (more rarely) to claim this in most cases[8] in total or partial satisfaction of the statutory legacy. It also enabled the surviving spouse to have her or his life interest redeemed by payment of a capital sum calculated as laid down by the Act.[9]

The provisions increasing the share of the surviving spouse in the deceased's estate were admittedly based on the assumption that in most cases the surviving spouse will also be the parent of surviving minor children. The Committee foresaw the possibility of hardship where this was not the case, and found this an argument for applying family provision to cases of intestacy. Today the surviving spouse is more likely not also to be the surviving parent of the deceased's minor children. There may even be surviving minor children of more than one former spouse of the deceased. The Act of 1952 provided,[10] however, that the Inheritance (Family Provision) Act 1938 be extended to cases of intestacy. This enabled the restricted class of dependants then entitled, to apply for family provision whether a will had been left or not.

3. The distribution on intestacy is now as follows:

(a) If the deceased left a surviving spouse and issue:
    (i) the surviving spouse takes:
        (1) all the personal chattels[11] and
        (2) £15,000 here called 'the statutory legacy' with interest at 4 per cent per annum from date of death, and
        (3) a life interest in half the residuary estate;[12]
    (ii) the issue take:
        (1) one half of the residuary estate on the statutory trusts[13] sons and daughters taking equally,

---

7. Section 1(2), amending the Administration of Estates Act, 1925, s. 46.
8. See Intestates Estates Act 1952, Sched. 2. The surviving spouse must have been resident in the home at the time of the intestate's death; the home must not be held on a tenancy with less than two years to run. If the home or part of it was used for purposes other than domestic purposes, or in some other circumstances, the right may be exercised only on the order of a court.
9. Intestates Estates Act 1952, s. 2, inserting s. 47A to the Administration of Estates Act 1925.
10. Ibid. ss 7 and 8 and third and fourth schedules.
11. As defined in the Administration of Estates Act 1925, s. 55(i)(x), viz.: 'carriages, horses, stable furniture and effects (not used for business purposes), motor cars and accessories (not used for business purposes), garden effects, domestic animals, plate, plated articles, linen, china, glass, books, pictures, prints, furniture, jewellery, articles of household or personal use or ornament, musical and scientific instruments and apparatus, wines, liquors and consumable stores' but not including any chattels used at the death of the intestate for business purposes nor money nor securities for money.
12. This means that where there is a surviving spouse and issue the surviving spouse is normally entitled to about £20,000 before interests for the issue arise.
13. As defined in the Administration of Estates Act 1925, s. 47(1), viz. in trust, in equal shares if more than one, for the child or children of the intestate living at the death of the intestate,

   (2) the interest in remainder expectant on the death of the surviving spouse.

(*b*) If the deceased left a surviving spouse and no issue but there is a surviving parent or brother or sister of the deceased or their issue:

   (i) the surviving spouse takes:
      (1) all the personal chattels
      (2) £40,000 statutory legacy with interest at 4 per cent from date of death, and
      (3) half the residuary estate absolutely;

   (ii) the surviving parent(s) take the other half of the residuary estate. If both parents of the deceased survive, it is divided equally between them;

   (iii) if there is no surviving parent, the residuary estate is held on the statutory trusts for the brothers and sisters of the whole blood and the issue of deceased brothers and sisters who take by representation the share to which their deceased parent would have been entitled.[14]

(*c*) If the deceased left issue but no surviving spouse, the issue take the whole estate equally between them on the statutory trusts.

(*d*) If the deceased left a surviving spouse but no issue and no surviving parent or brother or sister of the whole blood nor issue of such brother or sister, the surviving spouse takes the whole estate.

(*e*) If the deceased left no surviving spouse nor issue, then the following are entitled in the order given; those first entitled excluding more remote claims:

   (i) parent(s) of the deceased entitled equally
   (ii) brothers or sisters of the whole blood or their issue on the statutory trusts
   (iii) brothers or sisters of the half blood or their issue on the statutory trusts
   (iv) grandparent(s), if more than one in equal shares
   (v) uncles and aunts of the whole blood or their issue on the statutory trusts
   (vi) uncles and aunts of the half blood or their issue on the statutory trusts
   (vii) the Crown or the Duchy of Lancaster or the Duke of Cornwall, as *bona vacantia*.

---

who attain the age of 18 years or marry under that age, and for all or any of the issue living at the death of the intestate who attain the age of 18 years or marry under that age of any child of the intestate who predeceases the intestate, such issue to take through all degrees, according to their stocks (*per stirpes*), in equal shares if more than one, the share which their parent would have taken if living at the death of the intestate. No issue may take whose parent is living at the death of the intestate and so is capable of taking. By the Legitimacy Act 1976 s. 5(3) a legitimated person and any other is entitled to take any interest as if the legitimated person had been born legitimate. For the adopted person see the Adoption Act 1976 ss 39, 44, 46(3) and (4) and Chapter IX.

14. The share of the deceased parent is divided equally among that parent's issue.

In English law entitlement on intestacy is unconditional. That is, the spouse married a few minutes before the other dies, or who deserted the deceased thirty years previously to live in adultery, both come within the definition of surviving spouse for purposes of intestate succession.[15] Similarly the parent who has persistently failed, without reasonable excuse, to discharge the obligations of a parent has exactly the same rights as one who sacrificed to give his child every possible advantage. When in 1969 illegitimate children were given the same rights of succession on intestacy as those born legitimate,[16] it was deemed appropriate to give to their parents the same unrestricted rights of succession as the parents of legitimate children,[17] subject only to the presumption that the father of an illegitimate child predeceased the child until the contrary is proved.[18] Thus the mother who placed her child in the care of the local authority at the age of a few weeks and thereafter saw him rarely and under pressure; the father who denied paternity and contributed in no way to the maintenance or upbringing of his illegitimate child, now both have an absolute right to succeed to that child's property on his death intestate. The chances of such a child dying intestate without surviving spouse or issue and leaving property worth inheriting are remote but not infinitesimal.[19] Rights either of succession to property or of any other kind, which are founded on having procreated or given birth to an illegitimate child without more, need justification.

B. NO BENEFIT FROM CRIMINAL HOMICIDE

One restriction which still applies, however, to all rights of succession on intestacy or by will, is the common law rule that one who by a criminal act causes the death of another cannot succeed to that other's property. Thus in *Re Crippen*[20] the convicted murderer was entitled to leave all his property to his mistress, Ethel le Neve, but this could not permit him notionally to inherit and to transmit to her by his will the property of the wife he had murdered. There have been several cases recently in which the problems raised by failure of gifts in such circumstances have been considered,[21] the most bizarre to date being *Re Giles*.[22] There a woman who had spent several years in Broadmoor 'struck her husband a single blow on the head with a domestic chamber-pot' as

---

15. Until the Matrimonial Proceedings and Property Act 1970, s. 40 came into operation, the same applied also to the judicially-separated wife of a husband who died intestate, although if the wife died first her judicially-separated husband did not succeed on her intestacy: Contrast the Matrimonial Causes Act 1965, s. 20(3) with the Matrimonial Causes Act 1973, s. 18(2).
16. Family Law Reform Act 1969, s. 14(1).
17. Ibid. s. 14(2).
18. Ibid. s. 14(4).
19. Cf. *Aldrich* v. *Attorney-General* [1968] P. 281, where the husband (*H*) of the mother (M) of a deceased woman (*N*) sought to claim in *N*'s very large estate overseas as her lawful father.
20. [1911] P. 108. See also *Re Sigsworth* [1935] Ch. 89 and *Re Pollock* [1941] Ch. 21.
21. *Re Callaway* [1956] Ch. 559; *Re Peacock* [1957] 1 Ch. 310; *Re Dellow's Will Trust* [1964] 1 W.L.R. 451.
22. [1972] Ch. 544.

a result of which he died twelve days later. The wife pleaded not guilty to murder, but guilty of manslaughter by reason of diminished responsibility. It was held that, although she was receiving remedial and not punitive treatment, she could take no benefit under her deceased husband's will, consisting principally of their matrimonial home. It would have been otherwise had she been found not guilty by reason of insanity, since such a verdict amounts to an acquittal.

C. SUCCESSION TO STATUTORY TENANCIES

The provisions[23] for succession to a protected or statutory tenancy of a dwelling house depart from the general rules for succession to property of a deceased intestate. If the original tenant was a man who died leaving a widow who was residing with him at his death, then after his death the widow is the statutory tenant so long as she occupies the dwelling house as her residence. If those circumstances do not apply, then any person who was a member of the tenant's family[24] residing with him at the time of and for six months immediately before his death will be the statutory tenant. If there was more than one such member of the family they may agree which of them shall be the statutory tenant and in default of agreement the county court may decide. The 'first successor' may similarly transmit the tenancy at his death to his widow residing with him at his death, or failing her, to a member of his family residing with him at and for six months before his death.

D. CLAIMS FOR FINANCIAL LOSS SUFFERED FROM THE DEATH OF A MEMBER OF THE FAMILY THROUGH ANOTHER'S WRONGFUL ACT OR DEFAULT[25] (THE FATAL ACCIDENTS ACT)

The common law rule that it was not a civil wrong to cause the death of a human being,[26] which made it cheaper to kill than to maim, led to great hardship when the railways ushered in a new era of transport and gave a foretaste of the mortality to follow the mass use of the motor-car. This

---

23. The Rent Act 1968, s. 3 and Sched. I.
24. Not defined in the current or previous Acts. Under the previous legislation it had been held to include a mistress living with the deceased and their children: *Hawes* v. *Evenden* [1953] 1 W.L.R. 1169 C.A. and this was confirmed for the current legislation in *Dyson Holdings* v. *Fox*, [1976] Q.B 503 C.A. where the couple had no children. But see *Perry* v. *Dembowski* [1951] 2 K.B. 420 C.A. For further examples see *The Rent Acts*, by R. E. Megarry, 10th edn (1970) pp. 214–16.
25. See further any of the standard textbooks on the Law of Tort, viz. *Salmond*, Ed. R. V. F. Heuston, *Street*, or *Winfield and Jolowicz*.
26. Per Lord Ellenborough C. J. in *Baker* v. *Bolton* (1808) 1 Camp. 493.

rule was therefore abolished by the Fatal Accidents Act, 1846 (Lord Campbell's Act),[27] which provided[28] that: 'Whensoever the death of a person shall be caused by wrongful act, neglect or default[29] . . . such as would (if death had not ensued) have entitled the party injured to maintain an action and recover damages in respect thereof, then and in every such case the person who would have been liable if death had not ensued shall be liable to an action for damages, notwithstanding the death of the person injured.' The action must be brought within three years of the death[30] by and in the name of the executor or administrator of the person deceased[31] for the benefit originally of the wife, husband, parent, grandparent, child and grandchild of the person whose death was so caused.[32] The class of dependants on whose behalf the action may be brought was extended by the Fatal Accidents Act 1959[33] to include a brother, sister, uncle or aunt of the deceased or the issue of any such person. The Acts were consolidated by the Fatal Accidents Act 1976, which came into operation on 1 September 1976. By s. 1(4) of this Act:

(*a*) relationship by affinity is treated as relationship by consanguinity; relationship by the half blood as by the whole blood, and anybody's stepchild as his child; and

(*b*) an illegitimate person is treated as the legitimate child of his mother and reputed father.

Damages are to be 'proportioned to the injury resulting from the death to the dependants respectively and the damages recovered, after deduction of costs, are divided amongst the dependants as directed'. Particulars of the persons for whose benefit the action is brought, and of the nature of the claim, must be supplied to the defendant. Since the Law Reform (Contributory Negligence) Act 1945, the damages recoverable by the dependants are proportionately reduced by the deceased's responsibility for his contributory negligence.[34]

---

27. In operation as amended by the Acts of 1864, 1908 and 1959, until all except the Act of 1908 were repealed and replaced from 1 September 1976 by the consolidating Act of that year.
28. Section 1.
29. By s. 3 of the Carriage by Air Act 1961, this phrase includes references to any occurrence giving rise to a liability under Art. 17 of the First Schedule to that Act. By s. 14 of the Gas Act 1965, the gas authority's liability for damage caused by gas in or escaping from underground gas storage is also included. The phrase has been interpreted as including a breach of contract as well as a tort: *Grein* v. *Imperial Airways Ltd* [1937] 1 K.B. 50 C.A. Under the Coal Mining (Subsidence) Act 1957, s. 12 the National Coal Board is liable for death caused by subsidence, not necessarily resulting from any wrongful act, neglect or default. Other similar Acts incorporated are listed in Sched. I of the 1976 Act.
30. Law Reform (Limitation of Actions, etc.) Act 1954, s. 3. For death from collision at sea the period is two years, with discretion in the court to extend the period: Maritime Conventions Act 1911, s. 8.
31. Fatal Accidents Act 1976 s. 2. If there is no executor or administrator, or if he does not take action within 6 months of the death, the dependants may sue in the name of all or any of themselves.
32. Fatal Accidents Act 1846, s. 2 as extended by s. 5.
33. Section 1.
34. Law Reform (Contributory Negligence) Act 1945, s. 1(4), now Fatal Accidents Act 1976 s. 5.

It was quickly held[35] that damages were to be awarded for pecuniary loss alone, and could not include any solatium for mental suffering. In the words of Diplock L.J.:[36] 'When, after the lapse of centuries, Parliament in 1846 reintroduced the principle of blood-money, it was, as the courts soon decided, in order to protect the children of the poor rather than to punish the wrongdoer.'

The wrongdoers and their insurers have given ample evidence of their ability to protect themselves. The principle had been taken so far that damages were not recoverable for a child's loss of his mother's care, until a more humane approach was adopted in recent decisions.[37] If the loss is of income derived from the deceased's criminal activities, no damages are recoverable, as *ex turpi causa*.[38]

Secondly 'the pecuniary loss recoverable is limited to the loss of benefit in money or money's worth which, if the deceased had survived, would have accrued to a person within the defined relationship to the deceased, and would have arisen from that relationship and not otherwise'.[39] Thus if a father and son,[40] or husband and wife,[41] have also a business relationship, the damages recoverable for the wrongful death of one of them will not include loss of profit from that contractual relationship. If the deceased over-paid the dependant for the latter's business services, it is the excess payment alone for which compensation is recoverable.[42]

Since the action is for compensation for loss caused to the dependants by the death, in principle any financial benefit to the dependants must be brought into account.[43] But by the Fatal Accidents (Damages) Act 1908 no account was to be taken of any sum paid or payable on the death under any contract of assurance or insurance,[44] and the benefits exempted from being brought into account were considerably widened by the Fatal Accidents Act 1959.[45] Now under s. 4 of the 1976 Act no account is to be taken of any

---

35. *Blake* v. *Midland Railway Co.* (1852) 18 Q.B. 93, applied in *Franklin* v. *S.E. Railway* (1858) 3 H & N. 211 and ever since. But see now the Law Commission recommendations in Law Com. 56, considered *post*.
36. *Malyon* v. *Plummer* [1964] 1 Q.B. 330, 348.
37. *Hay* v. *Hughes* [1975] Q.B. 790 C.A., and *Regan* v. *Williamson* [1976] 1 W.L.R. 305, in which Watkins J. refused to equate the continuous care of a good mother with that provided by a housekeeper: Ibid. p. 309. The former approach was exemplified in *Pevec* v. *Brown* (1964) 108 S.J. 219.
38. *Burns* v. *Edman* [1970] 2 Q.B. 541.
39. Per Diplock L.J. in *Malyon* v. *Plummer* [1964] 1 Q.B. 330, 349.
40. *Sykes* v. *N.E. Railway* (1875) 44 L.J.C.P. 191.
41. *Burgess* v. *Florence Nightingale Hospital for Gentlewomen* [1955] 1 Q.B. 349. See the definitive analysis and judgement by Devlin J. at pp. 354 et seq.
42. *Malyon* v. *Plummer* [1964] 1 Q.B. 330 C.A.: The husband, probably for tax avoidance purposes, paid the wife £600–£800 p.a. for services to his one-man business which the Court of Appeal valued at £200 p.a.
43. *Grand Trunk Railway Co. of Canada* v. *Jennings* (1888)13 App. Cas. 800, 804. In *Baker* v. *Dalgleish S.S. Co.* [1922] 1 K.B. 361 C.A., it was held that the receipt of a Crown pension by the dependant in consequence of the death should be taken into account, as should the probability of reduction of the pension by the damages recovered for the death.
44. Section 1. See *Green* v. *Russell* [1959] 2 Q.B. 226.
45. Section 2. See *Humphrey* v. *Ward Engineering Services, The Times 28.5.75, where a widow's 'substantial' lump sum pension payment was disregarded.*

insurance money (including return of premiums); benefit under the Social Security Acts or any payment by a friendly society or trade union for the relief or maintenance of a member's dependants, or pension including a return of contributions and any payment of a lump sum in respect of a person's employment, or gratuity which has been or will or may be paid as a result of the death. The net result is that generally the only deduction made is of damages recovered under the Law Reform (Miscellaneous Provisions) Act 1934 for which a claim is likely to be joined to that under the Fatal Accidents Act. In the rare cases where the bulk of the estate consists not of the matrimonial home but of stocks and shares, some deduction is made for the accelerated value of the widow's gain from the estate. The Law Commission has suggested that this should no longer be taken into account.

The general approach to the assessment of damages expounded by Lord Wright in *Davies* v. *Powell Duffryn Associated Colliers Ltd*[46] has been generally accepted and followed.[47]

Because an assessment must be made of future loss to the dependants, the judge must attempt to assess their future prospects, and in claims by the widow damages assessed tended at one time to become not so much blood money as an inverse assessment of the widow's sexual attractions. Starting with a presumption that a husband's maintenance of his wife was pure bounty, it followed that when he was killed, she suffered financial loss. Her remarriage terminated the loss.[48] There were complaints that large and powerful companies who first killed a man through negligence or breach of their statutory duty thereafter placed his widow under surveillance and conducted enquiries in her neighbourhood about her sexual conduct, male friends and the likelihood of her remarriage. At the trial the judge was called upon to look over the claimant widow as she stood in the witness box and assess once and for all her chances of remarriage. If he thought them high, his award of damages would be low. The widow's legal advisers would of course advise her to appear as unattractive as possible in court, and the advisers to those responsible for her husband's death would do their utmost to cast doubt on her marital fidelity or at least to show that she was waiting only for the receipt of damages before remarriage.[49] Some judges were revolted at the duty of making this public assessment of the sexual attractions and remarriage prospects of the woman before them.[50]

---

46. [1942] A.C. 601, 611 et seq.
47. E.g. in *Bishop* v. *Cunard White Star Co., Ltd* [1950] P. 240. See also *Taylor* v. *O'Connor* [1971] A.C. 115, where account was taken of the tax situation and the effects of inflation.
48. In *Curwen* v. *James* [1963] 1 W.L.R. 748, the judge had reduced the damages awarded because the widow was a 'presentable young lady' who should have no difficulty in remarrying if so minded. He was right, as by the time an appeal was heard she had remarried, and the Court of Appeal therefore halved the damages awarded at first instance.
49. See e.g. some of the cross-examination reproduced in the Court of Appeal hearing of *Goodburn* v. *Thomas Cotton Ltd* [1968] 1 Q.B. 845, at pp. 851–2. A spokesman for the National Coal Board contended at a conference that the mere award of damages sufficed to render any widow remarriageable, and seemed persuaded of a moral duty to prevent this happening.
50. E.g. Phillimore J. in *Buckley* v. *John Allen and Ford (Oxford) Ltd* [1967] 2 Q.B. 637, 644–5: 'After all, whatever men may like to think, women do not always want to remarry.

Others insisted that it was their duty to persist in pricing the widow's prospects with first consideration for her remarriage prospects.[51]

In 1971 Parliament intervened to end this survival of the slave auction. It provided[52] that neither the widow's remarriage nor the prospect of it should be taken into account in assessing damages payable to a widow in respect of the death of her husband under the Fatal Accidents Acts. Any damages payable under the Acts to a person not under disability were also released from the control of the court.[53] The present provisions are not ideal. The whole question of civil liability for personal injury, including death, was in December 1972 placed in the hands of a Royal Commission on Civil Liability under the chairmanship of Lord Pearson. In the meantime the Law Commission published in July 1973 its *Report on Personal Injury Litigation – Assessment of Damages*[54] with an annexed draft *Law Reform (Personal Injuries) Bill*, of which no doubt more will be heard. This coincided with the publication by the Scottish Law Commission of its *Report on the Law Relating to Damages for Injuries Causing Death.*[55]

In this area of law also the basic theory survives that a man's primary dependant is his wife (and in rare circumstances a married woman's primary duty may be to maintain her incapacitated husband) and that, maintenance for the spouse being once assured, comparatively minor sums should be added to the damages for the dependent children's loss of a parent.[56] The Law Commission's proposals do not deal with this aspect of the matter, since their proposed tariff for damages for bereavement does not include bereavement of a minor child.

The Law Reform (Miscellaneous Provisions) Act 1934[57] abolished the rule that *actio personalis moritur cum personam*, so that an action for or against the deceased survived his death (with certain exceptions of very personal actions). If he had been killed by the negligence or default of another, his right of action could be pursued by his personal representatives and, as has been seen, such an action is normally joined to one on behalf of the dependants

---

There are quite a lot of rich widows who prefer to remain single. . . . It seems to me that this particular exercise is not only unattractive but is not one for which judges are equipped.'

51. *Goodburn* v. *Thomas Cotton Ltd* [1968] 1 Q.B. 845 C.A., per Willmer L.J. at pp. 850–1; per Davies L.J. at p. 854 and per Edmund-Davies L.J. at p. 856.

52. Law Reform (Miscellaneous Provisions) Act 1971, s. 4. But see *Thompson* v. *Price* [1973] Q.B. 838.

53. Ibid. s. 5. This ended the practice of retaining the widow's damages for administration by the court, which was sometimes very inefficiently carried out.

54. Law Com. 56.

55. Scot Law Com. 31.

56. See e.g. *Heatley* v. *Steel Co. of Wales* [1953] 1 W.L.R. 405 C.A.: £6000 awarded, of which £5000 to the widow and £1000 among four children. In *Voller* v. *Dairy Produce Packers* [1962] 1 W.L.R. 960, the damages to two children were reduced because their mother died two years after their father was killed. The court assumed their parents' house would be sold, resulting in an 'accelerated benefit' to them. A more humane approach was adopted in *Hay* v. *Hughes* [1975] Q.B. 790 C.A. and *Regan* v. *Williamson* [1976] 1 W.L.R. 305. For illegitimate children see *K.* v. *J.M.P. Co. Ltd* [1976] Q.B. 85 C.A. See also *Payne-Collins* v. *Taylor Woodrow Constructions Ltd.* [1975] Q.B. 300.

57. As amended by the Law Reform (Miscellaneous Provisions) Act 1971.

in their own right under the Fatal Accidents Act. Apart from this fact, the action has no especial significance in family law.

E. DECREE OF PRESUMPTION OF DEATH AND DISSOLUTION OF MARRIAGE

When a spouse disappears in circumstances suggesting that he or she is dead but the death cannot be proved, it has been possible since 1937[58] to obtain from the court a decree of presumption of death and dissolution of marriage. By the Matrimonial Causes Act 1973, s. 19(1), the burden of satisfying the court of the other partner's death is normally on the petitioner, but by s. 19(2), the continual absence for seven years of the other party, coupled with the lack of any reason for believing him or her to have been alive at any time during that seven years, raises a presumption of death.

As mentioned previously,[59] the English divorce county courts and High Court now have jurisdiction to make such a declaration and dissolve the marriage if the petitioner:

(*a*) is domiciled in England and Wales on the date when the proceedings are begun; or

(*b*) was habitually resident in England and Wales throughout the period of one year ending with that date.[60]

F. FAMILY PROVISION

During the eighteenth and nineteenth centuries and until 1938 English law incurred the odium of allowing a man 'to do as he liked with his own' even after his death, and to dispose by will of all 'his' property as he chose, leaving his wife and dependent children destitute. This applied even when much of 'his' property had been conveyed to him from his wife by law at the wedding ceremony. The doctrine of 'freedom of testation' was no inherent English vice. From Anglo-Saxon times there had been a custom, which came to be administered by the Church, of dividing a man's personal property among his wife and children. This was the right of *legitim*, or *reasonable part*, acknowledged and confirmed by the Magna Carta of 1215.[61] By 1399 the common law courts were declaring the reasonable part contrary to law, but since succession to personal property was a matter for the church courts, the attitude

---

58. Matrimonial Causes Act 1937, s. 8, now the Matrimonial Causes Act 1973, s. 19.
59. Chapter V, n. 176.
60. Domicile and Matrimonial Proceedings Act, 1973, s. 5(4).
61. Chapter 18: The King undertook to collect from the estates of his deceased tenants only what was due to him, and if nothing were owing to the King, all the chattels 'shall go to the use of the dead (saving to his wife and children their reasonable parts).'

of the common lawyers became important only later, when they had drastically curtailed the jurisdiction and effectiveness of the church courts. The reasonable part for the surviving spouse might in the early days vary according to local (ecclesiastical) custom, but the custom that eventually came to dominate was the tripartite division: one-third for the widow, one-third for the children, equally divided, with right of representation, and one-third which was the dead's part, over which alone he could exercise power of testation, and which increasingly the Church came to claim as her own. When there was no issue the widow's share was half the estate. It was probably the unpopularity of the Church in general, and her claim to one-third of a deceased's estate in particular, coupled with delays in administration and other abuses, that by the time of the Reformation had brought the whole system into disrepute.

By the time of Elizabeth I's accession in 1558 the system of *legitim* had broken down as a coherent system in the southern (ecclesiastical) Province of Canterbury (on which the common lawyers could exert more direct and continuous pressure), although it survived in certain areas as local custom.[62] It remained a coherent system in most of the Northern Province of York, where the Church retained popularity. The breakdown of feudalism and the growth of doctrines of unrestrained individualism and *laissez-faire* probably led to its gradual abolition by statute from 1692 to 1724,[63] when it was finally abolished in the City of London.[64] There can be little doubt that in other towns it survived even later,[65] and by borough custom married women long retained control of their own property. This does not support the view that the vesting in the husband by the wedding ceremony of a wife's personal property and the normal rights of ownership[66] in her freehold land for his life[67] was essential to the funding of commerce before the rise of the joint stock company.[68] If this were so, the reason why the towns, in which commercial enterprise was centred, were the last and not the first both to deprive a woman on marriage of power to deal with her property and to refuse a widow and children any rights in the property of the deceased father and husband, has yet to be explained.

As regards land held by her husband in freehold, in the early days a woman's

---

62. The Statute of Distributions 1670. s. 4, specifically saved the custom where it existed.
63. The Act of 1692 established 'freedom of testation' for all the inhabitants of the Northern Province except the cities of York and Chester; in 1696 the 'reasonable part' was abolished in Wales and the Marches, but women already married and children already born retained their rights. In 1704 the old custom was abolished for the City of York, and in 1724 for the City of London.
64. As part of a statute dealing with elections.
65. See C. S. Kenny, *History of the Law of Married Women's Property*. (1898).
66. Viz. management, control and receipt of income. In theory the husband could not alienate his wife's land, but in practice even this final attribute of ownership was his by virtue of the fine, subject to the separate examination of the wife to ensure her consent.
67. Initially the husband's right was for the duration of the marriage, but as soon as the wife gave birth to a child capable of inheriting her land, the husband's right was prolonged to the duration of his own life should he survive her.
68. A view advanced by Professor Sir Otto Kahn-Freund Q.C. in his Joseph Unger Memorial Lecture (delivered 29.1.71) 'Matrimonial Property: Where do we go from here?'

rights also varied and again the general rule developed that, if she survived her husband, the widow was entitled for her life to one-third of the income of the land of which he had held the fee. The land itself was administered by others (usually the male heir), after her husband's death. The Statute of Uses 1535 included devices for barring the widow's right to dower; these were taken further in the Dower Uses of Bridgeman's Conveyances, which came into prominence in Chancery after the Restoration of 1660. By the Dower Act 1833 a man was given the statutory right to bar his widow's right to dower either by deed or will. Dower and curtesy were both finally abolished in 1925.[69] Total freedom – or irresponsibility – of testation as against dependants thus formally reigned for just over a hundred years in England and Wales, from the Dower Act 1833 until the Inheritance (Family Provision) Act 1938 came into operation.[70]

New Zealand was the first common law country to introduce flexible restraints on testation in the interests of dependants by the Family Protection Act 1900.[71] The scheme of legislation spread to all the Australian States[72] and to the common law Provinces of Canada as Testators' Family Maintenance or Dependants' Relief Acts, before a restricted version was enacted in England in 1938.[73] The object was to allow a narrow class of dependants[74] of one who died domiciled in England to apply to the court, which might in its discretion grant them *maintenance* out of the *income* of the *net estate* during *dependancy*, provided they applied within six months of the grant of probate or letters of administration to the estate.[75] In 1952 the Act was extended to apply in cases of intestacy, and some anomalies were rectified.[76] Former spouses whose marriages had been annulled or dissolved and who had not remarried were permitted in 1958 to apply under new and different legislation,[77] which proved more favourable to the applicant than the provisions for widows

---

69. Administration of Estates Act 1925, s. 45.
70. 13 July 1939.
71. N.Z. Statutes. 64 Vict. 20.
72. See R. J. Davern Wright, *Testators' Family Maintenance in Australia and New Zealand.* 3rd edn, (1974).
73. See J. Laufer, 'Flexible restraints on testamentary freedom, 69 *Harv. Law Rev.* (1955–6) 277. The best account of the English legislation and its operation before the enactment of the Inheritance (Provision for Family and Dependants) Act 1975 is by E. L. G. Tyler, *Family Provision* (1971).
74. Viz. a surviving spouse who had not remarried, a son under the age of 21; a daughter of any age who had not been married, or a child of either sex who, by reason of some mental or physical disability, was incapable of maintaining himself or herself.
75. Intereference with the normal process of administration is the criticism most frequently made by those in the United States who prefer the fixed share, normally only for the surviving spouse or pretermitted heir, viz. a child not in existence when the will was made.
76. Intestates Estates Act 1952, s. 7 and Third Schedule. The Fourth Schedule reproduced the 1938 Act as amended.
77. Matrimonial Causes (Property and Maintenance) Act 1958, ss 3–6, which became the Matrimonial Causes Act 1965, ss 26–8A. This legislation was necessary because on divorce the court has power to order periodical payments only during joint lives unless the payments are secured on capital. Unsecured periodical payments cease on the death of either party or the remarriage of the person maintained: see Matrimonial Causes Act 1973, s. 28(1)(*a*).

and dependent children.[78] In 1966 the provisions were considerably extended,[79] in particular to allow greater use to be made of lump sum provision and more flexibility in the time for applications. The lump sum provisions cut across the principle of maintenance out of income[80] since a surviving spouse might remarry or a daughter marry or an incapacitated child recover soon after the award of a lump sum. Illegitimate children were brought within the category of those who could apply for provision in 1969.[81]

Previous decisions that a surviving spouse applying must prove at least the presumptive validity of her or his marriage to the deceased[82] were overruled by the Law Reform (Miscellaneous Provisions) Act 1970, s. 6, which allowed the survivor of a void marriage to apply under the Acts provided the marriage had not been avoided and the applicant had not been through a wedding ceremony with any third person during the lifetime of both the parties. The fact that the court could make only money awards remained a major drawback, and great hardship might be caused if the principal asset of the net estate was the matrimonial home, which must be sold before provision could be made for the applicant.[83] The overriding defect was that the legislation could be avoided by any testator minded to dispossess his dependants.[84]

Almost as important as the legislative changes was the changed attitude of those whose duty it was to administer the Acts. In the early days judicial references to the 'invasion' by the legislature of the freedom of testation traditional among Englishmen were commonplace, and there were numerous reminders of the caution with which the Act should be administered.[85] The last clear example of such an approach was that of Wynn-Parry J. in Re Andrews,[86] but Harman L.J. echoed it in 1966 and again in 1970.[87] In the meantime a

---

78. See Re Kay [1965] 1 W.L.R. 1463, 1469 per Russell L.J. In Re W. deceased The Times 28.4.75, an elderly woman was awarded £11,000 from the estate of £28,000 left by the former husband she had divorced 29 years previously.

79. By the Family Provision Act 1966, ss 2–8.

80. See e.g. Re Catmull [1943] Ch. 262 and Re Pugh [1943] Ch. 387 for restrictive interpretations of the income provisions, which were amended in 1952 and again in 1966.

81. Family Law Reform Act 1969, s. 18(1).

82. Re Peete [1952] 2 All E.R. 599; Re Watkins [1953] 1 W.L.R. 1323.

83. See, e.g. Re Ferrar's Application [1966] Ch. 126 C.A.

84. The first book on the legislation: The Inheritance (Family Provision) Act 1938, by M. J. Alberry Q.C. (1949) included as Appendix D: 'Settlement upon mistress and illegitimate child for purpose of evading the provisions of the Act.' The use of the term 'evading' is interesting in view of its scrupulous avoidance in tax avoidance schemes.

85. See e.g. Re Styler [1942] Ch. 388, per Morton J., and Laufer, 69 Harv. Law Rev. Widowers have generally received scant consideration: see Re Sylvester [1941] Ch. 87, Re Pointer [1941] Ch. 60, and the comments thereon in Re Styler. Some practitioners' books, e.g. Williams and Mortimer on Executors, Administrators and Probate, 15th edn (1970) still adopt the 'invasion' approach, p. 539.

86. [1955] 1 W.L.R. 1105; 'an invasion of that unqualified right of disposition'. The decision in the case was clearly right.

87. Re Bluston [1967] Ch. 615, 627 at G: 'English law ... unlike most or all other systems, allowed a testator ... complete testamentary freedom. This Act for the first time gave rights to dependants, but this innovation of the old law was strictly limited in particular in time ...' and Re Gregory [1970] 1 W.L.R. 1455 C.A. 1458 at F: 'The Act of 1938 was an invasion of the rights of English testators which ... ought to be sparingly used.' This decision

different attitude had become apparent, first expressed in a reported case by Wilberforce J. in *Re Sanderson, deceased,*[88] when he said that the Act had brought many strange circumstances before the court and remedied many gross injustices. For some years now the amended legislation has been administered by judges who learned it as part of English law and accept its principles. For example, in *Re Goodwin*[89] Megarry J. rejected the former doctrine of *Re Styler*[90] that an applicant must show that the testator had acted unreasonably in failing to make any or more ample provision, and held that the test is whether the provision in fact made was reasonable. In 1971[91] the Law Commission concluded that the surviving spouse was less amply protected under the legislation than the divorced former spouse under the amended discretionary judicial powers on divorce, and in 1974 it recommended[92] a considerable expansion of the legislation. A draft Inheritance (Provision for Family and Dependants) Bill was submitted; it received the Royal Assent on 12 November 1975 and came into force on 1 April 1976.

THE INHERITANCE (PROVISION FOR FAMILY AND DEPENDANTS) ACT 1975

This Act repeals and replaces all the previous legislation affecting all classes of applicants for family provision. It extends the powers conferred on the courts by the Family Provision Acts 1938–66 and the Matrimonial Causes Act 1965, ss 26–8A. As the Act has only recently come into force, the way in which its provisions will operate in practice cannot yet be clearly seen. By bringing together in one court applications from all those dependent on the deceased, however, it may mark the beginning of the end of the fragmented jurisdiction that has wreaked such havoc in our family law.

---

also illustrates the persistent attitude that if a man successfully evades his obligations during life the judges should not interfere with the continuance of evasion after his death.

88. *The Times* 2.11.63. For years few family provision cases reached the law reports, and judges themselves commented that many did not reach even the newspaper reports.

89. [1969] 1 Ch. 283, since adopted by Lord Simon of Glaisdale in *Re Shanahan* [1973] Fam. 1, and in the Court of Appeal in *Re Gregory* [1970] 1 W.L.R. 1455 and *Millward* v. *Shenton* [1972] 1 W.L.R. 711.

90. [1942] Ch. 388.

91. P.W.P. 42: *Family Property Law*, Part 3. Law Coms 52 (1973) and 61 (1974) went further than the Working Paper, in particular by rejecting the principle of maintenance for a surviving spouse in favour of recognising the survivor's right to claim a fair or reasonable share of the deceased's estate, i.e., capital. The Court has also, under the Inheritance (Provision for Family and Dependants) Act 1975, power to transfer or settle any assets forming part of the deceased's estate.

92. Law Com. 61: *Family Law: Second Report on Family Property: Family Provision on Death*, published 30.10.74. In connection with the 1975 Act see *Practice Note (Inheritance: Family Provision)* [1976] 1 W.L.R. 418 and S.I. No. 337 of 1976 introducing R.S.C. Ord. 99.

(i) THOSE ENTITLED TO APPLY

By s. 1(1), those entitled to apply to the court for provision include as previously, the surviving spouse[93] of the deceased, but now a surviving spouse (not judicially separated from the deceased at his death) who has remarried may apply. Applications from former spouses of a marriage annulled or dissolved or from spouses judicially separated at date of death are, however, still limited to those who have not remarried.[94] Any child of the deceased[95] of any age may apply, and so may anybody who, although not the deceased's child, was treated by the deceased as a child of the family in relation to any marriage to which the deceased was at any time a party. Most far-ranging of all, any other person may apply who, immediately before the death, was being maintained either wholly or partly by the deceased.[96] This will clearly include the mistress or cohabitee, even of the same sex as the deceased. The Act of 1938 was enacted primarily to protect the lawful widow and dependent children where the deceased had left most of his net estate elsewhere (usually to a mistress but sometimes to a charitable organisation). Now mistresses and illegitimate children are entitled to apply for provision from the estate, and an even more varied assortment of applicants may soon appear before the courts.

Where reasonable financial provision has not been made those entitled may apply. A surviving spouse (not judicially separated), is entitled to 'such financial provision as it would be reasonable in all the circumstances of the case for a husband or wife to receive, whether or not that provision is required for his or her maintenance'.[97] In respect of other applicants, it is such financial provision as it would be reasonable in all the circumstances of the case for the applicant to receive for his maintenance.[98]

(ii) ORDERS THE COURT MAY MAKE

These include not only orders for periodical payments or lump sums,[99] as previously, but also transfers or settlements of property comprised in the estate,

---

93. By s. 25(4) this includes one who in good faith entered into a void marriage with the deceased unless either that marriage was validly dissolved or annulled during the deceased's lifetime, or the survivor during the deceased's lifetime entered into a later marriage.
94. Section 19.
95. This includes an illegitimate child and a child *en ventre sa mère* at the deceased's death: s.25(1).
96. This means if the deceased, otherwise than for full valuable consideration, was making a substantial contribution in money or money's worth towards the reasonable needs of the applicant: s. 1(3).
97. Section 1(2)(*a*).
98. Section 1(2)(*b*).
99. By s. 2(2), periodical payments may provide for payments equal to the whole of the income of the net estate or of such part of it as may be specified, or of part or the whole of such part of the net estate as the court may direct to be set aside or appropriated for the making of the payments out of income. No larger part of the estate shall be so appropriated than will suffice at the date of the order to produce the income required for the payments ordered: s. 2(3). Section 25(3) confirms that the provision ordered may extend to the whole of the net estate. Lump sums may be ordered payable by instalments: s. 7.

or the acquisition of property not comprised in it, and its transfer or settlement;[100] or the variation of ante-nuptial or post-nuptial settlements (including testamentary settlements) made on the parties to a marriage of whom the deceased was one. Here variation may be ordered only for the benefit of the surviving party to or any child of that marriage, or of the family in relation to it. The court is also empowered to make such consequential and supplemental provision as it may consider fair and reasonable, or to confer on the trustees such powers as it may consider necessary or expedient.[101]

Guidelines as to matters to which the court is to have regard in exercising its powers are laid down in s. 3 of the Act, on the lines, *mutatis mutandis*, of those set out in s. 25 of the Matrimonial Causes Act, 1973 for financial provision and property adjustment orders under ss 23 and 24 of that Act. They include not only the probable financial resources and needs of the applicant, but also the financial resources and needs of, and the deceased's obligations and responsibilities towards, any applicant for an order, or any beneficiary of the deceased's estate; the size and nature of the net estate; any physical or mental disability of the applicant, and any other relevant matter,[102] including the conduct of any applicant or any other person. In the case of applications by a surviving spouse or former spouse the court is to have regard to the age of the applicant and the duration of the marriage and to the contribution made by the applicant to the welfare of the deceased's family, including any contribution made by looking after the home or caring for the family. In respect of applications by a surviving spouse (not judicially separated) the court is also to have regard to the provision which the applicant might reasonably have expected to receive if on the day on which the deceased died the marriage, instead of being terminated by death, had ended by a decree of divorce. In making this latter recommendation[103] the Law Commission was clearly trying to end a situation in which a widow receives less adequate protection than a woman who is divorced, but the wisdom of equating by statute the widowed with the divorced seems questionable. In dealing with children or children of the family, the court is to have regard, in addition, to the manner in which the applicant was being or might expect to be educated or trained. For applications from children of the family only, it is also to have regard to the

---

100. Section 2(1)(*e*): Law Com. 61, para. 116 explains that this power is intended primarily for use where the home does not form part of the estate or where the applicant wishes to move to a smaller home.

101. Section 2(4), confirming the interpretation given in *Re Preston deceased* [1969] 1 W.L.R. 317 to the previous law, but extending the courts' powers to deal with the additional property.

102. Law Com. 61, para. 36 supported Lord Denning's definition in *Wachtel* v. *Wachtel* [1973] Fam. 72 C.A., of the nature of the conduct of the other party relevant in matrimonial proceedings; viz. whether it would be 'repugnant to anyone's sense of justice' to make an order for financial provision. The applicant is presumably excluded from the company of 'anyone'. The provision is intended to include consideration of any written explanation left by the deceased, and s. 1(7) of the 1938 Act has therefore not been re-enacted. See also s. 21 as to the admissibility of statements made by the deceased, and Law Com. 61, paras 105–8.

103. Law Com. 61, para. 34, guideline (*k*).

extent of any responsibility the deceased had assumed for the applicant's maintenance, the period for which he had discharged it; whether he had assumed and discharged it knowing that the applicant was not his child and the liability of any other person to maintain the applicant. For other dependants of the deceased, the court is to have regard to the length of time, basis and extent to which responsibility was assumed and discharged. Account is to be taken of the facts known to the court at the date of the hearing, which may not correspond with those existing or known to the deceased at the date of his death.

The court may make interim orders[104] and orders for the variation or discharge of orders for periodical payments,[105] or in instalments for lump sums (but not variations in the total sum).[106] Orders may be made on the application of anybody entitled to apply for an order, the deceased's personal representatives, the trustees of any relevant property, or (in respect of periodical payments only) any beneficiary of the deceased's estate.[107]

(iii) PROPERTY AVAILABLE FOR FINANCIAL PROVISION

The new legislation seeks for the first time to provide effective anti-avoidance measures. Compliance with the previous legislation was voluntary. Anybody minded to avoid it had only to adopt one of the expedients for removing property from his net estate at his death,[108] since orders could be made only in respect of that net estate. The new Act attempts to deal with this in ss 8–13, as follows:

(a) By s. 8, the net estate will include the net value of money or property which the deceased during his life nominated anybody to receive after his death under existing legislation[109] or of which he disposed by *donatio mortis causa*;

---

104. Section 5. Personal representatives who pay out money under an interim order are protected from liablility for insufficiency of the estate by s. 20(2) unless when the payment was made they had reasonable cause to believe that the estate was not sufficient.
105. Section 6. This provision confirms the previous law but extends it to enable the court to discharge or temporarily suspend and subsequently revive any order, and not only, as previously, one in favour of surviving spouse.
106. Section 7(2).
107. The previous law is here extended to include all the new groups of possible applicants: former spouses may also apply to have any order varied. The inclusion of personal representatives, who may also be trustees of property, will enable them to apply before it is clear whether they have become trustees. The term 'beneficiary of the estate', by s. 25(1) includes a person in whose favour a nomination has been made, or the recipient of a *donatio mortis causa*, both types of property now included in the estate for family provision purposes by s. 8 of the Act.
108. These fall under two main headings: (i) disposal of the property and (ii) contracting to leave the property elsewhere by will: Law Com. 61, para. 189 and see Albery, *The Inheritance (Family Provision) Act 1938* (1949), Appendix D: 'Settlement upon mistress and illegitimate child for purpose of evading the provisions of the 1938 Act.'
109. Under a considerable number of statutes there is power for a depositor in such funds as the National Savings Bank, Post Office Savings Bank, and various funds of Trade Unions and Friendly Societies to nominate the recipient after his death of deposits made during his

(*b*) The court may, on an application for financial provision within six months of grant of representation only, sever the deceased's severable share of property on joint tenancy[110] at its value immediately before his death and, to the extent desired, treat it as part of his net estate;[111]

(*c*) If satisfied that, with the intention of defeating an application for provision, the deceased made a disposition within six years of his death for which full valuable consideration was not given, the court may order the donee or his personal representatives to provide a specified sum of money or other property from which financial provision can be made.[112] The value shall not exceed the net value to the donee at the date of transfer or of the deceased's death after deduction of capital transfer tax borne by the donee.[113] Once application is made in respect of one such disposition, the court acquires power to deal with other property which it is satisfied was so disposed of within six years of the death.[114] For these purposes a 'disposition' does not include any provision in a will, or a nomination, *donatio mortis causa* under s. 8, or any appointment made otherwise than by will under a special power of appointment, but includes any other payment of money.[115] The standard of proof is fulfilled 'if the court is of the opinion that, on a balance of probabilities, the intention of the deceased (though not necessarily his sole intention) in making the disposition . . . was to prevent an order for financial provision being made under this Act or to reduce the amount of the provision which might otherwise be granted by an order thereunder'.[116] The court is to have regard to the circumstances in which any disposition was made, any valuable consideration given, the relationship, if any, of the donee to the deceased, the conduct and financial resources of the donee and all the other circumstances of the case.[117]

(*d*) By s. 11[118] the court has similar powers where it is satisfied that the deceased made a contract to leave to any person a sum of money or other property by his will, or have such money or other property

---

lifetime. Such deposits do not therefore fall within the net estate disposed of by the will or on intestacy unless there are provisions to this effect. The Administration of Estates (Small Payments) Act 1965 Sched. 2 lists some such provisions, but not all. An upper limit of £500 for nominations is usual but not universal; for example in the National Savings Bank the limit is £10,000 and there are no limits for investment deposits. See Law Com. 61, para. 134(*a*) and nn. 149–150. Holders of deposits who pay out under a nomination are protected from responsibility by s. 8(1) of the 1975 Act.

110. Section 9; by s. 9(4) there may for this purpose be a joint tenancy of a chose in action.
111. By s. 9(2) the court is to have regard to any capital transfer tax payable in respect of the severable share.
112. Section 10 as modified by ss 12 and 13.
113. Section 10(3) and (4). If the property has been disposed of by the person to whom the deceased transferred it, the value is that at the date of its disposal, after deduction of capital transfer tax borne by the donee: s. 10(4).
114. Section 10(5).
115. Section 10(7).
116. Section 12(1).
117. Section 10(6).
118. As modified by ss 12 and 13.

transferred to that person out of his estate; that the contract was made with the intention of defeating an application for financial provision under the Act and that full valuable consideration for the contract was not given or promised. In such a case it may (i) order the donee to provide a specified sum of money or other property from which family provision can be made or, if all of it has not been transferred to the donee, (ii) order the personal representatives not to make any or any further payment or transfer, or only such as it may specify.

In respect of these contracts, the court may exercise its powers only to the extent that it considers the amount of any money to be paid, or the value of any property to be transferred, exceeds the value of the consideration for it. For this purpose it is to have regard to the value of the property at the date of the hearing.[119] The standard of proof that the contract was made with the intention of defeating an application for financial provision is the same as the standard for proving that a disposition was made with this intention,[120] but where no valuable consideration was given or promised, an intention to defeat an application for family provision will be presumed unless the contrary is shown.[121] In using its powers under s. 11 in respect of contracts the court is to have regard to the criteria applicable to dispositions of money or property under s. 10.[122] It cannot, under either provision, make an order in respect of part of the estate which has been distributed by the personal representative, who also is not liable for having distributed any such property before having notice of an application under either section.[123]

The court's powers to order trustees to provide money under these sections are limited to the aggregate of money covered by a disposition or a contract in the hands of the trustee at the date of the order and the value of property then in the trustee's hands representing or derived from such money. As regards dispositions or contracts for transfer of property other than money, orders for the trustees to provide property shall not exceed the aggregate value of such property then in the hands of the trustees, together with any property they then hold representing or derived from such property.[124]

The effect of these provisions is summarised in the definition of 'net estate' in relation to a deceased person, viz.:[125]

'(a) all property of which the deceased had power to dispose by his will (otherwise than by virtue of a special power of appointment) less the amount of his funeral, testamentary and administration expenses, debts and liabilities, including any capital transfer tax payable out of his estate on his death;

---

119. Section 11(3).
120. See s. 12(1) and n. 116 *ante*.
121. Section 12(2).
122. Section 10(6) and n. 117 *ante*.
123. Section 12(4).
124. Section 13.
125. Section 25(1).

(*b*) any property in respect of which the deceased held a general power of appointment (not being a power exercisable by will) which has not been exercised;

(*c*) any sum of money or other property which is treated for the purposes of this Act as part of the net estate of the deceased by virtue of s. 8(1) or (2) of the Act;

(*d*) any property which is treated for the purposes of this Act as part of the net estate of the deceased by virtue of an order made under s. 9 of the Act;

(*e*) any sum of money or other property which is, by reason of a disposition or contract made by the deceased, ordered under ss. 10 or 11 of the Act to be provided for the purpose of the making of financial provision under the Act.'

(iv) LINKS BETWEEN FAMILY PROVISION AND FINANCIAL PROVISION IN MATRIMONIAL CAUSES

When a party to a former marriage dies within twelve months of the date when a decree of divorce or nullity of marriage was made absolute, or a decree of judicial separation was made (which was in force, the parties being separated, at the death) the court may, if it thinks it just, treat an application by the survivor under the Inheritance (Provision for Family and Dependants) Act as if the decree had not been made. This applies only if either no application has been made by the surviving party for financial provision or property adjustment under the Matrimonial Causes Act, or an application was made but had not been finally determined at the time of the death. The object is to enable the court to make orders on a more generous scale in favour of the survivor, including a share of the assets of the estate not necessarily limited to maintenance,[126] and obviate the need for a separate application for family provision. The court may also, on or after granting a decree of divorce or nullity of marriage or judicial separation and with the consent of the parties, order that either is not entitled to apply on the death of the other for an order under the Inheritance (Provision for Family and Dependants) Act. Such an order will bar application by the judicially separated survivor only if the other party to the marriage died while the decree was in force and the separation was continuing, or by the former spouse only after the decree of divorce or nullity has been made absolute. This type of consent order will not affect applications by dependants other than the surviving spouse or former spouse, as for example, those on behalf of children of the marriage or of the family.[127]

By s. 16 of the Act, if an application is made for family provision by someone who, at the time of the deceased's death, was entitled to payments from the deceased under a secured periodical payments order under the Matrimonial Causes Act 1973, the court shall have the power to vary, discharge, or revive

---

126. Section 14.
127. Section 15.

that order or any instrument executed in pursuance of it. The court is to have regard to all the circumstances of the case, including any orders or interim orders it proposes to make for family provision and any change (whether resulting from the death of the deceased or otherwise) in any of the matters to which it was required to have regard when making the secured periodical payments order.[128] Section 17 gives the court powers other than those it possesses under s. 36 of the Matrimonial Causes Act 1973 to vary or revoke after the death of one party the terms of maintenance agreements entered into and providing for payments to continue after the payer's death. In particular, the powers are not limited (as are those in the Matrimonial Causes Act[129]) to written agreements.[130] The variation made takes effect as if made by agreement between the parties immediately before the death, as under the Matrimonial Causes Act.[131] Here again, the court is to have regard to all the circumstances of the case, including any orders it proposes to make for family provision and any change (whether resulting from the death or otherwise) in any of the circumstances in the light of which the agreement was made. Applications under the Matrimonial Causes Act 1973 for variation of either a secured periodical payments order or a maintenance agreement may be deemed to have been accompanied by an application for family provision and the court may then use its powers under either or both of the Acts and give consequential directions, except where there has been a consent order under s. 15 of the 1975 Act, barring application for family provision by the survivor. This should effectively link two of the stools between which applicants could formerly fall.[132]

(v) TIME FOR APPLICATION

'A time limit for applications must balance the interests of the possible applicants for family provision against the need for certainty in administering the estate'.[133] The Law Commission therefore recommended no change in the previous provisions. Section 4 of the 1975 Act accordingly provides that, except with the permission of the court, an application for family provision shall not be made more than six months after the date on which representation of the deceased's estate was first taken out.[134] The discretion for the court to extend the time for application enables it to deal with the gravest hardships encountered.[135] The personal representatives are, however, protected from personal liability only when they distribute the deceased's property more than six months after the date

---

128. Section 16(2).
129. Matrimonial Causes Act 1973, s. 34(2).
130. Inheritance (Provision for Family and Dependants) Act 1975, s. 17(4).
131. Section 17(3) of the 1975 Act is to the same effect as s. 36(4) of the 1973 Act, with 'varied' and 'variation' substituted for 'altered' and 'alteration'.
132. See Law Com. 61, paras 274–5.
133. Ibid. para. 144.
134. For this purpose, by s. 23, limited grants are to be left out of account.
135. See, e.g. *Re Hodgkinson* [1967] Ch. 634 C.A. (decided 1957); *Re Bluston* [1967] Ch. 615 C.A. *Re Kay* [1965] 1 W.L.R. 1463.

of taking out representation or under a court order.[136] They may also postpone for six months payment of any sum or transfer of any property under a contract made by the deceased if they believe that it was intended to defeat applications for provision.

The continuance of these provisions, coupled with the considerable extension of the class of possible applicants under the Act, has been attacked[137] as making it difficult or impossible for the personal representative to make any distribution to the lawful wife or minor children of the deceased until at least six months after taking out the grant of representation. It is hoped that the courts will make it clear that reasonable maintenance for a surviving dependent spouse and minor children is in all circumstances payable from the deceased's solvent estate from the date of death. In the last resort, an application could be made under s. 2 for an interim order under s. 5.

(vi) JURISDICTION

Section 22 of the Act re-enacts substantially the previous provisions, which limited the jurisdiction of the county court to cases in which the value of the property of which the deceased had power to dispose by his will did not exceed £5000. Power is given to the Lord Chancellor to fix a larger sum from time to time by statutory instrument, but the enactment of so low a limit on the county court's jurisdiction seems to hark back to hoary myths about the sanctity of the testator's most erratic or vindictive provisions. An upper limit of £15,000[138] at least would seem reasonable if the bulk of the estate is not in most cases to be swallowed up by legal fees.[139] There are the usual provisions for transfer of cases from the High Court to the county court or vice versa and an unusual provision that, should the upper county court limit be increased by statutory instrument, the county court will be entitled, as from the date when the instrument is laid before Parliament but before it comes into operation, to decline to transfer to the High Court applications in respect of estates exceeding the former but not the increased value.[140]

---

136. Inheritance (Provision for Family and Dependants) Act 1975, s. 20(1)(2).
137. Letter in *The Times* of 18.9.75. Interference with due administration is the principal reason advanced by most lawyers in the United States for opposing flexible restraints on testamentary dispositions.
138. The statutory legacy received by the surviving spouse on intestacy where the deceased left also surviving issue, additional to the personal chattels and a life interest in one half of the remaining estate. It was formerly the threshold for estate duty as it now is for capital transfer tax.
139. In *Re Parkinson, The Times* 4.10.75, even where the application was made to the county court the legal costs (including the appeal,) amounted to at least £1000 from an estate of less than £4000. The former matrimonial home had to be sold, so that the widow lost her home because she applied for provision.
140. Inheritance (Provision for Family and Dependants) Act 1975, s. 22(4)(*a*).

CHAPTER VII

The Effects of Separation or Divorce Between Spouses

Today divorce increasingly follows separation, with or without a court order[1] as an intermediate stage.[2] In either event, one immediate effect is that the income and property, if any, that formerly supported one household must now maintain and support two separate households, at least for a time and perhaps permanently.

The remarriage,[3] after divorce, of one or both former spouses may again affect both the personal and financial position of each individual and of any children of the former marriage.

When divorce was rare separation by agreement was normal, whether the agreement was oral, in writing or by deed. Now that divorce has become more accessible and acceptable and the powers of the courts have been considerably extended, they are increasingly required to make orders about the property, the parties' financial arrangements, and the arrangements for the custody, care, control and maintenance of or access to children. Sometimes, but today in a minority of cases, the courts are asked to approve the terms of agreements drawn up between the parties.[4]

---

1. Table II in Chapter V shows only 246 decrees of judicial separation granted in 1974. There are no statistics for non-cohabitation provisions in the magistrates' courts.
2. The *Finer Report* (Cmnd 5629), para. 3.1 points out that it is impossible to know whether the stability of marriage has changed from one generation to another. 'Nevertheless, the statistics of marriage breakdown are formidable.' And it concludes (para. 3.32) that as the result of earlier marriages and increased expectation of life, 'divorce has replaced death as the major factor in disposing of the marriages of couples in the younger age groups'.
3. A *de facto* relationship at any stage will have similar, but not identical, effects. Such relationships rarely leave a permanent record, and their precise effects and the ways in which they differ from the effects of a lawful marriage remain largely matters of (widely differing) surmise.
4. The Matrimonial Causes Act 1973, s. 7: The Matrimonial Causes Rules 1973, S.I. 2016 no longer include provisions for applications for the consideration of agreements between the parties. In *Smallman* v. *Smallman* [1972] Fam. 25 C.A., the parties made an agreement with a view to divorce 'subject to the approval of the court'. It was held that the husband could not

The kinds of orders made may be considered under the following heads, although some overlapping is unavoidable:[5]

A. For division or transfer of property either on application under the Married Women's Property Act 1882, s. 17, or the Law of Property Act 1925, s. 30, or the court's discretionary powers under the Matrimonial Causes Act 1973, s. 24(*a*) and (*b*) (as modified by ss 21, 25 and 30).
B. For variation of settlements under M.C.A. 1973, s. 24(*c*) and (*d*) (as modified by ss. 21, 25 and 30).
C. For other financial provision under the Matrimonial Causes Act 1973, ss. 21–3 and 26–33.
D. For maintenance under the Matrimonial Proceedings (Magistrates' Courts) Act 1960.
E. For possession of property under the Married Women's Property Act 1882, s. 17 as extended in respect of the matrimonial home by the Matrimonial Homes Act 1967,[6] or as ancillary to the court's powers under the Law of Property Act 1925, s. 30[7] or the court's discretionary powers under the Matrimonial Causes Act.[8]
F. The Enforcement of orders.

A. ORDERS IN RESPECT OF TITLE TO PROPERTY BETWEEN SPOUSES OR FORMER SPOUSES

Under the Married Women's Property Act 1882, s. 17, 'in any question between husband and wife as to the title to . . . property, either party may apply . . . in a summary way to any judge . . . and the judge may make such order . . . as he thinks fit'. It is traditional for property, particularly in the matrimonial home, to be held in the husband's sole name,[9] although both spouses have claims to it, either by agreement or by purchase.[10]

---

then resile from its terms. For the court's powers under ss 34–6 of the Act to vary maintenance agreements between the parties during the lives of both or after the death of one, see Chapter V, n. 17.

5. 'Although we have drawn a distinction between property rights and support rights they are, in fact, complementary': Law Commission P.W.P. 42, para. 0.20, p. 12. Support rights under s. 27 of the Matrimonial Causes Act are granted on proof of wilful neglect to maintain, although they are *semble* not enforceable whilst the parties are cohabiting and are restrictively interpreted.
6. As amended by the Matrimonial Proceedings and Property Act 1970, s. 38.
7. E.g. *In re Solomon (A Bankrupt)*, [1967] 1 Ch. 573; *Re Turner* [1974] 1 W.L.R. 1556; *Re McCarthy* [1975] 1 W.L.R. 807, and Matrimonial Causes Act 1973, s. 39, *ante* Chapter IV, and nn. 11–12 *post*.
8. See especially Matrimonial Causes Act 1973, s. 30 and *Danchevsky* v. *Danchevsky* [1975] Fam. 17 C.A.
9. But the Social Survey; *Matrimonial Property*, by J. E. Todd and L. M. Jones (1972) shows the rapid decline of the tradition as women increasingly seek stability in their lives by a proprietary right in their home: see further Chapter IV n. 49.
10. See Bagnall J. in *Cowcher* v. *Cowcher* [1972] 1 W.L.R. 425, and the criticism by Lord Denning M.R. in *Kowalczuk* v. *Kowalczuk* [1973] 1 W.L.R. 930, 933, at D, and by J. Levin, 'The matrimonial home—another round', 35 *MLR* (1972) 547.

Where spouses who have acquired the property in their joint names as trustees for sale for themselves as beneficial owners under the Law of Property Act 1925 subsequently separate, the spouse in possession normally resists demands for a sale. The general rule here is that, excluding bankruptcy,[11] where the parties are husband and wife and the property has been acquired as a matrimonial home neither party has the right to demand a sale whilst that purpose still exists.[12]

Under the Matrimonial Causes Act the courts have on divorce, nullity or judicial separation wide discretionary powers, first introduced in 1971,[13] to order transfers or settlements of property held by either party to a marriage; to vary ante-nuptial or post-nuptial property settlements, and to extinguish or reduce the interest of either party to the marriage under such a settlement. These are additional to their powers to order secured or unsecured periodical payments and to make lump sum orders.

The respective ambits of the three jurisdictions to deal with property are now of considerable importance.[14] In *Gordon* v. *Gordon*[15] Lord Denning M.R. said 'once there has been a divorce, applications under the Married Women's Property Act 1882, s. 17 should not be proceeded with', and 'the right way' is to take out proceedings under the Matrimonial Causes Act 1973, s. 24 and then determine all matters at issue between the parties 'according to the justice of the case'. He expressed similar views in *Wachtel* v. *Wachtel*.[16] Dunn J. adopted a different approach in *Glenn* v. *Glenn*[17] and considered there were two reasons in that case why the registrar should have referred the matter to a judge: (i) conduct had been raised, and (ii) when there were proceedings under both Acts the registrar should exercise his discretion to order transfer of the proceedings to a judge so that, in the event of an appeal, both appeals would come before the Court of Appeal.

It is not always possible, even if they consider it desirable, for the parties to leave the whole matter in the discretion of the court under the Matrimonial Causes Act. If they are domiciled or habitually resident say in Scotland but are litigating about land in England, their divorce is a matter for the

---

11. See Chapter IV nn. 104–7.
12. Per Salmon L. J. in *Rawlings* v. *Rawlings* [1964] P. 398, 418. Excluding bankruptcy, sales were ordered in *Jones* v. *Challenger* [1961] 1 Q.B. 176 C.A., *Rawlings* v. *Rawlings* [1964] P. 398, *Re Johns' Assignment Trusts* [1970] 1 W.L.R. 955, *Jackson* v. *Jackson* [1971] 1 W.L.R. 1539 and *Burke* v. *Burke* [1974] 1 W.L.R. 1063 C.A. (under the Married Women's Property Act 1882, s. 17). Sales were refused in *Re Hardy's Trust, The Times* 23.10.70. *Bedson* v. *Bedson* [1965] 2 Q.B. 666 and *Williams (J.W.)* v. Williams *(M.A.)* [1976] Ch. 278 C.A. In *Nielson-Jones* v. *Fedden* [1975] Ch. 222, the husband died after both parties had agreed that he should sell the house and use the proceeds. This was held not to defeat the wife's right to the whole beneficial interest by the *jus accrescendi.*
13. By the Matrimonial Proceedings and Property Act 1970, ss 1–9.
14. See S. Cretney, 118 *Solicitors' Journal* (1974) 431: '*The Matrimonial home after Wachtel*'; J. Neville Turner, 38 *MLR* (1975) 397: 'Confusion in English family property law – Enlightenment from Australia?' In Australia, the discretionary powers arise under Australian Federal legislation, whereas the Married Women's Property Acts are State legislation.
15. *The Times* 12.10.73 C.A.
16. [1973] Fam. 72, 93 at B.
17. [1973] 1 W.L.R. 1016.

Scottish courts, but the English courts alone can deal adequately with their English land. Moreover if one party is dead or insolvent the Matrimonial Causes Act does not apply.[18] There are many reasons why one or both parties may prefer to deal with their property under the Married Women's Property Act or the Law of Property Act,[19], but an overriding consideration may be the decision of the Court of Appeal in *Wachtel* v. *Wachtel*,[16] which has laid down general guide lines for the exercise of the courts' discretion under the Matrimonial Causes Act 1973. It has been generally applauded.[20] The one-third division, under which it is assumed that the husband is entitled to receive at least twice as much as the wife, was there described as a starting point but operated as a finishing point, and has been followed in most subsequent decisions.[21] The decision is therefore considered in some detail.

(i) *WACHTEL* V. *WACHTEL* [1973] Fam. 72 C.A.

(i) *The facts*

The marriage took place in 1954 when both parties were aged 28 and lasted until the wife left home on 31 March 1972. A son was born in 1958 and a daughter in 1961. The husband based his petition for divorce on the wife's adultery: she alleged his adultery and neither adultery was proved. Both parties were granted a divorce on the basis of the other's unreasonable behaviour. There was no appeal from the finding at first instance that they were equally responsible for the breakdown of the marriage.[22]

In 1956 they bought a house for £5000 in the husband's sole name with the help of a mortgage which was reduced from £5000 to £2000, while the house

---

18. *Re Nicholson deceased.* [1974] 1 W.L.R. 476.
19. See Cretney, 118 *Solicitors' Journal* (1974) 431, and nn. 41–4 *post.* The Court of Appeal has now held in *Williams (J.W.)* v. *Williams (M.A.)* [1976] Ch. 278, that such questions should not be decided in the Chancery Division under the Law of Property Act 1925, but in the Family Division under the Matrimonial Causes Act.
20. E.g. by the *Finer Report on One-Parent Families*, Cmnd 5629, which concentrated on some of the things the court said rather than the different things it did.
21. E.g. in *Harnett* v. *Harnett* [1974] 1 W.L.R. 219 C.A., Cairns L.J. at p. 224–5 stressed the importance of following, and Roskill L.J. at p. 227 that of 'loyally following' the decision of another division of the Court. In *Lombardi* v. *Lombardi* [1973] 1 W.L.R. 1276 C.A., one-third was applied to income, not only as between husband and wife, but as between husband and mistress in respect of profits earned in the business in which both worked. This seems contrary to the Equal Pay Act 1970 and the Sex Discrimination Act 1975. In *Gengler* v. *Gengler* [1976] 1 W.L.R. 275 the magistrates have been instructed to apply the one-third income rule to matrimonial orders in their courts. Scarman L.J. in *Trippas* v. *Trippas* [1973] Fam. 134 C.A. at 146 D–E said: 'there is nothing either in the so-called one-third rule or in the language of the Act of 1970 which precludes this court from doing rough justice on the basis of approximate equality'. The wife received £10,000 out of over £175,000 obtained by the husband after their separation but before their divorce. In *Hunter* v. *Hunter* [1973] 1 W.L.R. 958 C.A., the husband was ordered to pay the wife half the equity in the house in his sole name, which he had sold, but it is not really an exception to the one-third principle, since there was evidence there of a common purse. See also *S.* v. *S.* [1976] 3 W.L.R. 775 C.A.
22. Per Lord Denning M.R., p. 87 at H: 'The crucial finding of fact is that the responsibility for the breakdown of the marriage rested equally on both parties.'

increased in value from £5000 to at least £22,000 by the date of the divorce. The wife earned until 1958; thereafter she helped the husband as a receptionist in his dental practice, for which he credited her with a salary claimed as part of his expenses for tax purposes. The wife withdrew her original claim, based on contributions to its cost, to an interest in the house of which the husband remained in possession. The son of 14 was at a boarding school at the expense of his paternal grandfather. The daughter aged 11 lived with her mother. The Court of Appeal found that the husband's income could not be less than £6000 p.a., and that he 'appears not to have disclosed part of his income as a dentist'.[23] The wife's potential earning capacity on part-time work as a dental nurse was assessed at £750 p.a.

(ii) Guidelines and dicta

1. *Conduct.* Unless the conduct of one of the parties is 'both obvious and gross', so much so that to order one party to support another whose conduct falls into this category is repugnant to anyone's sense of justice, the court should not reduce its order for financial provision merely because of what was formerly regarded as guilt or blame.[24]

2. *The allocation of capital assets.* Since the court's discretionary powers were introduced in 1971, the question whether the wife had made financial contributions of sufficient substance to entitle her to a share in the house became 'of little importance', because the powers of transfer under the Act enabled the court to do 'what was just having regard to all the circumstances'.[25] The legislation of 1970 required the court to have regard to, *inter alios* 'the contributions made by each of the parties to the welfare of the family, including any contributions made by looking after the home or caring for the family'.[26]

If, therefore, the conclusion is reached that the home has been acquired and maintained by the joint efforts of both, it should be regarded as the joint property of both of them, no matter in whose name it stands when the marriage breaks down.[27]

---

23. [1973] Fam. 72, 97E.
24. Ibid. 90B–D. This is the authority followed in subsequent cases for disregarding conduct unless 'obvious and gross', e.g. *Harnett* v. *Harnett* [1974] 1 W.L.R. 219 C.A., *Campbell* v. *Campbell* [1976] Fam. 347.
25. [1973] Fam. 72, 92B. If the wife could here trace payments of her money towards the cost of the house, she may have been ill-advised to withdraw her claims under s. 17 of the Married Woman's Property Act.
26. Now Matrimonial Causes Act 1973, s. 25(1)(*f*), being the twelfth of thirteen 'matters to which the court is to have regard' in exercising its discretionary powers so as 'to place the parties, so far as it is practicable and, having regard to their conduct, just to do so, in the financial position in which they would have been if the marriage had not broken down and each had properly discharged his or her financial obligations and responsibilities towards the other'.
27. The passage usually cited by those who applaud the decision. There is here a false antithesis. Many wives contribute both in cash and in labour, time and skill. Mrs Wachtel did both, but the half share awarded to her at first instance was reduced to one-third on appeal.

3. *The one-third rule.* On breakdown of a marriage:

'The husband will have to go out to work all day and must get some woman to look after the house – either a wife, if he remarries, or a housekeeper, if he does not. He will also have to provide maintenance for the children. The wife will not usually have so much expense. She may go out to work herself, but she will not usually employ a housekeeper. She will do most of the housework herself, perhaps with some help. Or she may remarry, in which case her new husband will provide for her'.[28] '... A starting point at one-third of the combined resources of the parties is as good and rational as any other. ... There may be cases where more than one-third is right. There are likely to be many others[29] where less than one-third is the only practicable solution'. But one-third 'will serve in cases where the marriage has lasted for many years and the wife has been in the home bringing up the children. It may not be applicable when the marriage has lasted only a short time or where there are no children and she can go out to work'.[30] 'Most wives want their former husbands to make periodical payments as well to support them; because, after the divorce, he will be earning far more than she; and she can only keep up her standard of living with his help. He also has to make payments for the children out of his earnings, even if they are with her. We do not think she can have both – half the capital assets, and half the earnings'.[31]

(iii) The decision

1. The Court of Appeal reduced the lump sum payment to the former wife in respect of her share in the matrimonial home (which was accepted as being the

---

28. P. 94E. The passage implies that all women, but no man, must expect to do housework. There is no suggestion that a married woman earns her keep, sometimes abundantly. It is not true, as here implied, that fathers alone maintain their children, although most mothers do so in kind more than in cash. To look after her children a woman must forego more highly-paid work both in the present and the future. See *Milliken-Smith* v. *Milliken-Smith* [1970] 1 W.L.R. 973 C.A.
29. The qualifications clearly indicate that one-third is normally the maximum for a wife, and the courts assume that where sums are large the wife will be entitled to less than half the share of the husband. See Bagnall J. in *Harnett* v. *Harnett* [1973] Fam. 156, 164G. An exception was *O'D* v. *O'D* [1976] Fam. 83 C.A. It has been suggested, e.g. by S. M. Cretney, 36 *MLR* (1973) 653, 655, that less than a third of large sums may be a way of distinguishing 'family assets' from the husband's investment capital. Where the husband owns the capital it is, of course, he alone who decides how much of it he will release into 'family assets' and contemporary evidence of his intention is likely to be indirect and inconclusive.
30. [1973] Fam. 72, 95F. Thus the children also are entitled to a standard of living at one-half the level of that enjoyed by their father. This passage could mean that in a marriage without young children, where the wife 'can go out to work' she is entitled to none of the assets accumulated during the marriage, but it has not been so interpreted.
31. There had been no award of half the earnings in this case. Periodical payments are usually both temporary and unenforceable. The courts have refused to say so explicitly by making orders for amounts reducing annually until they disappear, as is done in some countries. But as soon as the husband acquires new 'dependants' he will be granted a reduction in the amounts payable to his wife or former wife and children, for change in circumstances, and the woman's maintenance is reduced or lost if she cohabits.

only substantial asset) from £10,000, or about half the value, to £6000, or less than one-third of it.

2. It confirmed the order for periodical payments of £1500 p.a. for the wife's maintenance bringing her income up to one-third of joint incomes[32] provided she earned £750 a year and the payments were made.

3. It reduced the order for maintenance of the 11-year-old daughter from £500 p.a. to £6 per week.[33]

(iv) The lessons of the case

1. In dealing with any property, including money, laymen and lawyers alike crave certainty. Judicial discretion can be exercised only round an accepted norm, and failure to include such a norm in the Matrimonial Proceedings and Property Act 1970[34] opened the way to reversion to the traditional one-third division adopted by the church courts. This will be applied as a rule because a rule is needed round which the parties can bargain out of court. The financial sanctions on litigation, despite legal aid, can be dramatic.[35]

2. The main justification advanced for the one-third 'starting point', and that only for the wife with children, and only after a long marriage, (at least according to *Wachtel* v. *Wachtel*) is that the man will continue to maintain his wife or former wife. But:

(a) the principle has been applied in *Lombardi* v. *Lombardi* to financial provision as between man and mistress working in a business together, where no such legal obligation is applicable;

(b) periodical payments for a wife or former wife rarely approach adequate maintenance for her; maintenance payments of £1 and £2 a week are scattered throughout the law reports.

(c) periodical payments are reduced as soon as the man acquires additional dependants, legal or illicit, and cease if the payee (usually the woman) remarries or cohabits or the payer (usually the man) dies. The woman may then apply amongst all his other dependants for family provision.

(d) periodical payments are usually made (though normally in arrears) by a professional man with a known address, at least until he acquires new dependants. Should he go permanently abroad they will cease. Where he is

---

32. Income (husband) £6000 plus (wife) £750. Wife's maintenance £1500 plus earnings £750 becomes £2250.

33. That is the only child for whose maintenance a father was liable was not entitled to one-twelfth of his income but to no more than one-twentieth of it.

34. The norm of equal division (subject to discretion) was put forward in the Matrimonial Property Bill, annexed to Law Commission P.W.P. 42, to which the House of Commons gave a second reading in January 1969. The Matrimonial Proceedings and Property Act 1970, and particularly s. 5, (now the Matrimonial Causes Act, 1973, s. 25) was falsely hailed as ushering in a system of matrimonial community of property. The courts have instead resiled from the former 'equity is equality', which may well have been misused (per Lord Reid [1971] A.C. 886, 897B) and reverted to assuming a woman's entitlement at a maximum of half a man's.

35. See *Till* v. *Till* [1974] Q.B. 558 C.A., and *Cooke* v. *Head* (*No. 2*) [1974] 1 W.L.R. 972 C.A., where the costs of litigation destroyed much of its purpose.

not easily traceable periodical payments are unlikely to be made regularly, and there is no effective form of enforcement short of a charge on capital.[36]

Most women with or without dependent children would be better off with more assets and no periodical payments. The unenforceable duty to maintain a wife and children prevents a rational approach to the problems the law should solve. The people most affected are the children, who are usually dependent on their mother after break-up of the marriage. They will live at her level, now fixed again at no more than one-half that of the husband.

The absurdity of long contests about the precise monetary contribution of each spouse to the acquisition of a particular asset, which the court may then set at nought by the exercise of its discretionary powers, has not escaped comment.[37] But the higher courts have repeatedly emphasised the irrelevance of conduct to property claims under the Married Women's Property Act,[38] and have held a woman's money to be of the same value as a man's. In the post-*Wachtel* situation, when the weight of the Court of Appeal has been decisively thrown against holding the balance impartially between the sexes, there are additional reasons why women should pursue their proprietary remedies, and why any attempt to reduce them[39] in favour of the court's view of 'the justice of the case'[40] should be resisted:

(ii) PROPERTY CLAIMS AND DISCRETIONARY ALLOCATIONS

Important features of the discretionary judicial powers are:

(i) The discretionary powers are no longer exercisable on the application of a party who has remarried following the grant of a decree of nullity or dissolution of marriage.[41]

(ii) The thirteen 'matters to which the court is to have regard', now set out in s. 25 of the Matrimonial Causes Act 1973, include the income of the

---

36. The *Finer Report*, Cmnd 5629, Table 4.9 and accompanying text is conclusive. Less than half the maintenance orders made are paid to the extent of 75 per cent. In a gross case, *Weisz* v. *Weisz, The Times* 16.12.75 C.A., a husband who had shown a determination not to pay anything to the wife (to whom he owed much) was ordered to transfer to her three-quarters of his property.

37. See, e.g. Jennifer Levin, 35 *MLR* (1972) 547; J. Neville Turner. 38 *MLR* (1975) 397.

38. E.g. Roxburgh J. in *Hickson* v. *Hickson* [1953] 1 Q.B. 420, 427 C.A.; Romer L.J. in *Cobb* v. *Cobb* [1955] 1 W.L.R. 731, 736 C.A. *Pettitt* v. *Pettitt* [1970] A.C. 777 H.L.

39. As suggested by Mr Neville Turner in the Australian context. His observation that in Australia litigation under the State Married Women's Property Act retains its popularity is further evidence that the profession will strive for certainty and rarely prefer judicial discretion.

40. As interpreted by the Court of Appeal in *Wachtel* v. *Wachtel*.

41. Matrimonial Causes Act 1973, s. 28(3). In *Marsden (J.L.)* v. *Marsden (A.M.)* [1973] 1 W.L.R. 641, Baker P. would not permit the former husband to pursue a claim under the court's discretionary powers after the former wife's remarriage. See also *Pace (formerly Doe)* v. *Doe* [1976] 3 W.L.R. 865.

parties. In *H*. v. *H*.[42] the wife had left the husband and four children for a richer man. She remarried after her application but before the hearing and the court reduced her share in the value of the former matrimonial home from one-third to one-twelfth of the value. It might be difficult to extend such a reduction to purely proprietary claims, and the decision may have been influenced by her conduct. In a claim under the Law of Property Act 1925 the county court judge's reduction of the woman's interest from one-half to one third was reversed by the Court of Appeal in *Leake* v. *Bruzzi*.[43]

(iii) Lord Denning's antithesis between the woman who contributes money to the home and the woman who contributes labour, time and skill, is inappropriate in most cases. All but a tiny minority of women do the latter; an increasing number do the former as well. Account should be taken of both, but while presumptions that a woman is entitled to half a man's share are applied, strict property claims should not be excluded.

On the other hand, an unfortunate decision was reached by the Court of Appeal under the Married Women's Property Act 1882, s. 17 in *Burke* v. *Burke*,[44] where it was held that after a divorce and his remarriage, a father might evict from his former matrimonial home, the two minor children of his former marriage as well as his former wife, so that he could sell it with vacant possession. The offer of suitable alternative accommodation should surely be a *sine qua non* for any physical parent seeking to evict minor children.[45] In reaching its decision, the Court of Appeal dissented from a dictum by Salmond L.J. in *Rawlings* v. *Rawlings*,[46] that: 'If there were young children the position would be different. One of the purposes of the trust would no doubt have been to provide a home for them, and whilst that purpose still existed, a sale would not generally be ordered.' It is thought that Salmond L.J. was right and the

---

42. (*Family Provision*: *Remarriage*) [1975] Fam. 9. See also *W*. v. *W*. (*Financial Provision*: *Lump Sum*) [1976] Fam. 107 and *Daubney* v. *Daubney* [1976] Fam. 267, where the former wife's interest in another residence was taken into consideration. In *Daubney* she had wisely invested tort damages received, whereas the former husband had contrived to lose his larger award. Similarly in *Martin* v. *Martin* [1976] Fam. 335 C.A., the former wife had brought the farm back to profitability after the husband left, whilst he had entered into disastrous financial transactions with his mistress, with whom he was suspected of hiding some assets. In *Calder* v. *Calder The Times* 29.6.76, the Court of Appeal took account of the husband's large reversionary interests contingent on surviving the life tenant of some Canadian settlements.

43. [1974] 1 W.L.R. 1528. See also *Griffiths* v. *Griffiths* [1974] 1 W.L.R. 1350.

44. [1974] 1 W.L.R. 1063 C.A. The most disturbing aspect of the decision in *National Provincial Bank* v. *Ainsworth* [1965] A.C. 1175, was that, by various dealings with the former matrimonial home, the father procured the eviction from their home of his minor children as well as his wife. The Matrimonial Homes Act 1967 does not deal with this problem.

45. Similar considerations apply to the eviction by a putative father of his illegitimate twin sons, which had been permitted at first instance in *Tanner* v *Tanner* [1975] 1 W.L.R. 1346 C.A. The Court of Appeal ordered the putative father to pay the mother £2000 compensation. See also *Colin Smith Music Ltd.* v. *Ridge* [1975] 1 W.L.R. 463.

46. [1964] P. 398, 419.

Court of Appeal wrong in *Burke* v. *Burke.* However in *Browne (form. Pritchard)* v. *Pritchard*[47] the court allowed an appeal by a former husband against the sale of the house in which he lived with his two sons aged 13 and 14, and held that there should be no sale until six months after the younger of the two sons was eighteen.

Even under the Married Woman's Property Act and the Law of Property Act, however, differences of approach exist and result in different answers. In *Cowcher* v. *Cowcher*[48] it was held that prima facie, and unless a contrary intention is proved, the parties are entitled on an implied or resulting trust in proportion to the contributions made by each respectively to the purchase price. This approach was criticised by Lord Denning M.R. in *Kowalczuk* v. *Kowalczuk,*[49] and in *Earley* v. *Earley*[50] a different Court of Appeal emphasized that account should also be taken of the financial burdens and commitments each party assumed.

Bagnall J. has drawn attention[51] to the fact that, by reason of the Law of Property Act 1925, ss 40, 52 and 53, claims in law or equity to any real property may require to be evidenced by deed or writing. Married people, even if they 'spend the long winter evenings hammering out agreements about their possessions'[52] are unlikely to reduce them to writing.[53] In *Gissing* v. *Gissing*[54] the court accepted that when the husband left her to live with a younger woman he assured the wife that she could retain the former matrimonial home, but since there was nothing in writing to this effect, he finally succeeded in evicting her. Mrs Merritt,[55] better informed, secured her house.

The jurisdiction under s. 17 extends to personal property abroad,[56] but has been held not to extend to loans from one spouse to the other.[57] It is available within three years after divorce and has also been used when one party is dead.[58]

---

47. [1975] 1 W.L.R. 1366 C.A., and see now *Williams (J.W.)* v. *Williams (M.A.)* [1976] 3 W.L.R. 494 C.A.
48. [1972] 1 W.L.R. 425, per Bagnall J. 431B–432D: 433–434A.
49. [1973] 1 W.L.R. 930, 933 at E. In that case it was held that the wife had no claim under s. 17 in respect of a house owned by the husband before the marriage, but that under the court's discretionary powers she might be given credit for contributions or improvements she had made.
50. *The Times* 20.6.75. Such considerations introduce a discretionary element which, in the present judicial climate, is likely to place women and minor children at a disadvantage.
51. *Cowcher* v. *Cowcher* [1972] 1 W.L.R. 425 at 430, 432 and 435–6.
52. Per Lord Hodson in *Pettitt* v. *Pettitt* [1970] A.C. 777, 810F.
53. *Fribance* v. *Fribance* (No. 2) [1957] 1 W.L.R. 384 C.A. is a rare example of an agreement that was not only clear but in writing. See 20 *MLR* (1957) 281.
54. [1971] A.C. 886, 889A.
55. *Merritt* v. *Merritt* [1970] 1 W.L.R. 1211.
56. *Razelos* v. *Razelos* (No. 2) [1970] 1 W.L.R. 392.
57. *Crystall* v. *Crystall* [1963] 1 W.L.R. 574 C.A.
58. Matrimonial Proceedings and Property Act 1970, s. 39. For use of s. 17 after the death of a party see *Re Nicholson decd.* [1974] 1 W.L.R. 476 and *Re Cummins* [1972] Ch. 62 C.A., although Law Com. 25, para. 61, p. 31 recommended that application under the section be not permitted after the death of one party. It seems that s. 17 is merely procedural, enabling the matter to be brought before the court. Where application has been made for family

Conduct of the parties. Cases since *Wachtel* v. *Wachtel* in which conduct has been considered relevant to property matters include *Cuzner* v. *Underdown*,[59] and *Bothe* v. *Amos*[60]. Both of these, like *Wachtel* v. *Wachtel*, raised the question of sexual conduct, particularly by a woman, a topic with which the divorce courts have inherited the church courts' excessive preoccupation.

Some cases, however, involve conduct or misconduct of a different kind. For example, *Bryant* v. *Bryant*,[61] *Jones (M.A.)* v. *Jones (W.)*,[62] and to a lesser degree *Hector* v. *Hector*.[63] There the husband had shown persistent cruelty and behaved badly. He was ordered to transfer to his wife the half share to which he had been held entitled in the home, which he had bought in his sole name. Violent disruptive conduct is different in kind from flighty or even promiscuous sexual conduct, and it is suggested that different considerations should apply to it from those applicable to a case like *Wachtel* v. *Wachtel*.

Even conduct that would not qualify under any of these heads has been held relevant in adjusting payments made by one party to a marriage after the other left without good cause, and a distinction has been drawn between deciding the shares of husband and wife at the point of separation and subsequently taking accounts between them.[64]

A new method of dealing with the matrimonial home when a couple with minor children were divorced was devised by the Court of Appeal in *Mesher* v. *Mesher*.[65] The house, held in the joint names of the former husband and wife, was there to be held on trust for sale, the rents and profits until sale to be held for the former spouses in equal shares. No sale was to take place while the daughter was under the age of 17 years or until further order. The former wife was to discharge all current outgoings but the capital payments, for example mortgage repayments, were to be discharged equally by the former husband and wife. The case was cited and followed by Bagnall J. in *Harnett* v. *Harnett*,[66] where a more complicated settlement was imposed, and in *Chamberlain* v. *Chamberlain*,[67] the court stressed the desirability of flexibility in decisions on financial provision and property adjustment, depending on the circumstances of the individual case.[68] This decision was in turn followed by Latey J. in *S.* v. *S.*[69]

---

provision and the court is seized of the matter, it has acted on the evidence produced to declare a resulting trust in favour of the purchaser. The facts in *Re Thornley* [1969] 1 W.L.R. 1037 C.A. were similar, but no resulting trust was declared. This may account for the Court of Appeal's unprecedented review of the exercise of discretion by the judge at first instance in awarding family provision.

59. [1974] 1 W.L.R. 641.
60. [1976] Fam. 46 C.A.
61. *The Times* 7.11.73.
62. [1976] Fam. 8 C.A.
63. [1973] 1 W.L.R. 1122 C.A.
64. *Cracknell* v. *Cracknell* [1971] P. 356, 362B.
65. *The Times* 13.2.73 C.A.
66. [1973] Fam. 156, affirmed C.A. [1974] 1 W.L.R. 219. Cairns L.J. at p. 224G said that conduct should be taken into account only in a very broad way.
67. [1973] 1 W.L.R. 1557 C.A. Here also there was to be no sale until the children had completed their education.
68. Contrast *Cumbers* v. *Cumbers* [1974] 1 W.L.R. 1331 C.A.
69. *(Note)* [1976] Fam. 18, (decided 1973). Maintenance of £4 per week was there allocated as

The discretionary powers under the Matrimonial Causes Act have been held to extend to a weekly contractual tenancy, which the Court of Appeal in *Hale* v. *Hale*[70] transferred from the former husband to the former wife after divorce, despite the landlord's opposition. However, while affirming jurisdiction to order transfer of a council tenancy where there was no covenant against assignment,[71] the Court of Appeal in *Thompson* v. *Thompson* refused to disturb the decision of a county court judge dismissing on the merits an application by the former wife for a transfer order.[72]

The courts have also held that the discretionary powers under the Matrimonial Causes Act include the right to decide which of two competing claimants may have possession of the matrimonial home, whatever the position as to ownership. In *Allen* v. *Allen*[73] the former husband was ordered to vacate the house in his sole name within two months so that the wife could return and make a home there for the three children, who had previously been separated, and a similar order was made in *Bassett* v. *Bassett*[74] pending the wife's suit for divorce. She was also granted injunctions against the husband's returning to or loitering near the home, or assaulting or threatening her or the child.[75] The discretionary powers have also been applied retroactively to make a property transfer order between parties divorced twenty years earlier.[76]

(iii) PROPERTY ADJUSTMENT BETWEEN COHABITEES NOT MARRIED TO EACH OTHER

The Matrimonial Causes Act 1973 does not empower the courts to adjust or transfer title to property between cohabitees not married to each other. The only law applicable is that between strangers, and there have been different

---

£3 per week for the child and £1 for the wife. Whatever the intention, such an allocation can only have the effect of encouraging the husband to believe that he is maintaining his wife and daughter, whereas he is failing to support either. Cf. *Wachtel* v. *Wachtel* [1973] Fam. 72, 94E, 'The husband . . . will also have to provide maintenance for the children. The wife will not usually have so much expense. . . .'

70. [1975] 1 W.L.R. 931 C.A. The landlord was the husband's father, but there was no covenant against assignment of the tenancy.

71. Not sharing the doubts expressed by Dunn J. in *Brent* v. *Brent* [1975] Fam. 1 at 8, whether a council tenancy constituted property for the purpose of the discretionary powers. The court in *Hale* v. *Hale supra* also disagreed with Dunn J.'s dictum to this effect.

72. [1976] Fam. 25 C.A. The couple had at first lived in the house when the wife's parents were the tenants. When the marriage was dissolved they had been there for twenty-five years. But the former wife had alternative accommodation whilst the former husband had none.

73. [1974] 1 W.L.R. 1171 C.A.

74. [1975] Fam. 76 C.A.

75. The dicta in *Hall* v. *Hall* [1971] 1 W.L.R. 404, which concerned a well-behaved professional couple living in a large house, were not applicable to those threatened with drunken violence in overcrowded accommodation.

76. *Chaterjee* v. *Chaterjee*, [1976] Fam. 199 C.A.

approaches to the application of resulting trusts. In *Diwell* v. *Farnes*[77] and *Ryan* v. *Ryan*[78] the court said that strict accounting would be applied, but a more liberal approach was adopted in *Cooke* v. *Head*[79] In *Eves* v. *Eves*[80] a married woman aged 19 years had cohabited for four years with a married man and they had two children. The man bought a dilapidated house, on which the woman worked hard, and when the arrangements broke down she was held entitled to one-quarter of the equity in it. Maintenance for the children was safeguarded by the order that while the father continued paying off the arrears of maintenance for them the house would not be sold.[81]

More complex facts were presented in *Horrocks* v. *Forray*,[82] which illustrates some of the pitfalls that may underlie such informal liaisons, and suggests caution in adopting simplistic solutions.

A more curious case was *Burgess* v. *Rawnsley*[83] where a man and a woman bought a house jointly, he contemplating marriage, but she intending only her sole occupation of the upper floor. When he died, she was held not entitled to his share by the *jus accrescendi.*

B. VARIATION OF SETTLEMENTS

The power to vary pre-nuptial or post-nuptial settlements[84] for the benefit of the parties to the marriage or children of the family[85] continues in s. 24(c) and (d) of the Matrimonial Causes Act 1973, and has not been displaced by the new powers for property adjustment or transfers first granted after 1970. But the courts have interpreted liberally the prohibition on application for such variation after remarriage following divorce,[86] first introduced by the Matrimonial Proceedings and Property Act 1970, s. 7(4) and now contained in the Matrimonial

---

77. [1959] 1 W.L.R. 624 C.A. This concerned the death intestate of a married man living with his mistress and their child. Willmer L.J. would have accorded the mistress equal rights in the assets of a joint enterprise.

78. *The Times* 4.5.63. See also *Richards* v. *Dove* [1974] 1 All E.R. 888.

79. [1972] 1 W.L.R. 518 C.A., especially Karminski L.J. p. 522E: the principles between man and mistress are 'in no way different from the principles applicable in the cases of husband and wife'. The mistress was given a one-third share in a house she never occupied, but on which she had spent money, time and labour. For the disastrous cost of litigation see *Cooke* v. *Head (No. 2)* [1974] 1 W.L.R. 972 C.A.

80. [1975] 1 W.L.R. 1338 C.A.

81. See also *Tanner* v. *Tanner* [1975] 1 W.L.R. 1346 C.A., Cf. *ante* n. 45.

82. [1976] 1 W.L.R. 230 C.A.

83. [1975] Ch. 429 C.A. See also *Hussey* v. *Palmer*, [1972] 1 W.L.R. 1286 C.A., where all the judges agreed that a mother-in-law should have a charge on property, for the improvement of which she had paid, but there was disagreement about the appropriate form of the action.

84. For the form of orders see *Jones* v. *Jones* [1972] 1 W.L.R. 1269, Dunn J.

85. Matrimonial Causes Act 1973, s. 24(1)(c). When the former husband died after making application and remarrying, his widow could not pursue the application as his administratrix. *D'Este* v. *De'Este* [1973] Fam. 55, Ormrod J.

86. *Jackson* v. *Jackson* [1973] Fam. 99; *Madden* v. *Madden* [1974] 1 W.L.R. 247.

Causes Act 1973, s. 28(3). The power was applied in *T.* v. *T.*[87] to extinguish the wife's joint interest in the matrimonial home where there had been very short cohabitation and little contribution, financial or otherwise, from her.

C. OTHER FINANCIAL PROVISION UNDER THE MATRIMONIAL CAUSES ACT

(i) MAINTENANCE PENDING SUIT

Under the Matrimonial Causes Act, the court has jurisdiction[88] on a petition for divorce, nullity of marriage, or judicial separation to make an order requiring either party to the marriage to make periodical payments to the other for any period during the time from the presentation of the petition to the date of its determination. Such interim orders are traditionally made on a conservative basis; a wife applicant may expect to receive an order bringing her income up to some 20 per cent of the joint incomes pending a full hearing.

(ii) FINANCIAL PROVISION BY PERIODICAL PAYMENTS OR LUMP SUMS IN MATRIMONIAL CAUSES[89] OR IN CASES OF WILFUL NEGLECT TO MAINTAIN[90]

Traditionally, financial provision after divorce or separation took the form of maintenance by way of periodical payments for which there was a plethora of different terms, depending on the type of action. 'Financial provision' has now replaced all these. Since 1949 a married woman has been able to obtain a maintenance order from the High Court without initiating some 'substantive matrimonial cause'[91] and since 1970 either spouse may do so, in a divorce county court or the High Court[92] on proof that the other has (being the husband) wilfully neglected to provide reasonable maintenance for the wife, or to provide, or make a proper contribution towards, reasonable maintenance for any child of the family[93] or (being the wife) wilfully neglected to provide or make a proper contribution towards reasonable maintenance for the applicant in

---

87. *The Times* 4.11.74.
88. Section 22.
89. Primarily under the Matrimonial Causes Act 1973, s. 23, as affected by ss 21, 25, 26, 28–33.
90. Primarily under s. 27 of the Act, as affected by ss 21, 25(3) and 28–33.
91. Law Reform (Miscellaneous Provisions) Act 1949, s. 5.
92. Matrimonial Proceedings and Property Act 1970, s. 6 and Matrimonial Causes Act 1967, s. 2.
93. Matrimonial Causes Act 1973, s. 27(1) expanded by s. 27(3) and (4). It must be shown that it would be reasonable in all the circumstances for the other spouse to maintain or contribute towards the maintenance of the child, and if the other spouse is not the child's parent the considerations under s. 25(3) must be taken into account.

a case where, by reason of the impairment of the applicant's earning capacity through age, illness or disability of mind or body, and having regard to the resources available, it is reasonable in all the circumstances to expect the respondent so to provide or contribute for any child of the family. Interim orders may be made. The statute does not say that the order obtained is unenforceable whilst the spouses are cohabiting, although it is usually assumed that this is so, and the authority sometimes cited to the contrary seems unconvincing.[94] Unfortunately, a restrictive interpretation has recently been re-affirmed of the jurisdiction to order financial provision on proof of wilful neglect to maintain a spouse or children. It has been held in *Gray* v. *Gray*[95] that uncondoned adultery by wife precludes any provision for her maintenance, since (i) s. 27 of the Matrimonial Causes Act 1973 represents a mere extension to the divorce courts of the jurisdiction in the magistrates' courts, and (ii) wilful neglect to maintain is governed by the common law rule that excludes any duty to maintain an adulterous wife. When the jurisdiction in the magistrates' courts is amended it is important that corresponding amendments should be made to these provisions.

Apart from these differences the kinds of orders that may be made for financial provision in matrimonial causes or on wilful neglect to maintain are similar, viz. for secured or unsecured periodical payments or a lump sum to the other spouse, or for secured or unsecured periodical payments or a lump sum to any person for the benefit of a child of the family or to that child.

Orders for periodical or lump sum payments cannot be separated completely from those for adjustments or transfers of property; references have already been made in the discussion of property orders to periodical payments or lump sums sometimes charged on real property as additional to or replacements for property orders. Applications for the kind of provision required should, however, be sufficiently specific.[96] The general principles laid down in *Wachtel* v. *Wachtel* are applied to all financial and property division, viz. the starting point is that the husband is presumed to be entitled to twice as much as the wife in respect of all property real and personal whether acquired during the marriage or accrued before it, and income actual and anticipated. The decision has been followed in pure financial provision cases.[97] It has recently been

---

94. *Caras* v. *Caras* [1955] 1 W.L.R. 254. It seems clear that the parties were not cohabiting in that case, though living separately under the same roof.

95. [1976] Fam. 324. The insertion of s. 27(8) in the 1973 consolidation Act provided a strong argument for the interpretation adopted.

96. In *Doherty* v. *Doherty* [1976] Fam. 71 C.A. the Court of Appeal held that, despite lack of clarity, the former wife's intentions had been made sufficiently clear and she should have been given leave to apply for a property transfer or a lump sum order, but in *Wilson* v. *Wilson*, [1976] Fam. 142 C.A. where only periodical payments had been applied for and there had been no application to amend the pleadings, it was held that no lump sum was recoverable.

97. E.g. *Lombardi* v. *Lombardi* [1973] 1 W.L.R. 1276. Reversion to the one-third division was first suggested in a financial provision case, viz. *Ackerman* v. *Ackerman* [1972] Fam. 225, in which at p. 234C Phillimore L.J. said: 'I would begin with the "one-third rule", bearing in mind that it is not a rule.' Where the marriage was short and the wife able to support herself no order or a purely nominal one may be made: *Krystman* v. *Krystman* [1973] 1 W.L.R. 927.

held[98] that a daughter aged 20, engaged in higher education, may be granted leave to intervene in a divorce suit between her parents in which the decree had been made absolute during her minority, so as to claim financial provision from both parents under the Matrimonial Causes Act 1973 s. 23.[99] The principal additional questions arising are:

(*a*) how freely the courts will order lump sum payments,
(*b*) the application of 'consent' orders, and
(*c*) the kind of order to be made where supplementary benefits are paid to the parties or one of them.

(*a*) LUMP SUM PAYMENTS

The Court was first given power to order payment of lump sums by the Matrimonial Causes Act 1963.[100] After 1970, however, the importance of this type of order greatly increased since periodical payments now cease on the remarriage of the recipient. The powers to deal with the husband's property first accorded under the Matrimonial Proceedings and Property Act 1970 have concentrated attention on the assets available and enabled the courts to charge the payment of lump sums on such property in appropriate cases. Both spouses are also becoming more aware of the possibility of obtaining a reduction of an order for periodical payments on proof of changed circumstances.[101]

At first the courts were hesitant to order payment of lump sums[102] and later said that such orders should not become commonplace amongst people of moderate means. These hestitations seem to be disappearing, and it has now been emphasised that the power to order lump sums cannot be ousted by

---

98. *Downing* v. *Downing (Downing intervening)* [1976] Fam. 288. Both divorced parents declined to complete financial statements or to contribute to local authority grants for her higher education. The divorce had been made absolute ten years earlier. Since the decision resulted in a compromise between the parties approved by the court no appeal is expected.
99. As qualified by s. 29(3). The court pointed out that, where orders are made in matrimonial proceedings for child maintenance to be paid direct to a child, the child alone can enforce payment of arrears, and that an adult may also enforce arrears accrued on a maintenance order under the Guardianship of Minors Act 1971 during his minority.
100. Section 5, following *Schlesinger* v. *Schlesinger* [1960] P. 191.
101. In *Calderbank* v. *Calderbank*, [1976] Fam. 93 C.A., the wife was ordered to pay the husband £10,000 from the proceeds of sale of the former matrimonial home wholly owned by her. She was also maintaining all three children. See Scarman L.J. at p. 593F that husbands and wives come to the judgement seat on a basis of complete equality. No 'starting point' has been laid down when the wife owns most of the capital, and husband applicants usually receive considerably less than half the property left with their former wives. See also *Griffiths* v. *Griffiths* [1974] 1 W.L.R. 1350.
102. *Hakluytt* v. *Hakluytt* [1968] 1 W.L.R. 1145, 1149 C.A., but *contra* was Law Com. 25 (1969), para. 9. The first awards reported were in *Curtis* v. *Curtis* [1969] 1 W.L.R. 422 and *Brett* v. *Brett* [1969] 1 W.L.R. 1187 C.A. See also *Millward* v. *Millward* [1971] 1 W.L.R. 1432 C.A., especially Edmund-Davies L.J. at p. 1434D. But in *Hunter* v. *Hunter* [1973] 1 W.L.R. 958 C.A., Edmund-Davies L.J. was a member of the court that declared lump sums useful when the parties were of small means. See also *Von Mehren* v. *Von Mehren* [1970] 1 W.L.R. 56, C.A., *Martin* v. *Martin* [1976] Fam. 335, C.A., *Calder* v. *Calder, The Times,* 29.6.76, C.A., and *S.* v. *S.* [1976] 3 W.L.R. 775, C.A.

any agreement between the parties.[103] The power has been exercised to cover the entire property of a spouse who disappeared.[104] Only one lump sum order may be made but it may provide for the payment of instalments or more than one lump sum.[105] On the other hand, if periodical payments were ordered, arrears which fell due more than twelve months previously may not be enforced without the leave of the court.[106] Application for a lump sum payment may, however, be made after a divorce if the former spouse's means have considerably improved.[107]

(*b*) CONSENT ORDERS

While the courts generally favour consent orders for financial provision, it is important that the terms be stated with sufficient precision to be enforceable.[108] In *Morss* v. *Morss*[109] such an order was held no longer enforceable because of the former wife's breach of its implied terms. Judges have differed on whether consent orders are or are not more difficult to vary than other kinds of orders.[110] The scope of this type of order was probably expanded with the extension of the special procedure for divorce without oral testimony in undefended petitions on grounds of adultery, two years' desertion, and five years' separation.[111] Consent orders are, of course, essential if any financial provision is required in divorces based on two years' separation with the respondent's consent.

(*c*) FINANCIAL PROVISION WHERE SUPPLEMENTARY BENEFITS ARE PAID TO ONE OR BOTH PARTIES

After the 1969–70 legislative reforms this matter was considered by the Court of Appeal in *Barnes (R.M.)* v. *Barnes (G.W.)*,[112] where the wife's decree of divorce had been made absolute in 1971, and the former husband remarried a

---

103. *Brockwell* v. *Brockwell, The Times*, 11.11.75. The wife agreed to renounce any claim to the matrimonial home, which was the only substantial asset. The Court of Appeal ordered a re-hearing of her application for a lump sum, even if it could be raised only on the security of the home.
104. *Ally* v. *Ally, The Times*, 24.8.71.
105. *Coleman* v. *Coleman* [1973] Fam. 10.
106. Matrimonial Causes Act 1973 s. 32, extended to magistrates' matrimonial orders in *Ross* v. *Pearson* [1976] 1 W.L.R. 224.
107. *Jones* v. *Jones* [1971] 3 All E.R. 1201 C.A. A lump sum was not ordered, but the annual provision was increased. In *Buchanan* v. *Buchanan, The Times* 21.5.73, the Court of Appeal reduced the lump sum payable where the husband's employment had ended.
108. *Practice Direction (Decrees and Orders: Agreed terms)* [1972] 1 W.L.R. 1313.
109. [1972] Fam. 264 C.A.
110. In *Wilkins* v. *Wilkins* [1969] 1 W.L.R. 922, Baker J. thought variation more difficult, but this was doubted in *Brister* v. *Brister* [1970] 1 W.L.R. 664.
111. S.I. 1975 No. 1359 from 1 December 1975.
112. [1972] 1 W.L.R. 1381 C.A.

month later. An order for maintenance of the former wife and three of the four children[113] who remained with her was made on divorce and registered in the magistrates' court for enforcement.[114] It was, however, insufficient for their maintenance, and she had been receiving social security payments (supplementary benefits). The Court of Appeal ordered that the sum of £1·50 per week for each of the four children should remain unchanged, but that the former husband should in addition pay £2 a week for the maintenance of his former wife. It might be enlightening to know the precise arguments for this insistence on a symbolic wording, when on the face of things the father and former husband was unable to support his children or their mother, his former wife.[115] In *O'Brien* v. *O'Brien and Smith,*[116] there had been an undefended divorce on the wife's petition. The former husband was patently unable to support his former wife or either of his two children by her, but wanted at public expense to have a judicial declaration about her conduct during the marriage. The Court adjourned generally the former wife's application for financial provision, saying that in such cases nominal orders should not be made, but the application be adjourned without a hearing.

Williams (L.A.) v. *Williams (E.M.)*[117] also concerned an order for financial provision made on divorce and registered for enforcement in the magistrates' court. The order, which was for £4 per week, was several hundred pounds in arrears, and both parties were receiving supplementary benefit. In this case, however, the 'diversion procedure' was in operation so that any sums the man paid were received direct by the Supplementary Benefits Commission, which was supporting him and probably providing any money he paid to it. The Divisional Court held that the magistrates were wrong in refusing to reduce the amount payable and also in doubting if the former husband was genuinely seeking employment, when the Supplementary Benefits Commission had better information.

D. MAINTENANCE UNDER THE MATRIMONIAL PROCEEDINGS (MAGISTRATES' COURTS) ACT 1960

Amendment of the Act may be anticipated soon after the publication of the Law Commission's Report on 21 October 1976, following its Published Working

---

113. Aged 11, 10, 8 and 7 at the time of the Court of Appeal hearing in 1972.
114. Under the Maintenance Orders Act 1958, considered *post* under enforcement.
115. A nominal order in favour of the wife will keep alive her right should the husband's circumstances improve. The *Finer Report on One-Parent Families*, Cmnd 5629–I Appendix 7 found no evidence that orders for children only are more regularly paid than those for both spouse or former spouse and children, although there is a popular myth that this is so.
116. [1972] Fam. 20. This is further evidence that it is the cost of legal aid that is the most important spur to 'no fault divorce'.
117. [1974] Fam. 55 See especially Finer J. at p. 62F and Baker P at p. 64B: 'it was the department that had legal aid, because the wife has no interest in this whatsoever. She cannot be either better or worse off'.

Paper No. 53.[118] The reforms are likely to fall somewhere between the unattainable (even if desirable) radical replacement of the magistrates' jurisdiction by an executive order, as suggested by the *Finer Report*, and the mild amendments recommended by the Law Commission Working Paper. Some defects of the Working Paper have been discussed in Chapter V, but the overriding characteristic of the magistrates' jurisdiction is not poor legislation but poor people. The Law Commission Working Party was in error in describing the magistrates' jurisdiction as a 'casualty clearing station'. It is and is likely to remain exclusively the poor people's and overwhelmingly the poor and ill-advised woman's court. It can never hope to do more than make partial arrangements for some redistribution of the inadequate funds available and for some protection of the children and the spouse in case of need.

Magistrates have recently been instructed,[119] in apportioning income between husband and wife in their courts, to adopt the one-third 'starting-point' laid down by the Court of Appeal in *Wachtel* v. *Wachtel*. In particular the court thought it would be unfortunate if a spouse with grounds for divorce were able to maintain herself in a better financial position by resorting to the magistrates than to the divorce court. The lower the joint income available, the greater is likely to be the deprivation of the wife who is judicially assumed entitled to no more than one-half of the share apportioned to the husband. Magistrates have also been directed not to enforce but to consider remitting maintenance more than twelve months in arrear for payment.[120]

E. POSSESSION OF REAL PROPERTY

At common law (i) husband and wife have a duty to live together until something happens to absolve them from that duty, and (ii) a husband has a duty to maintain his wife, which means in the first place to keep a roof over her head. In the acute housing shortage during and immediately after the Second World War which had also by long separation disrupted many marriages, the Court of Appeal in a succession of cases[121] applied these principles to extend to a married woman the protection afforded to her tenant husband under the Rent and Mortgage Interest Restrictions Acts 1920–39 and

---

118. Published on 1 December 1973.
119. By the Divisional Court in *Gengler* v. *Gengler* [1976] 1 W.L.R. 275. Magistrates were also referred to the considerations for income allocation set out in *Attwood* v. *Attwood* [1968] P. 591, 595–6. Strict application of the one-third 'starting-point' to the husband's gross (untaxed) and the wife's net (taxed) income in *Gengler* would have resulted in only a nominal order for the wife. The marriage had lasted three years and there were no children. Since the wife's expenses exceeded her earnings, however, the husband was ordered to pay her £3 a week.
120. *Ross* v. *Pearson* [1976] 1 W.L.R. 224.
121. The principal decisions are *Brown* v. *Draper* [1944] 1 K.B. 309 C.A., *Old Gate Estates* v. *Alexander* [1950] 1 K.B. 311 C.A., and *Middleton* v. *Baldock* [1950] 1 K.B. 657. See also Chapter IV note 122.

the Rent Acts. These precedents were specifically unaffected by the decision of the House of Lords in *National Provincial Bank* v. *Ainsworth*[122] and lay down that the wife's occupation is the husband's occupation; that the husband can neither revoke his wife's right to occupy the property of which he has the tenancy, nor contract out of his statutory right of occupation if she wishes to continue in occupation. If, however, a landlord obtains a possession order for non-payment of rent against the husband who is a statutory tenant, then the wife's possessory right is terminated.[123] No such rights inhere in the tenant's mistress and their young children, and therefore in *Colin Smith Music Co., Ltd.* v. *Ridge,*[124] when the male tenant surrendered his tenancy they could be evicted.

By the Married Women's Property Act 1882, s. 17, 'in any question between husband and wife as to the . . . possession of property, either party may apply. . . in a summary way to any judge . . . and the judge may make such order . . . as he thinks fit'. It has been held[125] that if real property is held in joint names, both joint tenants have a right of occupation. A judge (but not a registrar) has inherent power to order one spouse to leave, or to restrain him from entering the premises,[126] and by the Domestic Violence and Matrimonial Proceedings Act 1976 s. 4 either may apply for court orders. However, the court will not so order unless real need is shown.[127] The spouse's right of occupation is, however, terminated by divorce.[128] But even after divorce the court has power at common law to order one party to leave if real need is shown, and violence is not essential.[129] Unfortunately at present the magistrates' courts have no power to issue injunctions to prevent violence or stop one spouse entering or remaining in property occupied by the other.

When the House of Lords in *National Provincial Bank* v. *Ainsworth* declared non-existent the 'married women's equity' which some previous courts had applied only to the woman deserted and left in occupation of her husband's property[130] the Matrimonial Homes Act 1967 was passed to remedy the

---

122. [1965] A.C. 1175.
123. *Penn* v. *Dunn* [1970] 2 Q.B. 686 C.A. See also *Metrobarn Ltd.* v. *Gehring* [1976] 1 W.L.R. 776 C.A. The Law Commission has recommended that the spouse in occupation should be able to apply to the court to suspend execution of a possession order. See P.W.P. 42.
124. [1975] 1 W.L.R. 463 C.A. By the Family Law Reform Act 1969, s. 14(2) this and every other putative father has an absolute right of succession should these children die intestate leaving property 'as if the child had been born legitimate'.
125. *Gurasz* v. *Gurasz* [1970] P. 11 C.A.
126. There are many such decisions, including *Silverstone* v. *Silverstone* [1953] P. 174; *Maynard* v. *Maynard* [1969] P. 88, especially per Baker J. at 100B–C, and *Jones* v. *Jones* [1971] 1 W.L.R. 396 C.A.
127. *Gorulnik* v. *Gorulnik* [1958] P. 47 C.A., *Hall* v. *Hall* [1971] 1 W.L.R. 404 C.A. and *Montgomery* v. *Montgomery* [1965] P. 46. But see *Bassett* v. *Bassett* [1975] Fam. 76 C.A., discussed *ante* notes 74–5.
128. *Vaughan* v. *Vaughan* [1953] 1 Q.B. 762 C.A. *Morris* v. *Tarrant* [1971] 2 Q.B. 143, unless an occupation order is obtained before or during the divorce proceedings.
129. *Phillips* v. *Phillips* [1973] 1 W.L.R. 615 C.A., a case of noisy isolation and non-involvement in the troubles of wife and son. See also *Stewart* v. *Stewart* [1973] Fam. 21.
130. As in *Bendall* v. *McWhirter* [1952] 2 Q.B. 466 C.A. and many cases following that decision.

situation. By s. 1 of the Act, the spouse without a property right[131] is entitled to occupy the matrimonial home and her or his exclusion is illegal. Unfortunately there is no summary remedy for exclusion, and the only sanction is application to the court, especially since the police will rarely intervene in a domestic dispute. The occupation right may be valid against such third parties as the subsequent purchaser or mortgagee provided it has been registered, but is not enforceable against the trustee in bankruptcy of the owner spouse.[132] Nor is there any right of possession in the minor children, who are mentioned only among the circumstances to be taken into consideration by the court in exercising its powers. Contractual and statutory tenancies are included in the Act[133] but not council tenancies (which comprise two-thirds of all unfurnished lettings in the country), nor crown tenancies. To safeguard her or (unusually) his occupation rights the non-owner spouse should register either (i) a Land Charge Class F against the owner's name in the register[134] or (ii) in respect of registered land, a notice or caution against the title,[135] but the possessory right is not an overriding interest under the Land Registration Act 1925. Alternatively the non-owner spouse may obtain a court order before[136] or during[137] divorce or nullity proceedings, but if the proceedings are terminated without such an order having been made the right to it is lost when the marriage ends either by court order or by the death of the tenant.[138]

Unless the charge or caution under s. 2 of the Act was registered before the mortgage was created or the sale effected, the mortgagee or purchaser will have a claim to vacant possession ranking prior to that of the non-owner spouse.[139] It has been held[140] that if mortgage repayments are in arrears, the mortgagee need not give notice of the arrears to the spouse in occupation, whose only right is to redeem the mortgage if she[141] is able. Even if not in occupation, a spouse may register her conditional right of occupation as a charge under the Act,[142] although it cannot be enforced without an order of the court.[143]

---

131. As amended by the Matrimonial Proceedings and Property Act 1970, s. 38, this includes a spouse entitled under a constructive or resulting trust.
132. Section 2(5); *Bendall* v. *McWhirter* [1952] 2 Q.B. 466 C.A. is to this extent not revived. And see *Hounslow London Borough Council* v. *Peake* [1974] 1 W.L.R. 26 D.C.
133. Matrimonial Homes Act 1967, s. 7.
134. Ibid. s. 2(6).
135. Section 2(7).
136. Under s. 1(1)(*b*) or 1(2) or s. 7 for tenancies.
137. Under s. 2(2).
138. Unless the statutory tenancy passes to her or him under the Rent Acts.
139. *Miles* v. *Bull* [1969] 1 Q.B. 258; *Caunce* v. *Caunce* [1969] 1 W.L.R. 286.
140. *Hastings & Thanet Building Society* v. *Goddard* [1970] 1 W.L.R. 1544, and see *Halifax Building Society* v. *Clark* [1973] Ch. 307; the mortgagee is entitled to possession as against the mortgagor's spouse in possession unless there is a reasonable chance that the mortgagor or his spouse can, within a reasonable time, pay off the sums due.
141. The Act does not discriminate between the sexes, but the owner is more likely to be the husband and the non-owner the wife.
142. *Watts* v. *Waller* [1973] 1 Q.B. 153 C.A., overruling *Rutherford* v. *Rutherford* [1970] 1 W.L.R. 1479.
143. Under s. 1(1)(*b*): *Baynham* v. *Baynham* [1968] 1 W.L.R. 1890 C.A.

For some time it was thought that the principal use of the Act was to enable the spouse of the owner to bargain for a sum of money as the price of releasing her right of occupation and agreeing beforehand to be deferred to the rights of others.[144] The decision in *Wroth* v. *Tyler*[145] demonstrates the possible cost to all parties of ignoring the spouse's occupation right. Here a husband about to retire contracted to sell for £6000 the bungalow in which he lived with his wife and adult daughter. He also contracted to buy a cheaper bungalow in another part of the country.[146] The owner admitted that his wife and daughter, who were very close to each other, were both 'very cool' towards the proposed move. The day after contracts were exchanged the owner's wife entered notice of her right of occupation in the charges register against the husband's title. She did not tell her husband, and Megarry J. commented: 'One can only speculate on the wife's thoughts as she lived her daily life with the defendant, with this unrevealed secret in her mind.[147] On discovering her notice of occupation, the husband tried, by striking her, to persuade his wife to remove it from the register, but was not surprisingly unsuccessful. The husband could not complete his contract on due date. The value of the bungalow he had agreed to sell had risen to £11,500 at the date of the hearing, and damages of £5500, were awarded against him. The net result may have been to force the husband into bankruptcy, when the house would have been sold. It would be prudent to insist upon the written agreement of the spouse with a right of occupation before any contract is made for the sale of a matrimonial home with vacant possession, or to search the register before contracts are signed. If the right has already been registered, the notice, caution or land charge must be withdrawn.

By s. 1(2) of the Act as amended by the Domestic Violence and Matrimonial Proceedings Act 1976 s. 3, 'either spouse may apply to the court for an order prohibiting, suspending or restricting the exercise by either spouse of the right to occupy the home', and requiring either to allow the other to exercise such rights.[148] The High Court or a county court judge may also exclude the owner on the common law or other statutory principles previously discussed.[149]

The divorced, deserted or separated spouse occupying real property whose spouse or former spouse does not pay the mortgage instalments[150] or rent or rates[151] due, is liable to eviction unless the occupying spouse can make the

---

144. As permitted by s. 6(2)(3).
145. [1974] Ch. 30.
146. The wife gave no evidence at the trial. The court's version of what took place between husband and wife was therefore informed by the evidence of one party only.
147. One wonders what inhibited speculation on the husband's thoughts as he lived his daily life with the wife, knowing that he was seeking to force her to move from a district in which they had lived for twenty-three years and far from their daughter to whom she was very close.
148. The Act was amended following the decision in *Tarr* v. *Tarr* [1973] A.C. 254.
149. *Ante* nn. 6–8, 73–75, 124–126.
150. *Hastings and Thanet Building Society* v. *Goddard* [1970] 1 W.L.R. 1544 C.A.
151. *Des Salles d'Epinoix* v. *Kensington and Chelsea Royal London Borough Council* [1970] 1 W.L.R. 179 D.C., *Mourton* v. *Hounslow London Borough Council* [1970] 2 Q.B. 362 and *Metrobarn Ltd.* v. *Gehring* [1976] 1 W.L.R. 776 C.A.

required payments,[152] even though the divorced former spouse will be in occupation only by reason of a court order.

The court's powers under the Matrimonial Homes Act are, of course, additional to and not in derogation of its powers under the Law of Property Act 1925 and the Bankruptcy Act 1914 to order a sale with vacant possession, and its powers to order such a sale on an application either under the Married Women's Property Act 1882, s. 17 or under the discretionary powers contained in s. 24 of the Matrimonial Causes Act.

F. ENFORCEMENT OF PROPERTY AND FINANCIAL PROVISION ORDERS

By the Matrimonial Causes Act 1973, s. 30 the court may direct a proper instrument to be drawn up for securing financial provision or transferring property and, by s. 30(b), it is expressly empowered to defer the grant of the decree until the instrument has been duly executed. The court also has power under the Supreme Court of Judicature (Consolidation) Act 1925, s. 47 or the County Courts Act 1959, s. 74 to execute a conveyance of property[153] and it may issue a warrant for possession and sale of any real property. In *S.* v. *S.*[154] a receiving order was made against a husband who persistently refused to pay as ordered.

The court may, under s. 37 of the 1973 Act, restrain one party from disposing of assets or transferring them out of the jurisdiction[155] and set aside a disposition made in contemplation of or with the intention of defeating a claim for financial relief, unless it was made for valuable consideration (other than marriage) to someone acting in good faith and without notice of the intention. Intention to defeat a claim is presumed if the disposition took effect less than three years before the claim was made.

Where there is no capital, enforcement presents problems ranging from the difficult to the insoluble. The Matrimonial Proceedings (Magistrates' Courts) Act 1960, s. 13(1)[156] provides that maintenance orders shall be enforced in the same manner as affiliation orders. Under Part I of the Maintenance Orders Act 1958, orders granted in the High Court and the county court may be registered for enforcement in the magistrates' court and orders obtained in the magistrates' court may be similarly registered for enforcement in the county court or the High Court.[157]

---

152. The occupying spouse is entitled to make such payments under the Matrimonial Homes Act 1967, s. 1(5).
153. See *Danchevsky* v. *Danchevsky* [1975] Fam. 17 C.A.
154. *The Times* 23.6.73.
155. See *Benson* v. *Benson*, *The Times* 2.1.73.
156. See also the Magistrates Courts Act 1952, ss 52, 53 and 74. Payments are made to the clerk of the court and he tries to collect arrears.
157. The comparative popularity of enforcement procedures is shown by the fact that in 1974, 15,838 orders made in the higher courts were registered in the magistrates' courts, but only 64 made in the magistrates' courts were registered in the county courts and High Court: *Civil Judicial Statistics* 1974, Cmnd 6361, Table B12(vi).

Attachment of earnings was first introduced for maintenance orders in 1958, and extended to judgement debts by the Attachment of Earnings Act 1971. The Payne Committee on the *Enforcement of Judgement Debts*,[158] also recommended the establishment of an enforcement office, with local offices attached to the county courts in each district, which would from the start of enforcement be in a position to ensure the ordered control of the debtor's affairs which is fundamental to a proper system of enforcement. This recommendation was not implemented. An attachment of earnings order may be made by the High Court, county court or a magistrates' court. It is made on the debtor's employer on the application of the person due to make or to receive maintenance payments. Should the debtor leave his employment the order does not lapse but is now transferable from one employer to another. The debtor must have failed to pay one or more instalment of money due under a financial provision or maintenance order, and except on his own application, the court does not make an attachment of earnings order unless his failure to pay was due to the debtor's wilful refusal or culpable neglect. It is, however, no longer necessary that he should be a month in arrear before an attachment order can be made. The order must state the normal deduction rate, viz. the sum to be deducted from the employee's earnings and sent to the court, and the protected earnings rate, viz. the minimum sum that must be left free for the employee, sufficient to cover his subsistence. It has been held that, where the debtor has greatly increased the number of his dependants, the protected earnings rate may be below the supplementary benefit subsistence rate.[159]

The extent to which the Department of Health and Social Security should take over the onus of extracting money from the liable relative is probably not yet decided. In *Winter* v. *Winter*[160] Payne J. suggested that the Department should enforce payment in all courts where the parties were poor, but a Private Member's Bill to this effect was withdrawn. The *Finer Report*'s recommendation for a Guaranteed Maintenance Allowance payable by the Department for all those looking after minor children will not be implemented in the near future, but the Department's payments to (usually) women in this position are nevertheless considerable,[161] and child benefit should be operative by 1979. The *Finer Report* also published the Supplementary Benefits Commission formula for the 'liable relative',[162] which allows him (and those living with and dependent on him) the supplementary benefits scale plus either £5 per week or 25 per cent of

---

158. Cmnd. 3909 of 1969. The passage quoted is from para. 318.
159. *Billington* v. *Billington* [1974] Fam. 24 D.C. A registered disabled person did not pay the £1 per week ordered for the maintenance of his former wife. He had remarried a widow with three children, all of whom he had adopted. His protected earnings rate of £11 p.w. was below supplementary benefits subsistence rate. An enquiry would seem indicated to find out why such adoptions were allowed. They could not have been for the financial benefit of the children.
160. *The Times* 14.11.72.
161. According to the *Finer Report*, Cmnd 5629, para. 4.89, and Table 4.14, in 1972 the S.B.C. paid out some £144·55 million to divorced women, separated wives and mothers responsible for illegitimate children, who received a further £12 million from the men liable to support them. The Commission recovered about £12·52 million from the liable relatives.
162. Ibid. paras 4.188 and 4.189.

his net earnings (whichever is the greater) before he has any obligation to contribute to the maintenance of his wife or former wife or his children by her when they are receiving supplementary benefit. The *Finer Report* found nothing to criticise in this acceptance of the wage-earner's right to a higher standard of living than his minor children, and suggested its continuance should a Guaranteed Maintenance Allowance be introduced.[163]

Government Departments will also help in tracing missing spouses by providing their addresses to the court, but not to the other spouse or former spouse.[164]

Both the Payne Committee's Report on the Enforcement of Judgement Debts and the Finer Report on One-Parent Families have condemned committal to prison for non-payment of maintenance as guaranteed to produce no maintenance but add at least one to the number of those supported in secure conditions at great expense to the community. So far, however, such alternatives as administration orders for defaulters on maintenance orders have not been implemented.

G. INTERNATIONAL ENFORCEMENT OF PROPERTY AND MAINTENANCE ORDERS

The Maintenance Orders (Reciprocal Enforcement) Act 1972 has now been brought fully into operation[165] by Statutory Instrument. Part I of the Act replaces the Maintenance Orders (Facilities for Enforcement) Act 1920, for enforcement in one part of the Commonwealth of orders (including affiliation orders) made by magistrates or the sheriff in another. It was brought into operation from 1 April 1974,[166] and extends to Scotland. Orders in Council have been made under this Part, so that there is an extended scheme of reciprocal enforcement between the United Kingdom and certain Commonwealth countries[167] for maintenance, including affiliation, orders made in magistrates' courts or their equivalents. As under the 1920 Act, it is the creditor who obtains the order in the country of his residence. The country in which the debtor resides may enforce or, on application by the debtor, provisionally vary or revoke the

---

163. According to the *Finer Report*, Cmnd 5629, para. 5, 227.
164. *Practice Note* (*Disclosure of Addresses*) [1973] 1 W.L.R. 60.
165. Except for s. 22(2), which will repeal the previous legislation. All the Orders made under the earlier legislation, extending enforcement to a large number of Commonwealth countries and to South Africa, remain operative. As the legislation of these countries is amended to accept the principles accepted by the United Kingdom in the Act of 1972, further designations will be made under Part I of the Act.
166. By S.I. 517 of 1974.
167. At present Gibraltar; New Zealand; the Australian Territories and States except for Western Australia; British Columbia, Manitoba, Nova Scotia and Ontario. *Collister* v. *Collister* [1972] 1 W.L.R. 54 D.C. (decided under the Act of 1920) makes it clear that the Act does not give jurisdiction to make a maintenance order, but only to enforce one already made.

order; and the court that originally made it may then confirm or refuse to confirm the variation or revocation. [168]

Part II of the Act applies for the recovery of maintenance where the laws of the countries in which the debtor and the creditor respectively reside are fundamentally different. Its enactment will enable the United Kingdom to accede to the United Nations Convention of 1956 on the Recovery Abroad of Maintenance, [169] on which it is based. Under this Part it is for the country of the debtor's residence to make a maintenance order, and in so doing, it applies its own laws, thereby avoiding problems of conflict of laws. This Part of the Act was brought into operation on 12 April 1975, [170] and from that date thirty-seven countries have been designated as convention countries, that is, countries to which the United Nations Convention extends. The United Kingdom does not intend to ratify the Hague Conventions of 1956 on the Law Applicable to Maintenance Obligations towards Children, [171] or that of 1958 on their Recognition and Enforcement. [172] A further draft Hague Convention on the Recognition and Enforcement of Decisions relating to Maintenance Obligations was prepared in 1972 by the Hague Conference on Private International Law. This provides for recognition or enforcement by contracting parties of maintenance obligations if certain jurisdictional conditions are satisfied.

The delay of more than three years between the date of the Royal Assent to the Act of 1972 [173] and 12 April 1975, when Part II became operative, is indicative of the delays encountered in international implementation of such agreements.

Part III of the Act enables reciprocal enforcement machinery to be established by bilateral treaties where neither of the two earlier Parts of the Act is appropriate, for example with countries having a federal Constitution in which recovery and enforcement of maintenance is not the responsibility of the Federal Government, and the individual States cannot accede to the 1956 United Nations Convention. The first bilateral treaty under Part III was made with the Republic of Ireland, and came into force on 1 April 1975, applying the machinery of Part I of the Act with modifications.

Article 220 of the Treaty of Rome provides that 'Member States shall, so far as is necessary, enter into negotiations with each other with a view to securing

---

168. See In *re McK The Times* 14.7.76 where a magistrate in Sydney Australia had reduced from £3,000 to £275 p.a. an order made in the English High Court for maintenance of a former wife. The reduction was not confirmed and suggestions were made for improving the amount of information available on such applications.

169. Cmnd 4485.

170. By S.I. 423 of 1975, the Recovery Abroad of Maintenance (Convention Countries) Order 1975. Convention Countries include France (and many of her overseas departments and territories) Federal Germany and West Berlin; Austria; Belgium; Greece; Hungary; Israel; Italy; the Netherlands (Kingdom and Netherlands Antilles); Poland; Portugal; Spain; Sweden; Turkey and Yugoslavia.

171. Cmnd 4533.

172. Cmnd 4534.

173. 23 March 1972. The current practice of bringing statutes into operation by statutory instrument creates great uncertainty, which is compounded by delays of this order.

for the benefit of their nationals: the protection of persons and the enjoyment and protection of rights under the same conditions as those accorded by each State to its own nationals.' In 1968 the then six members of the European Communities accepted the provisions of a Convention on Jurisdiction and the Enforcement of Civil and Commercial Judgements, which has been in force since 1973. Property disputes between husband and wife are expressly excluded from the Convention, but maintenance is included. Negotiations have taken place in Brussels about the accession of the United Kingdom to the Convention, which must be expected at some time. The basis of jurisdiction is the domicile of the respondent or, as special jurisdiction, the domicile or habitual residence of the claimant.

CHAPTER VIII

Orders for the Care and Control of Children of Separated Parents

A. ONE-PARENT FAMILIES

The estimated number of children in Great Britain in 1971 living with one parent only because their parents are divorced or separated, or one of them has died, or the parents were never married to each other, is set out in Table III, produced by the Department of Health and Social Security:[1]

TABLE III

Estimate (in thousands) of Number of One-Parent Families with Dependent Children Resulting from Illegitimacy, Factual Separation, Death and Divorce: Great Britain 1971

Parent			Number of	
			Families	*Children*
Female:	single		90	120
	married		190	360
	widowed		120	200
	divorced		120	240
		Sub-total	520	920
Male			100	160
		Total	620	1,080

1. 'The Number of One-Parent Families in Great Britain', reproduced as Appendix 4 to The Finer Report on One-Parent Families. The Table above appears as Table 3.1 in the principal volume of The Finer Report, Cmnd 5629.

B. JURISDICTIONS OVER CHILDREN

The English courts rarely make orders for children of a widowed parent, male or female. The Guardianship of Minors Act 1971 provides[2] that on the death of a minor's father the mother, if surviving, shall be guardian of the minor either alone or jointly with any guardian appointed by the father; and (*a*) where no guardian has been appointed by the father or (*b*) in the event of the death or refusal to act of the guardian or guardians appointed by the father the court may, if it thinks fit, appoint a guardian to act jointly with the mother. The same provisions apply, *mutatis mutandis*, on the death of the mother. Applications for the court to appoint another guardian to act with the surviving parent, whether mother or father, are extremely rare. There would have to be irreconcilable disagreement between the surviving parent and the testamentary guardian[3] appointed by the deceased parent, or the guardians appointed by both parents when both have died[4] or evidence of abandonment of the child or gross misconduct by the surviving parent or guardian before the court's jurisdiction could be invoked.

There is a major lacuna where the parents have separated or divorced and the children have been in the care of one parent, who dies while the children are still minors. Unless the custodial parent has appointed a testamentary guardian, the surviving parent is solely entitled to guardianship of the children, and normally to their custody also. *Re F. (A Minor) (Wardship: Appeal)*[5] concerned a man who had broken up his marriage on forming a relationship with another woman, and the following year forced his wife out of the home. The wife, who took with her their daughter then aged 5, died after the divorce. The child was made a ward of court, and the Court of Appeal reversed the exercise of discretion by the trial judge and held that the father and the former mistress he had married were entitled to custody of the girl, now aged 9, in preference to the over-possessive maternal grandmother.

It has been held[6] that a step-parent has no parental powers in respect of a child, and by s. 5 of the Guardianship of Minors Act 1971 application may be made to be appointed a child's guardian only where there is no parent, no guardian of the person and no other person having parental rights with respect to the child. However, by s. 3 of the same Act, if the deceased parent did not appoint a guardian or the guardian appointed has died or refuses to act, the court may, if it thinks fit, appoint a guardian to act jointly with the surviving parent. It is not clear who is entitled to bring the matter before the court and no application of the provision has been reported. It

---

2. Section 3.
3. So-called although he may be appointed by deed as well as by will.
4. Guardianship of Minors Act 1971, s. 4.
5. [1976] Fam. 238 C.A. The Australian Family Law Act 1975 s. 61(4) provides that on the death of a custodial parent the other parent is entitled to custody of the child only if the court so orders.
6. *Re N. (Minors), The Times* 13.6.73. By the Children Act 1975 s. 33(3) a step-parent with whom a child has lived for the preceding three months may apply for custodianship only with the consent of a person having legal custody.

would seem desirable for legal advisers to consider it part of their duty to urge any parent who is granted custody,[7] or care or control of a minor child to appoint a testamentary guardian without delay.

The courts are therefore rarely concerned with appointing a guardian, because except for the above-mentioned provisions of the Guardianship of Minors Act 1971, that Act, the Guardianship Act 1973, and the Matrimonial Causes Act 1973 are concerned not with guardianship, but with custody or care. Before 8 May 1974 this might be divided with custody to one parent and care and control to the other; now usually custody to both parents and care to one only. The Children Act 1975 has introduced custodianship,[8] a form of custody exercisable by a non-parent even against the wishes of the physical parent or parents, but not severing the legal relationship between physical parent and child as would an adoption. Under the Guardianship of Minors Acts 1971 and 1973 and the Matrimonial Causes Act 1973 the courts may also allow access to the child (which means the right to visit and communicate with the child) either to a physical parent or to another adult with whom the child has been in a family relationship.[9] In respect of a legitimate child the following gradations of parental or quasi-parental authority are therefore recognised:

(i) Parent(s) with whom the child lives, and who exercise(s) all parental duties and authority.

(ii) Adopter(s), whose adopted child is treated in law as if born as a child of their marriage or (if a sole adopter) as if born to the adopter in wedlock.[10]

(iii) Guardian(s), usually testamentary or appointed by the court, but some-times still invoked at common law to find some residual authority in the father as natural guardian.[11] This relegates the other parent or adult entrusted with custody or care and control to the lower status of

(iv) custodial parent, with or without care.

(v) The custodian with a custodianship order under the Children Act 1975 is by definition never the physical parent,[12] but may by virtue of the court order retain care of the child against the wishes of the physical parent.

(vi) The non-custodial parent or other adult allowed access to the child.

---

7. In P.W.P. 53 the Law Commission pointed out that the rationale of the former 'split order' giving custody to one parent and care and control to the other had disappeared since the Guardianship Act 1973, s. 1 provided that both parents have equal rights to custody and upbringing of a minor, exercisable separately. But the amendments to the Guardianship of Minors Act 1971 contained in Sched. 2 to the 1973 Act, (e.g. those to s. 9), make no amendment to the references to (a) custody and (b) right of access to the minor.
8. Children Act 1975, Part II, ss 33–46.
9. *Newman* v. *Newman* [1971] P. 43 raises prospects of an embarrassment of families for and access to children.
10. Adoption Act 1976 s. 39.
11. E.g. *Re T. (Orse H.) (An Infant)* [1963] Ch. 238.
12. Children Act 1975 s. 33(4). It is understood that the word 'custodianship' was used to indicate that the holder of such an order could never be the child's physical parent. Whether this information is so important may be doubted.

Where the parents were married and separate, one or both may apply to the court for an order for care and control of or access to the minor child or children, and the jurisdiction invoked may then be either:

(i) the wardship jurisdiction exercised under the prerogative of the Crown as *parens patriae*, now vested exclusively in the Family Division of the High Court, or

(ii) the common law jurisdiction by habeas corpus for production of the child's person, which is also now vested in the Family Division of the High Court (such actions are now discouraged in favour of the wardship jurisdiction), or

(iii) the jurisdiction under the Guardianship of Minors Act 1971 and the Guardianship Act 1973, vested in:

(*a*) the Family Division of the High Court, and

(*b*) the county court of the district in which either party or the minor resides, and

(*c*) a magistrates' court in whose area of jurisdiction either party or the minor resides, except that the magistrates' court has no jurisdiction if the minor is over 16 years of age unless he is physically or mentally incapable of self-support, nor in respect of the administration or application of any property belonging to or held in trust for a minor, nor of the income from such property;[13] or

(iv) the jurisdiction exercisable in the magistrates' courts only under the Matrimonial Proceedings (Magistrates' Courts) Act 1960, ss 2(1) and 16(1), over a child of the family[14] under the age of 16.

On divorce, the primary jurisdiction is:

(v) Under the Matrimonial Causes Act 1973, ss 41–4, to make orders for the custody and education of any child of the family.[15] The jurisdiction is normally exercised by the divorce county court judges, but in exceptional cases and where the divorce (rather than the arrangement for the children) is contested, by the Family Division of the High Court. After divorce, however, the Wardship jurisdiction may also be exercised, or that under the Guardianship of Minors Acts invoked, while the poor who have previously obtained orders from magistrates' courts relating to children will frequently wish them to continue, whether they were made under the Guardianship of Minors Acts or the Matrimonial Proceedings (Magistrates' Courts) Act.

13. Guardianship of Minors Act 1971, s. 15(2). In *C. v. C.*, *The Times* 5.7.72 D.C., it was suggested that this subsection may inadvertently have changed the law on jurisdiction.

14. Defined in s. 16(1) of the Matrimonial Proceedings (Magistrates' Courts) Act 1960 as: '(*a*) any child of both parties and (*b*) any other child of either party who has been accepted as one of the family by the other party'.

15. Defined in s. 52(1) of the Matrimonial Causes Act 1973 as: '(*a*) a child of both those parties; and (*b*) any other child, not being a child who has been boarded-out with those parties by a local authority or voluntary organisation, who has been treated by both of those parties as a child of their family'.

Where the parents were not married to each other and the child has not become a 'child of the family' of one parent and her or his spouse the legislation still refers to the child and not the parent as illegitimate, and the jurisdiction is:

(vi) by the Guardianship of Minors Act 1971, s. 14, any of the courts exercising jurisdiction may make an order under s. 9 for custody of and right of access to such a child. It is also provided in s. 14 that 'the *natural* father of an *illegitimate* child' may apply under s. 9 for custody of the child, and if this is granted he is treated as the lawful father. In the event of his death while so entitled he may appoint a testamentary guardian for the child. Maintenance for an illegitimate child who has not become a child of the family cannot be obtained under the Guardianship of Minors Act 1971, but only under the Affiliation Proceedings Act 1957.

(vii) in addition, where British nationality depends wholly or in part on the legitimacy of a petitioner or the validity of any marriage, there is jurisdiction in the High Court (and in rare and minor cases in the county courts) under s. 45 of the Matrimonial Causes Act 1973, on a petition, a copy of which must be served on the Attorney-General under Rule 110, for a declaration as to the status of the petitioner. The Attorney-General is a respondent to such a petition and any decree made binds the Crown.[16]

Arrangements for the care of children by the local or other public authorities will be considered in Chapter X.

The Law Commission Working Party has drawn attention to some of the anomalies in these various jurisdictions over children in a table published as Appendix 2 to its Working Paper No. 53 on Matrimonial Jurisdiction in Magistrates' Courts.

The Working Paper suggested that there might be a uniform child custody and maintenance statute, perhaps as one of a series of statutes giving substantive relief in family law. In the meantime, it has suggested *inter alia* that a 'child of the family' should be defined in the same way in the magistrates' courts as in the divorce courts;[17] that magistrates should have power to make orders for the custody of minors up to full age; that the courts be empowered to leave equal custody rights with both parents but give care and control to one and order the other to contribute towards the child's maintenance;[18] and that magistrates be expressly given power to stay the execution of a custody order

---

16. In *The Ampthill Peerage* [1976] 2 W.L.R. 777 the Committee of Privileges held that a declaration of legitimacy obtained under the Legitimacy Declaration Act 1858 (the ancestor of the present s. 45) is binding for all purposes and on all persons, including Her Majesty, unless prejudicial to persons not parties nor cited or obtained by fraud.

17. The recommendation was first made three years after the Matrimonial Proceedings and Property Act 1970 amended the definition for divorce proceedings and by August 1976 no action had resulted. The definition of the same term used in another statute applying only to poor people should be amended automatically.

18. This is now the normal order in the divorce courts. It has been held that magistrates may make 'split' orders under the Guardianship of Minors Acts, but not under the Matrimonial Proceedings (Magistrates' Courts) Act 1960: *Wild* v. *Wild* [1969] P. 33.

and guidance in the use to be made of the power. Views were invited on whether the magistrates should be empowered to prohibit the removal of a child from the jurisdiction. The fact that the United Kingdom is now part of the European Communities and the mass scale of international traffic today would seem to warrant a major reappraisal of existing controls on the international movement of minors, at least until international agreement has been obtained on the law applicable to them and measures to ensure its enforcement.

The Law Commission made a number of recommendations, but did not consider some major anomalies of the legislation, e.g.:

> (i) All the legislation is conceived in terms of the right of one parent or guardian to have the court adjudicate in his dispute with another parent or guardian in respect of a child.[19] The child has no rights as such. For this reason, the Law Commission's recommendation that, when proposing to make a maintenance order 'in respect of' a child, the magistrates should have regard to the same factors as those borne in mind when ordering maintenance for a spouse and in addition 'the financial needs of the child',[20] is inappropriate.

Similarly, because of the assumption of the law that a man's primary duty is to 'maintain' his wife, an order is first made for her maintenance, and then a trifling sum added to it for maintenance of the child or children. It is doubtful if more than a minute proportion, if any, of the orders for child maintenance made in the magistrates' courts cover the actual cost of maintaining the child, and in the matrimonial jurisdiction of the magistrates' courts the questions relating to children are expressly deferred for consideration after those relating to husband and wife.[21]

Caution should be exercised in trying to equate the jurisdiction over 'illegitimate' children who have not become children of a family with that over legitimate children. So far this has led to legislative solecisms about the *natural* father of an *illegitimate* child and the grant to such a 'natural' father of absolute rights of succession on the intestacy of the child, whilst the courts are holding that he may with impunity evict the child from any home the father owns. The mother of an illegitimate child was not the father's wife and cannot have the rights of a wife, since in most cases the putative father has a lawful wife and legitimate children by her, and perhaps also by one or more former lawful wives. In rare circumstances it may be safe to pay an unmarried woman a lump sum in respect of her illegitimate child, knowing that it will be prudently applied for the child's benefit, but in the majority of cases some additional safeguards for the child are desirable. For similar reasons, the provision in the Children Act 1975[22] that 'except as otherwise provided by

---

19. See Guardianship Act 1973, s. 1. See also J. C. Hall, 'The waning of parental rights', 31 *CLJ* (1972) 248–65; J. Eekelaar, 'What are parental rights? 89 *LQR* (1973) 210–34.
20. P.W.P. 53, para. 144. The child has no independent financial needs; rarely are orders made for payments directly even to older children.
21. Matrimonial Proceedings (Magistrates' Courts) Act 1960, s. 4(2). Sections 4(3) and 4(4) are amended by the Children Act 1975, s. 91(1) but s. 4(2) is untouched.
22. Section 85(7).

or under any enactment, while the mother of an illegitimate child is living she has the parental rights and duties exclusively' seems wrong in principle and undesirable in practice. The position of the illegitimate child requires that his interests in particular should override any possible 'right' of either of his parents. Subsequent behaviour towards the child may of course give rise to assumptions in favour of the adult who has done the best he or she could for the child in the difficult circumstances created by the parents and not by the child.

(ii) The Law Commission does not refer to the outmoded vocabulary used in respect of children. For example in the Guardianship of Minors Act 1971, s. 1, orders are for 'custody and upbringing' of the minor; by ss. 9, 10 and 11, for 'custody of' and 'right of access to' the minor and by the Guardianship Act 1973, s. 2(2)(*b*) the court may 'commit the care' of the minor to a specified local authority or place him under the supervision of an independent person. Under the Matrimonial Causes Act 1973, s. 42 orders are for the 'custody and education' of any child of the family; by s. 43 for 'committing the care' of the child to a local authority, (also included in the Matrimonial Proceedings (Magistrates' Courts) Act 1960, s. 2(1)(*a*),) and s. 44(1) refers to a period during which the child is 'committed to the custody of any person'.[23] The Children Act 1975, s. 86 defines 'legal custody' as: 'so much of the parental rights and duties as relate to the person of the child (including the place and manner in which his time is spent)', but not including a right for anyone other than a parent or guardian to arrange the child's emigration from the United Kingdom. By s. 87 of the 1975 Act, a person has 'actual custody' of a child if he has 'actual possession of his person, whether or not that possession is shared with one or more other persons', and any person having actual custody without legal custody 'has the like duties in relation to the child as a custodian would have by virtue of his legal custody', and a child is deemed to have his home with the person who has his actual custody.

The Affiliation Proceedings Act 1957, as the Law Commission points out,[24] was a consolidation measure based upon a nineteenth century Act which itself had had 'a very long legislative history'. The Act employs throughout a quasi-criminal terminology, beginning with s. 1 under which the 'single woman' being the mother may apply by 'complaint' for a 'summons' to be served on the man 'alleged' by her to be the father. The quasi-criminal approach goes also to the substantive provisions, such as s. 4, requiring that the mother's evidence be 'corroborated in some material particular', like the evidence of a criminal accomplice. Even the Guardianship Act 1973, s. 1 is in terms of 'equality of parental rights', and many recent decisions adopt the same

23. On 'custody' see Pennycuick J. and the Court of Appeal in *Re W*. [1963] Ch. 556, 561 and [1964] Ch. 202. The parent normally awarded 'care and control' has custody of the person of the child but lacks final control on such matters as religion and education.
24. P.W.P. 53, para. 162. Unfortunately the Law Commission Working Party construed its terms of reference as excluding review generally of the 1957 Act.

approach.[25] The Children Act 1975, s. 85 speaks of parental rights and duties which is some, if an inadequate, advance.

On the other hand in recent years some members of the judiciary have appreciated that the medical disciplines of psychology and psychiatry may contribute to dealing with children whose homes have been disrupted.[26] There is now a more enlightened approach, but the predominantly accusatorial nature of the judicial proceedings relating to children is still inimical to solutions. The decision in *Re Thain*[27] which is cited and followed in various parts of the existing and former Commonwealth, has not yet been overruled. The courts show a notable reluctance to speak to the children themselves. One of the few cases in which this was done with significant effect was *Re S.*[28] in which Cross J. talked to a boy aged $13\frac{1}{2}$ years. In *H.* v. *H.*[29] a county court judge had talked to two boys aged 13 and 8 years under a pledge not to divulge anything they told him except to an appeal court, and the Court of Appeal sent the case back for re-hearing, saying that no pledge of secrecy should be given to children in such circumstances. In the magistrates' courts, Sir G. Baker P. said in *Re T.*[30] that there is no statutory authority for magistrates to see children in custody cases in their private rooms and

25. E.g. *Re D. (Minors)* [1973] Fam. 209, where a husband and father left wife and children to be supported at public expense until the wife remarried after a divorce. He was allowed to assert his 'parental right' of access to those children and refusal to allow their adoption by the remarried mother, when the assertion of those rights could cause most distress both to the remarried mother and to his then wife, by whom he had since fathered two more children.

26. Noticeably after the resentment in the medical profession at the suggestion by Harman L.J. in *Re C. (M.A.) (An Infant)* [1966] 1 W.L.R. 646, 675 at B, that expert medical witnesses gave evidence in favour of those paying them. The medical profession rightly pointed out that it was the solicitors who frustrated their attempts to see both parties, and the judges who refused to have court experts appointed, preferring to have conflicting evidence from experts retained by both sides. Since then the Court of Appeal has said that disputing parents should, where possible, co-operate in obtaining expert medical opinion: *B (M.)* v. *B (R.)* [1968] 1 W.L.R. 1182 C.A. 1184, confirming the observations to this effect of Cross J. in *Re S. (Infants)* [1967] 1 W.L.R. 396, 407 D.

27. [1926] Ch. 676 C.A. A girl aged 6 was there taken from the only home she had ever known, with her maternal aunt, and handed over in theory to her father. In practice the crucial person in the life of a girl of this age would be the stepmother, who would exercise day-to-day care. Eve J.'s finding at p. 684 that the child would be as happy and well-cared for in the one home as the other could not be substantiated, since the stepmother was never seen or heard by the court. The fact was ignored that the mother had, by her will, left some £12,000 to her husband for life or until remarriage and thereafter to her child. The chances that this sum did not bulk large in all considerations about the child are slight at the highest. In *Re C. (M.A.)* [1966] 1 W.L.R. 646 C.A., custody of a boy aged 17 months was given to his putative father rather than prospective adopters largely because of the impression made by the father's wife, with whom he had become reconciled. But again the wife had never seen the child, and custody was awarded to the putative father alone, so that he could have removed the child from his wife at any time.

28. [1967] 1 W.L.R. 396. Surely any reasonable parent or guardian would discuss such a matter with a boy of nearly fourteen years.

29. [1974] 1 W.L.R. 595 C.A.

30. *The Times* 16.1.74. In its P.W.P. 53, the Law Commission made no recommendation for the magistrates' courts to be given power to interview children.

they must not do so. Since then Maria Colwell[31] screamed to all the world that she did not want to visit her 'true'[32] (meaning physical) mother, but nobody listened. She was forced to do so and eventually handed over to the mother's 'care', where she was brutally assaulted, abused and exploited before being battered to death. This happened within the sight and hearing of social workers charged with supervising the child, who neither saw, nor listened to the complaints of neighbours. Clearly a child in such a position can talk of what he or she alone knows only under a pledge of secrecy. Now we know that Maria Colwell was right in resisting return to her 'true' mother and that she was forced from an orderly and happy home through misery to death, both the legislation and social welfare practice have been amended, but so far there are few signs of changed judicial attitudes.

Under the wardship jurisdiction, and under the Guardianship of Minors Acts since 1925, the courts have been enjoined to regard the welfare of the minor as the first and paramount consideration, and they have adopted an increasingly enlightened interpretation of this vague concept. Very young children are usually left with the mother, whatever her matrimonial conduct may have been, although sometimes even young children are removed from mothers who behave badly,[33] *pour encourager les autres.*[34] Quite young boys are sometimes handed over to a father who can show that he has a home and a woman who keeps it in order and provides regular meals.[35] The use of welfare reports has become more widespread, and the superior courts usually insist that there should be such a report before custody of young children is given to the father.[36] They have also emphasised that there should be one report by one welfare officer rather than two reports each from someone who has seen only one of the two competing households,[37] and have given guidance on how these reports should be presented.[38] They have emphasised the need for speed in dealing with children's cases,[39] and castigated those legal advisers who exploit the overlapping

---

31. See The Field-Fisher Report on The Care and Supervision provided by the Local Authorities and other Agencies in relation to Maria Colwell and the co-ordination between them. September 1974.

32. So-called in para. 33 of The Field-Fisher Report, *supra.*

33. Particularly as regards sexual misconduct: *Re L.* |1962| 1 W.L.R. 886, *B.* v. *B., The Times* 15.5.75 C.A. In *W.* v. *W., The Times*, 26.11.76 C.A., it was said that *Re L (supra)* should no longer be followed.

34. See Lawton L.J. in *B.* v. *B. supra.*

35. *Re B. (An Infant)* |1962| 1 W.L.R. 550 C.A., with Donovan L.J. dissenting, held that a boy of four should be removed from the mother with whom he had always lived and handed over to the care of his father, who had a married couple keeping house. Presumably if the father had dismissed the married couple within hours of receiving the custody order that would have been a ground for variation.

36. *Re O. (Infants)* |1971| Ch. 748 C.A.

37. *C.* v. *C., The Times* 9.11.72 D.C., and *B.* v. *B., The Times* 24.1.73.

38. In *Thompson* v. *Thompson, The Times* 12.3.75 C.A., Buckley L.J. is reported as saying that if hearsay is included in welfare reports, particularly on controversial matters, that fact should be made explicit. Judges have been heard to emphasise to magistrates that welfare reports should be made by the signatory to them, and not 'improved' by someone higher in the hierarchy who did not see the homes about which the report is made.

39. *Practice Direction (Wardship Applications)* |1966| 1 W.L.R. 1384; *Re W., The Times* 28.1.72, and *M.* v. *M., The Times* 30.11.72.

jurisdiction of the magistrates' courts and the divorce courts to delay decisions relating to children.[40] The Divisional Court has asked to be told the reasons for abandoning appeals from magistrates particularly where the order made is unusual on its face.[41]

There is increasing emphasis on evidence rather than assumptions relating to custody.[42] Lord MacDermott in *J. v. C.,* cited and endorsed this approach.[43] The House of Lords there held that a so-called 'unimpeachable parent'[44] has not an absolute right to reclaim the child he has for many years allowed to be brought up by others at their expense. The decision has been followed in *Re O.*[45] and *Re E.O.*[46] It may be significant that in all these cases the foster-parents were of the professional classes.

The question of access to children, that is the right to visit and talk to them by the parent who does not have the child living with her or him, frequently causes problems. Indeed, the distinguished authors of *Beyond the Best Interests of the Child*[47] have urged that all such rights be abolished, and that 'the custodial parent must decide under what condition he or she wishes to raise the child. The non-custodial parent should have no legally enforceable right to visit the child, and the custodial parent should have the right to decide whether it is desirable for the child to have such visits'.[48] This is unacceptable. The fact that the law cannot create personal relationships does not mean it should not seek to control the abuse of power arising from them, particularly when we have overwhelming evidence that gross abuse of such power is widespread.

A more constructive approach was adopted by the committee of Justice on Parental Rights and Custody Suits, which appended to its report[49] a proposed Visiting Code.[50] It suggested this should be handed and explained to and discussed with parents at the conclusion of custody suits. The code draws attention to the needs of parents and children alike to love and be loved by the other without the feelings of guilt engendered by open hostility between the parents, especially when the child is used as a weapon in parental warfare.

Following the nineteenth century aberrations that denied a woman all contact

---

40. *Jones* v. *Jones* [1974] 1 W.L.R. 1471 C.A. See also *H.* v. *H., The Times,* 13.11.76.
41. *Bell* v. *Bell, The Times* 10.12.75. The magistrates had entrusted the father with custody of one child and the mother with the other.
42. See Wilberforce J. in *Re Adoption Application 41/61 (No. 2)* [1964] Ch. 48, 53.
43. [1970] A.C. 668, 713.
44. So described in the report, but Ungoed-Thomas J. found him 'crude and boorish' and that he would be quite unable to cope with the problems of adjustment: See Lord Guest [1970] A.C. 668, 701E.
45. *The Times* 17.2.63 C.A.
46. *The Times* 16.2.73. See also *Re R. (An infant)* [1974] 1 All E.R. 1033, or *The Times* 18.1.74. There a girl (age not given in any available report) was given into the custody of her great-aunt and not her father where she had special needs and the mother could not care for her.
47. Professor Joseph Goldstein, Miss Anna Freud and Professor Albert J. Solnit (New York: The Free Press, 1973).
48. Ibid. p. 38.
49. *Parental Rights and Duties and Custody Suits* (Stevens & Sons, 1975).
50. Compiled by Dr Kenneth Soddy.

with her children if the slightest imputation could be made against her sexual behaviour (although 'mere' adultery was never ground for depriving a father of custody of his children) the settled view of the English courts after the Second World War was that access was the right of every parent and was 'not to be refused unless the court is satisfied the parent is not a fit and proper person to be brought into contact with the children at all'.[51] In *B. v. B. (An Infant)*[52] the Court of Appeal refused access to a father where a boy of 16 resolutely refused to see him without a court order, on the ground that when he reached 18 no court could compel the boy to see his father. Edmund Davies L.J. described the order of non-access as: 'a dreadful order . . . the impact on both parent and child must have lifelong consequences. . . .'[53] Access by the mother of five children was refused in *C. v. C.*,[54] where she had made a wild outburst in the court of first instance and was clearly not in control of herself. Again in *M. v. M.*[55] access was refused for an adoptive mother to a boy aged 7. Divorce proceedings were pending between the adoptive parents, in which the judge could reconsider the whole question of custody. In this case Wrangham J. said:[56] 'I for my part would prefer to call it (viz. access) a basic right in the child rather than a basic right in the parent', and Latey J. agreed.

After the nineteenth century litigation arising from sectarian (miscalled religious) differences[57] had died down[58] there have been sporadic reminders that attempts to score sectarian points at whatever cost to children may be seized upon. In 1973 a responsible government introduced a Bill that, if enacted, would have rendered absolutely binding any ante-nuptial agreement about the upbringing of children.[59] In the *Desramault* case the apologia for the decision handing a 8-months'-old girl over to the French father who had never previously seen her, and who immediately removed her to France,[60] included the statement: 'we felt under the circumstances she would have been happier as a French child and a Catholic in France with her father'.[61] What evidence was received of the chauvinist or sectarian convictions of an 8-months'-old child was not revealed. Today most of the decisions seem more evenly balanced,[62] but the

---

51. *S. v. S.* |1962| 1 W.L.R. 445 C.A. per Willmer L.J., 449.
52. |1971| 1 W.L.R. 1486 C.A.
53. Ibid. at p. 1493.
54. *The Times* 28.5.71.
55. |1973| 2 All E.R. 81 D.C.
56. Ibid. p. 85f.
57. E.g. *Reg.* v. *Andrews* (1873) L.R. 8 Q.B. 153, *Andrews* v. *Salt* (1873) 8 Ch. App. 622; *Re Agar-Ellis* (1883) 24 Ch.D. 317, most of the Barnardo cases including *Barnardo* v. *McHugh* |1891| A.C. 388 also known as Jone's case or Roddy's case; *Barnardo* v. *Ford* |1892| A.C. 326, also known as Gossage's case.
58. The twentieth century still saw *Re Carroll* |1931| 1 K.B. 317 (eventually overruled by *J.* v. *C.* |1970| A.C. 668), *re Collins* |1950| Ch. 498 and *Re M.* |1967| 1 W.L.R. 1479 C.A.
59. See 339 H.L. Deb. col. 39–40; vol. 340, cols 643–58, and Chapter III, n. 125.
60. The nearest approach to the law reports made by this case was in *The Times* 11.2.71 in which Pennycuick J. awarded custody to the mother on appeal, but pointed out the ineffectiveness of the order since the child was by then in France.
61. See statement by Mrs Peile, chairman of the Bench of magistrates responsible for the decision, *The Times* 29.7.72.
62. Thus *B.* v. *B.*, *The Times* 15.5.75 C.A., *ante* notes 33–4, is balanced by *H.* v. *H.*,

presence in England and Wales of large numbers of adherents of various major religions is a potential source of discord, particularly in relation to children.

C. THE GENERAL PRINCIPLES OFTEN APPLICABLE

The courts are rightly cautious about laying down any general rules of thumb relating to the custody of children, whose circumstances may be almost infinitely variable, and whose welfare is by statute paramount. One or two general assumptions, which may of course give place to contrary indications, seem to emerge, viz:

(1) The courts are reluctant to divide brothers and sisters, although in rare circumstances this may be done.[63]

(2) They will give custody to[64] or leave it with[65] both parents where they seem prepared to co-operate over the children. Today, however, they rarely divide the custody over time, as by giving custody to each parent for six months of the year, as this has been found very detrimental to the child.[66]

(3) Very young children are usually left in the mother's custody,[67] but custody of young boys[68] and even girls[69] has been given to the father, sometimes in an effort to punish the mother for (usually sexual) misconduct.[70]

(4) The courts sometimes deny[71] that there is any rule that a boy should be in the custody of his father.

(5) All orders in respect of children are subject to variation: there is always 'liberty to apply'.

The Times 7.5.75 C.A. There an order at first instance giving care and control of a boy of 5 to his father, an Egyptian Muslim, was reversed and his care given to the English agnostic mother. The learning of Arabic and instruction in the Muslim religion were held not to be overriding factors for a boy living in England.

63. As in *Re O.* (*Infants*) [1962] 1 W.L.R. 724 C.A. The husband was Sudanese and the mother English. The mother at first instance was awarded custody of both children, but the Court of Appeal found this unjust to the unexceptionable father, and held he was entitled to custody of the boy. See also Baker P. in *Bell* v. *Bell*, *The Times* 10.12.75 D.C.

64. *Jussa* v. *Jussa* [1972] 1 W.L.R. 881.

65. Guardianship Act 1973, s. 1.

66. It usually leads to the parents vying with each other for the child's favour. In any separation of the parents, the question of firm and consistent discipline for the child poses major problems.

67. *P.* v. *McK.*, *The Times* 28.6.73, and see *Re B.* (*T.A.*) (*An Infant*) [1971] Ch. 270.

68. E.g. *Re B.* (*An Infant*) [1962] 1 W.L.R. 550, a boy of 4. In *W.* v. *W. & C.* [1968] 1 W.L.R. 1310 C.A., the court said a boy of 8 was better with his father.

69. In *B.* v. *B.*, *The Times*, 29.11.72, both parents had behaved odiously (exchange of spouses) but the girl had remained in her father's care throughout.

70. As in *Re L.* [1962] 1 W.L.R. 886, but see *W.* v. *W.*, *The Times*, 26.11.76, *ante* n. 33.

71. As *obiter* in *Re C.* (*An Infant*) [1970] 1 W.L.R. 288. This case concerned an illegitimate boy whose mother was dead, but see *W.* v. *W. & C. supra* note 68.

D. EVIDENCE RECEIVABLE IN CUSTODY CASES

In *Re K.*[72] the House of Lords finally held that a parent is not absolutely entitled to see all the evidence before the court in relation to a custody application, but that knowledge of such evidence should only rarely be withheld, and only when the judge personally[73] has considered the matter and decided that disclosure of the evidence to the parent would not be for the child's welfare. It is thought that this decision impliedly overrules that of the Court of Appeal in *Fowler* v. *Fowler & Sine*,[74] that a judge should not interview the welfare worker in the absence of the parties and their advisers. It is clear that a parent is not entitled to demand disclosure of local authority records where the local authority is involved.[75]

E. THE INDIVIDUAL JURISDICTIONS RELATING TO CHILDREN

(i) THE INHERENT WARDSHIP JURISDICTION OF THE HIGH COURT (acting in the name of the Crown as *parens patriae.)*

(a) Since the enactment of the Law Reform (Miscellaneous Provisions) Act 1949, the child must be made a Ward of Court before the jurisdiction can be invoked.[76] The exercise of so venerable and sweeping a jurisdiction attracts considerable publicity, and steps have been necessary to prevent abuse of the procedure for publicity purpose.[77] A nominal settlement on the child no longer suffices to invoke the jurisdiction, and is not essential.[78] Once the child is a ward of court the court must assent to any important step in the ward's life.[79]

(b) In theory the jurisdiction overrides all statutory jurisdiction,[80] viz. under the Guardianship of Minors Acts or the Matrimonial Causes Act or by

---

72. [1965] A.C. 201.
73. Per Lord Evershed. Ibid. p. 219G. The House of Lords thought that only in special circumstances should confidential reports be submitted to the court.
74. [1963] P. 311 C.A.
75. *Re D. (Infants)* [1970] 1 W.L.R. 599 C.A. cf. *D.* v. *N.S.P.C.C.* [1976] 3 W.L.R. 124 C.A., and the dissenting judgement of Lord Denning M.R.
76. *Re E. (An Infant)* [1956] Ch. 23; *Practice Direction (Wardship Applications)* Ch.D., [1967] 1 W.L.R. 623; *Re N. (Infants)* [1967] Ch. 512.
77. *Practice Direction (Wardship Applications)* [1967] 1 W.L.R. 623, (abuse by a night club.)
78. *Re S.* [1967] 1 W.L.R. 396; *Re R. (P.-M.)* [1968] 1 W.L.R. 385, *A.-W.* v. *E., The Times* 29.11.74. On the historical controversy as to the extent to which the possession of property was essential, see Lord Eldon in *Wellesley* v. *Beaufort* (1827) 2 Russ. 1, *contra* Lord Cottenham in *Re Spence* (1847) 2 Phil. 247.
79. *Re S.* [1967] 1 W.L.R. 396; *Re R. (P.-M.)* [1968] 1 W.L.R. 385; *A.-W.* v. *E., The Times* 29.11.74, *Re D. (A Minor) (Wardship: Sterilisation)* [1976] Fam. 185 (sterilisation operation not to be performed).
80. *Re Andrews* [1968] Ch. 665.

habeas corpus, and the court's powers under it are more sweeping than under any statute.[81] In practice:

(1) If a custody order is in existence under the Matrimonial Causes Acts, the prerogative jurisdiction should not be invoked. Application should be made to the Family Division to vary or to the Court of Appeal to reverse[82] the existing order. On the other hand, the court may take jurisdiction where foreign courts are likely to be involved in the future, as in *Re L.*[83]

(2) The Family Division may, under the Matrimonial Causes Act 1973, s. 42, direct that the children be made wards of court,[84] but if this power is used its exercise has not been reported, and the prerogative jurisdiction is not used where a divorce judge is seized of the matter.

(3) The wardship court will rarely interfere with decisions in the magistrates' courts,[85] but sometimes it may do so, where circumstances have changed or remedies such as an injunction are needed.[86]

(4) Where the child is in the care of the local authority under the Children Act 1948, s. 1 the court will not accept wardship so as to substitute its discretion for that vested in the local authority by statute,[87] but it may do so where the facts are such as were not intended to be covered by the statute or likely to remove discretion from the local authority.[88]

(5) Similarly the jurisdiction cannot be invoked to supplement the Education Act 1944[89] or to interfere with the provisions of the Commonwealth Immigrants Act.[90]

---

81. E.g. in *Re X.* [1975] Fam. 47 C.A., it was not doubted that the Court might, for the benefit of its ward, censor publication of a book, although the Court of Appeal decided that the power should not in that case be exercised. See *Re F. (orse. A.)* [1976] 3 W.L.R. 813 C.A.
82. See *Brown* v. *Brown, The Times* 5.3.75 C.A. If there is a change of circumstances an appeal is inappropriate, and application should be made for variation of the order. See also *Practice Note (Infants: Matrimonial Causes) (No. 2)* [1972] 1 W.L.R. 1195 for ensuring so far as possible that the judge first deciding custody should consider applications for variation.
83. [1974] 1 W.L.R. 250 C.A.
84. *Re A.H. (Infants)* [1963] Ch. 232 and *Hall* v. *Hall* [1963] P. 378 C.A.
85. *Re K.* [1966] 1 W.L.R. 1241; *Re P. (A.J.) (An Infant)* [1968] 1 W.L.R. 1976.
86. *Re H. (G.J.) (An Infant)* [1966] 1 W.L.R. 706; *Re P. (Infants)* [1967] 1 W.L.R. 818; *Re N. (Minors) (Parental Rights)* [1974] Fam. 40; *Re D. (Minors)* [1973] Fam. 179.
87. *Re M. (An Infant)* [1961] Ch. 328 C.A., *Re T. (A.J.J.)* [1970] Ch. 336 C.A., *H.* v. *H., The Times* 17.10.72, and see S. Cretney, 33 *MLR* (1970) 696.
88. *Re L. (An Infant)* [1963] 1 W.L.R. 97 (foster-parents applying to adopt); *Re G. (Infants)* [1963] 1 W.L.R. 1169; *Re R. (K.)* [1964] Ch. 455; *Re S. (An Infant)* [1965] 1 W.L.R. 483 C.A., especially p. 491; *Re P.* [1967] 1 W.L.R. 818. See also *Re Y (A Minor) (Child in Care: Access)* [1976] Fam. 125 C.A., where a ward had been placed in local authority care under s. 7(2) of the Family Law Reform Act 1969, and the Court of Appeal pointed out that by the Matrimonial Causes Act 1973 s. 43(5) the exercise of the local authority's powers under Part II of the Children Act 1948 remains subject to the direction of the court.
89. *Re Baker* [1961] 1 Ch. 303; *Re B. (Infants)* [1962] Ch. 201. The Education Act has now been amended by the Children and Young Persons Acts 1963, ss 35–6 and 1969, s. 72.
90. *Re Mohamed Arif* [1968] Ch. 643 C.A.

(c) The jurisdiction may be invoked when the parents separate but no matrimonial proceedings are contemplated, or where there is a possibility that the child may be kidnapped and taken abroad,[91] or where there is dispute about custody of an illegitimate child whose mother is dead.[92]

It was announced on 2 November 1973[93] that in future the police will help to trace Wards of Court removed from a parent and hidden within the jurisdiction. It is hoped that a hard-pressed police force may soon find it possible to extend the area of such assistance.

(ii) HABEAS CORPUS PROCEEDINGS

This remedy was developed during the eighteenth century[94] primarily to enable a father to recover custody of his children from anyone unlawfully detaining them. Such actions are discouraged in favour of the wardship jurisdiction since, from October 1971,[95] the remedy by habeas corpus was transferred from the Queen's Bench Division and the inherent wardship jurisdiction from the Chancery Division to the Family Division.

(iii) JURISDICTION UNDER THE GUARDIANSHIP OF MINORS ACT 1971 AND THE GUARDIANSHIP ACT 1973

Only parents or guardians may apply to the court under these statutes unless there is none, in which event any person interested may apply to be appointed guardian.[96] It was long thought that s. 1 of the Guardianship of Infants Act 1925, re-enacted as s. 1 of the Guardianship of Minors Act 1971 (a 'pure' consolidation), had equalised the position of mother and father as regards parental rights over legitimate children and made the welfare of the child paramount at all times. Section 1 of both Acts reads: 'Where in any proceedings before any court ... the custody or upbringing of a minor ... is in question, the court, in deciding that question, shall regard the welfare of the minor as the first and paramount consideration. . . .'

The statute therefore came into operation when the proceedings were before

---

91. *Re O (Infants)* [1962] 1 W.L.R. 724 C.A.; *Re L. (Minors)* [1974] 1 W.L.R. 250 C.A.; *Re N. (Minors)* [1974] Fam. 40 D.C.
92. *Re C. (An Infant)* [1970] 1 W.L.R. 288.
93. *The Times* 2.11.73.
94. Largely by Lord Mansfield, see e.g. *R. v. Ward* (1762) 1 Wm. Bl. 386; *R. v. Delavel* (1763) 2 Burr. 1434. The mother used the writ to bring the matter before the court in *R. v. de Manneville* (1804) 5 East 221, but it availed her nothing as against the father's custody.
95. When by the Administration of Justice Act 1970, s. 1 and Sched. 1, all the High Court jurisdictions over children were centred in the division renamed the Family Division of that court.
96. Guardianship of Minors Act 1971, s. 5. There is no rule of law in England, as in most Civil Law countries, that every child must have a guardian, but today in England every child may have one. See *Re N. (Minors)* [1974] Fam. 40 D.C.

the court and no earlier. Until then the common law prevailed, and at common law parental rights were paternal rights until the court saw grave reason to order otherwise. Thus before 8 May 1974[97] the position was that the father of a legitimate child was entitled at common law to all parental rights. If the mother disagreed with any decision made by the father, she could take the matter before the court and the welfare of the child then became for the first time the first and paramount consideration. From 8 May 1974 the Guardianship Act 1973, s. 1 substituted the concept of equal rights and authority in both father and mother exercisable separately.[98] The right to custody of any one child is not susceptible of such division and the Children Act 1975, s. 85(1) defines the parental rights and duties as 'all the rights and duties which by law the mother and father have in relation to a legitimate child and his property', whether the child is legitimate or not. Except by separation agreements between husband and wife parental rights and duties are declared nontransferable, and by s. 85(3), 'Where two or more persons have a parental right or duty jointly, any one of them may exercise or perform it in any manner without the other or others if the other or, as the case may be, one or more of the others have not signified disapproval of its exercise or performance in that manner'.[99] It is hoped that this attempt to elaborate and apportion parental rights may be abandoned in favour of an approach from the child's viewpoint, even though this may appear mainly negative, viz. not to be suddenly removed from familiar surroundings; not to be evicted from his home by any physical parent; not to have his educational arrangements drastically changed without good reason; not to have his identity tampered with as by change of surname to suit the convenience of adults and not to be removed from one jurisdiction or culture to another without adequate warning and preparation. The law cannot however, ensure that a child is cherished, stimulated, and adequately cared for, and legal sanctions in this area are few and weak.

Subject to s. 1 of the 1971 Act (the paramountcy of the minor's welfare) the court may, on the application of the mother or father of a minor, make such order regarding (a) the custody of the minor and (b) the right of access to the minor of his mother or father, as it thinks fit, having regard to the welfare of the minor and to the conduct and wishes of the mother and father.[100] If a custody order is made, (whether or not in favour of one of the parents) it may make a further order requiring payment to that person by the parents or either of

---

97. When the Guardianship Act 1973 Parts I and III and Scheds 1—3 were brought into operation by S.I. No. 695 of 1974.

98. It was said that if this enactment had been in operation when Linda Desramault asked a magistrates' court for legal custody of her 8-months'-old child, it would have been unnecessary for the mother to apply for custody. The contention seems fallacious. After the 1973 Act came into operation the father had equal rights with the mother exercisable separately. He could have taken custody of the child without a court order at any time if no application had been made. See also n. 60 *ante*, and *The Times* 11.2.71.

99. The Australian Family Law Act, No. 53 of 1975, s. 64 obliges the court to make or vary orders in accordance with the wishes of any child over 14 unless there are special circumstances making it undesirable to do so. It will be interesting to see how the provision is interpreted.

100. Guardianship of Minors Act 1971, s. 9.

them of such maintenance for the minor as it thinks reasonable.[101] If one of the parents is given custody, the maintenance order is unenforceable and no liability thereunder accrues while the parents are residing together, and it becomes ineffective if they continue to do so for three months after the order is made.[102] After the child attains full age, the maintenance may be payable to him direct,[103] but no maintenance is payable after he reaches the age of 21. The court may also make orders for a child under 16 given to the custody of any person to be under the supervision of a specified local authority or a probation officer, and in exceptional circumstances, his care may be committed to a specified local authority.[104]

Where the father and mother disagree on any question affecting the minor's welfare, either of them may apply to the court, which may make such order as it thinks proper but not including an order for the minor's custody or for access to him. The provision has no application to an illegitimate child.[105] No decisions have yet been reported on such applications.

The Domicile and Matrimonial Proceedings Act 1973, s. 4 now provides that a child's dependent domicile shall be that of his mother if his parents are alive but living apart and the child has his home with his mother and has no home with his father; or if he had at one time his mother's domicile because his home was with her and he has not since had a home with his father. If the child has a domicile dependent on his mother when she dies, and he has not since had a home with his father, he will retain the deceased mother's domicile.

(iv) and (v) JURISDICTION OF THE MAGISTRATES' COURTS UNDER THE MATRIMONIAL PROCEEDINGS (MAGISTRATES' COURTS) ACT 1960, ss. 2(1)(d) AND 16(1) AND OF THE DIVORCE COURTS UNDER THE MATRIMONIAL CAUSES ACT 1973, ss. 41–4

As contrasts between the two jurisdictions have already been made they will now so far as possible be considered together. The classic distinction made between the two jurisdictions is that divorce does and separation or maintenance orders do not affect the status of the parties to the marriage. Neither affects the status of the children. Whether their parents are cohabiting, living apart, divorced, or remarried, children remain their parents' children. The real difference between the two jurisdictions is that the poor go to the magistrates and the more prosperous and better-informed resort to the divorce court,

---

101. Guardianship of Minors Act 1971, s. 9(2) as amended by the Guardianship Act 1973, Sched. 2, Part 1.
102. Ibid. s. 9(3). The law's refusal to enforce maintenance of any dependant until after the marriage has been disrupted and separate accommodation found means that usually the wife must find another home for herself and the children before she can attempt to obtain an order for maintenance.
103. Guardianship of Minors Act 1971, s. 12.
104. Guardianship Act 1973, s. 2(2).
105. Ibid. s. 1(3)(4) and (7).

(with the exception of those slightly too prosperous for legal aid, who may have to make do with the magistrates' jurisdiction if a divorce is likely to be contested). The Bedford College Survey[106] found that the level of maintenance orders made in the divorce courts was little if any higher than the totally inadequate level in the magistrates' courts. Divorce or separation alike generally mean poverty, at least for the wife and children.[107]

(a) Divorce jurisdiction contrasted with that of magistrates on separation or for maintenance. In one respect the divorce jurisdiction relating to children is different from that in the magistrates' court and that is that at least one of the parties urgently desires the divorce. The divorce courts have a sanction the magistrates' courts do not possess. In the divorce jurisdiction only, therefore, it is possible to insist that details of all children of the family are shown on the petition,[108] that the decree absolute of divorce may be withheld unless the court is satisfied about the arrangements made for the children, and that any decree absolute is void if it is pronounced without a declaration having been made by the court as to the arrangements made for the children.[109] This is probably the most important achievement of the Royal Commission on Marriage and Divorce 1951–5.[110]

In 1973 a survey was made of undefended divorce petitions in three county courts, including evidence concerning the children and questions asked by the judge. The results were published in the *Modern Law Review* for November 1975.[111] It was found that no questions were asked in court about the arrangements for the children in more than half the cases and the divorcing parties themselves often considered that the investigations made concerning the children were inadequate. Some judges seemed reluctant to call for welfare reports[112] either because they considered the welfare service was overworked, or because they thought such a report an implied criticism of the petitioner. Examples are given of gross cases in which no report was ordered. One difficulty is that viable alternatives for the arrangements made by the parents are neither obvious nor easy to make. Rarely will a suitable individual other than a parent be available to care for the child, and the lack of proper accommodation for children in the care of the local authorities is so notorious, especially in the large urban areas, that a court can rarely feel that the local authority is preferable to a parent who is not actively vicious.

Judicial notions about what is important are also out of step with those

---

106. Conducted by Professor O. R. Macgregor, Mr L. Blom-Cooper and Mr C. Gibson. See *Report of the Committee on Statutory Maintenance Limits*, Cmnd 3587 (1968) paras. 103–6 and *Separated Spouses* (1970).

107. See further the Finer Report on One-Parent Families, Cmnd 5629 (1974), paras 4.62–4.101 and Tables 4.3–4.10.

108. Matrimonial Causes Rules 1973, S.I. 2016, rr 8–9, Form 2, and *Practice Direction (Divorce: Children)* [1971] 1 W.L.R. 10.

109. Matrimonial Causes Act, 1973, s. 41.

110. Cmd 9678 (1956).

111. 'Judicial hearings of undefended divorce petitions', by Elizabeth Elston, Jane Fuller and Mervyn Murch of the University of Bristol, 38 *MLR* (1975) 609.

112. Under the Matrimonial Causes Rules 1973. S.I. 2016, rule 95.

of the community. The writers who examined undefended divorces point out that 'To many petitioners, questions of custody of children, maintenance for themselves and the children, and the sale of the matrimonial home were of far greater importance than the "licence to remarry".' It is difficult to contend that those petitioners were wrong.

By s. 42 of the Matrimonial Causes Act the court may, in any proceedings for divorce, nullity of marriage or judicial separation, before or on granting a decree or at any time thereafter, whether before or after decree absolute or on dismissing the proceedings,[113] make such order as it thinks fit for the custody and education of any child of the family who is under the age of 18. It may also direct that the child be made a ward of court. Where the application is based only on wilful neglect to maintain a spouse or child of the family, the orders made are effective only until the child reaches the age of 18.[114] On granting or making absolute a decree of divorce or granting a decree of judicial separation, the court may declare either party to the marriage unfit to have custody of the children of the family, in which event such a parent is not 'entitled as of right' to the custody of the children on the death of the custodial parent.[115] In exceptional circumstances the court may commit the care of a child under 17 years of age to the local authority until he reaches full age.[116] The child is then in the same position as if he had been taken into the local authority's care under the Children Act 1948, s. 1, except that a parent or other person is not entitled to demand his return. Any child in the custody of any individual may also be placed under the supervision of a welfare officer or a local authority.[117] The magistrates' courts have similar powers under the Matrimonial Proceedings (Magistrates' Courts) Act 1960, s. 2(1), to provide for the legal custody of any child of the family under the age of 16 years; commit the care of the child to a specified local authority, or to order a child committed to the custody of an individual to be supervised by a probation officer or a specified local authority. There are specific statutory powers to order access to any child of the family by either of the parties or by any other parent of the child, wherever a child is committed to the legal custody of some other person.[118]. In the divorce courts these are inherent powers but they are detailed in the Matrimonial Causes Rules.[119] The magistrates' courts also have statutory powers to order payment by the respondent or the complainant or by each of them of weekly maintenance for any child of the family.

(b) Children of the family.[120] Although the concept is differently defined

---

113. Matrimonial Causes Act 1973, s. 42(1)(*b*).
114. Ibid. s. 42(2), and see *D.(J.R.)* v. *D.(J.M.)* [1971] P. 132, under previous legislation.
115. Ibid. s. 42(3)(4). There are no direct reports of such orders, publicity for which, if they are made, would seem at least as desirable as publicity for orders depriving women of custody of their children because of their sexual conduct.
116. Section 43. The local authority must first be heard: s. 43(2).
117. Section 44.
118. Matrimonial Proceedings (Magistrates' Courts) Act 1960, s. 2(1)(*g*).
119. S.I. 2016 of 1973 rule 92.
120. See also *Practice Direction* (*Divorce: Children*) [1971] 1 W.L.R. 10 as to additional information required.

in the two jurisdictions, the general intention is the same, viz. to make orders for the children who were living with the contending parties as part of their family but not as foster-children. Some difficulties arose over the earlier definitions, first introduced in 1958, but they have been amended. The courts are noticeably disturbed when confronted by a woman much more sophisticated than a man, who has managed to unload her responsibilities on to him,[121] and in at least two cases[122] the woman's conduct was so out of line with what might be called normal sexual behaviour that it would be difficult and perhaps undesirable to frame legislation to cover it. There have been differing views, not yet resolved, on whether the unborn child may be a child of the family.[123] It has been held that a child may be a child of more than one family, so that a stepmother may be granted access.[124] Even if blood tests exclude the husband as the father of the child, the child may nevertheless be 'of the family'.[125] Both in the divorce court and in the magistrates' court it is provided[126] that, in making an order for maintenance[127] of a child of the family by one who is not his parent, the court should have regard to whether and to what extent the party on whom the order is made had assumed responsibility for the child's maintenance and to the liability of any other person to maintain the child. In *R.* v. *R. (Blood test: Jurisdiction) (Practice Note)*,[128] Sir G. Baker P., having decided in a particular case without the need for a blood test, that the mother's husband was not the father, said that Registrars should adjourn to a judge, and preferably a High Court judge, applications for a blood test unless all parties concerned consented to it. Such applications need no longer be heard in open court.[129]

Although the judges are reluctant to refuse a parent access to his or her child, it has been held[130] that either parent awarded custody is entitled to

---

121. As in *Bowlas* v. *Bowlas* [1965] P. 450 C.A. and *Snow* v. *Snow* [1972] Fam. 74, C.A.
122. *P.* v. *P.* [1969] 1 W.L.R. 898, at Bristol Assizes, and *A.* v. *A.* (*Family: Unborn Child*) [1974] Fam. 6.
123. In *Caller* v. *Caller* [1968] P. 37 D.C., it was held that an unborn child could be a child of the family, but the contrary view was taken in *A.* v. *A.* (*Family: Unborn Child*) [1974] Fam. 6. This may have been influenced by the behaviour of the mother in that case.
124. *Newman* v. *Newman* [1971] P. 43.
125. *W. (R.J.)* v. *W. (S.J.)* [1972] Fam. 152.
126. Matrimonial Causes Act 1973, s. 25(3) and Matrimonial Proceedings (Magistrates' Courts) Act 1960, s. 2(5). The wording differs somewhat, that of the 1973 Act being the amended version. It includes also the question whether, in assuming and discharging responsibility for the child, the party did so knowing that the child was not his or her own.
127. In the divorce court this now takes the form of secured or unsecured periodical payments or a lump sum.
128. [1973] 1 W.L.R. 115. This arose out of Lord Reid's dictum on blood tests in *S.* v. *McC. (Orse S.)* and *M. (D.S. Intervener)*; *W.* v. *W.* [1972] A.C. 24, 45.
129. *Practice Note* (Matrimonial Causes: Issues) [1975] 1 W.L.R. 1640 and Matrimonial Causes (Amendment) Rules S.I. No. 1359 of 1975; following *B. (L.A.)* v. *B. (C.H.) The Times* 18.2.75.
130. *Poel* v. *Poel* [1970] 1 W.L.R. 1469 C.A. held the remarried custodian mother may emigrate; *Nash* v. *Nash* [1973] 2 All E.R. 704 C.A., even to a country to which the father might be refused entry. *T.* v. *T. The Times* 4.11.70 C.A. concerned the custodian father. The magistrates' courts have no power either to prevent removal of a child from the jurisdiction or to accept undertakings not to remove him.

emigrate taking the child with him or her, thereby in practice rendering any right of access ineffective. The divorce court may still exercise jurisdiction under the statute when a parent has died,[131] and after decree absolute, it may grant an injunction of one spouse at the suit of the other where this is necessary for the welfare of the child.[132]

(vi) and (vii) CHILDREN OF PARENTS NOT MARRIED TO EACH OTHER

Children are still stigmatised as 'illegitimate' in our legislation because of the actions of others for which they have no responsibility. The child's parents, however, who were responsible for their actions, are called the father or the 'natural' father, or the mother, or 'natural' mother. If the child is adopted or declared free for adoption, the physical parent is now called the former parent.

Most systems of law discriminate against the child born to a woman who is demonstrably not her husband's child, either because she has no husband or because he cannot be the child's father. This discrimination may be attacked in two principal ways, either by legitimating or making quasi-legitimate (as by adoption) as many as possible of such children, or by diminishing the legal disabilities of the children who remain illegitimate. Too much emphasis on the first method may further depress the status of the children who cannot be legitimated. Since 1926[133] English law has adopted both methods, and the former legal disadvantages of the ex-nuptial child have been greatly reduced.[134]

(a) Legitimation and deemed legitimacy. At common law only the child born in lawful wedlock or within the gestation period after its termination[135] was legitimate, although if at the time both of the child's birth and of the subsequent marriage the father was domiciled in a country that recognised legitimation by subsequent marriage, the English common law would recognise the child as legitimate by operation of that foreign law.[136] In 1926 it was

---

131. *Bell* v. *Bell* [1961] 1 W.L.R. 1467.
132. *Stewart* v. *Stewart* [1973] Fam. 21.
133. Legitimacy Act 1926, which came into operation on 1 January 1927. It was a characteristic of the common law that bastardy was indelible, and this was confirmed at the Council of Merton, 1253.
134. They were principally confined to inheritance: a bastard could not be an heir. Blackstone in his *Commentaries*, Book I, Ch. 16 was emphatic that no other disadvantage attended bastardy at common law, such as exclusion from public office. In the days of serfdom the bastard was always a free man, since his father might have been free. Conversely he could not inherit land held by servile tenure, which in some periods may have been more valuable than freedom. For the persistence of old attitudes, see correspondence in *The Times* 14–31 July 1976, on the Status of Children born of A.I.D.
135. The child born within hours or minutes after the wedding ceremony is born in lawful wedlock, and this is the justification for licensing marriage below the normal age for pregnant girls in many common law jurisdictions overseas. For the marriage dissolved by divorce see *Knowles* v. *Knowles* [1962] P. 161.
136. *Dalhousie* v. *M'Dovall* (1840) 7 Cl. & F. 817; *Re Goodman's Trusts* (1881) 17 Ch.D. 266 C.A.

provided for the first time that if a man domiciled in England married the mother of his illegitimate child the child (if alive at the relevant time) would be legitimated from 1 January 1927 or the date of the marriage, whichever last happened,[137] provided neither of the parents was married to another person at the time of the child's birth. This proviso was repealed only from 29 October 1959.[138] By the Act of 1926,[139] provided the father was at the date of the marriage domiciled in a foreign country whose law recognised the legitimation of the child by subsequent marriage, it was no longer necessary that he be domiciled there at the time of the child's birth.

The Matrimonial Causes Act 1937, which introduced new grounds on which marriage might be voidable, provided also[140] that if the marriage was avoided because of the respondent's unsound mind or epilepsy or venereal disease, any child of the annulled marriage would be considered legitimate. No such provision was made for the marriage avoided for incapacity or wilful refusal to consummate, with the result that some children conceived before their parents' marriage became illegitimate when it was subsequently annulled.[141] The Law Reform (Miscellaneous Provisions) Act 1949[142] provided for the legitimacy of such children, and by the Matrimonial Causes Act 1973, s. 16 a decree of nullity granted after July 1971 in respect of a voidable marriage operates to annul the marriage only as respects any time after the decree has been made absolute, and the marriage shall be treated as existing up to that time. This equates the avoidance of a voidable marriage with the termination of a valid marriage and no question of the child's legitimacy therefore arises.

The children of void marriages were illegitimate until the Legitimacy Act 1959, s. 2(1) provided that if the father was domiciled in England, and if both or either of the parties reasonably believed that the marriage was valid either at the time of the act of intercourse resulting in the birth, or at the time of the celebration of the marriage if later, the child shall be treated as the legitimate child of his parents.[143] It is sometimes argued that if the marriage was thought to be valid at the time of the ceremony but later found to be void (as for bigamy), children conceived thereafter should be considered legitimate. Such arguments seem prompted more by sentimentality towards the parents than consideration for the child. The children of a polygamous marriage have been held legitimate on rather doubtful evidence.[144] Operating

---

137. Legitimacy Act 1926, s. 1, see *Battle* v. *A.-G.* [1949] P. 358; *MacDarmaid* v. *MacDarmaid* [1950] P. 218; *Newbould* v. *A.-G.* [1931] P. 75.

138. Legitimacy Act 1959, s. 1; now Legitimacy Act 1976 s. 2.

139. Section 8: but see *Re Hurll* [1952] Ch. 722; and now Legitimacy Act 1976 s. 3.

140. By s. 7(2).

141. *Dredge* v. *Dredge* [1947] 1 All E.R. 29, *Clarke* v. *Clarke* [1943] 2 All E.R. 540. *L.* v. *L.* [1949] 1 All E.R. 14 (insemination *ab extra*).

142. Section 4.

143. See now Legitimacy Act 1976 s. 1; see also *Sheward* v. *A.-G.* [1964] 1 W.L.R. 724; *Wynn* v. *Wynn* [1964] 108 S.J. 239. In *Hawkins* v. *A.-G.* [1966] 1 W.L.R. 978 reasonable belief was not established.

144. *Hashmi* v. *Hashmi* [1972] Fam. 36. No evidence as to the belief, reasonable or otherwise, of either party to the polygamous marriage in monogamous form in England appears to have been offered.

in the other direction is the provision in the Family Law Reform Act 1969[145] that the presumption of legitimacy of a child born to a married woman is now rebuttable on the balance of probabilities. Formerly the presumption in favour of legitimacy was strong, and the evidence required to rebut it had to be cogent and convincing. The presumption was shared by the Romans, on the principle that *mater semper certa est; pater est quem nuptiae demonstrant.* The first as well as the second part of the proposition has been disproved in practice.[146]

By Part III of the Family Law Reform Act 1969, in operation from 1 March 1972,[147] much of the need for legal presumptions has been displaced by the provision of scientific evidence in the form of blood tests. The courts may now order that blood tests be administered,[148] and the proliferation of tests is such that today it is claimed a blood test will exclude from paternity nine out of every ten men wrongly cited as the father.[149] The court will not compel a blood test, but if it is refused it may draw 'such inferences, if any, from that fact as appear proper in the circumstances'.[150] Anyone who has reached the age of 16 may consent to a blood test on his own behalf.[151]

(b) Illegitimacy. Much of the sting was removed from illegitimacy by the Family Law Reform Act 1969, which provided that an illegitimate child ranks as a dependant for purposes of family provision, and[152] that if parenthood can be proved he has the same rights of succession on the death intestate of either of his parents as a legitimate child.[153] Perhaps most important of all from the viewpoint of the child's status, the presumption was abolished that words of relationship such as child, son or daughter connote legitimate relationship only,

---

145. Section 26.
146. *Re Hamer's Estate* [1937] 1 All E.R. 130.
147. By S.I. 1857 of 1971. See also Blood Tests (Evidence of Paternity) Regulations 1971, S.I. 1861, and Magistrates' Courts (Blood Tests) Rules 1971, S.I. 1991.
148. Family Law Reform Act, s. 20.
149. See article by Dr Barbara Dodd, Reader in Blood Group Serology at the London Hospital, in the *Law Guardian*, 26.2.75: 'Blood Groups in Parentage Problems'. The information in Law Com. 16 (1968) *Blood Tests and Proof of Paternity in Civil Proceedings* is now out of date, but the haptoglobin test was a great advance when it was introduced. See *Holmes* v. *Holmes* [1966] 1 W.L.R. 187; *Stocker* v. *Stocker* [1966] 1 W.L.R. 190; *Re S. (Infants)* [1967] 1 W.L.R. 396; 1 All E.R. 202; *B.* v. *A.-G.* [1967] 1 W.L.R. 776 (estoppel) and *T. (H.H)* v. *T. (E.)* [1971] 1 W.L.R. 429. In *C.* v. *C. and C. (Legitimacy: Photographic Evidence)* [1972] 1 W.L.R. 1335, photographic evidence was admitted but not believed.
150. Family Law Reform Act 1969, ss 21 and 23, overruling *W.* v. *W.* [1964] P. 67 C.A. See also *S.* v. *S.* and *W.* v. *Official Solicitor* [1972] A.C. 24.
151. Family Law Reform Act 1969, s. 21(2).
152. Section 18. Any affiliation order terminates on the death of the person ordered to pay.
153. Section 14(1), balanced in s. 14(2) by an unqualified right of succession for both illegitimate parents, mitigated only by the presumption in s. 14(4) that the father did not survive the child unless the contrary is shown. By s. 15(4) of the Act, legitimate children rank as legitimate from birth for purposes of succession, but by s. 15(5), dignities, titles of honour and property devolving with them are not affected (re-enacting the Legitimacy Act 1926, s. 10(1) and the Legitimacy Act 1959, s. 2(3)). See also Children Act 1975 (Sched. I Part III and Legitimacy Act 1976 ss 5–7 for legitimated children and intruments concerning property.

unless the contrary intention clearly appears. The common law presumption is now replaced by the presumption that illegitimate as well as legitimate relationships are included, provided the reference is to a person who may benefit under the disposition, unless a contrary intention appears.[154] Illegitimate children are also included among children under a protective trust by the Trustee Act 1925, s. 33, and those who save a gift from lapse under the Wills Act 1837, s. 33. The Domestic and Appellate Proceedings (Restriction of Publicity) Act 1968 permits the court to hear *in camera* questions concerning legitimacy, and this was done in *Barritt* v. *A.-G.,*[155] an application under the Matrimonial Causes Act 1965, s. 39.[156]

The Legitimacy Act 1959, s. 5 provided that affiliation proceedings should be heard as matrimonial proceedings, that is, in private before specially constituted magistrates' courts under the Summary Procedure (Domestic Proceedings) Act 1937. The Affiliation Proceedings (Amendment) Act 1972, s. 3 extended this provision to applications for revival or revocation of orders, and permitted the magistrates to extend it also, if they thought fit, to applications for variation. Unless the child has become a 'child of the family' under the Matrimonial Causes Act or the Matrimonial Proceedings (Magistrates Courts) Act 1960, there is, however, no provision for affiliation proceedings under the Affiliation Proceedings Act 1957 to be heard other than in the magistrates' courts,[157] and appeals on fact take the form of a rehearing in open criminal (Crown) court.[158] Appeals by case stated on law are now heard by the Divisional Court of the Family Division of the High Court.

Until 1968[159] there was a very low limit on the maintenance that could be awarded in magistrates' courts for a wife and children, legitimate or illegitimate. Although this has now been removed, the Bedford College Survey found that most of the orders made for illegitimate children were for very small sums, well below the level of supplementary benefit.[160] It is probably still cheaper for a man to have an illegitimate than a legitimate child. By s. 4 of the Affiliation Proceedings Act, maintenance payments for the child cease when he attains the age of 13 (three years before the present minimum school-leaving age) unless the magistrates order that it shall continue until the age of 16. Thereafter the order is renewable only if the child is in full-time education or training, and in no circumstances after the child reaches the age of 21. In 1973 in all 4330 affiliation orders were made.[161]

---

154. Family Law Reform Act 1969, s. 15.
155. [1971] 1 W.L.R. 1713.
156. Now the Matrimonial Causes Act 1973, s. 45.
157. But if nationality is involved, a declaration of status may be obtained under the Matrimonial Causes Act 1973, s. 45.
158. Administration of Justice Act 1970, as amended by the Courts Act 1971, s. 8 and Sched. 1.
159. Maintenance Orders Act 1968, abolishing all such upper limits.
160. See *The Report of the Committee on Statutory Maintenance Limits*, Cmnd 3587 (1968); *Separated Spouses*, by O. R. MacGregor, L. Blom-Cooper and C. Gibson; and the Finer Report on One-Parent Families, Cmnd 5629, paras 4.89–4.90.
161. 5016 were applied for (compared with 20,993 'Married Woman Maintenance' orders applied for and 13,657 granted,) and 5787 'Guardianship of Minors' orders applied for and 4865 granted: *Civil Judicial Statistics 1973*, Cmnd 5756, Table M. No figures for affiliation orders are included in the 1974 statistics, Cmnd 6361.

Because of the reluctance of most unmarried mothers to apply for an affiliation order, they are sometimes encouraged to try to obtain the putative father's agreement to maintain the child, which may be enforceable.[162] It is impossible to know how many such agreements are in force and with what effect, but it seems that previous estimates of their number and effectiveness were exaggerated.

Provided the woman can prove the child's paternity within the four corners of the statute of 1957, she may obtain an affiliation order, which may produce some maintenance for the child. The father has, however, no other duty towards the child, such as providing a home for him.[163] He has no duties towards the mother[164] and the major cost of maintaining most illegitimate children who are not adopted is divided between the mother and the public, in the shape of the Supplementary Benefits Commission.

Despite the quasi-criminal vocabulary used throughout the Affiliation Proceedings Act 1957, it has been held[165] that affiliation proceedings are civil and not criminal proceedings, with the result that the putative father cannot refuse to answer questions about possible paternity on the ground of self-incrimination.

Without statutory authority magistrates usually refuse an affiliation order if there is evidence that the mother was consorting with other men at the time of the child's conception, and it is an unpopular man who cannot find a friend to testify to this effect. Blood group tests may reduce the incidence of such evidence.

The Affiliation Proceedings Act 1957, s. 1 provides that: 'A single woman who is with child, or who has been delivered of an illegitimate child, may apply by complaint to a justice of the peace for a summons to be served on the man alleged by her to be the father of the child.' Formerly the mother had to be 'single' at the time of application for the order, but since the Legitimacy Act 1959[166] it suffices if she was a 'single woman' at the date of the child's birth. The wording has remained unchanged, although it has long been held that a married woman may be a 'single woman' for purposes of the statute provided she is living apart from her husband[167] and has lost her right to his consortium and to be maintained by him.[168] Since the Affiliation

---

162. The consideration for the agreement is probably the undertaking not to apply for an affiliation order so long as maintenance is paid, and not to publicise the connection or harass the putative father.
163. *Colin Smith Music Co., Ltd* v. *Ridge* [1975] 1 W.L.R. 463 C.A., *Eves* v. *Eves,* [1975] 1 W.L.R. 1338, *Tanner* v. *Tanner* [1975] 1 W.L.R. 1346 C.A.
164. Except, if she applies to the magistrates, to pay the expenses incidental to the birth under s. 4(1)(*b*) of the Act, but the hearing before magistrates can only be held after the birth: Any order can therefore take effect only after the expenditure has been made. Layette expenses were held incidental to the birth in *F* v. *B The Times* 19.10.76.
165. *S.* v. *F.* [1967] 1 Q.B. 367, but see 372.
166. Section 4. See *Gaines* v. *W.* [1968] 1 Q.B. 782.
167. Contrast *Whitton* v. *Garner* [1965] 1 W.L.R. 313 D.C. with *Giltrow* v. *Day* [1965] 1 W.L.R. 317.
168. *Jones* v. *Evans* [1944] 1 K.B. 582.

Proceedings (Amendment) Act was passed in 1972, magistrates are no longer precluded from making an affiliation order if the mother does not give evidence,[169] but if she does, her evidence must still be corroborated 'in some material particular'. The corroboration frequently takes the form of letters written to the mother by the alleged father at about the time of the child's conception.[170] Dismissal of the mother's complaint amounts to a non-suit; if further evidence becomes available she may make a new complaint,[171] as there is no estoppel and *res judicata* does not apply in the magistrates' courts. By the Affiliation Proceedings (Amendment) Act 1972[172] the mother may now 'lodge her complaint' within three years of the birth (instead of twelve months as previously); or within twelve months of the man's return to England if she can prove that he ceased residing in England within three years of the birth; or later if, within three years of the birth, the man paid money for the child's maintenance; or.if before the birth she and the alleged father went through a wedding ceremony that was void because either party was under the age of 16 and she can prove that sexual intercourse took place between them less than twelve months before the birth. Only the mother or the child's legal guardian, or a person having custody of the child with the approval of the court (including a custodian not married to the child's mother) may apply for an affiliation order;[173] the child has no independent right. The mother must be resident but need not be domiciled in England.[174] In *Reg.* v. *Bow Road Justices*[175] the Court of Appeal overruled many old precedents and took jurisdiction in respect of children born abroad where both parents and children were ordinarily resident in England. However, if the putative father is a member of foreign armed forces serving in England, the courts have no jurisdiction to make an affiliation order against him.[176]

Since 1914 all payments under affiliation orders must be made to the clerk of the court and not direct to the mother. The Bedford College Survey found, however, that many clerks refuse to forward payments to the mother by post or to answer telephone enquiries as to whether money is available, but insist that she makes personal visits during working hours, only to discover that there is no money for her to collect. So pervasive is the attitude of making life as difficult as possible for the unmarried mother, and so likely are efforts to better the lot of mother and child to be diverted into providing rights

---

169. Section 1. Previously if the mother died or for some other reason could not give evidence, no order could be made.
170. *Jeffrey* v. *Johnson* [1952] 2 Q.B. 8 C.A., *Simpson* v. *Collinson* [1964] 2 Q.B. 80 C.A., *Corfield* v. *Hodgson* [1966] 1 W.L.R. 590 In *Reg.* v. *Notts. Justices* [1970] 1 W.L.R. 1117., evidence from a welfare officer was allowed of an admission of paternity made to her before the child's birth.
171. *Robinson* v. *Williams* [1965] 1 Q.B. 89.
172. Section 2. The Local Authority or the Supplementary Benefits Commission (formerly the National Assistance Board) have since 1948 had three years in which to recover maintenance for the child.
173. Affiliation Proceedings Act 1957, s. 5(3) and the Children Act 1975, s. 45.
174. *Buckeridge* v. *Hall* [1963] 1 Q.B. 613.
175. (Domestic Proceedings Court), ex parte Adedigba, [1968] 2 Q.B. 572 C.A.
176. *R.* v. *Wilson* [1953] 1 Q.B. 59.

for the putative father, that the legislative prohibition[177] on a physical parent adopting his or her child alone unless the other parent is dead or untraceable or there are other special reasons justifying the exclusion of the other parent, must be viewed with reserve.

It is no new phenomenon that ex-nuptial children proliferate amongst the poorest and least adequate members of society, and efforts to reduce their cost to the public account for the early legislation. Witness the preamble to the Statute of Elizabeth I:[178] 'Concerning bastards begotten and born out of lawful matrimony (an offence against God's law and man's law) the said bastards being now left to be kept at the charges of the parish where they be born, to the great burden of the same parish and in defrauding of the relief of the impotent and aged *true* poor of the same parish, and to the evil example and encouragement of the lewd life.' Not until the Poor Law Act 1844 was the mother given a personal right to recover very low maintenance for the child from the putative father. Where the child is in the care of the local authority, the local authority may apply for an affiliation order direct within three years of the birth.[179] Once the child has received supplementary benefit, the Supplementary Benefits Commission may itself take proceedings against the putative father within three years of benefit being received.[180] The predecessors of the Supplementary Benefits Commission, the National Assistance Board, have been far more successful in recovering maintenance for the child than the inadequate and poverty-stricken woman who is the typical unmarried mother.[181] If the Commission obtains an order against the father, it may after repaying expenditure from public funds transfer the order into the mother's name;[182] conversely, as in *Reg.* v. *West London S.B. Appeal Tribunal,*[183] it may recover maintenance unpaid under the mother's affiliation order and pay it over to her after deducting supplementary benefit already paid to her.

(viii) PARENTAL RIGHTS OVER THE EX-NUPTIAL CHILD

The original common law position, that the mother of an illegitimate child was in no better position than a stranger as regards the child,[184] was reversed in

---

177. Adoption Act 1976 s. 15(3).
178. 10 Eliz. 1, c. 3 (1576).
179. Children Act 1948, s. 26. See also Affiliation Proceedings Act 1957, s. 5(2).
180. Supplementary Benefits Act 1966, s. 24.
181. E.g. *N.A.B.* v. *Mitchell* [1956] 1 Q.B. 53 and *N.A.B.* v. *Tugby* [1957] 1 Q.B. 506 demonstrated that their powers were wider; *Clapham* v. *N.A.B.* [1961] 2 Q.B. 77 that they were better equipped to refute false evidence. See *Oldfield* v. *N.A.B.* [1960] 1 Q.B. 635 for the danger of lump-sum payments to the mother. See also *Payne* v. *Critchley and the N.A.B* [1962] 2 Q.B. 83.
182. Supplementary Benefits Act 1966, s. 24(6) and see *Payne* v. *Critchley and N.A.B. supra.*
183. *Ex parte Taylor* [1975] 1 W.L.R. 1048. The Commission recovered £958·75 from the father on an order for £2·50 per week obtained seven years earlier but never paid. The case is concerned with whether such a sum is income or capital in the mother's hands and the effects of holding it to be income.
184. *Re Ann Lloyd* (1841) 3 M. & G. 547.

1883,[185] and now by legislation,[186] whilst she is living, the mother has the parental rights and duties exclusively. The illegitimate child has always had a domicile of origin and of choice dependent on that of the mother.[187] Since adoption was first introduced in 1926 the mother's consent to the child's adoption (renamed agreement in 1975) has been required.

At common law the putative father had no rights in respect of his illegitimate child,[188] but by statute his position also has been greatly strengthened. With the mother's consent he may be entered as the child's father when the birth is registered.[189] After 1969[190] the birth may be reregistered with himself as the father with the consent of the child if over 16. It is no longer necessary that he and the mother call together in person for such entry. His acknowledgement of paternity may be by declaration or affiliation order presented by the mother. Secondly, since 1959[191] the putative father may apply to the court for custody of his illegitimate child, and if this is granted he is treated as the lawful father, or as the child's guardian for purposes of assenting to his adoption,[192] and if entitled to custody at his death, he may appoint a testamentary guardian. This provision is preferable to any system of unilateral acknowledgement of the child by the father, which exists in many if not most civil law countries. There it may be possible for the father to acknowledge the child without the mother's consent, and if he does so before the mother acknowledges the child[193] or in some other circumstances,[194] he may be granted all parental rights over the child. This gives him a powerful means of pressure on the mother throughout the child's minority. It may also give rise to a situation differing from a polygamous system only in that the father has no obligations towards the mothers of his children, but all the means of coercion over each mother that his parental rights over her child or children afford him.

---

185. *Reg.* v. *Nash* (1883) 10 Q.B.D. 454 C.A., confirmed by the House of Lords in *Barnardo* v. *McHugh* [1891] A.C. 388. The year 1883 also saw the decision in *Re Agar-Ellis* (1883) 24 Ch.D. 317 C.A. that the mother of legitimate children had, in the presence of the father, no rights of custody or even uncensored access to her children.
186. Children Act 1975, s. 85(7).
187. Until the law of married women's domicile was changed by the Domicile and Matrimonial Proceedings Act 1973, s. 1, this meant that if the mother was a married woman, her domicile was her husband's domicile, which was also the domicile of origin of the child who, by definition, had no connection with her husband.
188. *Re M. (An Infant)* [1955] 2 Q.B. 479 C.A.
189. Births and Deaths Registration Act 1953, s. 10 as amended and s. 10A as inserted by Children Act 1975, s. 93. See also Regulations S.I. 2049 of 1968, Reg. 18(4)(*b*) and Form I space 4, and Family Law Reform Act 1969, s. 27.
190. Family Law Reform Act 1969, s. 27.
191. Legitimacy Act 1959, s. 3(1)(3) now Guardianship of Minors Act 1971, s. 14.
192. Adoption Act 1976 s.72.
193. This applies in countries such as France and those that follow the Napoleonic Code in requiring recognition of the child by the mother. Maternal recognition was originally introduced as a measure of liberation for the mother, who might if she wished deny maternity.
194. E.g. in the U.S.S.R. under the New Fundamental Principles of Family Law introduced in 1968, once paternity is established either by recognition or a judicial finding, the father has the same rights and duties in respect of the child as the lawful father. See 18 *ICLQ* (1969) 397.

CHAPTER IX

Adoption

The law of adoption is one aspect of the law relating to the welfare of children whose parents are unable to provide a normal home background and upbringing for them. Recent amendments have been directed towards linking more closely the law concerning children in the care of the local authorities with the law of adoption, creating greater unity in child welfare law as a whole and enabling more children to be adopted instead of remaining indefinitely in the care of local authorities. Another recent development has been the limitation on the growing practice of physical parents adopting their own children, both legitimate and illegitimate.

At the end of the nineteenth century it became clear that Great Britain was among the few so-called 'advanced' countries without any legal institution of adoption. The English common law, with its absence of provision for adoption, was deemed to have been carried to the settled colonies in North America, Australia, New Zealand and elsewhere from the sixteenth century onwards. Unofficial adoption had of course always taken place and the lack of legal recognition meant that adults were free to make the arrangements that suited them. The law would not enforce such arrangements, nor did it attempt what would today be regarded as the most important function of our adoption law: viz. to safeguard the interests of the child concerned. Unofficial adoptions probably still continue, and one of the continuing brakes on adoption law is that, if too many safeguards are imposed in the interests of the child, the adults concerned may avoid the law and resort to unofficial arrangements with resulting loss of protection for the children.

A. HISTORICAL OUTLINES OF ADOPTION IN ENGLAND

Legal recognition and regulation of adoption came to the common law, like many nineteenth and twentieth century reforms, from the lands west of the

Atlantic. It was first introduced in a common law jurisdiction in Massachusetts in 1851,[1] and spread north to New Brunswick in Canada by 1873. Ten years later the English Court of Appeal in *Reg.* v. *Nash*[2] reaffirmed that no such institution existed in English law. It was held that the mother had an absolute right to recover possession of her child by writ of habeas corpus from a couple she had allowed to bring the child up for seven years, and that the agreement she had made to the contrary was unenforceable.[3] Unwanted children of the poor were often left to the mercies of baby farmers in the nineteenth and early twentieth centuries, and if the children survived, unscrupulous parents did not fail to reclaim them when they reached wage-earning age.

Public agitation for recognition of a law of adoption developed as part of the general movement to improve the law for the welfare of children. This was renewed after 1918, and in 1921 the Hopkinson Committee reported[4] in favour of legalising adoption. Between 1922 and 1924 in all six Bills were introduced into Parliament to this end, but without success. In 1925 the Tomlin Committee again reported[5] in favour of legalising adoption, and appended a draft Bill which formed the basis for the Adoption of Children Act 1926. This came into operation in England and Wales from the beginning of 1927 and marked the birth of English adoption law.

The law was amended in 1939, but the amendments became operative only in 1943.[6] The provisions were further expanded in 1949 and in 1950 the first consolidating statute was passed.[7] Following the report of the Hurst Committee in 1954[8] the law was amended by Part II of the Children Act 1958 which, before coming into operation, was replaced by the Adoption Act 1958.[9] The Houghton Departmental Committee on Adoption was set up on 24 June 1969

---

1. North American States such as Louisiana and Texas, which were strongly influenced by Roman Law institutions by way of the French and Spanish law, had recognised adoption earlier.
2. (1883) 10 Q.B.D. 434 C.A. In *Humphreys* v. *Polak* [1901] 2 K.B. 385, the Court of Appeal held that the informal adoptive parents might similarly disclaim their agreement and return the child to its natural parents at any time. These decisions were affirmed by the House of Lords in *Barnardo* v. *McHugh* [1891] A.C. 388.
3. The decision constituted a reversal of the previous common law view in *Re Ann Lloyd* (1841) 3 M. & G. 547, that the mother of an illegitimate child had no greater right to the child's custody than any stranger.
4. Cmd 1254. The committee also recommended supervision of children 'unofficially' adopted: B.P.P. 1921 Vol. IX.
5. Cmds 2401 and 2469: B.P.P. 1924−5 Vol. IX. A third report of the Child Adoption Committee, Cmd 2711, was devoted entirely to the protection of infant life under Part I of the Children Act 1908, and the inspection of voluntary homes under s. 25 of that Act: B.P.P. 1926 Vol. VIII.
6. Adoption of Children (Regulation) Act 1939, which regulated adoption societies, provided for the supervision of certain adopted children and further prohibited payments in respect of adoption. The Act should have come into force on 1 January 1940, but owing to the outbreak of war its operation was delayed. It was eventually made operative from 1 June 1943 by S.I. No. 378 of 1943.
7. Adoption Act 1950.
8. Cmd 9248: reviewed 18 *MLR* (1955) 274.
9. In operation from 1 April 1959 by s. 60(2): reviewed 22 *MLR* (1959) 500.

and published a Working Paper in 1970. In 1972 the Committee, by then under the chairmanship of Judge Stockdale, published its report[10] which formed the basis for the Children Act 1975 and the Adoption Act 1976.[11] Part of the 1975 Act came into operation on receiving the Royal Assent on 12 November 1975 and part on 1 January 1976.[12] A consolidating Adoption Act 1976 received the Royal Assent on 22 July 1976, but its provisions will be brought into operation by statutory instrument.[13] By August 1976 no new Rules[14] or Regulations[15] connected with either the 1975 or the 1976 Act had been published.[16] The 1976 Act repeals all previous Adoption Acts and Part I (ss 1–32) of the Children Act 1975. The Children Act 1975 provides in s. 105 for a review of the working of its provisions after three years' operation, and thereafter at five-yearly intervals. Presumably this will include its adoption provisions now repealed.

The following statistics demonstrate the accelerating popularity of adoption, now checked only by shortage of children available,[17] and in future also by the curbs placed on the adoption of children by their physical parents:

The figures prove that, while undeniably children need parents, the converse is also true; the need of parents for children, even the children of others, to bring up as their own, is also powerful.

The fact that English law first countenanced the legal adoption of children some fifty years ago means that the law has not been encumbered with too many concepts from different civilisations functioning in wholly different circumstances.[18] That children benefit considerably from adoption seems established,

---

10. Cmnd 5107 published October 1972.
11. Hereafter the 1975 and 1976 Acts.
12. Viz. ss 71, 72, 82, 108 and 109 and Sched. 3, para. 57 have been operative from 12 November 1975. See generally Stone, *Recent Developments in Adoption and long-term fostering in England and Wales* in *The Child and the Law*, I.S.F.L. (1976) and David Bradley: *Children Act 1975*, 39 M.L.R. (1976) 452.
13. Adoption Act 1976 s. 74(2).
14. These govern court procedure. Section 64 of the 1976 Act now provides for private hearings and adds that in the magistrates' courts the proceedings are to be domestic proceedings for the purposes of the Magistrates' Courts Act 1952. See also the 1976 Adoption Rules S.I. Nos. 1644, 1645 and 1768.
15. These govern adoption agencies, viz. local authorities and adoption societies. See ss 8–9 and 67 of the 1976 Act.
16. The consolidated Adoption Act 1976 contrasts favourably with the morass of statutes, repeals and amendments governing children in public care, which make knowledge of the law impossible for any but the specialist.
17. Some children are available in excess of available adopters, principally members of minority religious or racial groups, and those with mental or physical disabilities. The provision in s. 57(4) and (5) of the 1976 Act for the approval of schemes for payment to adopters may improve the likelihood of adoption of such disadvantaged children. In recent years physically handicapped children have been successfully placed for adoption in greater numbers. The 1976 Act in s. 7 now enjoins only that an adoption agency shall, in placing a child for adoption, have regard to any wishes of the child's parents and guardians as to the child's religious upbringing so far as is practicable.
18. For example, there is no problem of women who adopt children to ensure a larger *legitim* for themselves from their deceased husband's property, and only unmarried minors may be adopted in England.

TABLE IV
Extract from Registrar-General's Statistics for England and Wales for 1973
[TABLE T4.   Registration of Adoption Orders, 1927 to 1973. See Adoption Act 1958, s. 20 Adoption Act 1976 s. 50 (England and Wales)]

| Year | Number of Adoption Orders dealt with | | | | | | | Corresponding number of children,[b] i.e. entries made in Adopted Children Register | | | | |
	Total[a]	Provisional	High Court Total[a]	High Court Provisional	County Court Total[a]	County Court Provisional	Court of Summary Jurisdiction	Total	Quarter ending 31 March	30 June	30 September	31 December
1927–30	14,026		403		961		12,662	14,094	2,986	3,817	3,319	3,972
1931–5	22,708		276		1,432		21,000	22,732	5,212	6,011	5,198	6,311
1936–40	31,521		349		2,511		28,661	31,544	7,113	8,404	7,937	8,090
1941–5	58,732		266		7,916		50,550	58,819	12,409	14,081	15,991	16,338
1946–50	88,123		870		19,225		68,028	88,178	20,532	22,124	22,028	23,494
1951–5	66,743		392		21,654		44,697	66,765	16,692	16,425	15,848	17,800
1956	13,198		44		5,118		8,036	13,201	3,451	3,000	2,997	3,753
1957	13,401		44		5,553		7,804	13,403	3,351	3,380	3,020	3,652
1958	13,303		53		5,899		7,351	13,304	3,249	3,210	3,094	3,751
1959	14,105	71	46	1	6,529	70	7,530	14,109	3,102	2,958	3,947	4,102
1960	15,099	207	42	2	7,602	205	7,455	15,099	3,899	3,600	3,399	4,201
1961	15,997	249	55	1	8,678	248	7,264	16,000	3,702	3,801	3,901	4,596
1962	16,894	280	53	4	9,572	276	7,269	16,894	4,048	3,747	3,998	5,101
1963	17,782	196	74		10,443	196	7,265	17,782	4,548	4,347	4,297	4,590
1964	20,412	232	59	1	12,796	231	7,557	20,412	5,193	4,945	4,614	5,660
1965	21,033	171	55	—	13,499	171	7,479	21,033	5,398	5,080	4,726	5,829
1966	22,792	127	50	—	14,880	127	7,862	22,792	5,783	5,396	5,121	6,492
1967	22,802	173	45	1	15,086	172	7,671	22,802	5,906	5,642	5,016	6,238
1968	24,831	189	39	4	16,499	185	8,293	24,831	6,502	5,855	5,497	6,977
1969	23,705	173	31	2	15,623	171	8,051	23,708	5,792	5,645	5,469	6,802
1970	22,371	155	16	1	14,506	154	7,849	22,371	5,403	5,754	4,875	6,339
1971	21,495	123	40	—	13,619	123	7,836	21,495	4,701	5,557	5,287	5,950
1972	21,603	134	21		13,461	134	8,121	21,599	5,499	5,249	4,902	5,949
1973	22,247	167	34	1	13,825	166	8,392	22,247	5,879	5,773	4,997	5,599

a Provisional Adoption Orders, which were introduced on 1 April 1959 (see Adoption Act 1958, s. 53) are included in the total.
These Orders confer authority on a person not domiciled in Great Britain to take a child out of this country for adoption.
b The number of adopted children usually exceeds the number of Adoption Orders because the High Court does not issue a separate Order for each child where an adopter adopts more than one child at the same time.

TABLE V

Extract from Registrar-General's Statistics for England and Wales for 1973

[TABLE T5. Children adopted under orders registered in 1973, by legitimacy, sex and age (England and Wales)]

Age at adoption and sex	All children	Legitimate children							Illegitimate children						
		Total	Joint adopters		Sole male adopter		Sole female adopter		Total	Joint adopters		Sole male adopter		Sole female adopter	
			One or both a parent	Neither a parent	Parent	Not a parent	Parent	Not a parent		One or both a parent	Neither a parent	Parent	Not a parent	Parent	Not a parent
All ages P	22,247	9,254	8,101	1,118	1	13	7	14	12,993	5,576	7,341	4	7	25	40
M	11,474	4,615	4,042	555	1	7	6	4	6,859	2,809	4,007	4	5	13	21
F	10,773	4,639	4,059	563	—	6	1	10	6,134	2,767	3,334	—	2	12	19
Under 6 months M	1,046	35	2	33	—	—	—	—	1,011	16	995	—	—	—	—
F	917	52	1	51	—	—	—	—	865	19	845	—	—	—	1
6–8 months M	1,794	89	7	81	—	—	—	—	1,705	47	1,656	—	1	—	1
F	1,484	84	4	80	—	—	—	—	1,400	34	1,366	—	—	—	—
9–11 months M	415	37	6	31	—	—	—	—	378	28	348	—	—	2	—
F	370	39	2	37	—	—	—	—	331	33	296	—	—	2	3
12–17 months M	378	54	5	49	—	—	—	—	324	75	244	—	—	1	—
F	358	53	17	36	—	—	—	—	305	89	215	—	—	1	—
18–23 months M	324	49	12	36	—	—	—	1	275	142	132	—	—	1	4
F	283	42	17	25	—	—	—	—	241	139	101	—	—	—	2
2 years M	626	144	103	41	—	—	—	—	482	324	153	—	—	4	6
F	643	172	118	52	—	—	—	2	471	352	116	—	1	3	2
3–4 years M	1,895	717	641	74	1	—	—	—	1,178	966	202	—	4	3	5
F	1,791	704	633	69	—	1	—	2	1,087	922	160	—	3	1	1
5–9 years M	3,381	2,234	2,045	132	—	1	3	—	1,147	922	214	2	3	3	3
F	3,276	2,188	2,027	134	—	3	1	5	1,088	902	176	—	1	3	6
10–14 years M	1,366	1,087	1,027	53	—	4	3	1	279	228	46	1	2	1	1
F	1,414	1,127	1,070	54	—	3	1	—	287	238	42	—	1	1	5
15–17 years M	249	169	142	25	—	1	1	1	80	61	17	—	1	1	—
F	237	178	152	25	—	—	—	1	59	39	17	—	—	—	3

and the latest research[19] suggests that the illegitimate child in particular is likely to fare better if adopted than if brought up by an unmarried mother. This poses a dilemma as, with improved welfare provisions, the unmarried mother is showing increasing reluctance to offer her child for adoption.[20]

B. THE BALANCE BETWEEN PARENTAL RIGHTS AND THE CHILD'S WELFARE

The law of adoption, unlike that governing the custody of children since 1925, has never provided that the welfare of the child is the first and paramount consideration, because this might be interpreted to mean that the affluent could always take away the children of the poor on the ground that it was for their welfare to be rich, or at least richer than their physical parents. The statutes have always provided that before making an adoption order the court must be satisfied that it is for the welfare of the child. However, it is now laid down by s. 6 of the 1976 Act[21] that 'In reaching any decision relating to the adoption of a child a court or adoption agency shall have regard to all the circumstances, first consideration being given to the need to safeguard and promote the welfare of the child throughout his childhood; and shall so far as practicable ascertain the wishes and feelings of the child regarding the decision and give due consideration to them, having regard to his age and understanding.'[22]

The general principle has always been that no minor may be adopted (and only unmarried minors may be adopted)[23] except with the consent (renamed agreement after 1975) of every parent or guardian of his, unless parental consent is dispensed with on specified grounds. For the legitimate child this means that both mother and father must agree, but between April 1959 and 1976 only the mother's consent was required in respect of the child born outside marriage, and not that of the putative father unless he had been granted custody

---

19. E.g. *Growing Up Adopted* by J. Seglow, P. Wedge and Mia Kellmer-Pringle (1972) suggests that adopted children compare favourably in adjustment and general development even with legitimate children.
20. The existence of Supplementary Benefits and the fact that they are on a more generous scale than the kind of 'maintenance' ordered in the magistrates' courts has now become common knowledge.
21. Replacing s. 3 of the 1975 Act, which has been in operation since the beginning of 1976.
22. This is more positive and extends back to an earlier time than the provision in s. 7 of the 1958 Act. As welfare workers are always involved in adoption, the practical question of ascertaining the child's wishes is left to them, thus avoiding the difficulties which arise in custody disputes of interviewing children apart from their parents. The new formulation was considered in *Re B. (An Infant) (Adoption: Parental Consent)* |1976| Fam. 161 and *Re S., The Times*, 17.11.76 C.A.
23. S. 12(5) Before the age of majority was reduced to 18 from the beginning of 1970, the courts were reluctant to sanction the adoption of children nearing their majority, which might be a device to obtain British nationality without the need for naturalisation: *see Re A.* |1963| 1 W.L.R. 231. On different facts the adoption in *Re R. (Adoption)* |1967| 1 W.L.R. 34 was sanctioned.

of the child on application to a court.[24] Consent once given could be revoked up to the moment when the adoption order was made, and the parents were in practice asked more than once to confirm assent already given. Often parents withdrew their consent at a late stage, sometimes on discovering that the adoption would mean the cessation of the child allowance, and often through inability to make any firm decision. The law and practice have now been changed in several respects under the 1975 Act.

(i) FREEING THE CHILD FOR ADOPTION

The procedure has been changed so that, instead of the parent being required to consent in advance to every individual application to adopt the child, she (and he for the legitimate child or child in the custody of his putative father) will normally be asked to agree 'generally and unconditionally' to the making of an adoption order, under s. 18 of the 1976 Act.[25] If this agreement is given, or the need for it is dispensed with by the court,[26] the child will be declared free for adoption; parental rights will vest in the adoption agency, and no further agreement will be required before an adoption order can be made on a particular application.[27] By s. 21, on a joint application by both agencies involved, the court may by order transfer parental rights and duties from one agency to another. Before declaring the child free for adoption, the court must satisfy itself that each parent or guardian who can be found has been given an opportunity of making a declaration of non-involvement, viz. of declaring that she or he prefers not to be involved in future questions concerning the adoption of the child, and record such a declaration.[28]

---

24. Adoption Act 1958 ss 4(1)(*a*) and 57. Before the 1958 Act the putative father's consent was required if he was under an enforceable obligation to contribute to the child's maintenance. This led to great difficulties with putative fathers who had maintained the child voluntarily but whose consent was not required (*Re M. (An Infant)* [1955] 2 Q.B. 479 C.A.) or at the other extreme, the putative father who had killed the mother and then refused consent to the child's adoption, when his consent was required because an affiliation order created an obligation enforceable against him, e.g. *Re D. (An Infant)* [1958] 1 W.L.R. 197; *Re F.* [1970] 1 W.L.R. 192. Under the 1958 Act it was one of the duties of the child's guardian *ad litem* to bring to the court's attention any representations the putative father wished to make. See *Re Adoption Application 41/61 (No 2)* [1964] Ch. 48. See now Adoption Act 1976, ss. 18(7) and 72, *post.*
25. This is modelled on the practice in the United States. The principal difficulty is that the parental rights vest in a hierarchical institution, and there are disturbing examples from the United States of agencies who place the sanctity of their rules above the welfare of the child, see, e.g. the case of Laura Neuberger In *Re Jewish Child Care Association,* 5 N.Y. 2d. 222; 183 N.Y.S. 2d. 65, 156 N.E. 2d. 700 (1959); *In Re Alexander* (1968) 206 So. 2d. 452, Fla.
26. Considered *post. A Survey of Adoption in Great Britain* (1971) found an overall rate of dispensing with consent of about 6 per cent, pp. 70–1, with little difference between county courts and juvenile courts. Civil Judicial Statistics for 1974, Cmnd 6361, Table B 13 (ii) show a total of 37 adoption orders made in the the High Court and 13,384 in the county courts. No figures are available for the juvenile courts. Parental consent was dispensed with in 5 cases in the High Court and 924 cases in the county courts.
27. This can be made under s. 16 of the 1976 Act, under which the parent may also agree to the particular application for adoption if the child has not previously been declared free for adoption.
28. S. 18(6); another innovation, considered *post,* (iv) nn. 35–6.

It is also provided[29] that before declaring free for adoption an illegitimate child whose father is not its guardian[30] the court shall satisfy itself either that any person claiming to be the father has no intention of applying for custody of the child or that if he did apply for custody the application would be likely to be refused.[31] This could be held to endorse the practice condemned in *Re Adoption Application 41/61,*[32] of delaying the adoption of illegitimate children while attempts are made to ascertain the whereabouts and the views of fathers who have displayed no interest in their children and may be unaware of their existence. The section refers, however, to a person 'claiming to be the father', which should mean that any initiative remains with the adult, who must make a claim before his intentions become relevant. The previous rule remains unchanged, that the mother's consent to the child's adoption, either generally or on a specific application, is ineffective if given less than six weeks after the child's birth.[33]

(ii) COURT ATTENDANCE OF PHYSICAL PARENT NOT USUALLY REQUIRED

Another change in procedure is that, by s. 66(3) the rules will require that every person whose agreement or consent is necessary or must be dispensed with before an order can be made declaring a child free for adoption under s. 18 or for a particular adoption application under s. 16(1)(*b*) shall, if he can be found, be notified of a date and place where he may be heard on the application and of the fact that, unless he wishes or the court requires, he need not attend. This includes those whose agreement is needed to the making of an order for the adoption of a child abroad under s. 55 of the Act.[34]

(iii) ONLY ADOPTION AGENCIES MAY PLACE CHILDREN FOR ADOPTION

Section 11 of the 1976 Act prohibits any person other than an adoption agency from making arrangements for the adoption of a child, or placing a child for

---

29. Section 18(7).
30. By s. 72 of the 1976 Act, 'guardian' in the case of an illegitimate child includes the father where he has custody of the child by virtue of an order under s. 9 of the Guardianship of Minors Act 1971 or the corresponding Scottish Act.
31. A difficult concept. Court *A*, not having received an application for custody from the father, must decide that court *B*, if it received such an application with supporting evidence, would be likely to refuse it. Suppose court *A* is not prepared to make such a supposition, but when the father applies to court *B* his application is refused. Presumably application to have the child declared free for adoption must start again. This looks like preferring adults' 'rights' to the welfare of children.
32. [1963] Ch. 315 C.A. and No. 2 [1964] Ch. 48.
33. Sections 16(4) and 18(4). The Houghton Committee Working Paper was thinking of the mother being able to consent within days of the birth, but such ideas appear to have been discarded.
34. This provision allows the court to vest parental rights and duties in someone not domiciled in England and Wales, to enable him to adopt the child 'under the law of or within' the country in which he is domiciled, replacing s. 53 of the 1958 Act, now repealed.

adoption, unless the proposed adopter is a relative of the child or the action is in pursuance of an order of the High Court. This is fortified by s. 13, which provides that if the applicant or one of the applicants is a parent, step-parent, or relative of the child, or if the child was placed with the applicants by an adoption agency or in pursuance of a High Court order, the adoption order may be made when the child is nineteen weeks old, provided he has at all times during the preceding thirteen weeks had his home with the applicants or one of them. If these conditions as to the applicants or the placement are not fulfilled, the adoption order cannot be made unless the child is at least twelve months old and has at all times during the preceding twelve months had his home with the applicants or one of them. It is also provided by s. 22 that an adoption order shall not be made in respect of a child who was not placed with the applicant by an adoption agency unless the applicant has, at least three months before the date of the order, given notice to his local authority of his intention to apply for the adoption order. On receiving notice the local authority must investigate and report to the court, in particular whether someone other than an adoption agency placed the child with a non-relative other than in pursuance of a High Court order. The child in the meantime becomes 'a protected child' over whom the local authority has special supervisory duties and powers under ss 32–7 of the Act.

(iv) RE-VESTING OF PARENTAL RIGHTS

Where a parent has declined to make a declaration under s. 18(6) that he prefers not to be involved in future questions concerning the adoption of the child, ss 9 and 20 of the 1976 Act come into operation. Section 19 provides that within twelve months and fourteen days of the order declaring the child free for adoption, the adoption agency in which parental rights and duties were vested by the order must notify the former parent[35] whether an adoption order has been made, and if not, whether the child has been placed for adoption. Thereafter the agency must inform the former parent when the child is adopted or placed for adoption or ceases to be so placed, unless the former parent makes a declaration of non-involvement. In that event the agency must ensure that this declaration is recorded by the court that freed the child for adoption, and need no longer keep the former parent informed. If the child has not been adopted and is not placed for adoption twelve months after he was declared free for adoption, the parent may apply for a revocation of that order on the ground that he wishes to resume the parental rights and duties. Pending such an application the agency may not place the child for adoption without leave of the court. If the order freeing the child for adoption is revoked, all the parental rights and duties re-vest in the person in whom they were vested before the order was made.

---

35. The wording used is novel. Although there have long been provisions for a court to declare a parent unfit to exercise parental rights, it has never previously been provided that he (or more probably she) ceases to be a parent, or that she or he may be divested of parenthood subject to re-vesting.

If on the other hand the former parent's application is dismissed on the ground that to allow it would be contrary to the need to safeguard and promote the welfare of the child throughout his childhood, the former parent will not be able to make a further application without the leave of the court[36] and the adoption agency is freed of all further duties of keeping him informed.

(v) DISPENSING WITH PARENTAL AGREEMENT[37] TO ADOPTION

The only slight addition to the grounds on which the court may dispense with the parent's agreement to the child's adoption is if the parent has seriously ill-treated the child and, because of the ill-treatment or for other reasons, the rehabilitation of the child within the household of the parent or guardian is unlikely. The drafters of the Act appear to be relying principally on the changes in procedure to reduce the difficulties that have been caused by the great reluctance of the courts in the past to dispense with parental consent.[38] There has also been some change of attitude to withholding and particularly to withdrawal at a late stage of parental consent to adoption, exemplified for example in *Re W.*[39] in which the House of Lords held that it is sufficient to show that the parent was not acting reasonably in all the circumstances in refusing, or withdrawing, consent. It is not necessary to show culpability, or callous or self-indulgent indifference, or probable failure of parental duty, or potential lasting damage to the child. The grounds for dispensing with parental agreement are therefore,[40] that the parent or guardian:

(*a*) cannot be found or is incapable of giving agreement;
(*b*) is withholding his agreement unreasonably;[41]

---

36. Not to be given unless it appears to the court that because of a change in circumstances or for any other reason it is proper to allow the application to be made.
37. The 1975 Act changed the word from 'consent' to 'agreement'.
38. Rarely will the court dispense with the agreement of the father of a legitimate child, but it did so in *O'Connor* v. *A. & B.* [1971] 1 W.L.R. 1227, H.L.(Sc.) and in *Re B. (S.)* [1968] Ch. 204, where the Spanish father of a legitimate child had made no attempt at any time to discharge the duties of a parent, nor responded to applications made to him, except by threatening criminal proceedings against his wife for deserting him. In *Re D., The Times*. 16.12.76 the House of Lords found a homosexual father's refusal to agree to adoption of his son aged 8 by the mother and stepfather unreasonable, and dispensed with his agreement.
39. [1971] A.C. 682, reversing the decision of the Court of Appeal and adopting the contrary interpretation in *Re B. (C.H.O.)* [1971] 1 Q.B. 437. The Court of Appeal also affirmed the decision of a county court judge in *Re C. (L)* [1965] 2 Q.B. 449, that the mother of a child born outside marriage was unreasonable not to take account of the psychological effects on her child, to whom she had little prospect of offering a stable environment. Her consent was dispensed with. See also *Re S.* [1973] 3 All E.R. 88. Contrast *In re Application No. 4 of 1974, The Times* 1.5.75 C.A., where an unmarried Indian woman aged 25 was allowed to withdraw her consent a year after the child was placed, so that she could take the child to India and retain her on her return, and see *Re M. (An Infant)* [1973] Q.B. 108 C.A.
40. Section 16(2), also applicable to an order freeing the child for adoption under s. 18 by s. 18(1)(*b*), where the child is in the care of the adoption agency applying for dispensation.
41. Described in the 1968 Report of the Standing Conference of Adoption Societies, paras 124−9, as the most usual ground for application to dispense with parental consent.

(*c*) has persistently failed without reasonable cause to discharge parental duties in relation to the child;[42]

(*d*) has abandoned or neglected the child;

(*e*) has persistently ill-treated the child; or

(*f*) has seriously ill-treated the child and, because of the ill-treatment or for other reasons, the rehabilitation of the child within the household of the parent or guardian is unlikely.

(vi) REMOVING A CHILD FROM THE HOME OF PROSPECTIVE ADOPTERS

This area of the law has been considerably amended, so that now once the parent or guardian has agreed to the adoption order being made, she or he is not entitled, against the will of the person with whom the child has his home, to remove the child from the custody of that person while the application for an adoption order is pending, except with the leave of the court. If the child is in the care of an adoption agency that is applying for him to be declared free for adoption, no parent or guardian who did not consent to the application is entitled without the leave of the court, to remove the child from the custody of the person with whom the child has his home, against the will of that person.[43] If an application is pending for an adoption order in respect of a child who has had his home for the preceding five years[44] with the applicant, no person is entitled, against the applicant's will, to remove the child from the applicant's custody except by leave of the court or under statutory authority or on the arrest of the child. A similar prohibition applies for three months after notice of intention to apply for an adoption order has been received by the local authority or until application is made, if that happens earlier. The prohibition extends to the local authority itself if the applicant is a foster-parent or custodian and the child remains in the care of the local authority (unless a custodianship order has been revoked). Contravention of these prohibitions on removing the child is a criminal offence, and the offender is liable on summary conviction to three months' imprisonment or a fine of £400 or both. Provisions are made for the child to be returned and if necessary for premises to be searched[45] to find and return him.

---

42. First introduced by the Act of 1958, and applied *inter alia* in *Re P.* (*Infants*) [1962] 1 W.L.R. 1296 and *Re B.* (*S.*) [1968] Ch. 204.

43. 1976 Act s. 27(2).

44. Section 28. This provision is intended to apply principally to the foster-parent with whom the child is placed by the local authority. The foster-parent will now be able to apply for a custodianship order after the child has been in his home for 3 years, or after 12 months if parental rights are vested in a local authority, which consents: Children Act 1975, s. 33(3)(*b*) and (*c*). The foster parent may apply for an adoption order after the child has had his home with him for 5 years.

45. 1976 Act s. 29.

C. THOSE WHO MAY ADOPT

(i) An adoption order may be made in favour of more than one person only when it is made in favour of a married couple.[46] Both prospective adopters must now have attained the age of 21,[47] and at least one of them must be domiciled in a part of the United Kingdom or in the Channel Islands or the Isle of Man unless the application is for a Convention adoption order.[48] One person alone may adopt if she or he has attained the age of 21 and is unmarried, or if married, provided the court is satisfied that her (or his) spouse cannot be found, or the spouses are separated and the separation is likely to be permanent or the other spouse is by reason of physical or mental ill health incapable of applying for an adoption order.[49] A sole applicant must be domiciled in a part of the United Kingdom, or the Channel Islands or the Isle of Man unless the application is for a Convention adoption order.[48]

Before making the order the court must be satisfied that sufficient opportunities to see the child in the home environment with the sole applicant (or with both applicants together where a married couple applies) have been given to the adoption agency that placed the child for adoption or, in any other case, to the local authority within whose area the home is.[50]

(ii) An adoption order may not be made on the application of the mother or father of the child alone unless the court is satisfied that the other natural parent is dead or cannot be found, or there is some other reason 'justifying the exclusion of the other natural parent',[51] in which event that reason shall be recorded by the court. Where a step-parent is the sole applicant or there is a joint application by a parent and step-parent of the child, the court shall dismiss the application if it considers the matter would be better dealt with under the provisions of the Matrimonial Causes Act 1973, applying to child custody orders.[52] These are decisive moves against the adoption of children by their physical parents, not only when the children were born of a marriage that is subsequently dissolved, and the custodian parent applies to adopt,[53] but also when the child was born outside marriage. In 1973 over 5500 children born outside marriage were adopted by joint adopters, one or both of whom was a parent.[54] If the unmarried mother marries a man other than the child's father

---

46. 1976 Act, s. 14. Once made the adoption is valid although the marriage was void. *In re S. and A. F. (Infants) The Times*, 21.12.76 C.A.
47. Previously by s. 2 of the 1958 Act there was no age-limit if one of the adopters was the child's parent; otherwise if one of the joint applicants was 21 years old, and the other a relative of 21, or was 25 years old, they might adopt. Adoption by physical parents or step-parents is now strongly discouraged.
48. Viz. designed to be made under the Hague Convention for the Adoption of Children, and s. 17 of the 1976 Act discussed *post*.
49. 1976 Act s. 15.
50. Ibid. s. 13(3).
51. Section 15(3).
52. 1976 Act 15(4) and 14(3) and Children Act 1975 s. 37, providing for custodianship orders to be made on certain applications for adoption.
53. See *Re D. (Minors)* [1973] Fam. 209 D.C., *Re B. (A Minor) (Adoption by parent)* [1975] Fam. 127.
54. *Ante*, Table V.

and then dies, however, or for some other reason the child had never come within the provisions of the Matrimonial Causes Act, there would seem to be no impediment to adoption by a step-parent.

The Rules made in 1976 for adoption orders in all three courts still require a guardian *ad litem* for the child to be appointed in every adoption application. A reporting officer may also be appointed to witness agreements to adoption and perform other duties as required by the rules, and one person may fulfil both functions if the court thinks fit.[55] The Secretary of State will establish a panel of persons eligible for appointment.[56] A person employed by certain adoption agencies may, however, sometimes be ineligible.

D. ORDERS FOR LESS THAN FULL ADOPTION

The provisions for interim orders have been reworded by s. 25 of the 1976 Act. If the requirements preliminary to an adoption order are complied with the court may postpone determination of the application and vest the legal custody of the child in the applicants for a probationary period or periods not exceeding two years in all.[57] If the court refuses to make an adoption order for a child under 16, it may in exceptional circumstances order that the child shall be under the supervision of a specified local authority or a probation officer, or commit the care of the child to a specified local authority.

It is now also clearly established that conditional adoption orders may be made, for example providing for continued access to the child by the putative father, as in *Re J.*[58]

If a child has been placed for adoption by an adoption agency, he must be returned to the agency within seven days after the prospective adopter has notified it that he does not intend to retain the child's custody or if, before an adoption application has been made, the agency has notified him that it intends to withdraw the child, or if the application for adoption is refused by the court or withdrawn. For this purpose the expiry, without an adoption order having been made, of the period specified in an interim order, is equivalent to the refusal of an order. Where an application is refused, however, the court may, within the period of seven days, extend to a maximum of six weeks the period for the child's return. The same rules apply if the child was not placed by an adoption agency, but the prospective adopter has notified the local authority of

---

55. s. 65.
56. 1975 Act, s. 103.
57. See for a recent example of an interim order, *S.* v. *Huddersfield Borough Council* [1975] Fam. 113, C.A.
58. [1973] Fam. 106. The mother and her husband were allowed to adopt the mother's pre-nuptial son by a rich father on agreed conditions, the Official Solicitor to supervise the arrangements which were to include access for the father. See also *Re B. (M.F.) (An Infant) Re D. (S.L.). (An Infant)* [1972] 1 W.L.R. 102 C.A., *Re S. (A Minor) (Adoption Order: Access)* [1976] Fam. 1 C.A.

his intention to apply for adoption, except that if his application is refused by the court or withdrawn, the child need only be returned to the local authority if the authority so requires. Such a child is a 'protected child', in respect of whom the local authority has the exceptional duties and powers set out in ss 32–7 of the 1976 Act.[59]

E. ADOPTION ORDERS IN PRIVATE INTERNATIONAL LAW

The Adoption Act 1964 extended to those adopted by order of any court in the United Kingdom or the Isle of Man or any of the Channel Islands, the recognition of an adoptive relationship for the purposes of succession to property, insurance claims, registration of baptism and similar matters throughout the British Islands. The Act has now been repealed and replaced by the Act of 1976.[60]

To enable the United Kingdom to ratify the Hague Convention on the Adoption of Children[61] the Adoption Act 1968 was passed, but only after considerable delay was it brought partially into operation. The 1968 Act is also now repealed by the provisions in s. 17 of the Adoption Act 1976 for Convention Adoption Orders. These are not applicable where the prospective adopters and the child to be adopted are all United Kingdom nationals living in British territory. Applicants must, if a married couple, each be a United Kingdom national or a national of a Convention country and both habitually reside in Great Britain, or both must be United Kingdom nationals, and each habitually reside in British territory or a Convention country. If both applicants are nationals of the same Convention country the adoption must not be prohibited by a provision (specified for this purpose by order of the Secretary of State) of the internal law of that country. The child to be adopted must be a United Kingdom national or a national of a Convention country and habitually reside in British territory or a Convention country.[62] If the child is not a United Kingdom national the court (which for Convention orders is the High Court only) must be satisfied that provisions of his national internal law regarding consents and consultations (excluding those by or with the applicant and his family) have been complied with. The court also has power to dispense with the personal attendance of anyone who does not reside in Great Britain.

The 1976 Act, in s. 55, now provides for the court to vest in an applicant not domiciled in England and Wales or in Scotland, parental rights and duties relating to a child, if satisfied that the applicant intends to adopt the child

59. 1976 Act ss 30–31.
60. Ss 38(1)(c) and s. 59 extending to children adopted in the British Islands s. 12 of the Act concerning adoption orders and s. 49 covering transfer of death benefit insurance.
61. No. 13 of 15 November 1965.
62. The provision in the Children Act 1975 s. 24(2)(c) that the child must not be or have been married has not been re-enacted in the 1976 Act s. 17. See also ss 38(1)(e) and 40 for the effects of Convention Adoption Orders.

under the law of or within the country in which the applicant is domciled. This provision replaces the provisional adoption order under s. 53 of the Adoption Act 1958.[63] Without such an order it is an offence to remove abroad for purposes of adoption a child who is a British subject or a citizen of the Republic of Ireland.

F. THE EFFECTS OF AN ADOPTION ORDER

By s. 12 of the 1976 Act an adoption order, further defined in s. 38, is an order vesting the parental rights and duties relating to a child in the adopters, made on their application by an authorised court. It does not affect parental rights and duties so far as they relate to any period before the making of the order but it extinguishes pre-existing parental rights or duties whether vested in a parent (not being one of the adopters) or any other person and all duties of maintenance for the child arising by agreement or court order in respect of any period after the order has been made, unless such an agreement constitutes a trust or expressly provides that the duty shall not be extinguished by the adoption order. Previously, under s. 15(1) of the 1958 Act, an affiliation order was not extinguished if the child was subsequently adopted by his mother alone, and the mother could even apply for an affiliation order after adopting the child. Part IV of the 1976 Act now deals with the status of adopted children and provides that as from 1 January 1976, where the adopters are a married couple, the adopted child shall be treated as if he had been born as a child of the marriage (whether or not he was in fact born after the marriage was solemnised). In any other case the adopted child is treated as if he had been born to the adopter in wedlock (but not as a child of any actual marriage of the adopter). If a non-citizen of the United Kingdom and Colonies is adopted by a citizen, or by joint adopters of whom the adoptive father is a citizen, the child becomes a citizen from the date of the adoption. Otherwise, however, the provisions do not apply to the nationality or immigration Acts. It is declared that an adopted person is not illegitimate.[64] The expressions 'adoptive relationship', 'adoptive father', 'adoptive mother' and 'adoptive' relative of any degree may all be used, as may also the terms applicable to physical relationship without the use of the word 'adoptive'. As previously, however, adoption cannot affect the descent of any peerage or dignity or title of honour.

The status of the adopted child is made explicit in the Act in relation to succession to property. Provisions of the law of intestate succession will be treated as if contained in an instrument executed by the intestate, while of full capacity, immediately before his death. For the purposes of this part of the Act, that is in relation to adopted persons as well as property, a will or codicil is

---

63. Few such orders are made and previously a physical parent was the adopter or one of them in about half of these adoptions. See *ante* Table *IV*. The magistrates have no jurisdiction to make such orders.
64. Ss 39 and 40.

treated as made on the date of the testator's death. Any disposition (including the conferring of a power of appointment or the creation of an entail) depending on the date of birth of a child of the adoptive parent or parents is to be construed as if an adopted child had been born on the date he was adopted. He will therefore not lose his right to succeed under an instrument in operation before he was adopted. If two or more children were adopted on the same date they will be treated as if they had been born on that date in the order of their actual births. These provisions do not affect any reference to the age of a child. Examples of the operation of these rules of construction are incorporated in ss. 42–43 of the Act. Any interest vested in possession in the child before the adoption, or any interest expectant upon an interest so vested is, however, not affected.[65] It is presumed that no woman who attains the age of 55 years will adopt a child after execution of any instrument, and if she does so the child will not be treated, for the purposes of the instrument, as her child or as the child of her spouse.

There is still only one case in which an adoption order, once made, can be revoked.[66] Between the beginning of 1927 and 29 October 1959 a child was not legitimated by the subsequent marriage of his parents if his father was domiciled in England and either of his parents was married to another person at the time of his birth. On intermarrying during this period such parents frequently jointly adopted the illegitimate child of both of them. When from late 1959 it became possible for such a child to be legitimated by his parents' marriage, the Adoption Act 1960 was passed, enabling an adoption order to be revoked in those circumstances only, viz. that the child's parents had married each other and subsequently adopted their illegitimate child. Once the adoption had been revoked the child's birth could be reregistered as that of a legitimated child. The Act of 1960 has now been repealed and the provisions incorporated in the Act of 1976.[67]

However, the status of an adopted child cannot be entirely assimilated with that of a child born of his adoptive parents' marriage. The child remains within the prohibited degrees of marriage to his physical family, whose identity may be unknown to him.[68] An adopted person under the age of 18 who is intending to be married in England or Wales may now apply to the Registrar General and be told if the registers suggest that he and the person he intends to marry may be within the prohibited degrees of relationship under the Marriage Act 1949. Any adopted person who has attained full age may be given sufficient information to enable him to obtain a copy of his original birth certificate.[69] Counselling will be provided by the Registrar General and each local authority and each adoption

---

65. Ss 39, 40, 42(4).
66. In many U.S. State statutes adoption orders may be rescinded on the application of adopters, the adopted child or the adoption agency; e.g. New York Domestic Relations Law, ss 114 and 118.
67. 1976 Act, s. 52.
68. For the first time this is now explicitly provided for in the 1976 Act S. 47(1). See also Marriage Act 1949 Sched. I Part I as amended by the Children Act 1975 Sched. 3 para. 8.
69. 1976 Act, s. 51(1)(2). In Scotland people aged 16 years have long been able to obtain this information.

society for those who so apply, and before supplying the information directing the applicant to his birth certificate, the Registrar General will advise him that these counselling services are available. If the applicant accepts counselling, the relevant birth information will be sent to the counselling agency. Nobody adopted before 12 November 1975 may receive official information about registration of his birth unless he has first received counselling.[70]

Essential as are private hearings for adoption, they also have their dangers.[71] In *Re R. (M.J.)*[72] it was held that the judge had a discretion under the Administration of Justice Act 1960, s. 12 to disclose relevant parts of the transcript of an adoption hearing where the mother's husband, an undischarged bankrupt, was a joint adopter of the child and appeared to have made a considerable settlement on him. His trustee in bankruptcy was entitled to see the relevant parts of the transcript of the adoption proceedings.

G. INTEGRATION OF ADOPTION WITH CHILD WELFARE PROVISIONS

This is one of the major areas of recent change in the law of adoption. The duty of every local authority to establish and maintain within their area a full adoption service is laid down in s. 1 of the Act, which also provides that the facilities shall include: (*a*) temporary board and lodging where needed by pregnant women, mothers or children;[73] (*b*) arrangements for assessing children and prospective adopters and placing children for adoption; and (*c*) counselling for persons with adoption problems. These facilities will be provided in conjunction with the local authority's other services falling within the functions of its social services committee and with approved adoption societies in their area. The adoption agencies are now exclusively empowered to place children for adoption with non-relatives or to apply for children to be freed generally for adoption. Adoption societies will, however, now be approved nationally in England by the Secretary of State[74] for a period of three years at a time, and not by the local authority, although the Secretary of State will ask for the views of any local authority in whose area the society is likely to operate extensively, and take account of them. Before refusing an application, the Secretary of State will

---

70. 1976 Act, s. 51(3)(4)(5)(6).
71. See e.g. Roxburgh J. in *Re E., The Times* 24.3.60.
72. [1975] Fam. 89. A member of the trustee's staff tried to attend the hearing but was asked to leave by the court. A copy of the transcript later arrived anonymously at the trustee's office.
73. See the Finer Report on One-Parent Families, Cmnd 5629, paras 6.68–6.70. The committee found evidence of discrimination against unmarried mothers as regards local authority housing in some areas. It is not clear how tightly the duty to provide accommodation for pregnant women, mothers and children will be tied to the adoption service. *A Survey of Adoption in Great Britain* (1971) p. 44, found that some 16 per cent of children adopted by non-parents and some 3 per cent of those adopted by parents and step-parents were or had been in public care.
74. At present of the Department of Health and Social Security. See 1976 Act s. 3.

serve on the society a notice of his reasons and the society then has twenty-eight days in which to make representations, which will be taken into account in giving further consideration to the application. Similarly, before withdrawing approval of a Society, the Secretary of State will serve on it a notice setting out his reasons, and again the Society has twenty-eight days in which to make representations, of which account will be taken.[75] When approval of a Society has been withdrawn or has expired, the Secretary of State may direct the body concerned to make arrangements he thinks expedient as to children in its care.[76]

---

75. 1976 Act, s. 5.
76. Ibid. s. 4.

CHAPTER X

Failure of Parental Duties and Public Responsibility – Children in the Care of Public Authorities

When parents, guardians, or other relatives are unable or unwilling to discharge normal parental duties, two problems arise. The less important is the kind of sanctions that may be imposed on those who fail in their duty. They are few and for the most part ineffective. The important question is how best to deal with the children. The general solution to this major problem is by a system of public care, but the phrase covers a considerable area of family law that, until recently, had received inadequate systematic study, certainly by lawyers. This is no longer true,[1] but as often happens when an area is studied intensively, one of the first discoveries is how little is known. The records of successful public care of children are so meagre that the policies to be pursued are acutely controversial. Realisation of the social cost of adult recidivists has coincided with increasing knowledge of children's psychological development. Old attitudes are being discarded and new approaches attempted, but there are many pitfalls. As a result it is probably true to say that the law regarding children in public care is at present of all English family law the most disordered.

There are two main groups of children requiring public care: (i) those who have no parent or guardian or other family, or whose parents or other relatives are temporarily or permanently unable to provide a stable home background for them, and (ii) those who, in their home environment, have come into conflict with the law sufficiently seriously or frequently to call for temporary

---

1. The standard reference book is Clarke Hall and Morrison: *The Law Relating to Children and Young Persons.* H. K. Bevan's: *The Law Relating to Children* (1973) is easier reading, and like Clarke Hall and Morrison, its main emphasis is on children and public authorities. See also Mrs W. Cavenagh's *Juvenile Courts, The Child and the Law* (1967).

removal from their homes in an effort to prevent their progression into dis-ruptive and socially costly habitual criminals. The two groups of course overlap. There are conflicting views on the extent to which they should be segregated from each other, on what criteria, and with what consequences. There was a strong current of opinion when the Children and Young Persons Act 1969 was passed that all such children should be considered simply as children in need of care, for whom the public must seek to discharge so far as possible the duties normally assumed by parents, without segregating them in advance.[2] It is now recognised that some different approach is essential for children in different situations, but the time when and the criteria on which distinctions should be made are controversial and frequently muddled by irrelevancies. In the mean-time irreparable harm is done to children. We may read with astonishment cases fought right up to the House of Lords during the nineteenth century, on whether a particular child should be brought up in the Protestant or the Roman Catholic sector of the Christian faith. To many people today the question seems irrelevant to the child's welfare, which is the important issue. But later observers may be equally astonished that for some years the minimum age for criminal responsibility has been a matter of acute party political controversy. There has been insufficient political consensus behind some recent legislation in these areas to make the legislation effective when in operation, and the Children and Young Persons Act 1969 was not in full operation by the end of 1975.[3] Sweeping institutional reforms, like the Local Authority Social Services Act 1970[4] and the Local Government Act 1972 have been introduced just as major policy changes like the Children and Young Persons Act 1969 should have been implemented, and the implementation has fallen far short of the ideal. From late 1970, when the regional local authorities were asked to present plans for the reorganisation of community homes, acute financial stringency has accentuated the problem of how the high cost of providing secure accommodation for experienced young housebreakers,[5] should be shared between the local com-munity and the nation. The same financial stringency, coupled with a chronic

---

2. See 33 *MLR* (1970) 649. This not only contrasts with the approach of *Re Gault* (1967) 387 U.S. 1 in the United States, but has never been entirely accepted in this country. Thus Sir Leslie Scarman, when Chairman of the Law Commission, said in a lecture on *Family Law and Law Reform* at the University of Bristol on 18.3.66: 'it would be really the wrong way round if the juvenile courts should first assume the name "family court" and then either take over or be confused with the *genuine* family courts that society needs for dealing with disputes that frequently have nothing whatever to do with the *criminal law*' [Italics supplied]. The transfer of adoption proceedings from the juvenile court to the adult magistrates' court under the Children Act 1975, s. 21(3) was advocated on the ground that adoption should not take place in a criminal court. The juvenile court is however, the only court in which 'care' proceedings can be brought under the Children and Young Persons Act 1969, s. 1, and only one of the six grounds for such proceedings is concerned with guilt.

3. In particular, s. 4 and most of s. 5 have not been brought into operation.

4. In operation from 1 January 1971. See Jose Harris 33 *MLR* (1970) 530.

5. The Children Act 1975, s. 71 now provides for grants to be made by the Secretary of State to local authorities for expenditure they incur in providing secure accommodation in community homes other than assisted community homes. In 1972 the local authorities themselves were reorganised.

shortage of trained welfare workers[6] and a constantly increasing burden on each of them,[7] raises doubts about the continuing policy of widening the areas of social workers' activities.[8] It may be essential to curtail some activities that, however desirable, are especially burdensome. One factor not to be omitted from any financial calculation is that not only the adult but also the juvenile persistent offender is an expensive member of society, in terms both of cash and of demands on the working lives of others. Any expenditure on a young child that prevents him from joining the ranks of recidivist offenders is likely to be profitable, but without this result it will be merely one more item in a very large bill.

A final comment cannot be omitted from what may sound a catalogue of failure. There are two main streams of current legislation in the area, one starting with the Children Act 1948 and the other with the Children and Young Persons Act 1933. The 1933 Act has been amended not only by the Children and Young Persons Acts 1938, 1956, 1963 and 1969 and the Children and Young Persons (Amendment) Act 1952, but by the Children Acts 1948, 1958 Part I and 1975, the Education Act 1944, the Family Allowances Act 1945, the Magistrates' Courts Act 1952, the Family Allowances and National Insurance Act 1956, the Mental Health Act 1959, and the Child Benefit Act 1975. In the area impinging on the criminal law it has also be amended by several of the Criminal Justice and Criminal Justice Administration Acts, and such Acts as the Sexual Offences Act 1956. When the consolidation of the Matrimonial Causes Acts in 1950, 1965 and 1973 is compared with the way in which the Act of 1933 has been allowed to drift along for nearly fifty years, the charge that the lawyers neglect poor children is not easy to refute. When a consolidated Adoption Act 1976 was enacted and published eight months after the amendments of the Children Act 1975 nothing was done about the rest of the legislation. A consolidated Children and Young Persons Act (to include the current Children Acts) would be a major undertaking, but until it is done it is difficult to dispel the suspicion that social workers and others are encouraged not to bother too much about the letter of the law because it is too complex, must be sought in too many different places, and is virtually incomprehensible except to the specialist.

---

6. Less than half the social workers now employed are trained. The Police are also 'social workers' though rarely classified as such, and their numbers have also been seriously depleted.

7. The Head of the Social Services Department primarily involved in the Maria Colwell case was reported as saying that the resources of his department were stretched to the limit and could not cope with the bombardment of difficult cases, worse than at the time of Maria's death. There was an acute shortage of trained and experienced staff and of financial resources: *The Times* 15.10.74.

8. Section 32B of the Children and Young Persons Act 1969, as inserted by s. 64 of the Children Act 1975, provides for a guardian *ad litem* to be appointed for a child for certain proceedings under the 1969 Act, where there may be a conflict of interest between parent and child. It will be interesting to see who is appointed to the panels of guardians *ad litem* to be established by the Secretary of State under s. 103 of the 1975 Act. One earlier draft Bill would have provided for the child to be represented by 'an officer of a local authority or other person', another by 'an officer of a local authority or a solicitor, or both'.

A. OUTLINES OF THE DEVELOPMENT OF PUBLIC CARE FOR CHILDREN SINCE THE NINETEENTH CENTURY

When the country people flocked into the towns and factories and down the mines during the industrial revolution many of the traditional controls on their social behaviour broke down. Probably in hard times the principal breadwinner had always been the last to go without food, and babies tended not to survive bad harvests, but with the people herded together in factories and tenements the old social controls of the village were shattered. Children too were herded into the factories and the mines and in times of shortage were exposed on the highways to die or be rescued by the more affluent. Voluntary societies arose to counter some of the suffering and cruelty and were usually centred round the churches, including those of dissenters.

The parental duty to educate children was first imposed by the Factories Acts from 1802, but these were ineffective until a salaried inspectorate was appointed in 1833. The Poor Law Amendment Act 1868, s. 37 made it an offence for a parent to neglect those under the age of 14 in his charge. Many of the early provisions were eventually grouped together in the Prevention of Cruelty to, and Protection of Children Act 1889, the first great Children Act. This Act introduced the 'fit person' order for the removal of children neglected or ill-treated in their own homes. It was amended by the Acts of 1894 and 1908, and in 1891 the first Custody of Children Act was passed. It is still in operation,[9] and provides *inter alia* by s. 3 that, where a parent has abandoned or deserted his child, or allowed him to be brought up at the expense of others, including the public authorities, in such circumstances as to satisfy the court that he was unmindful of his parental duties, the burden shifts to the parent to prove himself a fit and proper person to have care of the child.

Much of this legislation was prompted by the revelations following the founding of Dr Barnardo's Homes and the sectarian litigation that ensued, culminating in *Barnardo* v. *McHugh*[10] and *Barnardo* v. *Ford*.[11] The parental duty of maintaining a legitimate child had been imposed by statute and it fell in the first instance on the father. He alone had parental rights until 1886 and his rights were paramount, at least until the child was before the court, until May 1974. For the illegitimate child the duty fell primarily on the mother, and this is the foundation of the present position, viz. that while living she has the parental rights and duties exclusively.[12] The courts held that the parental duty to ensure that the child was not neglected could not be delegated and was not, for example, displaced by a contract that the other spouse should discharge it.[13] The

---

9. Cited but not applied in *Re Gyngall* [1893] 2 K.B. 232 C.A. The Act today tends to be overlooked.
10. [1891] A.C. 388, *Jones's* case or *Roddy's* case.
11. [1892] A.C. 326; *Gossage's* case.
12. Children Act 1975, s. 85(7).
13. *Poole* v. *Stokes* (1914) W.N. 123, a hard case, resulting in the conviction of the father who had regularly paid maintenance for the children and asked a voluntary society to investigate when he heard that his estranged wife was neglecting them. See also *Brooks* v. *Blount* [1923] 1 K.B. 257, C.A.

offences of neglecting or abusing children are now principally contained in Part I of the Children and Young Persons Act 1933, as amended, but some duties are also contained in, for example the Licensing Act 1964[14] and the Sexual Offences Act 1956.[15] In *Reg.* v. *Lowe*[16] it was held that the wilful neglect by a father of very low intelligence resulting in the death of a child did not constitute manslaughter.

Originally if parents were unable to feed themselves and their children they were entitled to relief from their parish in workhouses under the Poor Law and, as mentioned above, this relief was extended in 1889 to include the 'fit person' order, under which children neglected or ill-treated could be removed from their homes into the care of the public authorities.

During the Second World War some gross cases of cruelty to young people came to light, and a committee was appointed under the chairmanship of Dame Myra Curtis to review the position. The Report of this committee,[17] though now thirty years old, is still salutary reading, and the *Field-Fisher Report on Maria Colwell*[18] makes it clear that many of the defects the Curtis committee found are with us still; in particular the failure of both public and private authorities to co-operate with others, to keep them informed, and to pool information.[19]

B. CHILDREN IN CARE – THE CHILDREN ACTS 1948–75

The principal recommendation of the Curtis committee was that the local authority should have general over-all responsibility for all the children within its area, and this was implemented by the Children Act 1948, s. 1, which provides:

Where it appears to a local authority with respect to a child in their area appearing to them to be under the age of 17:

(a) that he has neither parent nor guardian or has been and remains abandoned by his parents or guardians or is lost; or

(b) that his parents or guardian are, for the time being or permanently, prevented by reason of mental or bodily disease or infirmity or other

---

14. Section 168: prohibition on sales to and presence of minors on licensed premises.
15. See also Bevan, *Law Relating to Children*, chs 6 and 7.
16. [1973] Q.B. 702 C.A.
17. Cmd 6922 (1946).
18. *Report of the Committee to Inquire into and Report upon the Care and Supervision Provided by the Local Authorities and other Agencies in Relation to Maria Colwell and the Co-Ordination Between Them.* (1974).
19. Thus the Field-Fisher committee (majority report): 'What has clearly emerged, at least to us, is a failure of system compounded of several factors, of which the greatest and most obvious must be that of the lack of, or ineffectiveness of, communication and liaison.' Even within organisations, and particularly the schools involved, the fragmentation of information and the lack of confidence shown by the headmaster in the good sense of his class teachers is very striking. It was, however, not only the system but also the individuals who failed.

incapacity or any other circumstances from providing for his proper accommodation, maintenance and upbringing; and

(c) in either case, that the intervention of the local authority under this section is necessary in the interests of the welfare of the child,

it shall be the duty of the local authority to receive the child into their care under this section.

Section 1(2) provides that, having taken a child into care, it is the duty of the local authority to keep him in their care so long as the welfare of the child appears to them to require it and he has not attained the age of 18.

However, by s. 1(3)

Nothing in this section shall authorise a local authority to keep a child in their care under this section if any parent or guardian desires to take over the care of the child, and the local authority shall, in all cases where it appears to them consistent with the welfare of the child so to do, endeavour to secure that the care of the child is taken over either (a) by a parent or guardian of his, or (b) by a relative or friend of his, being, where possible, a person of the same religious persuasion as the child or who gives an undertaking that the child will be brought up in that religious persuasion. [20]

An important amendment by the Children and Young Persons Act 1963, s. 1 gave statutory affect to the practice of the richer and more enlightened authorities by providing that they might 'make available such advice, guidance and assistance as may promote the welfare of children by diminishing the need to receive children into or keep them in care', and in particular empowered them to make 'provision for giving assistance in kind or, in exceptional circumstances, in cash'.[21] This is contrary to the usual tendency, which is to bring the law into operation only when the harm has been done.[22] In the New York jurisdiction, Judge Justin Wise Polier has pointed out[23] that, when the parents' only defect is poverty, the further the child is removed from the parent the greater the expense and the less the chances of success.

Once a child has been taken into care under s. 1 of the 1948 Act, the local authority may bring s. 2 of the Act into operation, the effect of which (as amended by the Children Act 1975, s. 57) is that in certain clearly defined conditions (now extended), the local authority may pass a resolution vesting

---

20. Section 1(4) provides for children normally resident in one area taken into care in another and s. 1(5) matters to be disregarded in deciding the child's ordinary residence. They are not further considered.

21. The section is one of the principal levers used by social workers to gain admittance to the home and give timely support. See 27 *MLR* (1964) 61.

22. E.g. no maintenance orders will be made by magistrates whilst the spouses cohabit. Until the marriage has been disrupted the divorce courts will not attempt to enforce maintenance, and after then enforcement is usually impossible because further liabilities have been assumed. Similarly, under the Children and Young Persons Act 1969, s. 1(2)(a) the local authority may apply for a care order if the child 'is being ill-treated', although now at least under s. 1(2)(b) it is no longer necessary first to exhibit the bruises on each individual child.

23. *A View from the Bench* (1968) and other writings, far removed from judicial anecdotage.

parental rights in itself, but in every such case, 'unless the person whose parental rights and duties have under the resolution vested in the local authority has consented in writing to the passing of the resolution, the local authority, if that person's whereabouts are known to them, shall forthwith after the passing of the resolution serve on him notice in writing of the passing thereof'. The notice sent to the parent must inform him of his right to object within one month, and if he objects, the resolution lapses automatically fourteen days later unless, in the meantime, the local authority has taken the matter to the juvenile court. The juvenile court may now affirm the resolution if it finds that the grounds on which it was passed in the first instance were justified, and that at the time of the hearing there continue to be grounds on which such a resolution could be founded. Before 1976 the juvenile court could only affirm the resolution on grounds narrower than those on which it could be made in the first instance. The result was that very rarely would an authority pass a resolution without the previous written consent of the parent. If by any chance it did so and the parent objected, the authority was forced into immediate withdrawal.

Before considering in more detail the the difficulties arising from the legislation and the amendments made to it, it may be convenient to consider the extent to which these provisions are used. The Departments[24] publish as at the end of March each year a report: *Children in Care in England and Wales.* The report for 1975[25] shows that on 31 March of that year there was a total of 99,120 children in care, of whom 60,329 were boys and 38,791 girls.[26] This is approximately 6·5 per thousand of the estimated population under the age of 18 in England and Wales. During the twelve months to 31 March 1975 the 51,590 who came into care did so for the reasons given in Table VI.

Most of the children coming into care leave it very quickly. The largest number of children in Table VI under any one category is 12,660: those who came into care because of the short-term illness of a parent or guardian. They and the 2,399 in care because of their mother's confinement will probably remain for only a short time. In all, as against 51,590 children coming into care during the twelve months to the end of March 1975, 47,816 went out. For some years past, however, the number going out has been lower than the number coming into care, and there has been a steady build-up of children remaining in the care of the local authority throughout their childhood. Hence the attempts by the Children Act 1975 and the Adoption Act 1976 to make some such children available for adoption.

Of the total of 99,120 children in care nearly one-third, a total of 31,930 children, were boarded out with foster-parents. This is not only the most popular

---

24. Viz., the Secretaries of State for Social Services and for Wales.
25. Published July 1976, H.M.S.O.
26. The figures are taken from Part I, Table I showing the manner in which the children were accommodated, which is the only table showing their sex distribution. The discrepancy is striking and probably arises chiefly in relation to children in care by reason of an order under the Children and Young Persons Act 1969 (Table VI, n. c) where boys usually outnumber girls.

TABLE VI

Children in the care of local authorities in England and Wales
Circumstances in which Children Came into Care during the Twelve Months to 31 March
1975a

	England	Wales	Total Children
No parent or guardian	333	25	358
Abandoned or lost	1,165	68	1,233
Death of mother, father unable to care	558	18	576
Deserted by mother, father unable to care	3,528	156	3,684
Confinement	2,299	100	2,399
Short term illness of parent or guardian	12,169	491	12,660
Long term illness of parent or guardian	714	33	747
Child illegitimate, mother unable to provide	1,689	125	1,814
Parent or guardian in prison or remanded in custody	792	21	813
Family homeless because of eviction	372	43	415
Family homeless through a cause other than eviction	1,131	118	1,249
Unsatisfactory home conditionsb	4,646	284	4,930
Care Order under the Children and Young Persons Act 1969	10,778	531	11,309
Order under section 43(1) of the Matrimonial Causes Act 1973	428	22	450
Order under section 2(1) of the Matrimonial Proceedings (Magistrates' Courts) Act 1960	160	3	163
Order under section 7(2) of the Family Law Reform Act 1969d	22	2	24
Order under section 2(2)(b) of the Guardianship Act 1973	45	—	45
Other circumstances	8,240	481	8,721
Total	49,069	2,521	51,590

N.B. For statistical purposes one circumstance only is recorded against each case.
Children who had more than one admission to care during the year have more than one entry.

a Extracted from Children in Care in England and Wales March, 1975 Table I.
b More information on this group might be desirable, and in particular whether there are generic differences between these cases and those under the Children and Young Persons Act 1969, apart from the fact that the parents here apparently assented to the removal.
c please see n. 26 *ante*. There was an additional 1,800 children committed to care under an interim care order, remanded to care or detained in care after arrest.
d Power to commit Ward of Court to care of local authority.

method of accommodating children, it is also very much the cheapest.[27] The average cost was £7 per child per week. By contrast the 34,582 children in various types of community homes cost an average of £50 per child per week. Many of these of course will be 'problem' children of one kind or another and 6186 of them received education on the premises. The average weekly cost per head of the 4335 children in voluntary children's homes was £22 per week. There was a total of 8281 children in other accommodation at an average

27. Excluding children 'in other accommodation', which is not a homogeneous group, as explained. The House of Lords held in *Race Relations Board* v. *Applin* [1975] A.C. 259 that, since foster parents provide 'a public service' or are 'a section of the public', it was an offence under the Race Relations Act 1968 to seek to incite foster-parents not to accept for fostering the children of certain races.

weekly cost per head of £4 per week, which is described as an average of widely varying costs, affected by relatively low expenditure on children accommodated in other public establishments, such as hospitals and boarding special schools, or those who were largely independent, for example in residential employment or lodgings. All the costs given are exclusive of parental contributions collected by local authorities, which are estimated as amounting to £1,609,000. The costs given do not include administration, field work, or the cost of miscellaneous items which cannot be separately identified for children in care.

Under the Children Act 1948, s. 1(3) the local authority is not empowered to keep a child in care if any parent or guardian desires to take over its care, and the local authority has a positive duty to try to ensure that the care of the child is assumed by a parent, guardian, relative or friend of his. The *Field-Fisher Report* found: 'There is no doubt that it was generally believed that natural parents had the "right" to have their child back from care once they had established that they were fit to receive it,[28] and that this thinking influenced magistrates' courts.' This is why the standard Form of Undertaking to be signed by foster-parents before any child is given into their care contains the following two incompatible undertakings:

1. We /I will care for *C.D.* and bring him /her up as we /I would a child of our /my own, and
6. We /I will allow him /her to be removed from our /my home when so requested by a person authorised by [the council] [the organisation] [or by the council of the county /county borough where we /I live].

Clause 6 of this Form might be thought to amount to a written declaration of unfitness to care for any child, and raises the question not why there has always been an acute shortage of foster-parents, but how any respectable person could be induced to sign such an undertaking before receiving a child into his home. Because every foster-parent has signed such an undertaking, the occasions on which foster-parents have been able to resist removal of the child have been few, but the defect in the legislation has long been apparent. In *Re A.B.*[29] the Court of Appeal confirmed that the foster-parents must hand back to the local authority a girl aged 4 who had been in their care for three years, but refused to confirm that part of the order made in the court below that the local authority should then hand the child over to her mother, who did not propose to look after her. Instead, the mother proposed to hand the child to the putative father who, a year after she was born, had married another woman by whom he now had a legitimate son. The court clearly saw the danger of the illegitimate daughter becoming an unpaid drudge in her putative father's home.[30] Since then there have been many

---

28. In Maria Colwell's case, there was in any event a liberal attitude to her mother's fitness.
29. [1954] 2 Q.B. 385 C.A. And see *Krishnan* v. *Sutton L.B.C.* [1970] Ch. 181 C.A. for the beneficent effect of the law's delays in preventing the forcible return of an unwilling seventeen-year-old girl to her father after years of happy fostering. An elder sister was living with the same foster-parents.
30. Per Lord Goddard, ibid. p. 393: 'How far it is desirable for an illegitimate child to be living with the wife and the legitimate child of the father is perhaps a matter which deserves very

cases in which parents have suddenly discovered a yearning to be reunited with a child ignored for many years whilst it was brought up by others, usually at public expense, and publicity has centred on what the media have chosen to call 'tug-of-love' cases. They are all tug-of-power cases.[31] Maria Colwell was the most publicised in a long line of children snatched back by physical parents for reasons of spite or profit, and the continuous ill-treatment she received from her physical mother after her forced return to her was probably similar to that received by many such children. It was because Maria was actually killed that consciences were at last aroused and the law has been amended.

The Children Act 1948, s. 1 has now been amended to provide[32] that if the child has been in the care of the local authority or a voluntary organisation[33] for six months, no parent or guardian may remove him without giving twenty-eight days'[34] prior notice of intention to do so. The grounds on which the local authority may by resolution vest parental rights in themselves under s. 2 of the 1948 Act have been widened, and they may also now vest parental rights in a voluntary organisation having care of the child if the organisation so requests.[35] Among the grounds on which such resolutions may now be made are the fact that the child has been in the care of the local authority throughout the preceding three years,[36] or that a resolution is in force in relation to one parent who is or is likely to become a member of the household comprising the child and his other parent.[37] Where a parent objects to the passing of the resolution and the local authority decides to pursue the matter before the juvenile court, that court may now confirm the resolution provided: (*a*) the grounds on which it was passed were made out, and (*b*) at the time of the hearing there continue to be grounds for the resolution and (*c*) that it is in the interests of the child. A right of appeal to the High Court is now given from the decision of the juvenile court affirming or refusing to affirm such a resolution.[38]

The general duty of the local authority with regard to children in their care, set out in s. 12 of the 1948 Act, has also been amended and now

---

careful consideration. . . .' Donovan J. at p. 401 pointed out that the mother would not be 'taking care' of the child.

31. When King Solomon delivered his famous judgement on the partition of the baby whose maternity was disputed by two prostitutes, the true mother: 'moved with love for her child, said to the King: "Oh! sir, let her have the baby; whatever you do, do not kill it".' 1 Kings 3, *New English translation.*

32. By s. 1(3A)(3B), inserted by Children Act 1975, s. 56(1).

33. By s. 33A inserted by 1975 Act, s. 56(2).

34. By s. 1(3B) the Secretary of State may by statutory instrument amend the periods of twenty-eight days or six months.

35. Children Act 1975, s. 60. The powers so vested do not include those to consent to an adoption, or to freeing the child for adoption. The regulations under s. 33 of the 1948 Act must also be complied with before arrangements can be made for the child's emigration. The powers vested in a voluntary organisation may be vested in the local authority by a further resolution under s. 61 of the 1975 Act.

36. 1948 Act, s. 2(1)(*d*), as inserted by 1975 Act, s. 57.

37. Ibid. s. 2(1)(*c*): See also s. 2(5) as inserted by the 1975 Act s. 57.

38. Ibid. s. 4A as inserted by Children Act 1975, s. 58.

provides[39] that (1) in reaching any decision relating to a child, a local authority shall give first consideration to the need to safeguard and promote the welfare of the child throughout his childhood; and shall so far as practicable ascertain his wishes and feelings regarding the decision and give due consideration to them, having regard to his age and understanding, although by s. 12(1A) the local authority may act otherwise if necessary to protect members of the public.

Provisions have also been made for summoning before the court any person reasonably believed to be in a position to produce a child who has run away from accommodation provided for him by the local authority in whom parental rights over him are vested, and for searching premises on which such a child is believed to be. Failure to comply with a summons is an offence carrying liability to a fine of £100.[40]

A new type of order has been introduced by the 1975 Act.[41] This is the custodianship order, which differs from an adoption order in that it does not sever the legal relationship between the child and his physical parents and it is revocable.[42] A custodianship order may never be made in favour of a natural parent of the child.[43] While the order is in operation, the legal custody of the child vests in the custodian, although at the time of making the order or thereafter the court may provide for access to the child of his mother or father, for payment of maintenance for the child by either or both of his parents, and for variation and revocation of such maintenance orders.[44] Those entitled to apply for a custodianship order (who must within seven days of the application give notice of it to the local authority for the area in which the child resides[45]), include: (*a*) a relative or step-parent of the child applying with the consent of the person having legal custody,[46] and with whom the child has had his home for the preceding three months.[47] A step-parent may not, however, apply if the child

---

39. Children Act 1948, s. 12 as amended by Children Act 1975, s. 59. See also *Re Y. (A Minor) (Child in Care. Access)* [1976] Fam. 125 C.A. as to the father's right of access to a ward placed in the care of the local authority under the Family Law Reform Act 1967, s.7(2). And see *Re T. (A.J.J.)* [1970] Ch. 688 C.A., note 90 *post*.
40. Children Act 1975, s. 67.
41. Ibid. s. 33.
42. Section 35; the order may also be varied. Application for revocation or variation may be made by the custodian, the child's parent or guardian, a local authority, or any other person on whose application an order for access to or maintenance of the child was made under s. 34 of the Act, or who was required to contribute to the child's maintenance.
43. Section 33(4). It is understood that the term 'custodianship order' was intended to make clear that its holder was not the child's physical parent.
44. Section 33(1) and 34. By s. 44, the right of any other person to the child's legal custody is suspended while a custodianship order is effective.
45. Section 40 and see *post*, s. 40(2) and note 64 as to the local authority's duty to inquire and report.
46. Besides the step-parent applying with the consent of the parent who has custody (the child not having been the subject of a declaration under the Matrimonial Causes Act s. 41), this will also include the relative or step-parent applying with the consent of the local authority in whom parental rights are vested.
47. Section 33(3).

was a child of the family in previous divorce or nullity proceedings,[48] about the arrangements for whose welfare the court was required to declare itself satisfied under the Matrimonial Causes Act 1973 s. 41, (*b*) any person who applies with the consent of the person having legal custody of the child and with whom the child has had his home for a period or periods of at least twelve months, including the three months preceding the application,[49] and (*c*) any person with whom the child has had his home for a period or periods amounting to at least three years,[50] including the three months preceding the making of the application.[51] When application is made for a custodianship order by the person with whom the child has had his home for the preceding three years, it is an offence for any other person to remove the child from his custody except with the leave of a court or under statutory authority or on the arrest of the child.[52] The prohibition is specifically extended to the local authority in whose care the child is,[53] and there are provisions for the return of the child.[54] A person holding a custodianship order may also apply for an affiliation order.[55]

When revoking a custodianship order, the court may either commit the care of the child to a specified local authority (if there would otherwise be no one with legal custody, or it is considered undesirable for the person with legal custody to exercise it), or provide for the child to be under the supervision of a specified local authority or a probation officer.[56] Before the order is revoked an oral or written report must be requested from a social welfare officer or probation officer, unless the court has sufficient information before it for the purpose.[57] Either or both parents may still be ordered to pay maintenance for the child.[58]

On an application for an adoption order[59] the court may make a custodianship order if satisfied that the child's welfare would not be better safeguarded and promoted by an adoption order.[60] Similarly, on the application of either parent for a guardianship order under the Guardianship of Minors Act 1971, if

---

48. Section 33(5), but there are exceptions in s. 33(8), viz. when the parent is dead or cannot be found, or the child has been found not to be a child of the family concerned in the matrimonial proceedings.
49. Applicants here are likely to include a high proportion of foster-parents applying with the consent of the local authority or voluntary organisation in whom parental rights are vested.
50. The period of three years may be amended by the statutory instrument: s. 33(7).
51. For the most part applicants will be foster-parents who, after three years, need no consent from the local authority before applying for custodianship.
52. Children Act 1975, s. 41.
53. Ibid. s. 41(2).
54. Ibid. s. 42.
55. Ibid. s. 45.
56. Ibid. s. 36.
57. Ibid. s. 36(4). The wording seems sufficiently positive to call for a report unless the court is satisfied that it already has sufficient information. The usual reason advanced for not calling for a report, viz. the pressure on the social welfare officers, will presumably not be adequate.
58. Ibid. s. 36(5).
59. Including a Convention adoption order: s. 37. Where the adoption application is made jointly by a parent of the child and his or her spouse, the custodianship order is to be made in favour of the spouse alone.
60. Ibid. s. 37(1)(*a*)(*b*).

the court considers that legal custody should be given to someone other than the parent, it may make a custodianship order in that person's favour.[61] If a custodianship order vests parental rights or duties jointly in two persons who cannot agree, they may apply to the court, which may make such order as it thinks fit.[62] The court has general powers to call for reports from local authorities and probation officers in connection with custodianship orders.[63] On receiving notice of an application for a custodianship order[64] the local authority must arrange for a report to be made to the court. The contents will be prescribed by regulation, but they include the wishes and feelings of the child, having regard to his age and understanding, the means and stability of the applicant, members of the applicant's household and the wishes regarding the application, and the means, of the child's mother and father.

The Children Act 1958, s. 1[65] provides for the local authority to arrange for all foster-children[66] in its area to be visited. Visits are to be made (in accordance with regulations to be drawn up by the Secretary of State under s. 2A of the Act)[67] on specified occasions or within specified periods of time. All those maintaining a foster-child must, within eight weeks of the regulations coming into operation, give written notice to the local authority to this effect. It is thought that staff shortages may make it difficult for some local authorities to comply with these requirements. There is disquiet about the widespread subjection of large numbers of young children to the short-term ministrations of illegal child-minders, who are known to function on a daily basis in many of our major cities for the children of the poor, especially where the mother is in full-time employment, and for the children of some minority groups. It has not been possible previously to deal with this problem because of the shortage of local authority welfare workers and accommodation. On the one hand, the local authorities could not provide fostering for all the children in their area who needed it; on the other, they could not spare officers to search for the illegal child-minders. The crucial questions will be whether the local authorities will now be able to make enquiries both when they are advised of fostering arrangements and when no such advice is given to them, and how far they will then be able to provide better care for the children involved.

By s. 3A of the Act[68] the Secretary of State may require parents whose children are or will become foster-children to give specified information about the fostering to the local authority. The Secretary of State may also by regulation

---

61. Section 37(3); in this event the qualifications for a custodianship order are widened, as by s. 37(4) 'the applicant shall be treated (if such is not the case) as if he were qualified to apply for a custodianship order'.
62. Section 38.
63. Section 39.
64. Under s. 40(1): please see note 45 *ante* and s. 40(2)(3).
65. As amended by the Children and Young Persons Act 1969, s. 51.
66. Defined in s. 2 of the 1958 Act, (as amended by s. 52 of the 1969 Act) as: 'A child below the upper limit of the compulsory school age whose care and maintenance are undertaken by a person who is not a relative or guardian of his.'
67. As inserted by the Children Act 1975, s. 95(3).
68. Inserted by the 1975 Act, s. 96(1).

prohibit the publication of advertisements by parents or guardians seeking foster-parents for a child.[69]

Advertisements offering either to adopt children or to offer them for adoption have been and still remain illegal, and it has long been thought that the pages of advertisements that appear in some journals for foster-parents or foster-children were more or less public circumvention of the prohibition. We now have legislation, and the quality of its enforcement should become known in course of time.

C. THE CHILDREN AND YOUNG PERSONS ACTS 1933–69, AS AMENDED

The scheme of the Children and Young Persons Act 1969[70] was that, if a child or young person[71] was neglected, or not receiving proper parental care and guidance, or seriously or continuously coming into conflict with the law, it should not be the juvenile court[72] before which the child was brought that should decide how he should be treated. The function of the court was, if certain conditions were satisfied, to place the child in the care of the local authority, whose social welfare officers would then decide outside the court atmosphere what treatment was desirable. This was the compromise solution reached after many years of political debate. It was a compromise in that one of the principal aims of the reformers was to keep such children out of court altogether.[73] In the House of Lords' debate[74] on the Bill that became the Children and Young Persons Act 1969, Lady Wootton pointed out that juvenile courts are for other people's children. They are not intended for or used by the children of those who establish, administer, or preside over them. Moreover, the arguments against collecting together in large numbers adult offenders of all kinds are even more

---

69. Children Act 1958, s. 37(1A), as inserted by Children Act 1975, s. 97.
70. Although it comprised seventy-three sections and seven schedules, the Act was merely the latest in 1969 of the many amendments of the Children and Young Persons Act 1933, with all of which it must be read. See 33 *MLR* (1970) 649 and *Part I of the Children and Young Persons Act 1969: a guide for courts and practitioners*, Home Office (1970) and Cmnd. 6494: *Children and Young Persons Act 1969, interdepartmental observations on the Eleventh Report of the Expenditure Committee* H.M.S.O. (1976).
71. The wording is peculiar to this series of Acts. By the Act of 1933, s. 107, a child was anyone under the age of 14 and a young person anyone over the age of 14 and under the age of 17. This interpretation also applied to the 1969 Act, by s. 70, except for Part II, ss 35−59, and ss 27, 63, and 65 in which 'child' means a person under the age of 18 and a person who has attained the age of 18 and is the subject of a care order. By the Children Act 1975, s. 107, except where used to express a relationship, a child means a person who has not attained the age of 18.
72. There have been some special provisions for the trial of children since 1847, but the juvenile courts were first established by the Children Act 1908.
73. See, e.g. the Report of the Ingleby Committee on Children and Young Persons Cmnd 1191 (1960); the Government White Paper: *The Child, the Family and the Young offender*, Cmnd 2742 (1965) followed by *Children in Trouble* Cmnd 3601 (1968). The corresponding Scottish proposals were contained in *Social Work and the Community*, Cmnd 3065.
74. H.L. Deb. vol. 302 (19.6.69), cols 1186−9.

cogent when applied to children. Thus it is argued that we create more delinquents in the waiting rooms of the courts than are ever cured in the court room, and that the various kinds of homes in which children were accommodated[75] were training grounds for the more sophisticated adult criminals.

In Scotland the reformers have succeeded in keeping many of the young people outside the courts. They are dealt with instead at Children's Hearings, that is by committees of trained laymen sitting informally.[76] In England such a solution was not found possible. The compromise adopted was that, whilst the child would be brought before the court, it would normally only be possible for the court to entrust the child to the care of the local authority, which would then decide the appropriate treatment.

The English Act also compromised on or circumvented the question of the minimum age of criminal responsibility. During the debate on the Bill that became the Children and Young Persons Act 1963, an attempt had been made to raise the age of criminal responsibility from eight to twelve years. A compromise emerged at the age of 10 years.[77] While not directly raising the age of criminal responsibility in the 1969 Act to 14 years, the promoters sought to ensure that no proceedings would be possible other than 'care' proceedings for those under that age,[78] and that between the ages of 14 and 17 years 'care' proceedings would be usual, and only after exceptional safeguards would summary criminal proceedings be possible. These provisions were not introduced in their entirety.[79] Whether the 1969 Act might have been more effective if it had been introduced as a whole will never now be known.

The new legislation and its implementation have run into serious difficulties. Local authorities were given the responsibility without the means of discharging it. They had inadequate accommodation of any kind for delinquent

---

75. There is an excellent summary and description of these in *Caught in the Act*, by Marcel Berlins and Geoffrey Wansell (1974). This Penguin book is a helpful popular account of the state of the law before 1976.
76. Under the Social Work (Scotland) Act 1968, amended by the Children Act 1975, ss 66, 72–84. If the facts are disputed there must be a finding by the sheriff court. If the parents dispute the treatment proposed by the Children's Hearings (also called Children's panels) on the ground that it is unreasonable they may appeal to the sheriff within three weeks. There is also a right of appeal to the Court of Session. There is controversy about the 'exceptional offences' which may still be prosecuted in the courts.
77. Children and Young Persons Act 1963, s. 16, amending the Children and Young Persons Act 1933, s. 50.
78. 1969 Act, s. 4 prohibited any charge of a child (under 14) with an offence other than homicide. Section 5(1) provided that only a qualified informant might lay an information in respect of an offence if the alleged offender was a young person, and the conditions in which this could be done were minutely prescribed. None of these provisions was brought into operation. There were also elaborate precautions in s. 8 about taking finger prints of suspected young persons.
79. Section 4 has not been brought into operation. Of s. 5, only parts of s. 5(8) and 5(9) came into operation on 1 January 1971 by the Children and Young Persons (Commencement No. 3) Order 1970, No. 1498, which made operative ss 1–3, 9–23, 25–8, 30–2, 34, 61, parts of other sections and some schedules from the same date. Commencement No. 1 Order No. 1552 of 1969 and No. 2 Order 1565 had earlier activated other provisions, mainly in Parts II and III of the Act.

children, there was a grave shortage of secure accommodation, and there was overall shortage of welfare workers, particularly to staff residential accommodation. Expertise amongst the social workers was diluted on two separate occasions,[80] and the continuing financial stringency will ensure that the present shortage of local authority welfare workers will not be quickly relieved. Some probation officers, who were dissatisfied at losing many of their former duties in respect of children under the 1969 Act,[81] may well have welcomed increasing opportunities for them to augment the skills and manpower of the local authority social workers.[82]

The Children and Young Persons Act 1969 abolished the 'fit person' order that had been the hall-mark of the Children Acts since 1889, and substituted for it the 'care' order. By s. 1(1) of the 1969 Act, only a local authority or constable or authorised person who reasonably believes that there are grounds for making such an order may bring the child or young person before the court. The court must in the first place be satisfied that one of six conditions applies, viz. that either:

(a) his proper development is being avoidably prevented or neglected or his health is being avoidably impaired or neglected or he is being ill-treated; or

(b) it is probable that the condition set out in (a) above will be satisfied in his case, having regard to the fact that the court or another court has found that that condition is or was satisfied in the case of another child or young person who is or was a member of the household to which he belongs;[83] or

---

80. First by the disbanding of Children's Officers and their absorption into Social Services Committees under the Local Authority Social Services Act 1970, in operation from January 1971, and S.I. No. 1813 of 1970. (See also S.I.s Nos. 1143 of 1970 and 1221 of 1971:) then by reorganisation of local government areas by the Local Government Act 1972, which took effect in part from April 1973 and in part from later dates to 1 April 1974 (See S.I.s Nos. 373 and 375 of 1973).

81. The Children and Young Persons Act 1969, s. 9 placed on the local authority the duty of making investigations and providing the court (before which proceedings under s. 1 of the Act were heard) with information regarding the home surroundings, school record, health and character of the person in respect of whom the proceedings were brought. By s. 11, a supervision order meant an order placing the child under the supervision of a local authority or of a probation officer, and by s. 13(2) a probation officer was not to be designated unless the local authority so requested and a probation officer was already supervising another member of the household to which the child belonged. In Cmnd. 6494 para. 35 the Government admitted the diffiulties but was not prepared to change direction.

82. A number of probation officers left the service when the change was made. Many found their work with adult offenders tolerable only when they had the opportunity also of working with children. The probation service is a national service and its members might not be inclined to accept local government employment. Probation officers are, however, still in attendance at matrimonial proceedings in magistrates' courts and are asked for reports before child custody orders are made, and many of them, as welfare officers, fulfil similar functions in divorce county courts and the Family Division of the High Court.

83. In *Surrey C.C.* v. *S.* [1974] Q.B. 124 it was held that the court before which child *A* is brought may find that child *B* had been ill-treated although there had been no previous adjudication to this effect, thus eliminating the need first to display the bruises on child *B* before action can be taken.

(c) he is exposed to moral danger; or

(d) he is beyond the control of his parent or guardian; or

(e) he is of compulsory school age within the meaning of the Education Act 1944 and is not receiving efficient full-time education suitable to his age, ability and aptitude; [84] or

(f) he is guilty of an offence, excluding homicide. [85]

Before making an order the court must, in addition, be satisfied that the child is in need of care or control which he is unlikely to receive unless an order is made under this section in respect of him. If so satisfied and provided the child has not attained the age of 16 and has never been married the court may make one only of the following orders (except that orders under both (c) and (d) may be made at the same time):

(a) an order requiring the child's parent or guardian to enter into a recognisance to take proper care of him and exercise proper control over him; [86] or

(b) a supervision order; or

(c) a care order (other than an interim order); or

(d) a hospital order within the meaning of Part V of the Mental Health Act 1959; [87] or

(e) a guardianship order within the meaning of that Act. [88]

If the child is in danger of harm, a 'place of safety' order may be made for his immediate removal. [88]

Despite these elaborate provisions, about half the cases coming before the juvenile courts are disposed of by the infliction of fines. Where fines are inapplicable the 'care' provisions have worked badly, since the local authority have not sufficient boarding accommodation in the way of community homes [89] for children committed to their care, [90] and especially not sufficient secure

---

84. By s. 2(8) of the Act, such proceedings must be brought by a local education authority, and there are elaborate provisions for satisfying the conditions.

85. This 'offence condition' (s. 3) cannot apply to any child under the age of 10, who is *doli incapax*. It is elaborately controlled by s. 3 of the Act, running to nine sub-sections and over 1000 words.

86. Such an order can be made only with the consent of the parent or guardian: s. 1(5)(a).

87. See s. 1(5)(b) for the conditions that must be satisfied.

88. Children and Young Persons Act 1969, s. 28 *See Reg.* v. *Lincoln (Kesteven) County Justice, ex parte M. (A Minor),* [1976] Q.B. 957.

89. These are dealt with by Part II, ss 35–50 of the 1969 Act. The former 'approved schools' (created by ss 79–81 of the 1933 Act from the former reformatories and industrial schools) were abolished by the 1969 Act, s. 7(5) and their buildings and some of their staff were brought within the comprehensive system of community homes for which the local authorities were required to submit plans under ss 35–8 of the 1969 Act by 1 December 1969 (S.I. No. 1565 of 1969.) The remand homes and youth treatment centres were also brought within the comprehensive community homes system.

90. In *Re T. (A.J.J.)* [1970] Ch. 688, the Court of Appeal declared that there was 'no difference of substance' between the relationship between the local authority and the child under a 'fit person' order (now a 'care' order) and that existing where the local authority has vested parental rights in itself under the Children Act 1948 s. 2. If it is alleged that a local authority

accommodation. The shortage of welfare workers has been particularly acute in the residential establishments, and standards have also been variable. Local authorities have therefore left the children in their own homes, surrounded by their delinquent families and in association with their teenage gangs. When the child was brought again before the magistrates, all the bench has been able to do is to commit him again to the care of the local authority, which meant that some of these children could break the law with complete impunity until reaching the age of 17. Magistrates tell of children of 10 to 12 years of age with four to five hundred offences proved or admitted.

The public upon which these young delinquents have been granted a licence to prey have attempted at least to obtain compensation for the damage they have suffered, or to make the local authority liable for not carrying out its duties, impossible as this may have been. The result has been a number of cases brought against the local authority for payment of compensation or fines. In *Reg.* v. *Croydon Juvenile Court Justices* [91] the Divisional Court held that, where the child is in the care of the local authority, and living in a community home, fines may be imposed on the local authority in respect of further offences committed by the child. Subsequent decisions have resiled from so drastic a solution. Thus where the local authority sent the child to an independent community home in another county, and whilst on leave from there he committed further offences, the local authority was held not liable. [92] In *Lincoln Corporation* v. *Parker* [93] this was extended to the situation where the local authority had allowed the child to go home on leave, and whilst there he committed further offences. Even when the child was actually in the care of the local authority at the time of the offence, it was held in *Somerset County Council* v. *Kingscott* [94] that the local authority was not liable where it had not fallen short of the standard of care to be expected from a good parent, although three boys had committed further offences after absconding from the home.

On the other hand it has been held that a juvenile court was not justified in excluding the local authority children's officer from the trial when she attended the court. [95]

The Children Act 1975, s. 71 has inserted into the 1969 Act a new s. 64A under which the Secretary of State may make grants to local authorities in respect of expenditure incurred in providing secure accommodation in community homes other than the assisted community homes provided for in ss 39–40 of the 1969 Act. The Secretary of State also now has extensive powers under s. 98 of the 1975 Act, to inquire in public or in private into: the functions

has not properly exercised its discretion, the person making the allegation should be required to state on affidavit at the outset the precise grounds asserted and the facts alleged to constitute them, and the evidence should initially be confined if possible to determining whether those grounds existed.
91. [1973] Q.B. 426.
92. *Somerset County Council* v. *Brice* [1973] 1 W.L.R. 1169.
93. [1974] 1 W.L.R. 713. See also *Leicestershire County Council* v. *Cross* [1976] 2 All E.R. 491.
94. [1975] 1 W.L.R. 283.
95. *Reg.* v. *Southwark Juvenile Court* [1973] 1 W.L.R. 1300.

of the social services committee relating to children of a local authority; or of an adoption agency, or voluntary organisation relating to voluntary homes; or into a home maintained by the Secretary of State for the accommodation of children in the care of local authorities and needing particular facilities and services there provided; or the detention of a child under s. 53 of the 1933 Act.[96]

It has been suggested[97] that in place of about 730 secure places for children under 17 outside the prison system, which are expected to be available by 1978,[98] secure accommodation is needed for some 2500 children who are 'hard-core' persistent offenders under the age of 17, and who commit a disproportionately large number of offences. There are complaints of great variations in the attitudes taken by police forces in different areas, and it would seem elementary that close and harmonious working between the police force and the local authority staff should if necessary be imposed at all levels if the problem of chronic juvenile delinquency is to be contained.[99] The provisions under s. 32 of the 1969 Act for the arrest of those absconding from local authority care have now been strengthened by s. 68 of the 1975 Act, to provide for the arrest by the police of those absent from a place of safety, and by provisions for the search of premises in which absentees are believed to be hiding. On the other hand the provisions of ss 22 and 23 of the 1969 Act, under which a child or young person may be certified as unruly, are now subject to conditions to be prescribed by order of the Secretary of State.[100]

The outcome of some controversial provisions about separate representation of a child or young person is now contained in ss. 64 and 65 of the 1975 Act, which provide[101] that in all applications for an order under s. 1 of the 1969 Act, or for discharge of a supervision order or a care order made under ss 15 or 21 of that Act, or for an appeal to the Crown Court against an order made under s. 1 of the Act, or against dismissal of an application for discharge of a care order or supervision order, if it appears that there is or may be a conflict between the interests of the child or young person and those of his parent or guardian, the court may order that the parent or guardian is not to be treated as representing the child or young person. In that event, unless satisfied that to do so is not necessary for safeguarding the interests of the child or young person, the court shall appoint a guardian *ad litem* of the child or young person for the purposes of the proceedings, and may order the parent or guardian to be given legal aid to take part separately in them.[102]

The presence of a persistently or seriously delinquent child is an indication of family breakdown far more serious than the so-called matrimonial offences on

96. Viz. those under 18 convicted of murder or other offences for which an adult is liable to imprisonment for fourteen years or more.
97. By Marcel Berlins and Geoffrey Wansell: *Caught in the Act*, pp. 101–5.
98. According to the statement by Sir Keith Joseph in January 1973.
99. In Cmnd. 6494 (1976) para. 31 the Government welcomed the recommendation for strengthening consultation between police and social service departments and drew attention to the police juvenile bureaux.
100. 1975 Act, s. 69.
101. Section 64, inserting ss 32A and 32B to the 1969 Act.
102. 1975 Act, s. 65, amending the Legal Aid Act 1974, s. 28(1).

which much misplaced learning has been expended in the past. One strand significantly missing in the many words of the Children and Young Persons Acts is a recognition that production of offspring who persistently or seriously infringe the law is a mark of grave parental failure. The Court of Appeal has been moved to protest about the state of the law regarding treatment of these young people,[103] and further developments may be expected.

---

103. In *Reg.* v. *D. (a boy), The Times* 21.10.76, where the Court reluctantly confirmed a sentence of borstal training on a 15-year old boy with 'an appalling record,' as the only way of ensuring his immediate confinement in secure accommodation.

Bibliography

REPORTS AND OTHER OFFICIAL PUBLICATIONS CITED

A. THE LAW COMMISSION FOR ENGLAND AND WALES

B. THE SCOTTISH LAW COMMISSION

C. OTHER REPORTS AND OFFICIAL PAPERS

	page
Social Work and the Community, Cmnd 3065, Scotland (1967) .	256
A Survey of Adoption in Great Britain (1971), *see* Home Office	
Tax-Credit System, Proposals for a, Cmnd 5116 (1972) . .	76
Tomlin Committee *Reports on Child Adoption*, Cmds 2401, 2469	
and 2711 (1925)	226
United Nations:	
Convention on the Recovery Abroad of Maintenance, Cmnd 4485	
(1956)	195
Convention on the Reduction of Statelessness, Cmnd 1825	
(1962)	63
Demographic Yearbook	9
Wealth Tax, consultative paper Cmnd 5704 (1974)	83

WRITERS AND EDITORS AND THEIR WORKS REFERRED TO

Adoption, *Report of Standing Conference of Societies registered*	
for, (1968)	234
Albery, M. J. *The Inheritance (Family Provision) Act* 1938 (1949)	160, 164
Anderson, Sir J. N. D. (ed.). *Family Law in Asia and Africa*. .	40
Baxter, I. F. G. *Law Commission: First Report on Family*	
Property (1974)	96
Berlins, M. and Wansell, G. *Caught in the Act* (1974) . . .	257, 261
Bevan, H. K. *The Law Relating to Children* (1973) . . .	243, 247
Blackstone, Sir W. *Commentaries on the Laws of England* . .	14, 54, 217
Bodenheimer, Brigitte. *The Community without Community*	
Property (1971)	87
The Utah Marriage Counselling Experiment (1961). . .	105
New Approaches of Psychiatry, Implications for Divorce Reform	
(1970)	105
Bowlby, John. *Attachment and Loss* (1969)	2, 3
Child Care and the Growth of Love (1965)	2, 3
Bradley, David. *The Children Act 1975* (1976)	227
Brooke, Rosalind. *Information and Advice Services* (1972) . .	107
Caesar, Julius. *De Bello Gallico*	8
Calvert, Harry. *Social Security Law* (1974)	83
Cavanagh, Mrs. W. *Juvenile Courts, the Child and the Law* (1967)	243
Cheshire, G. C. *Conflict of Laws* (ed. North) . . .	48, 52, 54
Church of England	
Board of Social Responsibility: *Fatherless by Law?* (1966) .	19
S.P.C.K. *The Church and the law of Nullity of Marriage* (1955)	4
S.P.C.K. *Putting Asunder* (1966)	4
CIBA Foundation.	
The Family and its Future (1970).	2
Law and Ethics of A.I.D. and Embryo Transplant (1973). .	1
Clark, Homer. *Law of Domestic Relations* (1968) . . .	30

page

James, T. *'The English Law of Marriage': A Century of Family Law* 2
Jackson, J. *The Formation and Annulment of Marriage* (2nd edn, 1969) 27
   Matrimonial Finance and Taxation (1972) 130
Justice. *Parental Rights and Custody Suits* (1975) . . . 206
Kahn-Freund, Sir Otto. *The Law Reform (Husband and Wife) Act 1962* (1962) 65
   Inconsistencies and Injustices in the Law of Husband and Wife (1952–3) 88
   Matrimonial Property: Where Do We Go From Here? (1971) . 158
Kanowitz, Leo. *Women and the Law: The Unfinished Revolution* (1969) 56
   Sex Roles in Law and Society (1973) 56
Karsten, I. G. F. *Capacity to contract a polygamous marriage* (1973) 53
   The Recognition of Divorces and Legal Separations Act 1971 (1972) 141
Keesing's *Contemporary Archives* 9
Kenny, C. S. *History of the Law of Married Women's Property* (1898) 158
Laslett, Peter (ed.). *The World we have lost* (1965) . . . 2
   Household and Family in Past Time (1972) . . . 1, 2
Lasok, D. *The Legal Status of the Putative Father* (1968) . . 19
Laufer, J. *Flexible Restraints on Testamentary Freedom* . . 159, 160
Lecky, W. E. H. *England in the Eighteenth Century* . . . 29
Levin, Mrs. J. *The Matrimonial Home – Another Round* (1972) . 171, 177
Lowie, Robert H. *'Marriage' Encyclopaedia of the Social Sciences* 4, 5
Macdonald, Ian A. *The New Immigration Law* (1972). . . 61
Macgregor, O. R. *Divorce in England* (1957) 11
Macgregor, O., Gibson, C. and Blom-Cooper, L. *Separated Spouses* (1966) 78, 114, 214, 220, 222
McLaughlin, Jon M. A. *Court-connected Marriage Counselling and Divorce* (1972) 106
Mair, Lucy P. *African Marriage and Social Change* . . . 6
Maitland, F. *Law of Real Property. Collected Papers* . . . 148
Maitland, Pollock and. *History of English Law* 27
Manchester, A. H. and Whetton, J. M. *Marital Conciliation in England and Wales* (1974) 105, 106, 107
Megarry, R. E. *The Rent Acts*, 10th edn (1970) . . . 152
Mendes da Costa, D. *Formalities of Marriage* . . . 50
Micklethwait, Sir R. *The National Insurance Commissioners* (1976) 83
Morris, H. F. *Marriage Law in Uganda* 40
Morris, J. H. C. *Conflict of Laws* (1971) 48, 49, 52
Muller-Freienfels, W. *Ehe und Recht* 87

page

Law Reform Committee (9th Report): Liability in Tort between Husband and Wife, 24 *MLR* (1961) 481 65
Maintenance Agreements Act 1957, The, 21 *MLR* (1968) 57 . 108
Marriage (Enabling) Act 1960, The, 23 *MLR* (1960) 538 . 40
Matrimonial Causes and Reconciliation Bill 1963, The, 3 *Journal of Family Law* (Louisville, Kentucky) (1963) 87 . 108
Matrimonial Proceedings (Magistrates' Courts) Act 1960, The, 24 *MLR* (1961) 144 111
Matrimonial Property – The Scope of Section 17, 20 *MLR* (1957) 281 179
Polygamy by Estoppel, 24 *MLR* (1961) 371 41
Recent developments in Adoption and Long-term fostering in England and Wales: The Child and the Law, International Society on Family Law (1976) 227
Status of Women in Great Britain, The, xx *American Journal of Comparative Law* (1972) 592 11
Uncommon Law: Taczanowska v. *Taczanowski*, 20 *MLR* (1957) 505 51
Street, Harry. *The Law of Torts* 152
Sullerot, Evelyne. *L'emploi des Femmes et ses problemes* . . 12
Tacitus. *Germania*. 8
Life of Agricola 8
Temkin, Ms. J., Rees, W. M. and White, P. M. *The Lane Committee on the Abortion Act* (1974) 68
Todd, Jean E. and Jones, L. M. *Matrimonial Property* (1972), *see* Population Censuses and Surveys, Office of
Tolstoy, Dmitri. *Marriage by Estoppel* (1968) 41
Void and Voidable Marriages (1964) 38, 44
Turner, J. Neville. *Confusion in English Family Property Law. Enlightenment from Australia?* 172, 177
Tyler, E. L. G. *Family Provision* (1971) 159
Wadlington, Walter. *The Loving Case (1966)* 3
Weitzman, Lenore. *Legal Regulation of Marriage* (1974) . . 109
Wheatcroft, G. S. A. and Park, A. *Capital Gains Tax* (1967) . 79
Williams, Glanville. *Some Reforms in the Law of Tort* (1961) . 65, 66
Williams and Mortimer. *Executors Administrators and Probate* (1970) 160
Winfield and Jolowicz. *Textbook of the Law of Tort* . . . 251
Davern Wright, R. J. *Testators' Family Maintenance in Australia and New Zealand* (1974) 159

Index